THE BEST DEFENSE

THE BEST DEFENSE

ALAN M. DERSHOWITZ

Vintage Books
A Division of Random House
New York

First Vintage Books Edition, May 1983
 Published in the United States by Random House, Inc., New York, and simultaneously in Canada by Random House of Canada Limited, Toronto. Originally published by Random House, Inc. in 1982.

Library of Congress Cataloging in Publication Data
Dershowitz, Alan M.
The best defense.
Includes index.
1. Trials—United States.
2. Dershowitz, Alan M.
I. Title.
KF220.D37 1983   345.73'02   82-40426
ISBN 0-394-71380-X (pbk.)   347.3052

Manufactured in the United States of America

79B86

This book is dedicated with love to my parents
Harry and Claire Dershowitz
for encouraging and tolerating me through my Boro Park years
and to my children Elon and Jamin
for encouraging and tolerating me through my Cambridge years

ACKNOWLEDGMENTS

This book has been a labor of love. I was fortunate to have had the assistance of friends, family, and colleagues who made the work seem like fun even when it consumed long hours. My són Elon provided excellent editorial—and, even more important, common sense—suggestions. My son Jamin provided just the right degree of healthy skepticism. My brother Nathan and his son Adam read portions of the manuscript and made helpful suggestions. My mother, in addition to providing cookies and other nourishment during exhausting court proceedings, coordinated the family effort to recall our roots. And my father, in his own quiet way, has always been a source of support. My close friends and colleagues Jeanne Baker and Harvey Silverglate, who are supporting actors in several of the cases described in the book, were always there when I needed them. My editor, Rob Cowley, who is a master of his craft and of the art of gentle urging, helped at every turn. My publisher, Bob Bernstein, who has the knack of calling at just the moments when I most needed encouragement, urged me to write this book.

My students at the Harvard Law School played a central role. I used several chapters in my classes and received valuable feedback. Students—now distinguished young lawyers—such as Cynthia Hamilton, Joanne Crispi, James Witkin, Laura Hanft, and Marjorie Heins, provided invaluable help. Betty Arnquist, Wendy Roth, Blue Tabor, and Anne Mandelbaum contributed valuable criticism and editorial comments. Other students too numerous to mention also assisted in the research, including, most recently, Elaine Mandelbaum, Mark Fabiani, and Donna Levin.

My colleagues at the Harvard Law School encouraged me in my efforts while not always agreeing with my conclusions. I especially want to thank John Ely, James Vorenberg, Phillip Heyman, Susan Estrich, and Alan Stone. The support services at the Harvard Law School were also invaluable, especially the help of Kaye Tousley, Sylvia Madrigal, Pam Foley, Debbie Reimal, and the people at the word-processing and Xeroxing centers. Sandy Schoenfein of Random House displayed enormous patience and real expertise in her copy editing.

Finally, the actors in the chapters—clients, prosecutors, judges, other defense attorneys—provided the grist. I have tried to be fair to them all, but to the extent that fairness is constrained by truth, I hope I have erred on the side of the latter.

Contents

Introduction

A conspiracy of silence shrouds the American justice system. Most insiders—lawyers and judges—won't talk. Most outsiders—law professors and journalists—don't really know. Few of those who are outside the club ever get close enough to the day-to-day operations of the system to appreciate how it really works.

Some insiders won't talk because they have a stake in not exposing the dark underside of the legal profession. Others are afraid of reprisals. Indeed, the formal rules governing the legal profession discourage lawyers from publicly criticizing their "professional brethren," and encourage them to promote "public confidence in our courts" and in "the honor of our profession." Equally important is the informal understanding among insiders that they should criticize only within the club and not in public.

This dichotomy between insiders who know but won't say and outsiders who will say but don't know has deprived the public of a realistic assessment of the American justice system. In this book I try to break down that dichotomy. Although I am a law professor, I have been litigating cases at every level of our justice system for more than a decade. Because I do not rely on my legal cases for a living, I have less fear of reprisal than do most practicing lawyers. Because I insist that my students approach the law with rigorous honesty, I can hardly remain silent about the dishonesty I encounter in the real world of justice.

I was an outsider during the first years of my legal career. I had seen the system only from the perspective of its highest courts and its most elite institutions of learning. After graduation from Yale Law School, I was privileged to serve as law clerk to two of the finest and most humane judges in American history: Chief Judge David Bazelon of the United States Court of Appeals for the District of Columbia and Associate Justice Arthur Goldberg of the United States Supreme Court.

I began my teaching career at Harvard Law School as a naïve idealist with an abiding faith in the system: trust in the integrity of judges, in the good faith of prosecutors, and in the dedication of defense attorneys. I probably would have maintained these views and passed them on to my students except for a remarkable "accident" that occurred in 1972. A member of the Jewish Defense League accused of making a bomb that killed an innocent young woman happened to be a neighbor of mine in the Boro Park section of Brooklyn, where I grew up. Unable to get a "real" lawyer, he turned to "the kid who became a law professor." That case, with its bizarre twists and turns, introduced me to a world that no one wrote about in law books or taught in law schools. It started me on an odyssey—on a new legal education—the story of which I tell in this book.

During the course of this odyssey I have discovered some disturbing truths that are not part of our theory of law. I have learned that despite the constitutional presumption of innocence, the vast majority of criminal defendants are in fact guilty of the crimes with which they are charged. Almost all of my own clients have been guilty. A few, of course, have been innocent. There has been almost no correlation between the guilt or innocence of my clients and whether they served time or got off.

Taking Offense

Several of my clients have gone free because their constitutional rights were violated by agents of the government. In representing criminal defendants —especially guilty ones—it is often necessary to take the offensive against the government: to put the government on trial for *its* misconduct. In law, as in sports, the best defense is often a good offense. Hence the title of this book.

My own clients whose cases are described in this book have included defendants charged with the most unspeakable of crimes—such as mass murder. They have also included defendants whose acts should never have been regarded as crimes—such as starring in a pornographic movie.

I am not unique in representing guilty defendants. That is what most defense attorneys do most of the time. The Perry Mason image of the heroic defender of innocent victims of frame-ups or mistaken identification is television fiction. Occasionally truly innocent defendants are brought to trial; less frequently they are convicted. In some cases they have even been executed. But these cases—important as they are—are not the daily fare of the criminal lawyer. Any criminal lawyer who tells you that most of his clients are not guilty is either bluffing or deliberately limiting his practice to a few innocent defendants.

Since I earn my livelihood as a law professor, I can be selective about the cases I take. I could, if I wanted to, represent only defendants who I believe are innocent or decent. I deliberately do not do that. I select my cases without regard to whether the defendant is guilty or what I think of him personally. Nor do I consider the likelihood of winning. I try to explain why I regard the representation of a guilty and despicable defendant, with little prospect of winning, as a challenge—and, indeed, as one of the highest obligations of my profession.

I try to pick the most challenging, the most difficult, and the most precedent-setting cases. Because I am somewhat insulated from the pressures of the courts and the bar, I also feel a responsibility to take on cases from which other lawyers might shy away. I explain why I tend to become involved in direct confrontations with judges, with prosecutors, and with other defense lawyers. I also take on cases that raise novel issues suitable for class discussion, and I try to integrate my courtroom and classroom work. In Chapter 2, I tell about a murder case that my students helped me to win by providing the solution to a perplexing legal dilemma.

Lawyer of Last Resort

I am primarily, though not exclusively, an appellate lawyer—a lawyer of last resort. Defendants (and their lawyers) generally turn to me after the jury has rendered a verdict of guilty—and often after the appeal has been lost as well. They want me to try to obtain review in the United States Supreme Court or have them freed on a writ of habeas corpus. They are desperate. They have little hope of legal recourse. One of my clients, in prison after losing all of his appeals but still retaining his sense of humor, sent me a cartoon depicting two prisoners hanging from the wall of an escape-proof cell, in arm shackles and leg irons. One turns to the other, and with an eternally optimistic look on his face whispers: "Now here's my plan . . ." That cartoon hangs in my office as a constant reminder of the desperate plight of most of my clients.

Once I decide to take a case, I have only one agenda: I want to win. I will try, by every fair and legal means, to get my client off—without regard to the consequences.*

*This is neither a radical nor a transient notion. As a British barrister named Henry Brougham put it in 1820:

"An advocate, by the sacred duty which he owes his client, knows, in the discharge of that office, but one person in the world, that client and none other. To save that client by all expedient means—to protect that client at all hazards and costs to all others, and among others to himself,—is the highest and most unquestioned of his duties; and he must not regard the alarm, the suffering, the torment, the destruction which he may bring upon any other. Nay,

I do not apologize for (or feel guilty about) helping to let a murderer go free—even though I realize that someday one of my clients may go out and kill again. Since nothing like this has ever happened, I cannot know for sure how I would react. I know that I would feel terrible for the victim. But I hope I would not regret what I had done—any more than a surgeon should regret saving the life of a patient who recovers and later kills an innocent victim.

Convictions and Reversals

This book tells the story of a dozen of my most controversial and dramatic cases. Unlike many lawyers who have written books about their cases, I have deliberately included several that I lost. I was not happy to lose them, but they were as significant to me, to the development of the law, and—obviously—to my clients, as were my courtroom victories.

Most of the cases I describe are criminal, but a few involve civil liberties issues that arose in the context of noncriminal cases: the Park Service's closing of a nude beach on Cape Cod—allegedly for environmental reasons; Stanford University's firing of a militant professor; the CIA's lawsuit against Frank Snepp, a former agent; and a judge's commitment of a young woman to a mental hospital because she wanted to sue her psychiatrist. All of the cases, criminal or civil, pit individual citizens against large institutions: government prosecutors, universities, bureaucracies.

Nobody Wants Justice

There's an old story about the lawyer who has just won a big case for his client and cables him: "Justice has prevailed." The client fires off a return telegram: "Appeal immediately." The story underlines an important point about the realities of our legal system: nobody really wants justice. Winning is "the only thing" to most participants in the criminal justice system—just as it is to professional athletes. Criminal defendants, and their lawyers, certainly do not want justice; they want acquittals, or at least short sentences.

Prosecutors are supposed to be interested in justice: the motto on the wall of the Justice Department proclaims that the government "wins its point whenever Justice is done." But in real life, many prosecutors reverse the motto and believe that justice is done whenever the government wins its point. Prosecutors want to win especially when a guilty defendant tries to

---

separating even the duties of a patriot from those of an advocate, and casting them, if need be, to the wind, he must go on reckless of the consequences, if his fate it should unhappily be, to involve his country in confusion for his client's protection."

get off because of some governmental misconduct—a "technicality." In such cases, the law demands acquittal. As Justice Oliver Wendell Holmes put it: "It is a less evil that some criminals should escape than that the government should play an ignoble role." Although prosectutors are sworn to uphold this law, they often seek convictions in cases based on illegally obtained evidence. In such cases the prosecutors are not seeking justice. They, like the defendant who wants an acquittal, are seeking only one thing: to win.

I explain why most prosecutors (and defense attorneys) are as concerned about their won–lost ratio as any major-league pitcher. Their concern helps to explain why plea bargaining is so widespread: both the prosecutor and the defense attorney can add a "win" to their record—only the public sometimes loses, but nobody keeps a won–lost record for them. I believe that plea bargaining is one of the most destructive and least justifiable institutions in the American criminal justice system.

Well, you may think, at least judges are interested in justice. They have no stake in any particular result in a given case. Would that it were so! Most judges have little interest in justice. They, too, have their own agenda: many see themselves as part of the system of law enforcement, as adjuncts to the police and prosecutors. They want to make sure that criminals are convicted and sent away. Even if the law requires acquittal, many judges will do everything within their lawful power—and some things beyond it—to convict defendants who they believe should be in jail. Judges are also interested in the efficiency of the system, in making certain that there are no backlogs or traffic jams in the courts. Most important, they do not want their decisions to be reversed by a higher court. We will see in this book the lengths to which judges sometimes go to protect against reversals of "their" convictions; they regard a reversal as a personal and professional affront, even when the reversal is essential to achieving justice.

Black Robes, White Lies

I say some critical things about judges—from the lowliest magistrates to the Chief Justice of the United States. (I try to be as critical of judges who have ruled in favor of my clients as of those who have ruled against them, but I doubt that I managed to eliminate all the sour grapes from the bunch.) Indeed, one working title for this book was "Black Robes, White Lies." That would have been appropriate, because lying, distortion, and other forms of intellectual dishonesty are endemic among judges. In my twenty years of experience in the practice of law, I have been more disappointed by judges than by any other participants in the criminal justice system. That is partly because I, like so many others, expected so much of these robed embodiments of the law. When I began to practice, I naïvely assumed that other judges would be as honest in their approach to the law, as sensitive to constitutional rights, as concerned about human beings as were the two judges for whom I had clerked. I have been keenly disappointed. Beneath the robes of many judges, I have seen corruption, incompetence, bias, laziness, meanness of spirit, and plain ordinary stupidity. I have also seen dedication, honesty, hard work, and kindness—but that is the least to which we are entitled from our judges. If I emphasize the negative side of the judiciary, that is because it is more noteworthy than the positive, and also because it threatens to corrupt the integrity of the American legal process. I emphasize the negative as well because most lawyers overemphasize the positive. Non-lawyers are entitled to know the "whole truth" about our legal system, not just the part the legal profession justly boasts about on Law Day.

Rough Justice

In our adversary system of criminal law, the participants—criminal defendant, defense lawyer, prosecutor, police, and judge—seek to maximize their own personal and professional interests. Although nobody in the system seems interested in abstract justice, the irony is that the net result may well be a kind of rough justice.

Despite the prevalence of dishonesty, I have learned that the American system of criminal justice generally produces fairly accurate results: few defendants who are innocent are convicted. Some who are guilty are, of course, acquitted. And a large number are never brought to trial. But that is part of a system that boasts "better ten guilty go free than even one innocent be wrongly convicted." The corruption lies not so much in the *results* of the justice system as in its *processes.*

Most appraisals of the American criminal justice system tend to be polemical: supporters boast that the system is honest and fair and produces accurate results; critics complain that the system is corrupt and unfair and produces inaccurate results. Throughout this book I try to show that the issues are not that simple or clear-cut. The American criminal justice system *is* corrupt to its core: it depends on a pervasive dishonesty by its participants. It *is* unfair: it discriminates against the poor, the uneducated, the members of minority groups. But it is *not* grossly inaccurate: large numbers of innocent defendants do not populate our prisons. Nor can our system fairly be characterized as "repressive." There is more freedom to speak, write, organize, and advocate in America today than there is or has ever been in any country in the history of the world. My appreciation of American freedom and justice increased as a result of my exposure to the Soviet legal system described in Chapter 7. This does not mean that I believe there is *enough* freedom or *enough* justice here. There is not. But a comparison with other times and places lends perspective to our situation.

Part of the reason why we are as free as we are, and why our criminal justice system retains a modicum of rough justice despite its corruption and unfairness, is our adversary process: the process by which every defendant may challenge the government. I explain why I believe that defending the guilty and the despised—even freeing some of them—is a small price to pay for our liberties. Imagine a system where the guilty and the despised—or at least those so regarded by the powers that be—were not entitled to representation!

"The Whole Truth"

The courtroom oath—"to tell the truth, the whole truth and nothing but the truth"—is applicable only to witnesses. Defense attorneys, prosecutors, and judges don't take this oath—they couldn't! Indeed, it is fair to say the American justice system is built on a foundation of *not* telling the whole truth.

It is the job of the defense attorney—especially when representing the guilty—to prevent, by all lawful means, the "whole truth" from coming out. It is not only proper but obligatory for a defense attorney to object to the admission of truthful evidence if that evidence was improperly obtained or is prejudicial. In Chapter 11, I describe various types of defense attorneys, some of whom go beyond their proper roles as advocates, while others place their own interests above those of their clients.

Although the prosecutor has a greater obligation to present the "whole truth" than the defense attorney, he, too, must occasionally withhold it—at least from the public. But beyond these rare situations where suppressing some truth may be proper, we will see in this book that deviousness and even outright dishonesty by prosecutors have become a way of life in some cities. These high public officials, sworn to uphold the law, do not see their mendacious behavior as improper. They justify it as a form of civil disobedience, of a commitment to a higher law. The American system of justice has come to depend on the "white lie." Chapter 10 tells the sordid story of how the United States Attorney's office in New York City—widely regarded as the best in the country—tried to suppress the truth about Robert Leuci, the policeman whose life is depicted in the book and film *Prince of the City*.

The cases in this book also illustrate how judges—the best and brightest among them—distort records, pretend to believe lying government witnesses, pervert the meaning of cases, and ignore the arguments made in their courtroom. Dishonesty by judges may indeed be inherent in the common law system of deciding criminal cases. Distortion of the record is sometimes the only way a judge can convict the guilty without making bad law for the future. Oliver Wendell Holmes once commented that "hard cases, like notorious ones, often make bad law." Some judges seek to avoid that dilemma by simply distorting the hard facts of notorious cases to make them seem easy. By substituting easy facts for hard ones, the judge can make sure that a notorious criminal goes to jail, without establishing a dangerous legal precedent that could be applied to less notorious defendants. Such judicial legerdemain is often praised as "judicial statesmanship."

I recently heard a story about a highly regarded federal appellate judge that suggests how pervasive judicial dishonesty has become. In an opinion affirming a criminal conviction, the judge included a paragraph saying that he had read the entire transcript and satisfied himself that there was more than enough evidence of guilt to support the jury's verdict. A second judge drafted and circulated a memorandum wondering how the first judge could have read the transcript when the only copy had been locked away in the second judge's file drawer during the entire appeal. The first judge, caught in the act, withdrew his paragraph. The public never learned of the embarrassing incident, although the story has been circulating among insiders. The first judge continues to be honored at the bar for his judicial integrity. I will almost certainly be criticized by the insiders for telling this story.*

If a lawyer or a law student falsely represents that he has read a transcript, he surely will be disciplined. (Journalists and medical researchers who have made analogous misrepresentations have been fired and disgraced.) Yet I know of numerous instances where judges have made false claims about what they have read, distorted records, and engaged in other deceptions. Why judges are permitted to get away with—and indeed are often praised for—this kind of intellectual dishonesty is an important and largely unanswered question confronting the American legal system.

Cheat Elite

I tend to focus my harshest criticisms on the most elite legal institutions: the most powerful judges of the highest courts; the most respected prosecutorial offices with the best reputations for integrity; the most famous and successful defense attorneys. It would be too easy to attack obvious

*I did not hear the story from either of the judges; I heard it from a reliable source within the court who personally saw all the documents.

forms of corruption at the lowest levels of our justice system: bribery, cronyism, case fixing. Others, who are in a better position to observe these cancers, have already written about them. What I have seen all around me is how some respected members of my profession learn to cheat elite, are rewarded for their conduct, and then pass it on to their successors.

Throughout the book, but especially in Chapter 10, I provide examples of how some of the most respected members of my profession cheat elite and get away with it. I feel a special responsibility to expose the cheat elite form of corruption because I teach in an "elite" law school, and my students quickly become members of the professional elite. As members of that elite —as law clerks, prosecutors, partners in large law firms, judges—they are not so much in danger of succumbing to the more obvious forms of corruption. But they are constantly exposed to the temptation to cheat elite. What, for example, would a law clerk learn from observing the respected judge who falsely claimed to have read a transcript? What would a recent law school graduate learn from the behavior of the federal prosecutors in the *Prince of the City* case? "Cheat elite" is among the most insidious forms of corruption in the American legal system today, because nobody tells those who practice it that they are as corrupt as those who take bribes.

The Rules of the Justice Game

In the process of litigating these cases, writing this book and teaching my classes, I have discerned a series of "rules" that seem—in practice—to govern the justice game in America today. Most of the participants in the criminal justice system understand them. Although these rules never appear in print, they seem to control the realities of the process. Like all rules, they are necessarily stated in oversimplified terms. But they tell an important part of how the system operates in practice. Here are some of the key rules of the justice game:

Rule I: Almost all criminal defendants are, in fact, guilty.

Rule II: All criminal defense lawyers, prosecutors and judges understand and believe Rule I.

Rule III: It is easier to convict guilty defendants by violating the Constitution than by complying with it, and in some cases it is impossible to convict guilty defendants without violating the Constitution.

Rule IV: Almost all police lie about whether they violated the Constitution in order to convict guilty defendants.

Rule V: All prosecutors, judges, and defense attorneys are aware of Rule IV.

Rule VI: Many prosecutors implicitly encourage police to lie about whether they violated the Constitution in order to convict guilty defendants.

Rule VII: All judges are aware of Rule VI.

Rule VIII: Most trial judges pretend to believe police officers who they know are lying.

Rule IX: All appellate judges are aware of Rule VIII, yet many pretend to believe the trial judges who pretend to believe the lying police officers.

Rule X: Most judges disbelieve defendants about whether their constitutional rights have been violated, even if they are telling the truth.

Rule XI: Most judges and prosecutors would not knowingly convict a defendant who they believe to be innocent of the crime charged (or a closely related crime).

Rule XII: Rule XI does not apply to members of organized crime, drug dealers, career criminals, or potential informers.

Rule XIII: Nobody really wants justice.

One

GUILTY UNTIL PROVEN INNOCENT

1

The Boro Park Connection

The very idea of bombs being made in Boro Park, by Jewish boys, was unthinkable to those of us who grew up in that peaceable Brooklyn neighborhood. But the unthinkable was happening on that Tuesday afternoon in January of 1972. While most of the Orthodox Jews of Boro Park were going about their business, oblivious to the passions and fashions of the outside world, three earnest young men were arguing, in the style of Talmudic disputation, about the correct method for assembling bombs. The site of the argument was a shabby office on New Utrecht Avenue, in the shadow and echo of the West End elevated train line.

Just a block away, the bearded merchants of Thirteenth Avenue—the major shopping thoroughfare that attracts a polyglot clientele from throughout the city—were hawking their wares in a dialect made up of English, Yiddish, Hebrew, Spanish, and Italian. Young boys wearing yarmulkes were playing punchball in the schoolyard of the Etz Chaim yeshiva (the "Tree of Life" seminary) on Fiftieth Street. Housewives bedecked in *shaytls* (ritual head coverings) were baking bread and changing diapers in their semiattached houses on Forty-eighth Street. In midafternoon, men and boys, some garbed in the black outfit of their Hasidic sect, gathered in minyans (assemblages of ten or more males over the age of thirteen) to recite the afternoon prayers in countless makeshift congregations on every street and avenue. As part of the service, some men rose to recite the *Kaddish,* the traditional Jewish prayer for the dead.

The boys in the building on New Utrecht Avenue did not pause to recite their prayers on that afternoon. They had to finish making the bombs—bombs whose deadly effects would soon require a Jewish father to rise and recite the *Kaddish* for his murdered daughter.

This is the true story of a tragic murder and the dramatic legal case that grew out of it. The action centers on three characters, all of whom grew up in Boro Park: the young man who was accused of making the bombs; the detective who broke the case; and the lawyer who defended the young man by trying to discredit the detective. It is a first-person story, because I was the lawyer.

"Whoosh"

The next morning, a Wednesday, Solomon Isaievich Hurok was hard at work in his elegant office on the twentieth floor of a glass tower at the corner of Fifty-sixth Street and Sixth Avenue in midtown Manhattan. Sol Hurok had emigrated from Russia in 1905, and his origins in Pogar, the Ukraine, had much in common with those of many Boro Parkers. But the similarity ended there. Hurok was as cosmopolitan as the Boro Parkers were parochial. For almost fifty years he was the man behind the marquee that read: "Sol Hurok Presents." The bald-headed man with the beaver fedora and silver-tipped ebony cane, shouting countless "Bravos" from the back of the hall, was the embodiment of the impresario. It was Hurok who introduced Rubinstein, Pavlova, Chaliapin, and the Bolshoi Ballet to the United States.

The eighty-three-year-old Hurok was putting the finishing touches on the American premiere of Russia's Osipov Balalaika Orchestra. He had no doubt that it would be an artistic success. He worried, however, about threats against the orchestra that had been made by a militant group calling itself the Jewish Defense League. The JDL, as it was known, opposed cultural exchanges with the Soviet Union as long as it refused to let Jews emigrate to Israel. In recent months, smoke bombs and ammonia cans had been hurled into concert halls. Once a crate of live mice had been turned loose in the audience. But the performances had resumed with little damage and no serious injuries.

As the impresario was arranging for extra security for the forthcoming concert, two neatly dressed men in their twenties entered the reception area of his office and politely inquired about an upcoming concert. They were asked to wait while the information was checked. Instead they quickly departed, leaving behind an ordinary-looking briefcase made of imitation leather. Inside, unheard, was a tiny Micronta timer, ticking away.

At precisely the same time, two other young men left an identical briefcase in the midtown Manhattan office of Columbia Artists Management, Inc., which also brought Soviet performers to the United States.

Before anyone had even noticed the briefcases, a loud, strange *whoosh* emitted from them. Pink and blue flames burst out, engulfing the rooms in smoke and filling them with heat. At Columbia's headquarters, terrified workers smashed through the ground-floor windows and ran into the street. At Hurok's suite, the maze of connecting offices and conference rooms was encased in hermetically sealed glass: the windows would not open. The air conditioning spewed out deadly fumes. Hurok nearly suffocated. Rescued by firemen, he was carried to a waiting ambulance, barely conscious.

Iris Kones, a twenty-seven-year-old assistant in Hurok's accounting department, and two fellow employees tried to escape the smoke by lying face down on the floor. When the firemen found them, the two others were unconscious, their faces buried in the deep carpet, their hair singed. The rescuers managed to revive them. But Iris Kones was pronounced dead of asphyxiation.

The outcry at this crime was universal. Perhaps the most eloquent response came from the Russian poet Yevgeny Yevtushenko, who had achieved international prominence particularly through his poem commemorating the massacre of Jews at Babi Yar during World War II. Yevtushenko, in New York for a poetry reading, requested permission to tour the burnt-out offices. The following night he read a new poem—entitled "Bombs for Balalaikas"—to a hushed crowd at the Felt Forum in Madison Square Garden:

> Poor Iris,
>   victim of the age,
> you've fallen,
>   fragile,
>   dark-eyed
> Jewish girl suffocated by smoke
> as though in a Nazi gas chamber.
> It's hard to vent out poisoned air.
> Damn you, servants of hell
> who seek coexistence between peoples
> by building bridges of cadavers.

Jewish leaders, too, denounced the bombing. The rabbis of Boro Park joined the crescendo of condemnation. At the funeral services for Iris Kones, the president of the board of rabbis prayed that "there were no Jews involved . . . This is not our way."

The chief of the bomb squad of the New York City Police Department believed, however, that Jews were involved. Within minutes of the bombings, anonymous callers had telephoned the Associated Press and NBC with identical messages: "Soviet culture is responsible for the deaths and imprisonment of Soviet Jews." The calls ended with the JDL motto: "Never again."

The JDL denied involvement. Rabbi Meir Kahane, founder and head of the organization, issued a statement from Jerusalem, where he was visiting, calling whoever was responsible for the crime "insane." Bertram Zweibon, vice chairman and general counsel of the JDL, blamed the bombing on provocateurs of the radical left seeking to discredit the JDL.

A five-month investigation, under the joint auspices of the local police and the FBI, produced few leads. Then, on June 16, 1972, a federal grand jury in New York indicted three young members of the Jewish Defense League for the murder of Iris Kones. Although her death was unintended, it was the result of a felonious bombing. Under the law, therefore, it was considered felony-murder—punishable by death.

"A Matter of Life and Death"

On the day the indictment was handed up, I was camping in Grand Teton National Park. A park ranger located me with a message: "A guy named Elephant is trying to reach you. Says it is a matter of life and death." The ranger's mention of the caller's name abruptly transported me from the splendors of the Wyoming mountains back to my boyhood memories of the Brooklyn streets. Marty Elefant had lived two doors away in Boro Park. I vaguely recalled that he had become a lawyer, but I had been out of touch with him for nearly twenty years. When I reached him in New York, he asked me if I remembered Sheldon Seigel from Fiftieth Street. "Sure," I said. "How has he been?"

"Sheldon's just been indicted for first-degree murder," Elefant answered gravely. "He's facing the death penalty. They say he was the bomb maker for the Jewish Defense League and that he made the bomb that killed the girl in Sol Hurok's office in January. It's an absolute frame-up," he assured me. "They can't prove a thing, but Sheldon's in big trouble and he's scared. He needs a lawyer right away. Will you represent him?"

As I thought about Elefant's question, I recalled my earlier encounters with Sheldon Seigel. A quiet, morose kid. Tall, gawky, pockmarked. A bit strange perhaps, but no mad bomber. Boro Park simply did not produce murderers. Comedians like Buddy Hackett and Jackie Mason, yes! Baseball players like Sandy Koufax! Assorted writers, doctors, lawyers, and rabbis; some petty thieves and several notorious nursing-home operators. But not murderers!

The Boro Park in which Sheldon and I had grown up was virtually free of crime—at least violent crime. Burglaries were infrequent, and when they occurred, were invariably attributed to outsiders. There were street fights, of course; I'd taken part in more than my share. But bombings, shootings, and murder? I had never so much as heard of an armed robbery. I'd never seen, or heard of, a Boro Parker owning a gun.

Growing Up Jewish in Boro Park

Boro Park is an amoebalike area with ever shifting and imprecise boundaries. Like other Brooklyn enclaves—such as Flatbush, Brownsville, and Bedford-Stuyvesant—Boro Park is not an officially designated governmental unit; it is an informally agreed upon neighborhood. Its central core is the one-square-mile area within which nearly 100,000 Jews, most of them Orthodox, make their homes. At the periphery, both geographically and politically, live several thousand Italian, Puerto Rican, and Scandinavian families.

The people of Boro Park are an amalgam of East European Jews, reflecting the overlapping waves of immigration that began near the end of the nineteenth century and continues to this day. Boro Park is unique among American Jewish neighborhoods in that it has always been Jewish. Unlike the Lower East Side of Manhattan, which was Irish before it was Jewish, and has since become heavily Puerto Rican, the first occupants of the small tract houses built at the beginning of the twentieth century on the site of rural farms were Jewish immigrants seeking to escape from the crowded ghettos of Manhattan.

My own paternal great-grandfather—whose family emigrated from the Polish *shtetl* of Pilzer in 1883—was among the first Jews to make the move from Manhattan to Brooklyn. During the first decade of this century, the family moved into an old attached house with high stoops. (The high stoops gave rise to the uniquely urban sport of stoop ball.)

Known to all as Reb Zecharia ("Reb" being a diminutive of "Rabbi"), my great-grandfather established one of the first Orthodox *shtibles,* or small family synagogues, in Brooklyn. My grandfather Louie was the cantor, and his seven sons and assorted nephews and cousins comprised the choir. "Reb Zecharia's Shtible," as it is still referred to today, became a gathering place, social center, and benevolent society for the small Orthodox community. During the late 1930s it decided to hire a professional rabbi to conduct services; one was brought over from Europe, but the congregants were not satisfied. After two weeks the newly hired rabbi was fired, given a small amount of severance pay, and sent on his way. A new rabbi was brought over from Europe, but he, too, was unceremoniously fired in a matter of weeks. This process continued until dozens of rabbis had passed through the "turnstile *shtible*" or the "Rabbi-of-the-Month Club," as it began to be called. Everybody in the neighborhood understood this charade for what it was: a small-scale rescue operation designed to save European rabbis who were endangered by Nazism. For nearly a decade it succeeded in circumventing the restrictive immigration laws, by claiming a "need" for imported rabbis to lead the fickle congregation.

When the *shtible* was first established there were few full-time rabbis or cantors, so my great-grandfather and grandfather both commuted back over the bridge to Manhattan to earn a living. Reb Zecharia, like so many of his contemporaries, worked in a sweatshop. The shop he worked in, which made pocketbooks, was located in a building just east of Washington Square, site of the ill-fated Triangle Shirtwaist factory. On the Saturday of the great fire in 1911 that engulfed the building and killed 145 workers, Reb Zecharia was at home. It was the Jewish Sabbath. He learned two lessons from this: he vowed that his children would never become factory workers and would never work on the Sabbath.

Reb Zecharia's son Louie began selling matches on street corners when he was eight years old and eventually worked as a printer and box maker. He met Ida, an immigrant from Zhikov, at the turn of the century. They soon married and my father, Harry, was born in 1909. Recently our family gathered to celebrate my father's seventieth birthday. My uncles regaled us with stories of his past. Each recounted tales of his fighting prowess: how he took on four Irish toughs, how he broke the nose of a neighborhood bully, how he climbed a tree in chase of a kid who had assaulted his younger brother. It was remarkable to see these mild-mannered men of my father's generation—now rabbis, lawyers, teachers, and businessmen—recalling the glory days when the fist was foremost and my father the undisputed champ.

After several years of public high school my father went to work as a salesman on the Lower East Side of Manhattan, where he and a partner eventually opened a small men's work-clothes store, which sold "wholesale" during the week and "retail" on Sunday.

My maternal grandfather arrived with the second wave of Polish immigrants in 1907. Unwilling to serve in the Polish army, he fled the small city of Przemysl, a center of Jewish learning and Hasidism, leaving behind three brothers and scores of other relatives. Thirty-five years later, all but one brother would be murdered along with 17,000 other Jewish townsfolk when the Nazis reached the city, but only after an armed defense by Jewish resistance fighters. The remaining brother fled the approaching Nazi troops and made his way to Siberia and eventually to Israel.

My mother's father originally moved to Scranton, Pennsylvania, where a relative had settled. The only job he could get was as a *shochet,* a ritual slaughterer of kosher animals. As unable to take the knife to their throats as he was to fire a gun at faceless targets, he returned to lower Manhattan, where he worked as a peddler to earn passage for his wife and three children still in Poland. After their arrival—and after two of the babies died of diphtheria—my mother was born and the family moved into an apartment on the Lower East Side of Manhattan until they, too, were able to afford the move across the East River to Brooklyn.

My mother, an excellent student, graduated from high school at the age of sixteen in the summer of 1929. Her career at City College was cut short when she had to get a job to help support her family, which was hard hit by the Depression. She never returned to school and has worked as a bookkeeper ever since.

My parents were married in 1937, and I was born two years later. After my brother's birth in 1942, we moved into a small house on Forty-eighth Street near Sixteenth Avenue in Boro Park. Originally built for one family, the house had been converted to a three-family residence. My mother's brother and his family moved in upstairs, while my father's cousin and his new bride moved into the basement.

During the years we were growing up, Boro Park was a close-knit neighborhood with a vibrant street life: punchball, stickball, marbles, and ring-a-levio occupied the untraveled avenues (we called them "gutters") and unused driveways. (Few residents had cars, and the sight of a taxi signified an emergency or an important outside visitor.) Many trees grew in our part of Brooklyn, but we hated them because they interfered with the flight of the ball, causing "do-overs." Sewers were essential to our young lives, not because of what they carried away, but because their covers served as bases and as yardsticks of our comparative manliness: I was never better than a one-and-a-half-sewer punchball hitter, which put me just over the midpoint of our unofficial standings.

Although by this time Brooklynites had abandoned the "duhs," "dats," and "toids," our accent was still distinctive: we referred to it as a "duh Kings English," since Brooklyn was in Kings County; the neighboring "Queens" English was slightly more refined; but Bronx English was incomprehensible even to us. I vividly recall my first recitation as a student at Yale Law School during which my accent was openly laughed at by several students. A few days later, however, they met Professor Abraham Goldstein —from Brooklyn by way of City College—whose accent made mine sound almost Midwestern. Perhaps in reaction to the Brooklyn stereotype, our parents, especially those who prided themselves on their American birth and did not want to be confused with the "greenies," took special pains to correct our diction at every opportunity. To this day, whenever my mother-pays one of her frequent visits to court to hear me or my brother argue a case, she invariably keeps a list of Brooklynisms that have unconsciously—consciously, if I am before a Brooklyn judge—crept into my speech.

Among the other families that moved to Boro Park were the Seigels. Sheldon Seigel was born in 1946, and his family moved into a two-family brick house two blocks from ours.

Sheldon and I attended the same Boro Park yeshiva, where we had some of the teachers who had taught our fathers—and where we shared a common characteristic: we both did poorly and were considered troublemakers. I recall my Cs and Ds in math and spelling, but even more painful were my Fs—and even F minuses—in conduct, deportment, and effort. My parents were called to the principal's office with such regularity that a classmate once asked if my mother worked at the school. I was always bored in class and had an attention span measurable in seconds. (My teachers didn't speak in the sophisticated language of "attention span" or "hyperactivity"; they described my plight in more earthy terms: I lacked *sitzfleish,* literally "enough meat on my rear end to allow me to sit still long enough to learn anything.") I never read, except comic books, and I spent every free minute playing basketball in our makeshift driveway court or punchball or stickball in the street in front of our house.

Many of our teachers—especially in religious subjects—were newly arrived immigrants from Europe's displaced-person camps. Several of our classmates had also experienced Hitler's concentration camps. But I do not remember any discussion—not a single one—either in class, in the schoolyard, or even at home, about the Holocaust. It was in the air; it was part of the experience of many of our friends and neighbors. Virtually everyone had lost relatives. The reminders were all around us: in the tattooed numbers we could see on the wrist of a classmate when he rolled up his sleeve to punch the "spaldeen"; in the fatherless or motherless families; in the "extra brother" some kids had; in the memorial prayers on holidays. We all knew. We did not ask.

Nor were we, as kids, concerned about other Jewish issues: secular Zionism was slightly suspect to our Orthodox parents; Soviet Jewry was simply unknown to us; and anti-Semitism was a distant abstraction in our homogeneous enclave. (I remember thinking that David Tartakoff, my next-door neighbor, must be a Gentile because his family did not wear yarmulkes, and they played the radio on the Sabbath.) As kids all we wanted was to be Americans: our heroes were Duke Snider, the Lone Ranger, and Franklin Delano Roosevelt; our aspirations were like those of other American kids. We spent endless hours arguing over what nicknames to affect when we made it to the major leagues: my friend Tsvi Groner settled on "Ted" (and decided to be a pitcher, since he could then work out his rotation to avoid playing on Saturday); Zolmon Eisenstadt would become "Zack"; and I practiced answering to "Red" (a handle that would quickly have become anachronistic—or anachromistic—since my hair has darkened to light-brown). We did, of course, exhibit some ethnic pride, as evidenced by the premiums attached to baseball cards of Jewish ballplayers, such as Cal Abrams and Sandy Koufax. The enhanced ethnicity of Boro Park today is reflected by the change in trading cards: instead of collecting baseball players, the Hasidic kids now collect and trade cards bearing the likenesses of famous religious leaders, such as the Bobover and Satmar rabbis.

We prided ourselves on toughness and street smarts. Fighting was a daily activity and an initiation rite for every new kid in the neighborhood. The rules were known to all: fists and feet were permitted, but hair-pulling, eye-gouging, and pounding heads on concrete were taboo. No implements—knives, belts, razors—could be used, though they could be carried, "just in case!" "Just in case" meant the Italian kids from the other side of the elevated, who periodically invaded our section of the neighborhood, or whom we would encounter at the Loew's 46th movie theater located on the boundary between Rome and Jerusalem, as New Utrecht Avenue was known. The interreligious battles were far more ferocious and hazardous than the others: you could really get hurt, though I don't recall getting anything worse than a few deep cuts, several broken teeth, and one concussion. These wars of ethnic pride were infrequent, but we were always ready with our garrison belt buckles sharpened and our razor blades secreted in our wallets. Those encased razor blades saw no more action than the condoms that we also carried "just in case."

We all belonged to "Social-Athletic Clubs," a euphemism for gangs. Mine was the "Shields S.A.C." and we sported chartreuse-and-black jackets, which our yeshiva promptly banned—my first experience with censorship. We circumvented the prohibition, however, by storing them in the basement of a member's house near the school and donning them at the close of the school day.

In Boro Park you always knew exactly where you stood in the eyes of the community. I was near the middle. Good but not outstanding in athletics, I was fairly popular among my male peers primarily on the strength of my fighting skills and sharp tongue. But my dreadful grades and deportment in school made me a pariah among parents, and I was actually banned in several homes lest my bad influence be transmitted. (I recently felt some silent satisfaction when I successfully defended a relative of one of the mothers who had banned me; he had been charged with bribery.) Since a career in medicine or engineering seemed out of the question, the neighborhood girls were told by their parents that I was a boy with no future.

After completing Etz Chaim, I proceeded to Yeshiva University High School, conveniently located only three blocks from Ebbets Field, the home of our local heroes, the Brooklyn Dodgers. My high school education consisted primarily of sneaking into the late innings of Dodgers home games, playing basketball for the school varsity (which in my case meant a lot of bench splinters), and periodically running for office in class and schoolwide elections. My only quasi-academic interest was in debating, which seemed like a form of verbal street fighting. I always did well on standardized tests, but my teachers were convinced that I must have been cheating. After a high grade in a statewide history Regents exam, my teacher called me in for a solemn talk in which he reminded me that I was a "75 student," that I had always been a "75 student," and that I would always be a "75 student." He suggested that I consider a craft.

My mischievous ways remained with me throughout high school. On one occasion when a teacher threw me out of class for being "fresh," my friend Jake Greenfield and I went up to the roof and made a stuffed dummy out of my leather jacket, cap, and a pair of pants. As I stood holding the dummy near the end of the roof, Jake went downstairs to the classroom and started yelling that I was on the roof threatening to jump. The teacher ran to the window; I let the dummy drop. It fell past his frightened and guilt-ridden eyes while Jake screamed, "He jumped, he did it!"

Another time the kid sitting next to me in class lifted an athletic supporter from my gym bag and tossed it at the rabbi. Finding my incriminating name tape on the offending item—my mother sewed name tapes onto every item we owned, from handkerchiefs to baseball mitts—the rabbi kicked me out of class. My friend Jake, never one to pass up an opportunity, cautioned the rabbi that I had a "gang." When I reached the street I told two drunks who were coming down Bedford Avenue that they could get free drinks if they went to the classroom and said, "Dersh sent us." As soon as they walked in and spoke their lines, Jake piped up, "That's Dersh's gang, I recognize them." The rabbi made a beeline for the door. I was suspended for several weeks and made to sit in the library reading old copies of *Life* magazine, to the apparent mutual satisfaction of everyone involved, except my mortified parents.

Eventually I was graduated from high school without academic distinction but with a reputation as "a wise guy with a good mouth on him." The first draft of my yearbook put it aptly when it said I had a "mouth of Webster and a head of Clay." My mother made them change it. Because of my glib stupidity, the principal suggested that I become "something where you use your mouth but don't need much brains." He suggested that I become a lawyer—if I could make it through school. My mother filled out an application for me to attend Brooklyn College, and after passing an entrance examination I was enrolled in the B.A. program. Suddenly my interests began to spark and I became a good student— motivated to do well in order to get into a first-rate law school.

Even during the years I was disgracing my parents with my inadequate school performance, my home life was warm and loving. Sheldon Seigel was not so fortunate. His mother died when he was seventeen, and within a year and a half his father married a woman whom Sheldon never got along with. It was the talk of the neighborhood. She constantly berated Sheldon for his immaturity, his irresponsibility, and his unwillingness to support himself. The tension in the home was palpable, and Sheldon more and more escaped into his love of cars and things mechanical. Skinny and unathletic, Shelley had few friends. He made people around him uncomfortable.

My younger brother had been Shelley's camp counselor one summer at a Jewish camp in upstate New York. He remembered Sheldon as a surly and scheming loner who repeatedly put his scientific talents to mischievous use. Once he wired his own microphone into the camp communications system and broadcast phony messages, throwing the campers and counselors into a frenzy.

After high school Sheldon began attending classes at the downtown campus of City College. His academic career was checkered and included brief stints at New York City Community College, the University of Southern California, and the uptown campus of City College. He finally graduated in 1971 with a degree in architecture. I remembered hearing that Sheldon had joined the JDL and not understanding why, since he had never been particularly active in, or committed to, Jewish causes when I knew him.

The bombing and murder charge just didn't fit. I was certain that if Sheldon was a killer, this could not have been kept from the ever prying eyes and ears of the extended family that was Boro Park. In our neighborhood there were no skeletons hidden in closets, because there were few closet doors. Privacy was a distant abstraction in a community of party lines, shared walls, and overlapping families. Everybody knew—and still knows—everybody by his or her family kinship. Though I've been away from Boro Park for twenty years, I am still "Harry and Claire's older kid." I recently overheard someone refer to me as "You know, the one who used to be the troublemaker and now is the lawyer for the troublemakers."

"Every Jew a .22"

Several years after I had left Boro Park for Yale Law School, Rabbi Meir Kahane founded the Jewish Defense League. Originally conceived as a small Jewish self-help organization directed at preventing assaults upon elderly Jews by toughs from other ethnic neighborhoods, the league's membership grew rapidly as it became increasingly militant.

Its initial concerns were local. It provided protection to Jewish teachers in racially troubled schools; it barricaded the doors of Manhattan's elite Temple Emanu-El to prevent the black activist James Foreman from demanding reparations; it protested the coddling of criminals; and its young members beat up several American Nazis carrying signs reading "Gas the Jews."

In the beginning the JDL even displayed a sense of humor when it picketed the major-league-baseball draft demanding that the "Racist, Imperialist Mets" draft a designated quota of Jewish ballplayers to reflect their ethnic proportion in the New York area.

But local humor turned to international terror as the JDL set its sights on bigger targets: the Soviet Union for its repression of Jewish religious practices and emigration; and Arab countries and organizations for their war against Israel. Its weapons quickly escalated from the walkie-talkie and the picket sign to the rifle and the bomb. Invoking the Holocaust, the league adopted the motto "Never again." JDL bumper stickers proclaimed: "Every Jew a .22."

Although Rabbi Kahane and his league had attracted considerable attention, it had not received the support of any significant segment of the Jewish community. It did, however, capture the imagination of many young Jews, particularly from the lower-middle-class sections of Brooklyn and Queens. Spurred by the romantic vision of a rabbinic warrior equally at home with rifle manuals or Talmudic discourse, these kids—I was to meet some as young as thirteen years old—formed a small army of devoted and disciplined followers. They took paramilitary training at a summer camp located in the Catskill Mountains, just a rifle shot away from Grossinger's. The huskier kids became a rumble of pushing and shoving bodyguards, appropriately named the *chaya* squad—the Hebrew word for animal. Those with a scientific bent formed a munitions squad, constructing bombs and other weapons. Some became sharpshooters.

Sheldon Seigel was recruited into the league by a friend on the Jewish holiday of Simchath Torah in 1969. Simchath Torah is celebrated throughout the Jewish world by dancing in the streets. During that year's festivities, the celebrants outside a synagogue on the outskirts of Boro Park had been attacked by some hooligans from the surrounding areas. As word of the attack spread through Boro Park, the JDL rounded up some kids to do battle; a friend of Seigel's was summoned, and Sheldon went along. After witnessing the vulnerability of the bloodied faces of the helpless victims—

most of them elderly—Seigel decided to join the league. Other youngsters were recruited into the organization after similar experiences. As one young man said, "It used to be you hit a Jew, he turned the other cheek. We are saying you hit a Jew, you gonna be hit back."

When I returned to Boro Park to visit my family, the "issue" of JDL violence was often discussed. Everyone had strong feelings about Kahane and his following among Jewish juveniles: some admired them, others despised them. But even among the detractors, I sensed a modicum of secret pride.

On one occasion, at a Boro Park street rally during the 1970 gubernatorial campaign, I was introducing Basil Patterson, the Democratic candidate for Lieutenant Governor. Patterson, a black, was roundly booed by a contingent of JDL protesters carrying racist signs. I was mortified and outraged. When the rally was over, I remained behind and tried to lecture the JDL kids on racism and civility, but they would have none of it. They began to push and shove, and eventually the police had to be called to rescue me.

As the league grew more militant, it began to have a disruptive impact on Soviet-American relations. League members were alleged to have used explosives at several Soviet facilities; to have shot bullets into Soviet diplomatic residences; and to have threatened kidnappings and murders. A tragedy seemed inevitable.

No one imagined, however, that the JDL's first fatality would be a defenseless and innocent Jewish woman who died without knowing who her assailants were or what they could possibly have had against her.

Those arrested and indicted along with Sheldon Seigel on June 16, 1972, for "causing the death of one Iris Kones" were two of his closest friends and long-time comrades-in-arms, Stuart Cohen and Sheldon Davis.

Stuart Cohen had first encountered Rabbi Kahane during a course in Jewish philosophy taught by the rabbi at the Yeshiva High School of Queens. Cohen quickly became a devotee of Kahane. Though quiet and small, Cohen became a squad leader at the summer training camp in the Catskills, a spokesperson for Rabbi Kahane's ideology, and a key person in the league's inner circle.

Sheldon Davis came to the league from a different background. Before encountering Kahane, he had all but abandoned his Jewish heritage. An honor science student in Jamaica High School in Queens, Davis had been considering an Army career when he met Kahane, who persuaded him to devote his scientific talents to the Jewish Defense League.

The statute under which the three were indicted carried the death penalty. These young zealots had thus become the first federal defendants to face the electric chair in New York since the Rosenbergs were executed for espionage in 1953.*

"One of Them"

My old neighbor Marty Elefant, having outlined the case over the telephone, came back to his question. Would I represent Sheldon Seigel in the murder case?

I had never actually tried a case at that time, having gone straight from law school to a pair of judicial clerkships and then on to teach at Harvard Law School. Although I had consulted on several cases and had argued a few appeals, this was vastly different: I was being asked to assume responsibility for the defense of a murder suspect whom I knew personally.

How could I presume to take on a murder case of this complexity as my first real trial? But then, how could I turn down a case involving someone I had known as a kid? Why should I represent a bunch of JDL hoodlums who had roughed me up a couple of years before? But aren't Jewish hoodlums entitled to representation? Still, couldn't they get another, more experienced—or at least more sympathetic—lawyer? It sounded like a straightforward murder prosecution rather than a civil liberties case. But Elefant had mentioned wiretaps, illegal searches, harassment, and other civil liberties issues. How could I turn down the chance to try out all of my classroom theories in such an exciting—and real—case?

As I turned these questions over in my mind I heard myself answering Marty Elefant's request. No, I could not actually represent Sheldon Seigel, since my teaching duties that year would make it difficult to commute from Cambridge to New York City on a regular basis; but I would try to get a good New York lawyer to take the case, and I would serve as a consultant on the constitutional issues.

I arranged to travel from Wyoming to New York to begin the process of finding a lawyer to represent Seigel. Knowing many civil liberties lawyers who had willingly represented all sorts of violent radicals while disclaiming sympathy with their means, I anticipated no difficulty in persuading one of them to lend his or her talent to a Jewish reactionary facing a murder charge. But the answer was the same all over town. "Why should I represent those thugs when I thoroughly disagree with their tactics?" When reminded that they also purported to disagree with the left-wing revolutionaries they had willingly represented—Black Panthers, Weathermen, and SDS mem-

*The case was being tried in federal rather than state court because a new federal statute had been enacted granting the federal authorities jurisdiction over all crimes involving the use of explosives in buildings "affecting interstate and foreign commerce."

bers—these attorneys were quick to come up with distinctions. Several Jewish lawyers claimed that when they represented or contributed to the defense of Black Panthers, no one could accuse them of espousing their aims or means; but when a Jewish lawyer represented a Jewish organization, it might be taken to imply political agreement. Some civil libertarians denied that there were civil liberties issues in the case, but when pressed, acknowledged that their ability to recognize a civil liberties issue is often sharper when the defendants are from the left than from the right.

In the end, it became clear that I could not fulfill my commitment to secure Seigel a good New York lawyer. I suggested to Elefant that they get a court-appointed or legal-aid attorney. He responded that the JDL—distrustful of outsiders—would never accept a lawyer who was paid by the government. They trusted me because I was "one of them." The Boro Park "connection" was a sufficient assurance that I would never turn on them, as other lawyers might.

And so, after more prodding and reflection, I decided to enter the case as Sheldon Seigel's lawyer. The decision, or so it now seems to me, was made out of mixed motives of guilt, ego, excitement, commitment to civil liberties, religious loyalty, regional parochialism—and probably an unconscious desire to please my family. I did not suspect then that this decision would change my life. It would expose me to the threat of disbarment and physical violence. It would make some friends and family turn against me. It would move my legal career in a new and totally unexpected direction.

What They Don't Teach in Law School

Having made my decision, I did not have the foggiest notion of where to begin. They didn't teach that sort of thing in law school. (Now I try to.) I turned to one of my former students, Harvey Silverglate, who had been practicing criminal law in Boston for four years. He urged me not to try to handle a case like this alone, gently reminding me that I barely knew how to find the Federal Courthouse and had no experience in preparing the necessary pre-trial motions and complying with other such technical requirements. He offered a role reversal: he would become my teacher for this case. I willingly assumed the status of student, and we got down to the hard work of preparing a defense.

During the summer of 1972 we met several times with Seigel, his two co-defendants, and their lawyers to devise a strategy. The defendants assured us that they were innocent and that the bombing was the work of another Jewish militant organization, named Betar (whose hero was the then minority leader of the Israeli Knesset, Menachem Begin).

We were skeptical. Notwithstanding the constitutional rhetoric that a defendant must be presumed innocent until found guilty, a wise defense attorney always presumes the guilt of his client, at least as a working premise. I proceeded on the assumption that the JDL defendants, including my client, were guilty as charged.

After a summer of planning, we had our first court hearing on September 8 to argue preliminary motions. The judge assigned to the case by lot was the Honorable Arnold Bauman, newly appointed to the bench by President Nixon.

Bauman's appointment at age fifty-eight followed a varied career both in public service and private practice. He began his law practice near the end of the Depression in the New York District Attorney's office under Thomas Dewey, investigating organized crime. During World War II he enlisted in the Navy, where he rose to the rank of lieutenant commander. He retained a military bearing—sometimes an overbearing—throughout his career, which was enhanced by his striking resemblance to George C. Scott (particularly in his role as Patton). After the Navy he entered private practice for several years only to rejoin the ranks of the prosecutors, this time as chief of the Criminal Division of the United States Attorney's office. Later he resumed private practice, where he achieved distinction as a criminal lawyer specializing in the representation of white-collar defendants.

As a judge he was intelligent, autocratic, and humorless. Known as a "prosecutor's man," he constantly reminded defense attorneys of the "high regard" in which he was held by his former colleagues and their successors in the United States Attorney's office. Bauman commanded, and sometimes demanded, visible offerings of respect; never for himself personally, he assured us, but rather for the office he believed he personified. Indeed, he generally referred to himself as "This Court," conjuring up the image of a large building garbed in a somber black robe. He often boasted that "This Court" had never been reversed by the court of appeals.

The lawyers drifted into the courtroom at about 9:45 A.M. for the scheduled ten o'clock hearing. At 10:03 Judge Bauman ascended the bench. Adopting the tone of a grade school teacher, he announced, "Gentlemen, my court starts at ten o'clock and that does not mean ten-fifteen. I want that understood now and in all proceedings throughout this or any other case in which either side appears before me."

Each lawyer was then introduced to the court. Stuart Cohen's chief counsel was Barry Ivan Slotnick, a seasoned local criminal-defense attorney whose clients had included Joe Colombo, the alleged organized-crime boss who had been shot at a rally of the Italian-American Civil Rights League. Slotnick was slick and fast-talking and wore flashy suits; but he was no mere mouthpiece. He was an able, hardworking, and successful trial lawyer. He used his flamboyance as a supplement to, rather than as a substitute for, his considerable legal talents.

Representing Sheldon Davis was Bert Zweibon, one of the founders of the JDL and Rabbi Kahane's hand-picked successor. As a lawyer, Zweibon had specialized in administering estates. ("*My* clients," he would tell me whenever the JDL defendants gave us any trouble, "just lie there; they never complain and they have all the time in the world.") Zweibon's role with the JDL had given him "on-the-job training" as a practicing criminal lawyer; he had participated—either as attorney or defendant—in most of the JDL trials. The government was unhappy with Zweibon acting as counsel for one of the defendants, since it regarded him as an accomplice to the crime. But Zweibon remained on.

The chief prosecutor was Henry L. Putzel III, a smart young assistant United States Attorney whose father was the Reporter of Decisions for the United States Supreme Court. Roly-poly, gentle, and funny, "Pete," as he was known, did not fit the stereotype of the prosecutor.

His assistant, Joseph Jaffe, on the other hand, looked exactly like a prosecutor is supposed to: tall, dark, and macho, he was always surly, taciturn, and suspicious. Joe saw the dark side of everything and was constantly threatening somebody with something. (He was later elected District Attorney of Sullivan County, which includes the Borscht Belt hotels where Seigel and I had both worked as teenagers.)

Judge Bauman, the defendants, the defense lawyers, and the prosecutors were all Jewish. Many observers drew immediate parallels to the Rosenberg case, in which all the participants were also Jewish; these parallels became even more striking when it was revealed that the presiding judge in the court of appeals was to be the same man who had sentenced the Rosenbergs.

The introductions completed, Judge Bauman made it clear that this was the most serious and important case in his thirty-six-year legal career and that he would treat it as a capital case—one carrying a possible death penalty—although he doubted that the death penalty could actually be imposed. (Several months earlier the Supreme Court had decided in *Furman* v. *Georgia* that most existing death-penalty statutes were probably unconstitutional.)

During the course of the hearing I made a motion that was later to prove a mite embarrassing. I raised the possibility that the government may have obtained its information about the Hurok and Columbia Artists crimes from an undercover agent planted within the JDL—a secret operative whom the government was unwilling to "surface." I argued that if there was such an undercover agent, he might be privy to the defense team's confidential discussions of legal strategy. Perhaps my suspicions should have been aroused by the prosecutor's cryptic response: "We are aware of the case law . . . and the defendants have their remedies at the appropriate time." But the reality of what was hiding behind those Delphic words was so far beyond what anyone suspected that the hints went unnoticed.

The next weeks were filled with difficult investigative work. I began to read about bombs and munitions, learning the effects of mixing potassium nitrate and sugar (traces of which were found at the scene of the Hurok bombing). I consulted munitions experts in an effort to establish that incendiary devices did not constitute "explosives" within the meaning of the statute.

The Search for the Informer

During these weeks, I became increasingly suspicious that there must be an informant or undercover agent within the JDL. It made sense that the government would try to plant a "mole" within the organization; that is standard practice in dealing with a subversive organization. But the JDL was not an easy organization to infiltrate: close-knit, exclusively Jewish, xenophobic, drawn from a few parochial neighborhoods, the league had successfully thwarted an earlier effort by the government to plant a Jewish undercover policeman within its membership. It took almost no time for league members to see through "Richie Rosenthal's" cover and to expose him as a cop. It was obvious from Richie's ostentatious tattoo—an affectation shunned by traditional Jews—that he didn't come from Boro Park. Other efforts had also failed, mainly because of the dearth of Jews in the ranks of the police and the FBI.

The government's attitude in the succeeding weeks seemed to confirm my suspicions that it indeed had an informant. Despite its acknowledgement that it had neither eyewitnesses nor fingerprints, it seemed suspiciously overconfident.

Suddenly a hideous idea occurred to me. Could the informer be one of those already charged with the crime? Maybe that explained why the government wasn't trying to make a deal with any of the defendants. Could it be that they didn't need a deal because one of the defendants himself was already an informer?

The idea seemed preposterous at first. Each of the three defendants had long been committed to the JDL. None was a cop—that we knew for sure. Each knew the others since childhood. Each trusted the others with his life. Moreover, the code of Boro Park—a code I knew well—condemned the turncoat and informer more seriously than any criminal. Indeed, in one of the eighteen prayers recited three times a day by Orthodox Jews it is said that informers shall have no hope of redemption either in this world or in the next.

I began to look at all the data again. Which of the three did the puzzle most closely fit? I started to snoop around and ask a lot of questions about past plans that had been thwarted. I looked carefully at the old indictments, both state and federal, and noticed that one of the current defendants was named in several of them. I learned everything I could about those cases: the nature of the evidence; how the crime was brought to the attention of the police; how the case was ultimately resolved. I discovered that the indictments naming my "suspect" had something in common: each involved a crime that had mysteriously been solved with no apparent clues, leads, or witnesses. Each could have involved a secret informant. After completing my amateur sleuthing, I was ready to test my hunch.

On the eve of the Jewish holiday of Succoth, I picked up my home phone in Cambridge and placed the most painful telephone call of my legal career. "I've come to the conclusion that you are the informant," I told the listener on the other end of the line. The response was silence at first, then sobbing, and then more silence.

"Thank God you know," Sheldon Seigel finally whispered. "I've wanted to tell you a hundred times, but I was sure you'd hate me and abandon me. Please help me get out of this mess."

My initial reaction was unmitigated fury. He was absolutely right! I did hate him and I most certainly did want to abandon him, get out of the case, and let him fend for himself. After all, when I agreed to become his lawyer I had taken his case to defend a *landsman*, a fellow Boro Parker, a kid from the old neighborhood—not a stool pigeon. How could I ever trust Seigel again. For months he had tricked me and my colleagues into believing that he was a murder suspect, when all the while he was working for the other side, probably reporting every detail of our strategy right back to the prosecutor. I hastily searched my mind for any statements I might have made to him that I would not want the government to know about. I thought of the months of wasted time—uncompensated time—I had spent trying to build a defense to a murder charge that he knew all along he would never face. (The selfish thought did occur to me that if he had been *paying* for all that time, he probably would have told me sooner, so as not to spend *his money* needlessly.)

I screamed at Seigel over the phone, "Why in hell didn't you tell me, your own lawyer?" He replied softly, "I didn't trust you not to tell the other JDL lawyers." As angry as I was, I couldn't help thinking that his explanation did seem plausible, since I had been brought into the case by Marty Elefant, a JDL lawyer. Seigel had no reason to see me any differently from the others. I assured him that when I represent a client, that client is my only concern and I would never share a confidence with other lawyers unless my client instructed me to do so.

I asked Sheldon how long he had been working for the government. "It isn't that way at all," he said. "I don't *work* for them. They *forced* me to give them information. They threatened to kill me if I didn't, and they promised me I would never have to testify against my friends. Now they want me to testify against Cohen and Davis in the Hurok case. I don't want to do that. Can they make me? What can I do?"

I was still inclined to drop him. But I agreed to meet with him in person before making my final decision, and to give him a chance to tell me his story. We agreed to meet the next day in Brooklyn.

Within minutes I called Harvey Silverglate and told him what I had learned. Harvey was flabbergasted but adamant: "We have to get out of the case. I don't work for the government. And I don't represent finks. Let the government get him a lawyer. He's their boy." I explained to Harvey that the issue was more complicated than it seemed, that Seigel claimed he had been coerced into becoming an informant, and that his rights might have been violated. Harvey was not convinced. "Every fink has his excuse," he said, "but it's not my job to make the government's case easy."

Eventually Harvey reluctantly agreed that he would stick with me whatever I decided to do, but that he himself would not participate in the case if Sheldon became a government witness. We agreed not to tell Sheldon of Harvey's position in order to avoid influencing him. I made up my mind that Seigel's decision whether or not to testify for the government would not determine whether I would remain his lawyer.

On the flight to New York for the meeting, I recalled a visit with my younger brother, Nathan, an experienced criminal defense lawyer, while I was preparing the murder defense. We were discussing the possibility of an informer when my brother jokingly asked, "How do you know it isn't your client?" With the patronizing air of an older brother, I had assured him that he didn't know what he was talking about. He reminded me that he knew Sheldon a lot better than I did, having been his camp counselor. "That kid's a bag full of trouble; he's sneaky; he's a loner; and he develops loyalty to the last person who's nice to him. Keep your eye on him." I had totally forgotten that conversation while trying to put the finger on the informant. I wanted to call my brother and commend him on his prescience, but I didn't feel that I could violate Seigel's confidence even to my own brother.

I also thought—with embarrassment—of the strident motion I had made in Judge Bauman's courtroom, charging that *my client's* rights were being violated by an informant. Sitting on the Eastern shuttle, I wondered whether Judge Bauman had been aware of the awkwardness of my position when I made that motion.

When Silverglate and I got to New York, we met with Seigel at a small kosher cafeteria in Brooklyn. We told him that this was his last chance. He had to tell us the whole truth. If he ever lied to us or misled us again, we were through. We had to know everything.

Seigel's Tale

Sheldon told us that after he joined the JDL in 1969, he began to "hang around" its Boro Park headquarters, which served as a combined command spot and social club. Since Sheldon was good with electronics, he was assigned to the munitions squad, where his ability to construct bombs of every type—smoke, incendiary, and explosive—won him the respect of his peers. He made friends and became something of a hero for the first time.

Among his admirers was a beautiful young woman with flowing blond hair and soft blue eyes named Tova Kessler, whose entire family—father, mother, and brothers—were all devoted and militant JDL activists. A romance began to bloom. Encouraged by the militancy of the Kessler family, Sheldon became more and more involved in the planning and implementation of JDL operations.

Sheldon's first major project reached fruition in April of 1971. At 5:30 P.M., the chief engineer of a Manhattan building that houses Amtorg, the Soviet trade mission to the United States, received a phone call announcing that the building was about to be bombed. The caller ended his warning with the JDL motto: "Never again." Within minutes, the building was cleared and the area cordoned off; dozens of police arrived, including Albert Seedman, Chief of Detectives, and several other high-ranking police officials. One bomb exploded; another was defused seconds before it might have killed the Chief of Detectives, Chief of Intelligence, and Chief Inspector, all of whom were standing within feet of the device. The police officials had come away from their brush with death with an important prize: for the first time, they had in their possession an unexploded and intact JDL bomb. It consisted of several red DuPont dynamite sticks wired to an 89-cent Union Carbide 1.3 volt battery, which was connected to a kitchen timer bearing the brand name Micronta.

With this valuable investigative tool, the police set out to find the bomb maker. A team of detectives from the explosive-arson squad was assigned the task of tracing the component parts. The team was headed by an experienced demolitions expert named Santo Parola. In addition to his expertise with bombs, Parola had one other important qualification for the job: he was the only detective on the bomb squad who had grown up in Boro Park. He was familiar with the kinds of kids who had joined the JDL.

Parola had grown up in the Italian section of Boro Park, near Sixtieth Street and Eleventh Avenue. He was a few years older than I. His father had emigrated from Italy to Pennsylvania, and then to Boro Park, where he worked as a shoe-store clerk. Like both Seigel and me, Santo had been a troublemaker of sorts. A notorious street fighter, Santo—or Sam, as he was called—hated school, both the "special trades" high school and the parochial school that his father made him attend. But he was a popular kid, good at Boro Park street games. "I was a two-sewer man," he once bragged to me during a courthouse break. I told him that I was duly impressed, having never been more than a one-and-a-half-sewer man myself. (Silverglate, who had grown up in New Jersey, didn't have the vaguest idea of what we were talking about: he asked whether a two-sewer man was anything like a second-story man.)

Although Sam grew up on the "Rome" side of the border, he had lots of friends from what he called "Jew Town." "They were the smart kids who were going to college, but some of them wanted to become 'hard guys' or 'rocks,' so they would hang around with us and wear pegged pants, a cigarette pack in their rolled up sleeve, and a garrison belt. It was almost as if having an Italian pal gave a Jewish kid a tough image. It also worked the other way: if an Italian kid had a Jewish friend, that made him look smart." Sam understood the interaction between the two groups, and this understanding would play an important part in his dealings with Seigel and me.

After leaving school, Parola enrolled in the Army as a combat engineer. Later he worked in demolition and electrical wiring. But his first love was the police force, which he joined at twenty-five. His rise to the rank of detective was rapid. By twenty-seven, he was a highly regarded detective. By thirty-five, he had investigated all the major bombings in New York City. His rate of success was extraordinary.

Now his job was to find the person or persons who bought the components for the Amtorg bomb. Since the dynamite and the battery were common items, his attention focused on the Micronta timer, which was sold exclusively by Radio Shack, a chain of electronics retail stores. Sifting through a recent pile of sales slips, Parola discovered a bill dated April 10, 1971—just days before the Amtorg incident—that included two Micronta timers and a package of copper wire. The sale had been made in Radio Shack's Boro Park store, just around the corner from JDL headquarters. The purchaser had given his name as "Feldman" and his address as "6136

Eighth Avenue." Parola visited the address and found no such person living there. He returned to the Radio Shack store and gave his calling card to the manager, a police buff, and told him to keep his eyes open for "Feldman."

Within a few weeks the excited manager called: "Feldman" had just been in the store, buying some copper wire, batteries, and electrical tape. The manager had noted Feldman's license-plate number. A quick check revealed that the car, a yellow Volvo, was registered to a man named Irwin Seigel.

Sheldon soon began to notice that he was constantly being followed by two plainclothes policemen in a battered old Pontiac. Seigel's response was to go on the offensive. He began to photograph his tails. On one occasion he filed a formal complaint with his local police precinct about being followed by two unidentified persons. On another, he stopped a patrol car and told the police that he was being tailed by two hoodlums; the uniformed police pulled the Pontiac over and asked plainclothesman Parola to identify himself, much to the amusement of Seigel.

On the morning of June 4, 1971, the day he was to graduate from City College, Seigel was driving the yellow Volvo along with another JDL member, Izzy Danzinger. They were being followed that day by a detective named Jeremiah Howard. The scene was something out of a Keystone Kops movie: when the cars stopped at a red light, Seigel jumped out of the car and snapped pictures of his tail. After a circuitous journey through the streets of Manhattan, Sheldon drove his car into a garage in midtown, where he left it. Howard moved in, and without a warrant, searched the Volvo and discovered timers, wires, batteries, and gunpowder. When Seigel and Danzinger returned to the car, they were arrested and charged with possession of explosives. The yellow Volvo, Sheldon's pride and joy, was seized and held as evidence.

Seigel and Danzinger were now suspects in the Amtorg bombing. But the police had bigger things in mind. What they needed most was a window into the impenetrable councils of the JDL. Parola was instructed to use the evidence as leverage against one of the suspects to "turn him around" so that the police could get the desperately needed information about the JDL's plans.

Parola, who had never actually met Seigel or Danzinger, could hardly have known where to begin his unenviable task. In an effort to figure out the best approach, he learned all he could about each of the suspect's background and habits. As a Boro Park kid himself, Parola already knew a great deal about the kind of people and neighborhood ties with which Seigel and Danzinger had grown up. He knew about the ethic of loyalty and the disgrace of informing; about the haunting feelings of guilt that many Jews experience for their impotence during the Holocaust; about their deep feeling of identification with Soviet Jewry; about Jewish ambivalence toward violence.

After studying both suspects and their backgrounds, Parola decided to focus his efforts on Sheldon Seigel. He learned that Seigel, having been released on bail, was spending the summer as an electrician and handyman at an Orthodox Jewish summer hotel in the Catskill Mountains. (My own roots at that hotel were deep: two of my uncles had worked there as kids; and I had spent some time there myself.) Parola called Seigel and said he wanted to talk to him about his car. Seigel, anxious for the return of his cherished vehicle, agreed to meet the detective on an abandoned country road several miles from the hotel. Parola found Seigel at the appointed spot and began what would be the first of hundreds of clandestine conversations.

Parola started out by expressing his sympathy for Soviet Jews and his dislike of the "Ruskies." Then he asked Seigel if he had ever heard of Al Seedman. Seigel shook his head. "Well, you damn well should!" Parola shouted. "He's one of your people and you nearly blew his fuckin' head off."

Seigel slumped his shoulders and said, "I don't know what you're talking about."

Parola told him about the Amtorg bomb and how close it had come to killing the Chief of Detectives. "These guys are out to break your balls, and they will unless you tell us about it."

Seigel was unmoved. "You guys must think I'm a real schmuck. I'm not telling you shit about anything."

Parola turned away and began to open the trunk of his car. Seigel watched with anticipation as he removed a shovel. "What are you gonna do with that," Seigel asked, "plant a tree for Israel?"

Parola wasn't smiling. "No, you wise-ass prick, we're gonna plant *you,*" he said, raising the shovel menacingly over Seigel's head. "We're gonna do to you what we used to do to pushers when we were in narcotics. How do you think we got them off the street? Not through the courts, you can bet your ass. There are a lot of planted pushers in the empty lots of Harlem."

Seigel backed away in fright. "Wait a minute," he said, no longer the wise guy. "Maybe we can talk."

Parola told Seigel that the government was planning to throw the book at him in the Amtorg case and that the only way he could help himself was by providing information about future JDL operations. He said that the police weren't interested in names; all they wanted was enough advance warning to thwart any bloodbath. Parola then mentioned Sheldon's brother, who, as the registered owner of the car in which the materials were found, might be brought into the case unless Sheldon came up with some information. Parola also offered to help Seigel get his Volvo back.

Seigel agreed to think it over. Parola told him that if he decided to cooperate, he should call a special number that had been installed exclusively for his calls. He was instructed to use the code name Angelo. Parola, in turn, would be called Steve Horowitz.

Two days after Parola arranged for the return of the car, "Angelo" called the special number and "Steve Horowitz" picked up the phone. "Some people," Seigel whispered into the receiver, had decided to plant a dynamite bomb at the Soviet estate in Glen Cove, Long Island. Without another word, Seigel hung up. A bomb team was quickly dispatched, and the unexploded bomb was found and disarmed. Parola was pleased. For weeks he had stalked the JDL and Sheldon Seigel in the hope of snaring what he called "his kosher canary." Now it had paid off. But the care and feeding of a canary is a delicate task. For weeks following this tip, Seigel refused to sing. In his mind, it had been tit for tat: he had gotten his Volvo back, and, in return, had helped the police prevent a major bombing. He didn't owe Parola another thing.

It was time for the next stage of Parola's assignment. Seigel had to become an informant who was willing to name names and provide information on a continuing basis. Parola kept reminding Seigel that he faced twenty years in prison for the Amtorg bombing. "You know that for all that time you won't get a single decent meal. And what's worse, you won't get laid once—at least not by a broad."

Sheldon was scared. Parola kept reminding him that the materials in the car matched the components used in the Amtorg bomb and constituted "scientific evidence" of his guilt.

Seigel didn't know what to do or where to turn. He had a lawyer in the Amtorg case, one of the cadre of JDL lawyers who were randomly assigned by the league to represent arrested members. Seigel could not tell his JDL lawyer about his conversations with Parola for fear that the JDL would learn of his treachery. Nor could he tell his girl friend, Tova Kessler, whose allegiance to the league transcended even her love for Sheldon. Sheldon was desperately anxious to marry Tova, and he knew what would happen if she found out he was a fink.

Seigel felt the pressure mounting as Parola tightened the noose: unless Seigel named names, the prosecutors would throw the book at him, haul in his brother, expose him as an informer—and take the car back. Seigel began to waiver: he wanted assurances that if he did turn in his friends, no one in the JDL would ever find out that he was the source. Parola gave him what he wanted. "I swear on the lives of my own kids," he solemnly assured him. Parola even came up with a gimmick for guaranteeing that he could never testify about anything that Seigel told him. "We ain't advising you of your rights, understand? You know about *Miranda* and that stuff. If we don't give you your rights—if we don't read you the card—then we can't testify about what you told us."

Finally, on an August night, while Parola and Seigel were sitting in a parked car under the West Side Highway, Seigel agreed to talk. They went to a deserted office of the explosive-arson squad and Seigel nervously began to tell how he had constructed the Amtorg and Glen Cove bombs. He identified those who had assembled the bombs, planted them, and made the calls.

Parola suggested that Seigel meet with the federal prosecutor in charge of the Amtorg and Glen Cove cases, Assistant United States Attorney Thomas Pattison of the Eastern District of New York. These cases were being tried in the Eastern District, encompassing Brooklyn and Long Island, because the bombs were made in Brooklyn, and Glen Cove is on Long Island. At that meeting, which Seigel attended without a lawyer, Pattison assured him that he would not be prosecuted for the Amtorg or Glen Cove bombings. But he told him that he would have to be indicted and arrested along with the others in order to maintain his cover. Seigel demanded something in writing. Pattison agreed to write out a letter that he would give Parola to hold. Quickly he scribbled a few words on a piece of official United States Justice Department stationery and gave it to Parola in a sealed envelope:

> [I]t is the intention of the U.S. Attorney's office to apply for a grant of immunity for Mr. Sheldon Seigel concerning the . . . bombing of Amtorg and the attempted bombing at Glen Cove.

Seigel went before the secret grand jury and testified about the Amtorg and Glen Cove crimes. The following day, the federal grand jury indicted Seigel and six others for the bombings. They were all arrested—including the "sham" defendant Sheldon Seigel.

A few weeks after the indictment, a sniper fired four shots from a high-powered rifle into a bedroom window of the Soviet mission to the United Nations, near Manhattan's Park Avenue, barely missing the four young children who were asleep in their beds. The rifle, found in an airshaft near the roof of Hunter College across the street, was a new .243-caliber Remington fitted with an expensive telescopic sight. The miss did not seem deliberate. This time there had been no warnings.

The U.S. ambassador in Moscow was summoned to the Kremlin in the middle of the night for an extraordinary rebuke. The Soviet Ambassador to the United Nations criticized the United States government and the City of New York for failing to prevent outrages by "Zionist hoodlums." Veiled threats to pull the UN out of "Jewish" New York City were voiced. Mayor John V. Lindsay—a vocal opponent of the JDL—was criticized as a supporter of Zionist excesses. Only the poor marksmanship of the sniper prevented a full-scale diplomatic disaster. Parola was told that he had to get Seigel to finger the sniper. The police had to make an arrest. The pressure—both international and domestic—was intense.

"Steve Horowitz" called "Angelo," but Seigel wasn't interested. Parola, whose orders had come directly from the Police Commissioner, began to hint—at first vaguely and then more specifically—that he could still be prosecuted on Amtorg and Glen Cove, notwithstanding the immunity letter. He also told Sheldon that any immunity would be conditional on his willingness to testify at the public trial of the other defendants. Seigel began to panic. Would he have to choose between being prosecuted or being exposed as an informer? Parola had promised that he would never have to make that terrible choice; that he would never be revealed to his friends. Now the reality began to sink in. What a fool he had been to trust Parola. The police were just playing with him; sucking him in deeper and deeper until he had no one to turn to—except them. He was learning, the hard way, that this is how the government plays in the deadly game of trial by informer, especially when, as is often the case, it's the only game in town; the only way of breaking an important case.

The government was closing the trap. Sheldon had no place to turn; no one to seek advice from, except Parola. Finally he had an inspiration! He would place his trust in the one thing in his life he had always been able to depend on—his talent for technology. He devised a simple but effective way of recording his conversations with the authorities. He installed a $29.95 Sears cassette recorder under the front seat of his car with an activating mechanism beneath the dash that could be turned on and off with his long legs. In this way he was able to record hours of conversation with Parola and Pattison.

The Tapes' Tale

Until Seigel mentioned the existence of the tapes to me, I had been skeptical of his story. Much of it seemed like rationalization for actions he was ashamed of. It is not uncommon for informers to claim that they have been threatened, tricked, or even tortured into cooperating. Moreover, I was certain that even if Seigel's uncorroborated version was absolutely true, no court would believe it in the face of contrary testimony by a policeman and an assistant United States Attorney. So when Seigel told me that he had tape recordings, I wanted to hear them as soon as possible. He warned me that they might not be playable, since he had left them in his car trunk for months. I asked Seigel if anyone else knew of their existence. He said no. I instructed him not to tell anyone.

Sheldon brought me a handful of battered and soggy cassettes. With some trepidation, we put one into a machine. Amid the static, grunts, and curses, we heard conversations that were music to our ears.

These cassettes, which are now in my possession, are a unique collection (and an invaluable teaching tool)—perhaps the only existing recordings, obtained surreptitiously, of government agents at work, using every trick to obtain information from a reluctant informant.*

The initial conversations were about the shooting into the Soviet mission, which had occurred a week earlier. (The fatal Hurok bombing was still three months into the future.) Seigel, aware that the tape was running, says little.

PAROLA: Just the fucking name of the guy. They can't use you for anything. I can't possibly produce you, I can't. All I want to know is one thing: you don't have to tell me nothin' else after that, do you know or don't ya?

SEIGEL: No.

PAROLA: That's the God's honest truth. Or don't make any fuckin' answers at all, and I'll draw my own conclusion. You hear me? 'Cause all I'm askin' for is a crummy, fuckin' favor, that's all. I told ya, I can't hurt the guy, I can't do nothin' to the people that're involved. I probably pick 'm up, I'll probably harass the shit out of 'em a little bit, but that's about as far as I can go with it, 'cause I can't use you, I could break the fuckin' people's balls is all I can do, just break their balls. But I'll know who it is, I'll go out, I'll pick 'em up, I'll make like I know the fuckin' end of the world is coming, but I can't fuckin' say where I got the information, and I can't produce you at all, I can't. And if I could just push this one a little with even bullshit information, I don't mean it's gotta be the right guy, it can't be some fuckin' phony.

. . .

*When these tapes were played in court, the judge remarked that Seigel should teach the FBI the secret of his recording technique, since the quality of Seigel's recordings exceeded any FBI tapes that the judge had heard. The secret, it turns out, was nothing more exotic than the $29.95 Sears cassette recorder. The FBI, on the other hand, relies primarily on expensive Kel sets that transmit the conversations over radio frequencies.

SEIGEL: Uh, huh.
PAROLA: Just mention a nice name to me so that I could get into the good graces downtown again, huh. So's maybe I can get promoted.

. . .

I might, may make an arrest, I might harass the shit outta him, but I'd never be able to prove it in a thousand years. All you gotta do to make me obligated to you, and I fulfill my obligations.
SEIGEL: If I was to make ya obligated to me, there's no way you could fulfill your obligations. What are you going to do?
PAROLA: Yeah, you never could tell, Shel, you never could tell. Supposing someday you need a favor? . . . [F]ive years from now, ten years from now, you might just fuckin' need a favor. You might just need a favor and you bet your ass I'd do it. Anything short of killin', and then it depends who the guy is who you want killed.

This theme of violence pervaded Parola's pleas for cooperation. It was almost never direct. Sometimes it was stated half in jest. But it was always there, as if to remind Seigel of the shovel in the trunk that originally helped loosen his reluctant tongue.

At one point he told Seigel how he treats people who "play games" with him.

PAROLA: . . . I'm gonna get a little fuckin' pissed off and I'm gonna start to put the pressure on. I'm gonna start breakin' fuckin' balls instead of tryin' to be Sam the nice guy.

Sometimes the threats are directed at Seigel himself.

PAROLA: . . . You're not going to jail on either one of them. And if . . . you ever say that I said it, I'm gonna deny it, and I'm gonna meet ya some fuckin' night, and I'm gonna run ya over with a truck.

. . .

[Y]ou . . . ever rat on me, boy, I'll fuckin' brain ya that I told ya. If you can't help me, you're no fuckin' good to me, Shel, I'll have to run you over next time I see you. . . . Did you hear what I said, you fuck, don't play games with me.

But neither the requests for a personal "favor" nor the threats of violence seemed to be working. So long as Seigel believed that he was safe from prosecution on the Amtorg and Glen Cove bombing charges, he had no reason to risk his friendships—indeed, perhaps, even his life—by giving Parola more information. It was necessary, therefore, to plant a seed of doubt in Seigel's mind about his immunity and the letter promising it.

Sensing that he needed legal advice, Seigel hinted to Parola that he might have to talk to a lawyer. Parola urged him not to and offered whatever advice was necessary. Here, for example, was Parola's legal advice if Sheldon refused to divulge the name of the sniper:

PAROLA: You'll be prosecuted you'll be in the same shoes, only you'll be hurt a little worse, 'cause they'll throw the fuckin' book at ya. If they convict ya, they'll throw the book at ya. Don't think they can't withdraw any agreement they made.

Parola also suggested that Seigel might be forced to testify at the trial if his value as an undercover source was diminished by his reluctance to continue providing information:

PAROLA: What did you tell the guy, that you would testify as a last resort, didn't you?
SEIGEL: Except I knew I wasn't.
PAROLA: What makes you think I can't convince a federal jury that this is the truth? You don't think I can twist a jury's fuckin' head? Hey, when I testify, I'm not the same guy sitting in this car, you know.
SEIGEL: Neither am I.
PAROLA: I don't curse.

Seigel began to panic about the prospect of being exposed through public testimony.

SEIGEL: What happens if I come to court, and we say that he promised immunity and he didn't give me immunity?
PAROLA: I'm not going to change my testimony to suit anybody. As long as I tell the truth, there ain't nothing anybody can do to you. [I'm] not gonna lie. I know what he'll probably ask me to do but I'm not gonna do it.

Seigel then reminded Parola of the gimmick they had earlier worked out whereby Parola, by failing to warn Seigel of his "rights," would be precluded from testifying.

SEIGEL: Did you tell Pattison yet that you'd get on the stand and say that you didn't, ah, offer me or that you didn't, ah, didn't advise me of my rights first?
PAROLA: Did I say this? Of course.
SEIGEL: You told him already?

PAROLA: I already said this to the whole fuckin' bunch of them. I said, I never advised him of his rights.

SEIGEL: You told 'em.

PAROLA: Is that the truth or ain't it?

SEIGEL: Yeah.

PAROLA: You know, I could turn around right now and say, of course I did, of course I advised him of—

SEIGEL: Did you tell 'm that if it comes to the stand. That you'd tell that also?

PAROLA: Of course. Hey, I'm not lyin' for nobody, Shel.

Thoroughly confused about his rights, his vulnerability, his status, and the meaning of the immunity letter, Seigel arranged a meeting with Assistant United States Attorney Pattison and Sergeant Parola in Seigel's Volvo. Pattison advised Seigel that he should plead guilty to the very crimes for which he had been promised immunity.

PATTISON: [I]f you plead guilty then they will know that they can't even cross-examine you on this. If you aren't prosecuted, they can make mincemeat of you. They'll say [this] guy's lying his ass off because he's getting a totally free ride. He didn't even have the nerve to plead guilty to what he did. And, he expects you to believe him, never!

SEIGEL: If I plead guilty, I could be a witness against them.

PATTISON: Right. And see, then, they'll know that they can't even cross-examine you on being granted . . . immunity. You see what I mean?

Pattison pointed out that if an accomplice receives formal immunity—"a free ride"—the lawyer for the defendants "can argue to the jury this guy got such a break that he would say anything against anyone. He would testify against his mother." But if the accomplice is not granted formal immunity, then the defense attorneys cannot make that argument.

Seigel asked how he could be sure that he won't be sentenced to prison. Pattison had a convincing answer:

> It's my opinion, and take it for what it's worth, I've been around the block a couple times . . . and you can count on us, and you can count on the judge, to tell him everything that's occurred and to recommend to him that you be allowed to start a new life . . . for yourself out on the West Coast.

Pattison had already assured Seigel that the particular judge assigned to the Amtorg and Glen Cove bombing cases—the Honorable Mark Constantino—generally followed his recommendations. Having told Seigel that if he pleaded guilty he would not be sentenced to prison, he described the advantages of this over the immunity.

PATTISON: You'll have the respect of everyone involved. As a guy who made a mistake and who's willing [to] tell the truth but to possibly suffer whatever consequences might arise out of it, you know what I mean? *But of course, you and I know that, with our recommendation and with our aid you'll be out on the West Coast. You know what I mean?* [My italics.]

SEIGEL: Uh, hmmm.

PATTISON: Can you see my point?

Pattison's "point" was subtle, and, in my view, dubious, both legally and ethically. He was saying, in essence, that while the government was assuring Seigel that he would serve no time, it was keeping that important fact from the lawyers for the other defendants.

Experienced defense attorneys have long suspected that prosecutors sometimes assure prospective witnesses that they will not be sentenced to prison, but advise them to deny on the witness stand that any "promises" were made. Generally they protect themselves by giving a veiled assurance that is—or, at least, can later be defended as—something short of a promise. In the taped exchange Pattison never quite expressly promised Seigel that he would receive no prison sentence, but the message was unmistakable. The absence of the magic word "promise" was designed to leave Seigel free, at a trial of his co-defendants, to deny that he was *promised* a free ride. This would have led the jury to infer—erroneously—that Seigel was not, in fact, assured a free ride in exchange for his cooperation and testimony.

Pattison was really hoping that the Amtorg and Glen Cove cases would never come to trial. He expected that if Seigel pleaded guilty and indicated a willingness to testify against his co-defendants, the lawyers for the co-defendants would recommend that their clients plead guilty. They would make this recommendation because of their ignorance that Seigel had immunity and an assurance of no imprisonment. If the lawyers were to become aware of the immunity letter and the secret assurances given by the prosecutor, they probably would not plead their clients guilty; instead they would seek a jury trial and try to make "mincemeat" out of Seigel on the ground that he was getting a free ride.

I believe that this kind of prosecutorial trickery is not uncommon. Indeed, in the course of his conversation with Seigel, Pattison referred to it as "the name of the game." But I am aware of no other tape recording, or other hard evidence, catching the culprit with the smoking gun the way this tape does.

As the result of these conversations, Seigel eventually did plead guilty to the Amtorg and Glen Cove bombings. Some of the other co-defendants pleaded guilty as well, and sentencing was deferred.

All the while, Parola relentlessly continued his interrogation of Seigel. He offered him money. He agreed to arrest one of Sheldon's competitors for Tova's affections. When all else failed, he again threatened to use the shovel: "You gonna jerk us off one time too many, and then you know what happens? I get the fuckin' shovel again. But this time the dig will be for real."

Finally Parola's persistence paid off. Seigel told him that the police had arrested the wrong person for the shooting into the Soviet residence, and that he thought someone named Gary had done it. The police arrested a seventeen-year-old JDL member named Gary Shlain as he was boarding a flight to Tel Aviv. The police were able to make a convincing case against Shlain without revealing their source of information. Seigel's secret role as informant was safe—at least for the moment.

Seigel hoped that the same could be done with the Amtorg and Glen Cove cases. But the government wanted more information. Parola was instructed to tell Seigel that they would try to keep his identity hidden in these cases, but only if he continued to come up with "good information" about future JDL operations.

It was at this point that Seigel's real value as an inside source became apparent. Over the next few weeks he told Parola of several planned operations that would endanger the lives of scores of Soviet diplomats and their families and that, if successful, would surely set back the prospects for détente.

The first plan was already operational. A drone airplane with a six-foot wingspan had been constructed by the JDL. The plane, carrying six TNT sticks, could be guided by a radio-controlled mechanism located in a moving automobile. They would direct the plane to the Soviet mission on Park Avenue and guide it from the automobile onto the roof of the mission, where its powerful payload would be detonated by remote control.

The second plan involved the basement of the Soviet mission and was potentially more deadly, if less futuristic. The JDL had shadowed a certain Soviet diplomat and discovered that he visited a woman friend at approximately the same time every week. During these visits he parked his car in an easily accessible place. The JDL planned to attach a timed dynamite device to the underside of his car. After the car was readmitted to the heavily guarded garage under the Soviet mission, it would detonate and cause a deadly explosion.

Other operations, still in the planning stages, involved portable mortars to fire shells into the Soviet estate at Glen Cove, and a carefully designed plan to assassinate Soviet Ambassador Anatoly F. Dobrynin in the driveway of the Soviet embassy in Washington.

When Parola communicated these plans to his superiors, the reaction was horror: if "Angelo's" information was accurate, the JDL seemed to be contemplating a full-scale urban guerrilla war against the Soviet Union.

A high-level meeting was convened in the Waldorf Towers apartment of George Bush, the U.S. Ambassador to the United Nations. Attending the meeting were representatives of the U.S. Secret Service, the FBI, UN Security, the Treasury Department, the New York District Attorney's office, the Justice Department, and the U.S. Attorney's office. Also in attendance were Chief Seedman and Sergeant Parola. Bush explained that he was expressing the direct commands of President Richard Nixon when he ordered that the JDL must be prevented—at any cost—from carrying out actions that could jeopardize our relations with the Soviets. He proposed that a task force be assigned to every known JDL terrorist. These teams would act as "virtual baby-sitters" for JDL activists. Parola was directed to keep the pressure on Seigel. "Now more than ever," they were told, " 'Angelo' has to keep the flow of information coming."

As a result of the information Seigel provided, this battalion of federal and state baby-sitters—with Parola as its front-line operational arm—was able to locate the drone airplane in the basement of a Boro Park home and prevent its death mission. They were also able to thwart the planned assassination in Washington, as well as the bombing and mortar plans. As Chief Seedman put it: "The only effective warning device we have against [the JDL carrying out its plans] is a cooperative 'Angelo' slumped in a car with . . . Parola."

But informers are a strange and unpredictable breed, especially "inside" informers like Sheldon Seigel who are not originally planted into the organization by the government but who are recruited from within its ranks. In order to prove his continued loyalty to the organization, the informer—often with the knowledge and implicit approval of the government—must continue to engage in criminal activities. Indeed, he may sometimes be stimulated to *create* violence in order to be able to deliver his "good information."

For example, most of the plans revealed by Seigel involved precisely the kind of technology and imagination at which he excelled. Did he devise them—consciously or unconsciously—in order to be able to earn points by disclosing them? Even as Seigel was informing Parola about the detailed plans to shoot the Soviet Ambassador in Washington, he was hard at work in the Boro Park headquarters of the JDL manufacturing the incendiary devices that would be planted at the Hurok and Columbia Artists offices.

The Hurok and Columbia bombings in January of 1972 caught the government totally off guard. They had all the hallmarks of a JDL job, yet Seigel hadn't given Parola a word of warning. Soon after the bombings, Parola met with Seigel and asked him who was responsible. For several weeks Seigel consistently denied that the JDL was involved. Parola was told to offer him money: $5,000 was put on the front seat of his car. Seigel reacted angrily, saying that he could not be bought.

Finally Chief Seedman authorized Parola to offer Seigel the one thing he desperately wanted: an absolute guarantee that if he told them who was responsible for Iris Kones' death and the Columbia bombing, he would never be revealed as the informant at any trial. Parola told Seigel that he was authorized to offer that guarantee in return for the names of the perpetrators of the Hurok and Columbia bombings. Relying on this promise, Seigel told Parola the names of the people involved—and that he himself had made the bombs.

When Seigel told me this, I asked him if he had it on tape. A recording of a guarantee that Seigel would never be called as a witness at the Hurok and Columbia bombings trial would prove invaluable in the event Seigel decided to refuse to testify against his co-defendants. Seigel sadly shook his head. The recorder hadn't been working that day and there was no tape of the crucial conversation. I told Seigel to keep that fact to himself.

Even without a corroborative tape recording, I was inclined to believe Sheldon's account of Parola's promise: it was entirely consistent with the earlier tapes and it had a ring of truth.

Seigel told us, however, that the government was denying that Parola had promised him anything in return for the names of those responsible for the Hurok and Columbia bombings. It was planning to call him as its star witness at the Hurok-Columbia case and to reveal him as the undercover agent who had been providing information against the JDL for nearly a year.

Sheldon was near the end of his rope. What could he do? Did he have to testify? Would we help him?

To Stay or Not to Stay?

Silverglate and I were emotionally drained after hearing this tragic tale of violence, corruption, and double-dealing. We didn't know whom to be more angry at: Sheldon and the JDL for committing inexcusably reprehensible acts, or the government officials for deliberately violating Seigel's constitutional rights and denying the promises they had made. While the government's actions may have been understandable in light of the need to prevent violence and diplomatic crises, they were nonetheless illegal, at least in our view. They raised serious civil liberties issues. Though informers may generate little sympathy among civil libertarians, they do have constitutional rights worthy of protection. The rights and remedies available to a government witness—as distinguished from a defendant—were, and are, in a state of constitutional confusion. This case, if we were to remain in it, could provide an excellent vehicle for challenging the questionable practices used by the government in its dealings with informants and witnesses. Moreover, Silverglate and I agreed that Seigel had been taken advantage of, and that he desperately needed legal assistance. With some hesitation about representing a double agent who had deceived us for so long, we agreed to remain in the case.

We decided to adopt a completely neutral stance toward both the government and the JDL. We would dissociate ourselves from the ongoing preparations being made by the other defendants and their lawyers. And we would not in any way attempt to influence our client's decision as to whether or not to testify. The decision was his to make, with the benefit of the best legal advice he could get.

Seigel had made up his mind that he was not going to testify *voluntarily* against his friends. He wanted to know exactly what the government could legally do to "make" him testify so that he could weigh the risks.

The general rule is that a witness who is given immunity from prosecution must testify and can be held in contempt for refusing to do so. The grant of immunity is said to serve as a substitute for his constitutional privilege against self-incrimination, since nothing the witness says can be used against him in a criminal trial. Seigel was aware of this, because Parola and Pattison had told him that he would have to testify, or go to jail.

But there was another side of the coin that the government had never told Seigel about: there are circumstances—exceptional ones, to be sure—under which a witness, even after a grant of immunity, can lawfully refuse to testify. For example, a federal statute provides that the government may not make any use of information obtained from an unlawful wiretap. Thus, the Supreme Court has held that if a witness, even one with immunity, is asked a question based on information secured from an unlawful wiretap, he may lawfully refuse to answer such an improper question ("improper" because it was based on information derived from the unlawful wiretap).

At about the same time that Seigel told us his story, the government disclosed that the FBI had used wiretaps against the JDL and Sheldon Seigel. A wiretap had been maintained at the JDL headquarters between October 1970 and July 2, 1971, and another on Seigel's home phone between December 15, 1971, and March 1, 1972. Several of Sheldon's conversations had been tapped. Both wiretaps had been conducted pursuant to authorization given by Attorney General John Mitchell. Despite a 1967 Supreme Court decision requiring warrants for wiretaps, the government had not sought one. The Nixon Administration's legal position had been that a warrant was not required for wiretaps in "national security" cases involving either foreign or domestic organizations that endangered the security of the United States. In 1972, however, the Supreme Court had rebuked the Nixon Administration by holding, in a case involving Students for a Democratic Society, that the prior approval of a neutral judge—rather than that of a potentially partisan Attorney General—was required in all cases involving domestic organizations. The Court left open the question of whether a court order would be required in cases involving "a foreign power" or agent.

When we learned of the existence of the wiretaps, we asked for all Justice Department and State Department memoranda dealing with the taps. Many of the documents were classified; we requested their declassification. Eventually we obtained much (but not all) of what we asked for, and it proved extremely revealing.

The Government's Secret Memoranda

The secret memoranda—disclosed here for the first time—revealed that the United States government was under intense pressure from the Soviets to control the JDL. After windows were broken at the Aeroflot offices in New York, the Soviet Union called off a "four power talk" scheduled for the next day, placing "responsibility" squarely on the shoulders of the United States government. Disruptions of performances by visiting Soviet artists led to the cancellation of a scheduled American tour of the Bolshoi Ballet and Opera (sponsored, of course, by Sol Hurok). The memoranda expressed concern that Soviet authorities might use the JDL disruptions as "an excuse" to "end or postpone the Soviet-American SALT negotiations looking toward strategic arms limitations."

Soviet protests alleged that the JDL could not possibly be carrying on its systematic harassment without the active "complicity" and "connivance" of American authorities. One typical message from Soviet Ambassador to the UN, Jakob Malik, contained the following flamboyant, if ungrammatical, accusation: "that the authoritative U.S. authorities [cannot] be so powerless to deal with the group of hoodluming Zionist element who are propagating ultrachauvinistic racist and fascist ideology of 'chosen people' that creates animosity hatred in your country towards the people of other nations and that openly proclaimed the worsening of relations between the U.S.A. and the USSR as its goal." (Ironically, a government task-force report categorized the JDL as a group "of left-wing political orientation" because J. Edgar Hoover regarded all anti-Nazi groups as left-wing.) Other Soviet cables protested that "none of [the] criminals have been punished thus far," and offered to give the American authorities the "addresses of [the] person causing these idiotic things if the [Justice] Department could not find him."

A confidential State Department memorandum urged the Justice Department to secure indictments against the JDL perpetrators, arguing that this would "measurably improve the ability of the United States to deal with the Soviet Union on substantive foreign policy issues."

When a Soviet court sentenced two Jews to death for planning to commandeer a Soviet plane and fly it to Sweden, the JDL immediately threatened to execute four Soviet diplomats if the death sentences were carried out. Secret State Department cables revealed that U.S. diplomatic personnel were worried that the JDL was capable of implementing its threats. On the eve of the scheduled execution, the State Department put its diplomats on maximum alert, but the sentences were commuted to life imprisonment. (Little did I then suspect that I would soon become one of the lawyers for these dissidents and travel to the Soviet Union in an effort to secure their release.)

In light of the JDL's potential to disrupt Soviet-American relations, FBI Director J. Edgar Hoover wrote a memorandum to Attorney General Mitchell requesting authorization to install wiretaps on their telephones. Characterizing the league as "the most militant pro-Jewish organization active in the United States," Hoover claimed that the "White House has expressed its concern." Fearing that JDL activities in support of "the Jewish race" could create a situation of "international embarrassment to this country," Hoover requested authorization by Mitchell to install wiretaps in order to secure "advance knowledge" of JDL activities. The authorization was granted and the taps installed.

After reviewing the secret memoranda, we sought a ruling that the JDL wiretaps were unlawful because there had been no prior judicial authorization. Whatever else the JDL was, we argued, it was a domestic American organization. Despite its mission to further the interests of "the Jewish race"—in J. Edgar Hoover's words—the JDL did not enjoy any international support; even the Israeli government, in whose interests the JDL sometimes claimed to be acting, deplored it and condemned its violence.

The government prosecutors argued that the JDL was an international organization and that the Supreme Court's decision governing domestic organizations was inapplicable to it. Henry Putzel, the chief prosecutor, stood up to make the argument, but Judge Bauman interrupted:

THE COURT: You mean somebody wants to contend that . . . a wiretap of the Jewish Defense League . . . had something to do with the international relations of the United States?

MR. PUTZEL: [M]y face is not as straight as it might otherwise be. [I]f the Court should hold that this is not a foreign intelligence situation but a domestic intelligence situation, then—

THE COURT: I so hold.

To this day I do not understand why the government did not push its international-relations argument harder, nor why Judge Bauman was so eager to dismiss it. The State Department documents lend support to the conclusion that the wiretaps "had something to do with the international relations of the United States," even if the JDL was a domestic organization. This might have been an ideal test case for the government to seek a broad construction of the foreign-intelligence exception to the warrant requirement. But Judge Bauman ruled, and the remainder of the case was litigated, on the unchallenged premise that all of the wiretaps were unconstitutional.

In light of this ruling we asked the government to make the wiretap tapes available so we could listen to them and determine whether the testimony sought from Seigel was "tainted" by the illegal wiretaps and was thus a "fruit of the poisonous tree." The concepts of "taint" and "fruit" are traditional legal metaphors for the causal connection between the challenged evidence and the original government illegality. For example, if the government searches a house illegally and discovers drugs, the drugs are "tainted" and constitute a "fruit of the poisonous" search. If, however, during the course of the illegal search, the police discover an address book containing the name of a witness who leads them to drugs, it is less certain that the drugs would be regarded as tainted by, or the fruits of, the original illegal search. The court might hold that the original "taint" had become "attenuated" by the questioning of a live witness and that the drugs were not the direct "fruits" of the government's illegality.*

If we could prove that the questions the government sought to ask Seigel at the trial were based directly on information the government had obtained

*Courts love to use imprecise metaphors such as "taint" and "fruit" because of their inherent ability to expand or contract with the context, which accords the judges broad discretion in applying them to specific situations.

from the wiretap, we might be able to persuade Judge Bauman that these questions were indeed tainted fruits of the poisonous tree. We might then secure the ruling we wanted: that Seigel would not have to testify against his friends at the Hurok trial.

We awaited receipt of the tapes so that we could listen to every word and nuance in search of clues linking the testimony sought from Seigel to the information obtained from the wiretap.

But we were never to hear the tapes: Putzel announced that the tapes of the wiretaps had been "routinely" and "inadvertently" erased and reused after the FBI had made summary "logs" of their contents. A "log," Putzel informed us, was "a chronological series of notes made by the agent who listens to the tapes." We were given the logs, which proved extremely unhelpful, containing as they did only the briefest summaries of those conversations deemed "relevant" to the FBI monitoring agents.

Even the summary logs, however, revealed the intrusive scope of a wiretap. The recorded conversations over the Seigel phone ranged from dog food and cars to bombs and rifles, and involved every member of the family and numerous friends. It was an embarrassing experience for me to read even the summary logs, since I personally knew so many of the people who were speaking and who were spoken about in the wiretapped conversations.

A study of these logs disclosed that the FBI had learned from the wiretaps—as early as February 1971, two months before the Amtorg bombing and four months before the search of the Volvo—that Seigel was a JDL activist. By March they had learned that Seigel was involved in the purchase of guns for the JDL. By May—several weeks after the Amtorg bombing but before Seigel had been identified by the Radio Shack salesman—the wiretaps had disclosed that Seigel was concerned that the authorities might be looking for him in connection with the Amtorg bombing.

Seigel's Dilemma

This was the situation facing Seigel: if he testified against his friends, the government would drop all charges against him. He would go free, and if necessary, relocate on the West Coast. But relocation was not what Seigel wanted, since it would have required complete separation from the community in which he had been raised and in which he had built his life. If, on the other hand, he refused to testify, the government would throw the book at him. He would be charged with contempt, and the government would seek the maximum sentence, which, under a leading case, could be as long as the Hurok defendants' maximum sentence—life imprisonment. He would receive the maximum sentence under his plea of guilty in Brooklyn.

And he would be prosecuted and sentenced for possession of explosives in the New York State case.

We advised Seigel that the odds were against him. We had a chance of obtaining a ruling that he would not be held in contempt for refusing to testify, on the ground that the government had secured his cooperation unlawfully. We also had a chance of vacating his guilty plea in the Brooklyn federal court because of his immunity letter. There was also some possibility of having the state's prosecution dismissed on the ground that the search of the Volvo had been unlawful. We cautioned him, however, that the likelihood of succeeding simultaneously on all three challenges was remote; and that if we failed on *any one* of them, he would spend a considerable amount of time in prison—if he refused to testify.

Sheldon then asked us if it would be possible for him to postpone his decision until *after* we had obtained these rulings; in that way he would know exactly what he faced if he refused to testify. This was a tough question. The law has never made it easy for witnesses to challenge the government. The general rule is that a witness may test his refusal only *after* he has been held in contempt.

Despite this rule—established by the Supreme Court—we decided to try to figure out some way of getting an advance legal ruling before Seigel had to make his critical decision. Instead of simply waiting for the government to call Seigel as a witness—which is what the government expected us to do—we went on the offensive and brought a lawsuit against the government.

Our tactic was to place the government on the defensive; to put Parola, Pattison, and the other government officials on trial for *their* conduct before the government could put the JDL defendants on trial for the killing of Iris Kones.

Taking Offense

When a criminal lawyer represents a guilty defendant—and the vast majority of criminal defendants are guilty—his only realistic alternative may sometimes be to put the government on trial. The American legal system is unique in permitting this turnabout. The United States Constitution does not expressly provide for putting the government on trial. But the Bill of Rights does impose important restrictions on the government and its agents: the Fourth Amendment restricts the government's power to search and seize (which has been construed to include wiretapping); the Fifth Amendment prohibits the government from compelling any person to be a witness against himself in a criminal case. In order to implement these amendments, the Supreme Court has developed what has come to be known as "exclusionary rules"—rules that exclude illegally secured evidence from consideration by the jury or judge.

Exclusionary rules were not originally regarded as part of our constitutional fabric. There was one type of evidence, however, that was generally excluded even during the earliest days of American justice: a coerced confession. This exclusion was derived from English law and was based on the fear that a confession obtained by torture might well be false and could result in the conviction of an innocent defendant.

The courts gradually expanded the Fifth Amendment exclusionary rule to cover cases in which there was little likelihood that the confession was false, even though it was obtained by coercion (for example, where the confession was independently corroborated by other witnesses or by physical evidence). In these cases the courts freed defendants not because there was any real doubt about their guilt, but because their constitutional rights had been violated. Instead of focusing on the guilt or innocence of the defendant, the developing exclusionary rule began to focus on the conduct of the police and prosecutors in eliciting the challenged confession. The government could thus be put on trial by the defense attorney. If the police or prosecutors were found "guilty" of violating the defendant's Fifth Amendment rights, then the confession could be excluded and the guilty defendant set free.

The Supreme Court eventually applied the constitutional exclusionary rule to the Fourth Amendment as well.* In 1961 the Supreme Court, in *Mapp* v. *Ohio,* held that physical evidence of guilt—even the most reliable and indisputable—must be excluded if it was secured by "official lawlessness" in violation of the Fourth Amendment. The Court has also applied the exclusionary rule to illegal wiretaps. It thus became permissible for a defense attorney to try to establish that the evidence against his client was obtained by "official lawlessness." By closing the courtroom doors to illegally obtained evidence, the Supreme Court had opened them to mini-trials in which the government was the defendant and its "official lawlessness" was on trial. (In recent years the Supreme Court, especially under Chief Justice Warren E. Burger, has riddled the Fourth and Fifth Amendment exclusionary rules with exceptions and limitations; but a skilled defense

*This application was not as natural as it had been in the context of the Fifth Amendment. The Fifth Amendment speaks in language suggestive of an exclusionary rule: "nor shall [any person] be compelled in any criminal case to be a witness against himself . . ." The Fourth Amendment, on the other hand, speaks in far more general terms: "The right of the people to be secure in their persons, houses, papers, and effects, against unreasonable searches and seizures, shall not be violated, and no Warrants shall issue, but upon probable cause, . . ." The Constitution does not specify the remedy for violation of these rights.

attorney—even today—can put the government on trial for its conduct.)

The "official lawlessness" that we wanted to put on trial ran the entire gamut from the use of warrantless wiretaps to the search of the Volvo, to the manner by which Seigel had been coerced into becoming an informer, and, finally, to the broken promises that the government had made in order to ensure his reluctant cooperation.

The first problem we encountered was that there was no established mechanism by which a witness—as distinguished from a defendant—could raise such charges and put the government on trial. A *defendant* could move to exclude the incriminating evidence that the government was seeking to introduce against *him* at his trial. But Seigel himself would not be on trial in the Hurok-Columbia case; there would be no evidence introduced against *him;* he would be called simply as a witness against others, and asked some questions. Seigel would actually have been in a better position had he been a *defendant* on trial for murder in the Hurok-Columbia case than he was as a witness with immunity from prosecution: as a defendant he would have been entitled to put the government on trial for the tactics it had used to secure the evidence—both verbal and physical—against him; as a mere witness, his rights were far more problematic.

We decided to try something that had never been tried before: we would ask the court to put Seigel on trial for murder. This may sound like a bizarre, indeed suicidal, strategy for a criminal defense lawyer, but it was really quite safe. We were confident that the evidence of Seigel's complicity in the Hurok-Columbia case had been secured by illegal means and that without it he could not be convicted of murder. Our motion, which we knew would never be granted, would serve as a dramatic gesture demonstrating that the government was attempting to get indirectly what it was not entitled to get directly: namely, punishment of Sheldon Seigel for his role in the Hurok-Columbia bombings—a role the government had discovered by its "official lawlessness."

The trial was scheduled to begin in February 1973. We came to court on a Friday morning ready to unveil our unorthodox legal maneuver. The tension was high as Assistant U.S. Attorney Henry "Pete" Putzel and his assistant, Joseph Jaffe, took their seats at the government's counsel table. Sitting behind them at the defendant's table were Sheldon Davis and Stuart Cohen with their lawyers.

We chose to sit at a separate table to emphasize our independence both of the government and of the defendants. Harvey Silverglate and I were joined by Jeanne Baker, a young Northeastern University Law School student who was working as a research assistant for Silverglate.

Judge Bauman entered the packed courtroom and inquired of Mr. Putzel,

"What is the state of the Union?" Moving slowly, almost teasingly, to the lectern, Putzel announced that "the Government has a motion for severance." Every lawyer in the room realized immediately what that meant: a motion for "severance" is the government's way of separating the real defendants, who are to stand trial, from an informant, who will not—at least not at the same time. It is a motion dreaded by defense lawyers because it generally signifies that one of the defendants has turned informer. A prospective government witness must be "severed" from his co-defendants, because the Constitution forbids the government from calling any defendant as a witness at his own trial.

Before Putzel could state the reason for his severance motion, I rose and asked that the motion be heard in the judge's chambers rather than in the public courtroom. The reason for this request was obvious: if Seigel had indeed been promised that he was not going to be exposed as the informant and if that promise was legally enforceable, surely he should not be publicly exposed by the government *before* our legal arguments could be heard and decided. Putzel's response established the tone of the government's position on this issue: "I have no knowledge of any promises that were made to Mr. Seigel as to the confidence that he would be kept in." Without listening to our argument, the judge ruled that the severance motion should be heard in open court.

We had lost the opening round.

Putzel proceeded: "The basis for our [severance] motion is that Mr. Seigel gave the information in this case [and] testified before the grand jury and was promised that at an appropriate time, which is now, he would be conferred immunity for his testimony. . . . Mr. Seigel will be called as a Government witness. . . ."

The JDL crowd that filled the courtroom gasped in disbelief and then anger. Never before had a turncoat been uncovered in the organization. The fear of an informer was constantly on their minds, but who could have imagined that it was their premier bomb maker? (Soon both Seigel and I would receive threatening letters reminding us that under Jewish law an informer must not be suffered to live.)

The government next made a motion to have the court bestow immunity on Seigel.

I objected.

Judge Bauman looked at me incredulously, as if I had made a slip, and asked, "You object to immunity from criminal prosecution?"

"Yes, we do," I replied. "Our position is that we would like to see the Government *prosecute* our defendant and not give him immunity."

The judge shook his head in disbelief and said, "[I]n all my experience this is the first time the Government has ever offered immunity where a defendant has declined it."

Putzel demanded a one-month delay to "investigate whether any improper pressures" had been brought to bear on Seigel. We suspected that the government wanted the month to put some pressures of its own on its reluctant star witness. Sensing the advantage of speed, I moved for a hearing on Monday and assured the court that all our papers—motions, affidavits, and legal memoranda—would be completed by then. As I was saying this, Silverglate was tugging at my sleeve and practically shouting, "We haven't even started; we can't have anything ready by Monday." I whispered back, "We will if we have to." And we had to. The judge set the hearing for Monday on condition that all papers were filed by that time.

Hurrying back to Boston, we rounded up volunteer law students and set up an around-the-clock production line for the completion of the necessary papers. By Sunday night we had finished, and we drove to New York to begin preparation for the next morning's hearing.

Since our client could not afford to pay for hotel rooms, a JDL supporter had offered the use of his office-townhouse on East Thirty-eighth Street in Manhattan as an evening work place and dormitory. When we arrived at midnight we couldn't quite figure out what kind of place it was. Equipped with a swimming pool and sauna, its walls were covered with red velvet and floor-to-ceiling mirrors. There was a hidden room that appeared from behind a mirror at the touch of a button. The upstairs rooms were protected by electronic eyes that sounded an alarm when anyone came up the stairs. Its several bars were completely stocked, and its refrigerators were filled with caviar and pâté. We noticed that none of the dozen or so beds had blankets but that there were hundreds of freshly laundered sheets and towels. There was no heat at night.

We fantasized about the activities that must have gone on in the house on Thirty-eighth Street as we converted it into a makeshift law office, equipped with a small law library, a typing area, a cassette-tape center, and an interview room. We were to spend many nights there listening to tapes, preparing cross-examinations, and drafting legal memoranda.

Since it was freezing when we arrived at the unheated house, we held our meeting in the sauna. At about one o'clock Seigel wandered in and told us that he had found an additional tape under the spare tire of his car. It was unraveled and seemed unplayable, but we finally made it work. Jeanne Baker was assigned the task of determining whether it contained anything useful for the next day's hearing.

Around four in the morning I heard a loud shriek from upstairs. Harvey and I ran up the stairs (setting off the electric-eye alarm) to find Jeanne sitting on her bed staring at the tape recorder and mumbling, "I found it. I found it."

We asked what it was and she replied, "I found proof that the government first learned about Seigel from the wiretaps."

I asked Jeanne to play the critical portion of the tape. This is what I heard Parola say to Seigel: "You know about the shit that was bought in the store and how we came to get all this information. You know it's"—and here there was a slurred word that could either have been "not" or "done"—"on wiretaps."

I stopped the tape in disappointment and said, "How are we helped by that? Parola just said, 'You know it's *not* on wiretaps.' " Jeanne and Harvey replied in chorus, "What, are you deaf? It says, 'You know it's *done* on wiretaps.' " We listened again, and again, and again, perhaps a dozen times. Harvey and Jeanne stuck to their interpretation. I began to waiver. The context in which the disputed remark was made supported either version.

PAROLA: If we wanted to prosecute the first case, don't you think we got a good chance of knockin' you over if we really push?

SEIGEL: Not much.

PAROLA: Supposing I decide to testify. You know about the shit that was bought in the [Radio Shack] store and how we came to get all this information. *You know it's [done? not?] on wiretaps.* [My italics.]

SEIGEL: What's that have to do with the first case?

PAROLA: *'Cause that's how we stumbled onto you.* What do ya think fingered ya? We did. We checked that store out again, and we found out you bought those batteries, and we said that you're up to no fuckin' good. We said we better watch this kid 'cause they're up to no fuckin' good, and *we never had your name before.* Said this is a fuckin' oddball name. *We never had this kid before. That's how we stumbled onto ya.* You know that. If you don't know it you're stupid or your fuckin' lawyer's dumb.

The crucial word—"done" or "not"—was slurred and nasal, in typical Brooklyn fashion. By listening carefully I could hear a muffled "d" sound and perhaps an "n" sound, but couldn't really make out the word. The more I listened, the more it sounded like "none"; I was still not convinced it was "done." Since I came from the same neighborhood as both Parola and Seigel, I fancied myself something of an "expert" on Boro Park accents. Brooklyn instinct said it was "not," but Cambridge rationality cautioned that it might be "done." As an advocate, I was obliged to argue my client's position that this conversation was proof of Parola's admission that the police had stumbled onto Seigel through the wiretaps. Seigel himself did not particularly remember the conversation and wasn't sure what Parola had said, but—quite understandably—urged us to argue the version that would help him most. In any event, we were not prepared to play the tapes in court yet, or even to disclose their existence. We had some other surprises in store for the government, and the tapes were to be our ace in the hole.

Bleary-eyed with fatigue, we arrived at the courthouse at ten o'clock. I began presenting Seigel's legal position.

MR. DERSHOWITZ: [A]t the beginning there were wiretaps. . . . The links in the chain were as follows:
First came the wiretap; and the revelation that Mr. Seigel had a relationship to Amtorg.
Then came the search of his car and the discovery therein of evidence relevant to the Amtorg case.
[W]e will show . . . that Mr. Parola was able to [turn Seigel into an informant] solely as a result of the information derived [from the wiretaps and the search.]

I pointed out the substantial handicap under which we had been placed, since the actual tapes of the wiretaps were not in existence. The FBI's destruction of the tapes—whether deliberate or accidental—violated the federal wiretaps statute, which requires the safekeeping of all tape recordings made of wiretaps conducted by federal agents. We argued that the government should not be permitted to profit from its violation of the law. The government lawyers responded, ingeniously, that the federal statute required the preservation only of those tapes of wiretaps made *pursuant* to the statute; but the wiretaps at issue here were not made pursuant to the statute, they were unauthorized by statute and hence illegal. Thus, according to the government, the tapes could lawfully be destroyed. In other words, while we argued that one wrong (the warrantless wiretaps) plus one wrong (the destruction of the tapes) equaled two wrongs, the government argued that the first wrong canceled out the second wrong. The court reserved judgment and asked the government to call its first witness.

The Wiretaps

The government called a string of witnesses—FBI agents and Parola—who denied any connection between the FBI wiretaps and Parola's activities. Parola swore that he was not aware that there had been any wiretaps. This was difficult for us to understand, since the justification for conducting the wiretaps was to alert local law enforcement officials to planned JDL violence, in order to prevent it.

To bolster its contention that Parola had discovered Seigel without help from the FBI wiretaps, the government presented its theory of how Seigel was found. It claimed that a detective named McKeegan had independently developed Sheldon Seigel as a suspect in *another* bombing. Parola and McKeegan just happened to be in the same room, Parola testified, when Parola mentioned the yellow Volvo used by a man named Irwin Seigel who made the purchases of wire and batteries at Radio Shack. Suddenly McKeegan "jumped up" and exclaimed that *he* was "looking for a guy named Sheldon Seigel" who owned a yellow Volvo registered in his brother's name.

Detective McKeegan was in the hospital and was not available to answer the inevitable question that Parola's testimony left open: how had *he* learned of Sheldon Seigel and classified him as a bombing suspect? Did McKeegan's information derive from the tainted wiretaps?

Judge Bauman, realizing that McKeegan's absence left a gap in the government's case, ordered the still-convalescing McKeegan into court to testify.

Our plan was to examine McKeegan and Parola out of the hearing of the other in order to establish—and probe—any inconsistencies in what we suspected was a fabrication. Just before Parola took the stand, Jeanne Baker overheard him offer McKeegan the keys to his car and suggest that since McKeegan was still convalescing, he should go home. She immediately interrupted the conversation and summoned a government lawyer, demanding that McKeegan remain in the courthouse to be available for recall to the stand. Parola then took the stand, and after some questioning, a recess was called. The speed with which Parola tore out of the courtroom alerted us that something was up and I rushed out after him. The corridor was empty, so I headed for the men's room and found both officers standing near the window. Parola was urging McKeegan to "get out of here" and go home. In fact, McKeegan took Parola's car and fled the courthouse faster than a criminal who had just seen his face on a "Wanted" poster. We immediately brought this lavatory conference to the attention of the judge, but neither Parola nor McKeegan were admonished for defying the order not to discuss the case or for disregarding our request that McKeegan remain available for recall.

"I Had to be Crazy"

The second area of inquiry at the hearing concerned the search of Seigel's car and the seizure of the bomb-making material. The government's version of this crucial search rested on the testimony of Detective Jeremiah Howard, who had searched the Volvo and found the material. Howard's account was that in the course of his surveillance duties he trailed Seigel from Brooklyn to Manhattan. Stopped in heavy traffic at a long red light, Howard got out of his car and walked right up to the Volvo. There, according to his testimony, he saw Izzy Danzinger, Seigel's companion, making a bomb in the front seat. Later, when Seigel parked his car in the garage, he left the door open with the bomb lying in plain view between the two front bucket seats. Howard gave this testimony with a straight face, despite his acknowledgment that Seigel knew he was being followed and even got out of his car to take a photograph of Howard—a candid picture that we were able to produce.

Judge Bauman appeared quite ready to accept Howard's bizarre account of Seigel's behavior, an account requiring him to believe that Seigel and Danzinger would commit a serious crime in plain view of the police. (A classic test of legal insanity is whether the criminal would commit the crime "with the policeman at his elbow.") Addressing the defense lawyers, Bauman said:

> I see nothing untoward in this man's handling of the event. . . . I suggest that . . . you address yourself to the facts as they have been testified to here . . . I mean, one must not permit legal jargon to interfere with common ordinary everyday sense.

Detective Howard's story had carefully included all of the elements that one finds daily in police testimony when warrantless searches and seizures are challenged by the defense: the officer invariably testifies that there was probable cause to believe that contraband would be found, that there were emergency circumstances justifying the failure to obtain a warrant, or that the contraband was in the officer's plain view.*

Judge Bauman's acceptance of Howard's testimony eventually changed,

*A retired New York State Criminal Courts judge has written about the problem of perjurious policemen. Irving Younger—who had served a term as an assistant U.S. Attorney in Judge Bauman's favorite office—put in print what every lawyer whispers about but none had dared to publish:

> Every lawyer who practices in the criminal courts knows that police perjury is commonplace.
>
> Policemen see themselves as fighting a two-front war—against criminals in the street and against "liberal" rules of law in court. All's fair in this war, including the use of perjury to subvert "liberal" rules of law that might free those who "ought" to be jailed. And even if his lies are exposed in the courtroom, the policeman is as likely to be indicted for perjury by his co-worker, the prosecutor, as he is to be struck down by thunderbolts from an avenging heaven.

after the occurrence of two fortuitous events. First, we managed to find the attendant who had been on duty at the parking garage. He testified that he had driven the yellow Volvo inside the garage and had accompanied Detective Howard and the squad of policemen who had searched the car. He told the court that he was certain that there was no bomb in view, and said that he would have "had to be crazy" to drive the car down the garage ramp if there had been a bomb in the front seat. The second fortuitous event was that shortly after he appeared as a witness, Howard was suspended from the police department on charges of accepting a bribe.

Guerrilla Lawfare

The final area of inquiry involved our claim that Parola had promised Seigel he would never be called as a witness. The key witnesses on this issue were Seigel and Parola. A classic one-on-one credibility contest seemed in the offing. And no one in the courtroom had any doubt how that would come out—no one except Seigel and his lawyers, who were the only ones aware of the existence of Seigel's surreptitiously recorded tapes.

We had spent many hours trying to decide on the most effective way to capitalize on our little secret. Our ultimate goal was to prove that Parola had specifically promised that if Seigel gave him the names of those responsible for the Hurok and Columbia bombings, he would not be called as a witness. But that crucial promise was not on tape. We had to get Parola to admit on the witness stand that he had made it.

We planned to break down our cross-examination of Parola into four phases. First, we would allow Parola to believe that there were no tapes of his conversations with Seigel and that he could lie with impunity in the expectation that his testimony would be contradicted only by Seigel's own words. We would elicit answers from him that we knew—while he did not—would be exposed as lies by his own words as recorded by the hidden tape machine.

During the second phase we would incorporate into our questions some verbatim quotations from Parola's conversations with Seigel, thus planting in his mind the possibility that Seigel had recorded some, if not all, of their conversations.

During the third phase we planned to continue to read to Parola what appeared to be "verbatim quotations" from a "transcript" of a conversation involving the Hurok-Columbia bombings. In fact, we *would* be reading from a transcript, but it would not be a transcript of a *tape:* it would be a rough reconstruction of the conversations as Seigel remembered them and had recounted them to us. We hoped that Parola would believe that we were reading from a transcript of a tape recording and therefore admit that he had indeed made the promises contained in our quotations.

In the final phase we would play the tapes themselves in order for the court to know precisely which statements were recorded and which were not.

We knew that this strategy posed considerable risks because it required the lawyer conducting the cross-examination to mislead the witness, the government, and the judge—at least for a time—into believing, or at least suspecting, that we had tapes of certain conversations that were not, in fact, recorded.

We put the issue to several authorities on legal ethics and were advised that although it was a close question, there was nothing wrong with what we had planned for Parola. We knew that we were skirting near the edge of permissible advocacy, but we were confident that our tactic was justified under the circumstances.

I decided to conduct the cross-examination of Parola myself. I had two reasons. First, there was some virtue in my obvious inexperience: during the first phase of cross-examination, it was important for Parola to be lulled into a sense of confidence, if not arrogance. It was critical to our strategy that he believe he had nothing to fear other than contradictions by Seigel and some ineffective cross-examination by a neophyte courtroom lawyer. Second, if anyone was going to be criticized for the misleading nature of the cross-examination, I wanted to be the one, since I was the chief counsel and the tactic was mine.

The first phase of the cross-examination began with routine questions designed to put Parola at ease. After a while I began to ask him about conversations that we had on tape:

Q: Did you ever tell [Seigel] that the reason you did not advise him of his rights [was] so that the information he gave you could never be used in evidence against him?
A: No, sir, I did not.
Q: Did you ever have such a discussion with him?
A: No, sir, I did not.

Unbeknownst to Parola, we would later show he had precisely that conversation with Seigel—and more than once.

Q: Did you ever promise him that he would never have to be publicly revealed if he gave you the information in the Amtorg case?
A: No, sir.

Again the tapes would disclose that Parola had repeatedly assured Seigel that he would not be publicly revealed if he provided the information.

Q: In regard to information that you were seeking from Mr. Seigel relative to a shooting into the Soviet Mission, did you at any point tell him that if he gave you information about that, that you would never call upon him to testify at any trial or ever reveal him as an informant?
A: Oddly enough, Mr. Seigel volunteered that information to me.

The tapes would, of course, demonstrate beyond any doubt that Seigel did not "volunteer" this information; that Parola had to extract it from a reluctant Seigel over a period of weeks and only after making repeated promises that he would never be revealed as the source of the information.

Parola was digging himself deeper and deeper into our trap: one answer after another was untrue. He had to know that they were false, but he did not suspect that we could *prove* they were false. Indeed, during a recess break he bragged to Jeanne Baker about how well he was handling my cross-examination: "That professor boss of yours, he may be smart in the classroom, but he sure don't know how to cross-examine a cop."

The time had come for phase two: Parola had to begin to suspect, and then to believe, that we had tapes of his conversations with Seigel.

After the recess I walked up to the lectern with a folder of transcripts in my hands. (At the same time, Harvey placed a box of tape recordings on our counsel table. Fearful that the government might simply seize the tapes and learn what was—and what was not—on them, Harvey had left the real tapes in his briefcase and placed musical recordings in the cassette boxes on the table. Even the nature of the music generated disagreement: Harvey wanted *Götterdämmerung,* but Seigel vetoed any music by Wagner; they finally settled on Beethoven.) I asked the court for permission to quote "obscenities" in my continued cross-examination of Parola. Judge Bauman solemnly responded that it had been his constant practice "to take the language as it was in fact used." This reference to obscenities produced immediate titters from the courtroom crowd. (My mother, who was present, was later to bawl me out for not obtaining *her* permission to use the dirty words.) Reading from the transcripts, I asked Parola whether he had ever had "the following conversation with Mr. Sheldon Seigel":

> You're not going to jail on either one of them, and if you ever say that I said it, I'm gonna deny it and I'm gonna meet you some fuckin' night, and I'm gonna run you over with a truck.

Parola did not immediately understand what was happening.

A: No, sir, I deny that.
Q: You are certain that you never said anything about running him over with a truck?
A: I never said anything like that.

I continued to press the witness. I asked him if he had ever made the following statement:

> You ever fuck me up like that when I tell you something, you ever rat on me, I will fuckin' brain you.

Parola became a little less certain about his answer: "I don't believe I made that statement."

Slowly, it was beginning to sink in: Parola's relaxed composure began to change. He asked for water. His face grew pale. His fingers trembled. He almost dropped the glass of water.

At this point Assistant U.S. Attorney Putzel interrupted my cross-examination with a series of objections. His purpose was plain: he wanted to give Parola time to comprehend his dilemma and reflect on his answers. The objections were overruled, but Parola got the message:

> The only thing I can say to that, Counsel, is that I would use that type of language at times. . . .

Parola's tune began to change. His self-confident denials gradually softened into evasiveness and forgetfulness: "I don't remember, but it sounds familiar"; "I possibly would say something like that"; "I would have said something like that in order to keep the rapport with the informer."

It was becoming clear to everyone that we had tapes that could prove that Parola had repeatedly lied in his earlier testimony.

The partisan JDL crowd, which had been given little to cheer about up to now, began to understand what was happening. Judge Bauman admonished them: "Some of the audience is getting a little exuberant. Unless they contain themselves I am going to have them removed."

The government lawyers were in a panic; their entire case hung on Parola's quickly evaporating credibility. Putzel tried to cut his losses by seeking immediate disclosure of whatever tapes we had:

> We have got obviously the clear inference from Mr. Dershowitz that he's got some verbatim transcriptions here of tapes, which would not surprise any of us.

The court gave a Delphic response:

> Are you altogether sure it wouldn't surprise any of you.

Putzel then made his request:

> [I]f there are tapes and transcripts, can't we just [get them] and not play footsie . . .

We stood in poker-faced silence awaiting the judge's response. Our strategy—indeed the entire case—hung in the balance. If Judge Bauman granted the request, we would have had to make a full and accurate disclosure, listing what we had and what we did not have on tape. The government's request could not have come at a worse time, from our point of view. We had succeeded in destroying Parola's credibility. But we had not yet been able to prove our crucial contention: that Parola had, in fact, promised that Seigel would not be called as a witness in the Hurok-Columbia case if he disclosed the names of those responsible for the bombings. We could succeed in proving this only if Parola continued to believe that we had tapes of the conversations about which we were questioning him. And we were ready to begin questioning Parola about the untaped conversations he had had with Seigel during the Hurok-Columbia investigation.

Judge Bauman called a recess to consider his decision. The tension was broken by my mother, who had baked a batch of tollhouse cookies and began to distribute them indiscriminately to the lawyers, the defendants, and even Sam Parola. (My mother never came to court without a baked offering.) My mother noticed my nervousness and attributed it to lack of sleep and food. She gave me more cookies and a coffee-flavored hopje.

I waited with concealed anxiety for the judge's ruling and felt a tremendous surge of relief when he came back to the bench and announced his ruling:

> [Professor Dershowitz is] entitled to examine this witness as to his credibility and as to the substantive facts.
>
> Now, he may do it by playing the tape for him, or he may do it in his own way. . . .
>
> Go ahead.

The time had come for the high point of our cross-examination: Parola had to believe that the conversation I was about to read to him was on tape. We had asked Sheldon to recall the crucial conversation about the Hurok bombing with as much precision and detail as he could. He came up with a draft that contained the substance, but it lacked Parola's style and earthy language. My Boro Park background proved invaluable as I edited it to reflect the street argot I had grown up with.

What we came up with sounded *to us* like Parola. The important question was whether it would sound like Parola *to Parola.*

Casually, as if I were simply continuing the interrupted examination, I asked Parola if he recalled having the following conversation with Sheldon Seigel:

PAROLA: Hey, where you been?
SEIGEL: What do you mean?
PAROLA: I told you two o'clock, didn't I?
SEIGEL: No. You told me between two and two-fifteen.
PAROLA: Hey, don't get cute. Hey, look, you got to do us a favor. If you can help us on the Hurok thing I would appreciate it. The whole place is gonna—

Suddenly the judge interrupted me and asked me to give a "copy of that" to the court reporter so that he could transcribe it without having to slow me down. I began to panic: right in the middle of the key question I would have to turn over to the court reporter the "transcript" I was reading from. But it wasn't a transcript! It was simply an account in Seigel's own hand writing. The jig was up. I had blown it by not having Seigel's account typed in transcript form. I didn't know what to do. But then the judge finished his remarks: "Otherwise, you will have to speak more slowly." We were saved. I slowed down my presentation and proceeded:

[PAROLA:] I promise you, Shelley, just give us the names and leave the rest to us. If we can't prove it without ya, then we can't prove it.

I turned away from the "transcript" and looked Parola straight in the eye. "Do you remember having that conversation in substance?"

Parola looked away and mumbled, "In substance, I could have had that conversation."

I looked at Jeanne and Harvey. Their eyes were aglow with success and anticipation. It had worked—so far. Parola believed that we had the Hurok conversations on tape. I turned back to the transcript and continued to read:

PAROLA: Once we know who did it, you don't think we can turn these guys? Are ya kidding? We'll get it out of them. I'm tellin' ya, we can do it.

SEIGEL: What if someone finds out?

PAROLA: No one's going to find out. You won't even have to go to the grand jury in this one. We can do this whole shmeer without even using you.

When I asked Parola whether he recalled the substance of that conversation, he again turned away and said vaguely that it "sounds familiar."

By this time Judge Bauman was beginning to become impatient with Parola's obvious evasiveness. When Parola responded to a question about another conversation by saying, "I possibly would say something like that," the judge snapped at him, "What do you mean possibly? Did you or didn't you?" The tide had turned. The government realized that and again began to interject objections. But Judge Bauman seemed to know exactly what we were doing. In fact, he made a remark that led us to suspect that he had seen through our little ploy and that he was somewhat skeptical about whether we really had tapes of all—or indeed any—of the conversations:

THE COURT: [T]he asking of questions does not constitute evidence, and particularly in a non-jury matter, where you are before a Judge who has had some pretty wide experience in criminal cases.

[Dershowitz] is going to have to decide if such a tape exists, and whether or not he is going to offer it.

All the while, Judge Bauman was becoming increasingly interested and involved in the cross-examination. At one point, in reading from the transcripts, I began to act out the roles of the participants. This drew an immediate objection from the government:

MR. PUTZEL: Your Honor, I will object to the dramatics.

MR. DERSHOWITZ: I'm sorry.

THE COURT: I understand your pain [Mr. Putzel], but it is pretty exciting stuff.

At another point, Judge Bauman virtually took over the cross-examination:

THE COURT: Take it sentence by sentence.

MR. DERSHOWITZ: [Reading] "Look, just tell me who did the Hurok thing. Just give me their fucking names."

THE COURT: In March of 1972 did you have such a conversation with Mr. Seigel?

MR. PAROLA: Yes, I could have had that conversation relative to Hurok, your Honor.

MR. DERSHOWITZ: [Reading] "We will never use you as a witness, we will build the case around you. We will use your leads."

THE COURT: Did you say to him in that conversation—and don't tell me you could or couldn't have—I want to know did you or didn't you?

MR. PAROLA: I believe I have testified on the record, your Honor, that I did, in fact, say to Mr. Seigel that we could build a case around him.

Judge Bauman was now helping to conduct my cross-examination. I continued:

[Reading] "We ain't going to use you. We just ain't going to, won't have to, we can make the case without you."

THE COURT [voice rising]: Did you say that?

MR. PAROLA: In those exact words, I don't recall, your Honor.

MR. DERSHOWITZ: Did you give the substance of that statement to Mr. Seigel?

MR. PAROLA: In substance I would say yes.

THE COURT: Then it is a fact, isn't it, that at some point in time you said to Seigel: "We will never use you." Is that correct?

MR. PAROLA: My conversations, your Honor, with Seigel: "We would never use you if we can build a case around you."

THE COURT: I didn't put that "if" part in. I am asking you whether you ever told it to him without the "if."

Read that language, Professor, please. The last few lines of that.

MR. DERSHOWITZ: [Reading] "We ain't going to use you. We just ain't. We won't have to. We can make the case without you."

THE COURT. Did you say that to him?

MR. PAROLA: That sounds familiar to me, your Honor. I don't recall exactly if those words are the words.

THE COURT [shouting in anger]: Just don't interrupt me. I take it when you say "that sounds familiar," that that means that you recollect that in substance, if not in those words?

MR. PAROLA: In substance, sir.

THE COURT: Yes.

Parola thus admitted that he had promised Seigel he would never be called as a witness in the Hurok-Columbia case.

Our strategy had worked better than we had dared hope for: Parola had denied most of the conversations that we had on tape; and he had admitted virtually all of the conversations that we did not have on tape.

By the end of phase three of the cross-examination, there was no one in that courtroom—not the judge, not the government, not even Parola himself—who wasn't convinced that Parola had been exposed as a liar. Parola skulked away from the witness stand frightened and embarrassed; Putzel looked at him angrily; and Judge Bauman did not hide his contempt for the officer who had been stupid enough to get caught red-handed. Indeed, the judge characterized the events of that day as a "debacle."

The time had come for the denouement of the examination: the playing of the tapes. We were anxious to play the tapes as soon as possible, while Parola's testimony was still fresh in everyone's mind. We also wanted to assure Judge Bauman that the suspicions he had expressed earlier—that we might be bluffing about the tapes—were only partly correct; that we did have tapes of some, although not all, of the conversations we had asked Parola about.

Immediately after completing the third phase of the cross-examination, I announced that "we would now like to play the tapes of the recorded conversations in order to refresh Officer Parola's recollection about various statements that he does not recall having made."

The government balked at this offer, and instead proposed that they receive the tapes so that they could play them, have them tested by the FBI for authenticity, and prepare a transcript. The judge adjourned the hearing until the government could complete its homework.

Although we were under no legal or ethical obligation to inform the court or the government at that time that all the conversations were not on tape, it now seems clear to me that we made a blunder in not doing so. By allowing the government lawyers to "discover" this "gap" and themselves disclose it to the court, we allowed the false impression to be created that we were trying to hide something.

In any event, that critical court day ended with the partisan JDL crowd greeting Seigel with shouts of congratulations. Those who, the day before, had despised him for his treacherous betrayal today praised him for his ingenuity and loyalty. Some even suggested—though I doubt that anyone really believed it—that Seigel had carefully orchestrated the whole bizarre scenario in order to discredit the government and expose its sordid mode of operations. Newspaper stories the next day announced the destruction of the government's key witness by the surreptitiously recorded tapes.

Turning the Tables on Us

Over the weekend, while we were busy preparing the transcripts of the Parola tapes, Judge Bauman was apparently beginning to appreciate the implications of his testimony. Until Parola's credibility crumbled, the judge did not have to face up to the difficult legal issue raised by our motion: whether a policeman's promise that an informer would not be called as a witness was legally enforceable. He could, as so many judges routinely do, choose to believe the policeman's denial. But this avenue seemed blocked after the disclosure of the tapes and Parola's admission that he had indeed made the promise.

When Judge Bauman next appeared in court, on Tuesday, it was to consider a motion brought by the other defendants in the Hurok case. Neither Seigel nor we were in court that day. But Judge Bauman repeatedly made a point of advertising his doubts about *our* motion:

> I am going to want to talk to Professor Dershowitz about just what it is that he is asking . . . me to do. [T]o stop the government from calling a witness at a trial not yet commenced? [O]n what authority does he claim I have such power, because I am unaware of it. I never heard of it.
>
> In all my previous experience going back well over thirty years I have never heard of such a thing in words of one syllable.

Now that the facts were going our way, Judge Bauman was having second thoughts about the law.

During that week we sent the government our tapes. The prosecutors played them and discovered, of course, that the Hurok promise was not included in the recorded material. Putzel called me in Cambridge, expressing anger at our "little trick," but admiration at our cleverness. He also advised me that Judge Bauman wanted me in his "robing room" on Friday afternoon for a status report on the tapes and transcripts. Since it was simply to be a "housekeeping" session, I came alone without my co-counsel and without any papers, expecting to spend no more than half an hour in the courthouse. That Friday session turned out to be the most threatening afternoon in my legal career.

As soon as I sat down, Assistant United States Attorney Joseph Jaffe immediately rose, and in a well-rehearsed speech, accused me of having "grossly, grossly misled the Court and misled the witness Parola." Jaffe charged that I had confused Parola by reading apparent "quotations" that were not on tape. Judge Bauman seized on this "monumental mistake" and informed us that "based on these representations, *you* demoralized that witness and led me to the conclusion that he was a liar." Appearing to forget that the tapes themselves—and not our "representations"—had conclusively proved that Parola *was* a liar, Judge Bauman began to treat Parola as a victim and me as his assailant. Sounding more like a prosecutor than a judge, Bauman began his attack:

THE COURT: Now, I want to suggest to you, sir, that in this court, at least, one expects lawyers to keep their punches above the belt . . .

MR. DERSHOWITZ: Your Honor, I do not think there were any punches below the belt.

THE COURT: You and I then, sir, have two different ideas of the level at which one practices law. . .

MR. DERSHOWITZ: I just don't understand your argument, your Honor.

THE COURT: Don't get the idea I am arguing with you, sir. I am expressing the opinion of the Court.

MR. DERSHOWITZ: If, in fact, he testified one way, thinking there were no tapes, and testified another, thinking there were tapes, I don't understand how anything but truth has been searched [out].

Judge Bauman was not convinced:

THE COURT: Is it your view that you can ask questions that were, in fact, taken from a wiretap or a tape recording and in the middle of real questions, for instance, make up a little question, which you slip in there, which never existed. . . .

MR. DERSHOWITZ: When you say never existed, are you suggesting made up?

THE COURT: Yes.

MR. DERSHOWITZ: No, that would not be proper. If you are asking whether it would be proper in the middle of conversations, which the witness assumed were on tape, to ask him about conversations which we believe occurred, but which were not recorded on tape, most affirmatively yes.

THE COURT: Indicating by your actions, mannerisms, readings and other attitudes in the courtroom that it was on tape?

MR. DERSHOWITZ: By all means, yes.

THE COURT: You and I have a diametrically different view.

MR. DERSHOWITZ: I guess we do, your Honor.

THE COURT: I regard it as a reprehensible practice.

MR. DERSHOWITZ: If you would explain to me—

THE COURT: I am not in the business of answering questions. You do understand that, don't you.

MR. DERSHOWITZ: I do not understand what is wrong with that in any way.

THE COURT: I can't help you, then.

We were obviously at loggerheads. I asked Judge Bauman to "keep an open mind" on the issue, at least until we had a chance to respond to the government's charges in writing. But the "court" could not wait to make its ruling:

THE COURT: I authorize and direct that those questions and answers be stricken from his testimony.
Is that, as the expression goes, perfectly clear? . . . Now, I want to save Professor Dershowitz the trouble of briefing it because I simply rule that that is totally improper procedure, and if I'm wrong, the Court of Appeals can tell me so.*

Thus, in one fell swoop, Judge Bauman had ruled that he would ignore the tape recordings, Parola's obvious lies, and Parola's reluctant admissions that he had made the crucial promise. Suddenly the lying cop had become the bastion of truth and his cross-examiner had become the unethical shyster. Judge Bauman strongly implied that in his written decision he would formally charge me with unprofessional conduct for my misleading cross-examination.

Defending My Own Conduct

I left the courtroom angry at Judge Bauman's criticism and capricious ruling, but determined that these would not be the last words on our cross-examination of Parola. Despite the judge's desire to save me "the trouble" of submitting a brief on the propriety of my cross-examination, I decided to prepare a defense of my conduct.

Several days later we returned to court armed with a memorandum on the propriety of the cross-examination technique used against Parola. It cited numerous legal authorities in support of the proposition that it "has long been regarded as the essence of effective cross-examination, especially of a lying witness, to convey the impression that the cross-examiner has more, less, or different evidence than he actually has." The brief cited numerous examples similar to those used against Parola that were regarded by the authorities as "classic" instances of effective cross-examination.

We had even discovered that Abraham Lincoln, as a trial lawyer in Illinois, reputedly used a tactic not so different from ours. Francis Wellman,

*Judge Bauman's abrupt termination of discussions without explanation reminded me of Ring Lardner's description of a conversation between a son and his father. When the son asked his father whether he was lost, the father terminated the discussion. Lardner puts it this way: "Shut up he explained."

in his classic treatise on *The Art of Cross-Examination,* gives the following "instructive example of cross-examination": A man named Grayson was charged with murder, and his mother engaged young Abraham Lincoln to defend him. Lincoln asked an alleged eyewitness how he had observed the crime. "By moonlight," he answered. Lincoln then removed an almanac from his pocket and read that there was no moon on the night in question. Believing himself trapped by the almanac, the witness broke down and confessed to being the killer. Wellman then recounts the rumor "frequently stated by members on the Illinois circuit to this day . . . that Lincoln played a trick . . . by substituting an old calendar for the one of the year of the murder."*

Judge Bauman was not impressed with our legal research. He continued to treat me in a personally abusive manner.

THE COURT: I had in mind this morning to caution you not to address me again in the manner in which you addressed me [last Friday].

MR. DERSHOWITZ: I really don't understand what your Honor is saying.

THE COURT: I am sorry about that. Proceed. I will hear you.

MR. DERSHOWITZ: Are you suggesting my tone of voice or the loudness of my voice or in what manner—

THE COURT: It isn't customary for me to respond to questions.

MR. DERSHOWITZ: Let the record simply reflect that I am now speaking in a quiet tone of voice and with the utmost respect that I can muster. (As I said these words I was thinking of Mae West's retort to the judge in *My Little Chickadee* when he asked her if she was trying to show contempt for the court. West answered, "No—I'm doing my best to hide it.")

*This Lincoln story, like so many others, is partly apocryphal. The actual facts appear to be as follows: Lincoln produced an almanac, showed it to the witness, and asked him the following questions:

> Q: Does not the almanac say that on August 29 the moon was barely past the first quarter instead of being full?
> A: (No answer.)
> Q: Does not the almanac say that the moon had disappeared by eleven o'clock?
> A: (No answer.)

The defendant was acquitted. The almanac was probably for the correct year (a copy of it is available at the Harvard library), but Lincoln's characterization of its *contents* was somewhat misleading: the almanac does describe that night's moon as barely past the first quarter; the implication of that description is that its lighted portion was barely more than one fourth. But a more careful review of the almanac disclosed that the lighted portion exceeded three fourths of the moon; it was nearly fully lighted. And it did not disappear until several hours after the witness had sworn he had seen the crime. (A check with the Harvard Observatory confirmed this.) But the witness was confused by Lincoln's misleading show of erudition and could not answer the questions. Lincoln apparently never informed the court of his misleading statements (if he was indeed aware, as I suspect he was, that they were misleading).

At that point Harvey Silverglate tugged at my sleeve and whispered, "Alan, this has got to stop. Bauman has *you* on trial. We have to show him we mean business. Why don't you call for a recess and let me handle it from here." Always willing to learn from my teacher, I asked for a recess to discuss the matter in the judge's chambers.

Harvey took over and explained the problem to Judge Bauman:

MR. SILVERGLATE: The problem is we feel we are entirely in the right. We have law to show it and it is quite difficult to proceed to the defense of Sheldon Seigel when we feel that every time Mr. Dershowitz says something, either his tone is mistaken for being hostile or his words are taken to be disrespectful.

THE COURT: It is inappropriate for counsel to address questions to the Court. You know that.*

MR. SILVERGLATE: He certainly is entitled to find out to what he had to respond.

THE COURT: What's the nature of this application?

MR. SILVERGLATE: We feel it would be appropriate for the Court to disqualify itself.

At the mention of the word "disqualify," Judge Bauman stiffened. The rules provide that if a judge has shown certain kinds of partisanship at a trial, he must remove himself from the case. It is a badge of dishonor for a judge, especially when it is demanded by counsel. Silverglate had deliberately raised the issue in the privacy of the judge's chambers so as not to embarrass him in public, but the issue could not be kept under wraps for long. Judge Bauman's entire tone changed after this exchange. He addressed me directly:

THE COURT: I see no reason why you should not continue with your customary vigor to represent your client.

. . .

I think we ought to start all over again and see if we can't go forward. I had in mind to express my view in rather strong terms of that kind of procedure on cross-examination in an opinion. By way of easing your mind, I tell you now that I do not propose to write anything . . . about this question.

But I do want an end to these personal things.

We accepted the judge's assurance and began to return to the courtroom. Before we could leave, Judge Bauman called me back and said that he

*Where Judge Bauman got this notion is a mystery. Lawyers constantly address questions to judges.

wanted to tell me something "off the record." With an avuncular smile he assured me that he would not have gotten so upset at my cross-examination if I had been some "ordinary street lawyer." "But you're a Harvard law professor. You teach law students. I have to hold you to a higher standard of ethics."

I told the judge that "if I were to impose on myself what you call 'a higher standard of ethics,' then I would be imposing on my clients a lower standard of advocacy. That wouldn't be good law or good ethics. I propose to continue to resolve all ethical doubts in favor of my client and to continue to teach my students to do that if they become defense attorneys."

Judge Bauman's behavior toward me during the remainder of the hearing was exemplary.

"It's Done on Wiretaps"

We returned to the courtroom ready to play the tapes that we had decided to offer in evidence. The FBI had concluded its check of the recordings and reported—to our relief—that they were genuine and had not been tampered with. But there was that one critical passage that was ambiguous: in the fall of 1971 Parola made the statement to Seigel in which he either said "You know *it's done* on wiretaps . . ." or "You know *it's not* on wiretaps . . ."

The tape was played and then replayed for the judge:

THE COURT: It sounded like, "not on wiretaps," but I will listen to it again. Play it two or three times.
(Tape played.)
THE COURT: I am mistaken. "You know it's done on wiretaps" is what it is.

We had won the crucial issue; the judge had heard the slurred remark our way.

The hearings were now over. Judge Bauman had promised a quick decision, but week after week went by without word from his chambers. One of the favorite pastimes of lawyers is to speculate about the meaning of delay in decisions, whether they be jury decisions or judicial decisions. Silverglate, the eternal optimist, saw the passage of time as a good sign: "He's really reading our papers." I, the eternal pessimist, saw only gloom: "He's writing a long opinion putting every last nail in our coffin." Jeanne Baker, the eternal pragmatist, was already preparing the appellate papers, confident that there would be an appeal whichever way Judge Bauman decided the Hurok motions.

There was other work to be done on the case while we waited for Judge Bauman's decision. Assistant U.S. Attorney Thomas Pattison was holding the Amtorg guilty plea over Seigel's head as an additional threat in the event that he refused to cooperate.

We had to find a way, therefore, to remove that threat. Accordingly, we brought a lawsuit in the Eastern District of New York seeking to withdraw Seigel's guilty plea on the ground that the immunity letter precluded it.

By this time it was widely known within government circles that Seigel had recorded conversations with government lawyers and agents. No one knew precisely what Seigel had recorded, since we had turned over to the government only the tapes relevant to the Hurok case, not those relevant to the Amtorg case.

In our negotiations with Pattison, we let it be known that his conversations with Seigel were among those that had been surreptitiously recorded. Pattison's fear of a cross-examination, like Parola's, may well, in my view, have contributed to his decision to "recommend" that the judge permit the withdrawal of the guilty plea without a hearing. The judge accepted Pattison's recommendation, and Seigel's guilty plea was withdrawn.

On April 25, 1973—the same day that Judge Constantino authorized the withdrawal of Seigel's plea in the Eastern District—Judge Bauman rendered his decision. It was almost as if a court jester had said to us, "I have some good news and some bad news." The bad news, contained in Judge Bauman's detailed 38-page opinion, was that Seigel would be required to testify at the Hurok murder trial.

Judge Bauman's Opinion

Judge Bauman found as a fact that there was "nothing in this record that supports Seigel's contention" that Parola had promised Seigel that if he furnished the names of those involved in the Hurok bombing, he would not be required to testify.

This was simply not true. Parola had admitted on cross-examination that "in substance" he had told Seigel "we will never use you"; Parola's partner, Joseph Gibney, had testified that he had given Seigel a "blanket assurance" that he would not be exposed or have to testify; and the tapes demonstrated conclusively that in other contexts Parola repeatedly assured Seigel that the government "can't use you for anything. I can't possibly produce you."*

*The best proof that Parola had given the disputed promise in exchange for the Hurok information ultimately came from Chief Detective Seedman, the man who had personally authorized the promise in exchange for the Hurok information. In his book, *Chief!*, published shortly after the conclusion of the Hurok trial, Seedman quotes Parola as follows: "Give us

Judge Bauman also decided to believe Parola's testimony that he was unaware of the wiretaps and "never received information concerning Seigel from wiretap sources or from the F.B.I." Of course, there was the problem that Judge Bauman had concluded at the hearing—after several plays of the tape—that Parola had told Seigel that he *had* been discovered by wiretaps. ("You know it's *done* on wiretaps . . . that's how we stumbled onto you.") The solution to this problem was simple. Judge Bauman just changed his mind again about what he had heard:

> I am inclined to agree with the government, . . . that the context supports a reading of "not."

Not content to rest his finding on the context, Bauman relied squarely on Parola's credibility:

> At the hearing Parola was confronted with this entire passage and insisted that he had said "not." I must attach some importance to this recollection. It carries even greater weight, in my view, because Parola consistently denied any knowledge or use of the J.D.L. wiretap in the face of persistent and at times, unfairly confusing cross examination.

Incredibly to us, particularly in the atmosphere of the Watergate scandals, a federal judge chose to "believe" a policeman whose testimony had been repeatedly shown to be false by his own statements, surreptitiously recorded and preserved on tape. Totally ignoring the tapes, Gibney's testimony, and the cross-examination—except to characterize it as "unfairly confusing"—Judge Bauman blithely asserted that Parola was telling the truth.

I have no doubt that *every* person who heard Parola's testimony and the tapes—the judge, the prosecutors, courtroom observers—believed that Parola had lied. Yet Judge Bauman stated in his opinion that he *believed* and *relied* on Parola's truthfulness. Nothing could demonstrate more graphically, and more distressingly, the virtual impossibility of persuading

---

the names of the kids who did this Hurok thing, and I think we can get a promise that not only will you walk away from everything else—but the DA won't reveal you. Otherwise, Shel, it's going to happen in open court right out in front of your people." Seedman writes that after this conversation Seigel asked Parola, "Will you still make good on that promise not to reveal me?" Parola responded, "For the good stuff, we sure will, kid." Seigel then asked, "Suppose I tell you who made the bomb they used at Columbia Artists Management." Parola responded, "That's the good stuff, all right." Seigel again demanded an assurance that he would not be disclosed: "You swear you won't reveal me?" Parola gave him that assurance: "We swear, kid." Only then did Seigel disclose his own participation and the names of the others. Did the prosecutors interview Seedman in preparation for the Hurok hearing? If not, why didn't he come forward with this crucial information?

some judges that *any* policeman is ever lying. Police perjury, and the way some segments of the American judiciary encourage it, is simply a fact of life that most criminal lawyers cynically accept as readily as they accept the inevitability that most defendants will also lie but will not be believed.

There are circumstances, however, under which even a policeman's testimony strains credibility to the point that it cannot possibly be believed—especially if the police department itself has expressed its distrust in the officer, as it had done by suspending Jeremiah Howard, the officer who had conducted the search of Seigel's car. Judge Bauman concluded that Seigel's account of the car search was more credible than Howard's. He held the search of the Volvo unconstitutional and ruled that "the Government will not be permitted to ask any questions of Seigel based on the contents of his automobile." But he did not discuss the implications of this holding: that the search and seizure of Seigel's car and the resulting discovery of the "scientific evidence" linking him to the Amtorg bombing was the key that Parola used to unlock Seigel's potential as an informer.

Judge Bauman's opinion was typical, in many respects, of judicial decision making in cases involving the so-called "exclusionary rule." He did not quarrel with us over the law, since he knew that any legal error he might make would be reviewable by the court of appeals. Instead, he resolved most of the critical *factual* issues against us. It is a fundamental rule of appellate review that findings of *facts* made by a district judge cannot be overturned by a court of appeals except in extraordinary situations. The reasoning behind this rule is that the district court has actually seen and heard the live witnesses and is thus deemed in a better position to assess their credibility than would an appellate court reading a "cold" transcript. The "law," on the other hand, is within the special province of the appellate courts; it comes from the pages of books rather than from the mouths of witnesses. Many district judges—acutely aware of their power to make law through facts—consciously tailor their fact-findings to achieve the legal results they desire, thus effectively tying the hands of the appellate courts.

All the participants in the legal process are aware of this charade, but little can be done about it except in clear cases of abuse.

Judge Bauman's opinion was a masterpiece of this genre. We realized that it would be difficult to overturn on appeal. Judge Bauman had repeatedly and proudly reminded us that he had never been reversed by the court of appeals. (Many judges have a way of personalizing the process so as to make it appear that *they,* rather than the defendants, are the subjects of the appeals.) Now we understood why he could boast of this record: his decision seemed consciously designed to withstand appellate reversal.

At this point Seigel's future looked bleak. We had obtained an advance ruling as to whether Seigel would have to appear as a witness, but it had come out mostly against us. If Seigel was called but refused to testify, a contempt conviction seemed almost certain; and a stiff sentence for criminal contempt was likely.

"It Is Not My Intention to Obstruct Justice"

Having won the opening round, the government moved quickly to begin the Hurok murder trial. With the momentum on their side, the prosecutors were anxious to call Seigel to the witness stand while Judge Bauman's decision was still fresh. We were obliged to inform Seigel of our professional opinion that the likelihood of success in the court of appeals was anything but certain. We continued to decline to give Seigel our own personal advice as to whether or not he should testify against his friends. (Indeed, our own personal views differed among ourselves.) That was his decision to be made on the basis of the best professional judgments—really predictions or "guesstimates"—about what the courts were likely to do.

We decided to file our appeal immediately, in the expectation that by the time Seigel was called as a witness and held in contempt (if he should refuse to testify), the case could be argued without delay. Speed was important because we expected Judge Bauman to order Seigel's confinement without bail after a finding of contempt, since by the time Seigel was called to the stand, the Hurok jury would already be sitting, and the judge would be reluctant to keep the jurors in a state of limbo during lengthy appellate proceedings. It was crucial to our strategy that Seigel remain out of jail pending appellate review. We wanted him to be able to make up his own mind. This meant keeping him free of pressures by the government and the court, on the one hand, and by the Jewish Defense League, on the other. Sheldon had recently married Tova Kessler, and she had become a pillar of support for his refusal to testify. We feared that if the government could get him into their custody, away from his lawyers and wife, they might again apply the kind of pressure that had produced results in the past.

At long last, the trial of the Hurok defendants opened. The courtroom was filled with JDL supporters, many in yarmulkes and some in prayer shawls. Every spectator was searched for weapons by a special squad of U.S. marshals. Judge Bauman admonished several JDL supporters to stop "davening" in the court. (He explained that davening was a form of prayer in which those praying sway back and forth in rhythmic concentration.) At one point a woman stood up and gave the judge "the evil eye"—an ancient Jewish curse—provoking Bauman to threaten to expel her "if you do that again."

After much bickering and ethnic guessing by both sides about what "kinds" of jurors would be most sympathetic, a jury was impaneled. (The defense lawyers had surmised that Irish and Italian jurors would be more sympathetic to JDL defendants than WASP, black, or even Jewish jurors.) Assistant U.S. Attorney Joseph Jaffe made the opening statement, informing the jurors that the government's case rested almost entirely on the testimony of Sheldon Seigel.

Tension was high as the judge said impatiently, "Get Mr. Seigel on the stand." Everyone waited for our next move. Would Seigel testify? Would he refuse and be held in contempt? What sentence would the judge impose? Sheldon Seigel, dressed in an ill-fitting suit and an open shirt, walked slowly up to the wood-paneled witness stand. He shifted around nervously as he took his seat. The tension mounted as Assistant U.S. Attorney Henry Putzel put the first incriminating question to a slumping and morose Sheldon Seigel: "Is it not a fact, sir, that on Tuesday, January 25, 1972 [the day before the Hurok bombing], you met with Stuart Cohen and Sheldon Davis at the headquarters of the Jewish Defense League?" At this point even we did not know for certain what Sheldon would do.

He reached into his pocket, and with cold determination, pulled out a sheet of paper. It was the statement I had prepared for him to use in the event he decided not to testify. He began to read, stumbling over some of the words:

> I respectfully decline to answer on the ground that I was promised by government officers that I would not have to testify if I provided certain information, and on the ground that my identity was learned as the result of [illegal] wiretaps [and searches].
>
> I believe that my respectful refusal to answer these questions is based on just cause and it is clearly not my intention to obstruct justice but only to see that justice is done to me, and my constitutional rights are secure.

Putzel was visibly upset at Seigel's scripted performance and snapped, "Who prepared that statement for you?" Judge Bauman responded, "Obviously his lawyer did. I don't think it makes much difference." Putzel then asked Seigel whether it was his "intention to refuse to answer any questions on the grounds of the Fifth Amendment to the Constitution?" Seigel responded, "No, I'm not." Putzel expressed surprise; it was the first time in his experience that a reluctant witness had not automatically invoked the Fifth Amendment when asked incriminating questions.

Putzel continued to ask incriminating questions; Seigel repeated his litany in response to each. Finally Judge Bauman leaned forward and stared directly at Seigel.

> Mr. Seigel, I want to inform you of the following: In refusing to follow the direction of the Court you are subjecting yourself to punishment for contempt of Court.

The judge continued to stare at Seigel as the frightened witness sank lower and lower into his seat, averting his eyes from those of the judge. But he persisted in his refusal to answer the government's questions.

The government—quite predictably—then moved to have the court confer immunity on the witness. I rose to object on the ground that the statute authorized the conferring of immunity only after a witness had invoked his privilege against self-incrimination. We had purposely decided to have Seigel plead everything but the Fifth, in order to throw a monkey wrench in the government's plans. But Judge Bauman saw through our ploy and reminded the government lawyers that since Seigel had not invoked the privilege against self-incrimination, there was no *need* to confer immunity on him; he could be compelled to answer the questions; and he could be punished for contempt for his refusal to do so.

The judge then formally held Seigel in contempt of court and ordered his confinement until he changed his mind and agreed to testify.

Normally, when a witness is held in contempt, he is immediately carted off to jail in order to be pressured into complying with the order of the court. I asked the court to allow Seigel to remain free on bail pending the decision of the court of appeals. I told the court that I would be ready to argue the appeal "at 2:30 this afternoon, if necessary," thus demonstrating that I was not seeking delay for its own sake. I also reminded Judge Bauman that he had written a lengthy opinion on the issues we had raised, and that surely this must mean that the issues on appeal were serious and important ones.

We doubted that our request would be granted, since the Hurok trial was under way and the jury had been sworn. The government wanted swift action. We were concerned, as well, that Judge Bauman might be influenced by a recent highly publicized interview in which Sol Hurok had bitterly protested the continued freedom of the JDL bombers who had nearly killed him. Hurok had touched a responsive chord when he complained that he could not "understand the simply terrible judiciary system we have in this country. These people have been brought into court a number of times, they have been proven guilty, and still the trials go on."

To our surprise, Judge Bauman agreed with us and allowed Seigel to remain free on bail on the express condition that "Mr. Dershowitz expedite the appeal." Within minutes, Putzel and I were before a panel of the court of appeals, which imposed an extremely tight schedule, under which all briefs and arguments would have to be completed within twelve days. The Hurok trial would be postponed and the jury sent home while everyone awaited the action of the court of appeals.

The Court of Appeals

The United States Court of Appeals for the Second Circuit is an important court with a distinguished tradition. Its jurisdiction covers the entire state of New York, as well as Connecticut and Vermont. Since the United States Supreme Court reviews very few cases, the courts of appeal are—for practical purposes—the courts of last resort for most criminal defendants. Past members of the Second Circuit have included such giants of the law as Learned Hand, John Harlan, Jerome Frank, and Charles Clark. (It has also had its share of judicial midgets.) Its courtroom, located on the seventeenth floor of the Federal Courthouse overlooking the Brooklyn Bridge and the Wall Street financial district, is an austere but impressive setting. The court itself consists of nine active judges and several senior judges, who rotate in panels of three. The particular panel that will hear and decide a given case is a well-guarded secret until several days before the actual argument: this secrecy is designed to prevent lawyers from tailoring their briefs to the predilections of individual judges. It makes the appellate lawyer's job all the more difficult and challenging, since individual judges have very different views of the law, especially in the criminal and constitutional areas; and an argument that may be well received by one judge may offend another.

There was one judge about whom I was particularly concerned: Chief Judge Irving R. Kaufman. As a young district judge, Kaufman had presided over the last capital case in that courthouse: the infamous Rosenberg spy trial in 1951. The storm that surrounded his imposition of the death penalty has still not subsided. Although he had built a well-deserved reputation as an independent and effective court of appeals judge, he has remained under constant attack for his actions in the Rosenberg case. Among the criticisms hurled at Kaufman by some was that, as a Jew, he leaned over backwards to demonstrate his lack of favoritism toward his co-religionists. I was worried that he might do exactly that in a case involving the most notorious Jewish organization in the world. I was hoping for a panel of non-Jewish judges who could more easily remove themselves from the emotional component of the case and limit themselves to its complex legal issues.

The panel was announced: the presiding judge was Chief Judge Irving R. Kaufman. His associate judges were two rather elderly men: Judge J. Joseph

Smith of Connecticut and Judge Frederick van Pelt Bryan, a district court judge from New York, who had been assigned temporary duty on the court of appeals. As soon as I learned the composition of the panel, I went to the Harvard Law School library to read every relevant case decided by Kaufman and his colleagues. Appellate argument can often become a very personal encounter, with considerable discussion about the proper interpretation of a particular case written by one of the sitting judges.

My reading of Judge Kaufman's court of appeals opinions gave me some encouragement. He was not a government man: he often chastised the United States Attorney's office (as well as defense counsel). He obviously enjoyed a good argument. And he was prepared—at least on occasion—to free obviously guilty criminals in order to enforce the principles of the Constitution. Several lawyer friends of mine, when they heard that Judge Kaufman was presiding, called to caution me about his acerbic manner with counsel who had not done their homework.

With all this in mind, I prepared for the oral argument, which I knew could be crucial. Oral argument in an appeal is the only direct encounter with the judges. It is the only opportunity to learn what is on their minds and to respond to their concerns. Cases are often decided in the fifteen or twenty minutes that a lawyer is given to argue his case before the judges.

Normally the arguments before the court of appeals are not the kind of spectator sports that some trials have become. The small audience generally consists exclusively of the judges' law clerks, an occasional defendant sitting in the spectators section, and other lawyers waiting their turn to argue. On that hot Tuesday in June, only one case was scheduled; and the courtroom was packed to overflowing with JDL supporters, the press, family members, and virtually the entire United States Attorney's office.

The clerk announced the entrance of the court with the traditonal "oyez, oyez" (pronounced o-yea, which led Marty Elefant, who was present that day to observe the appeal, to mimic it by whispering "oy vay, oy vay," the traditional Yiddish cry of desperation). He proceeded to call the case of *Seigel* v. *The United States of America.* I approached the lectern and began to describe the circumstances under which Seigel had become an informant. Almost immediately, Chief Judge Kaufman interrupted to ask a question about the destruction of the wiretap tapes. It was apparent that Kaufman had read the briefs and record of the case with great care, since the issue he was asking about had not been discussed in Judge Bauman's opinion, nor had we emphasized it in our brief. (Harvey Silverglate had persuaded me to mention it in our brief in order to "preserve" it in the event we had to go to the Supreme Court.)

Judge Kaufman's question took everyone by surprise. But it is the job of an appellate lawyer to anticipate every question that might be asked, and we had done our homework. As I began to formulate an answer, Jeanne Baker handed me a file folder neatly marked "Tape Destruction." It contained the relevant cases, statutes, and record references with the critical sentences underlined in red. Sensing that the other judges were interested in this issue as well, I discarded my original argument outline and focused on the legal consequences of the tape destruction. Attempting to weave the other arguments into my discussion, I contended that the FBI's unlawful destruction of the tapes had made it far more difficult for us to prove that the government had discovered Seigel by means of the wiretap. The questions came fast. The judges had obviously not yet made up their minds. (In many cases, the judges clearly have closed minds about a case; indeed, it is not uncommon to argue before judges who have not read the briefs—and probably never will.) The government, represented by Henry Putzel, was questioned just as vigorously—also about the tape destruction. At the close of the argument, Chief Judge Kaufman assured us that the court's decision would be handed down within a few days, since the resumption of the suspended Hurok trial hung in the balance.

A good lawyer always anticipates the worst for his clients. (It continues to amaze me that criminal *defendants* remain eternally optimistic about their prospects even as the prison gates are closing behind them.) As we awaited the court of appeals' decision, we continued to discuss with Seigel the legal consequences of his decision to testify or not to testify.

Two weeks after the oral argument I received a phone call at my Harvard office from the court of appeals. A clerk informed me that the court had rendered a unanimous decision reversing Judge Bauman's contempt order. I arranged for the opinion to be put on the next plane and it arrived at my office within a few hours.

"The Constable Has Blundered"

The opinion—written by Chief Judge Kaufman—opened with a description of the death of Iris Kones, which it said, was caused by "senseless and cowardly acts of violence." It then proceeded to describe the legal issues as "set in a context that unfortunately highlights the seamiest aspects of the criminal law and its enforcement." "Given the context," the court observed,

> . . . it should hardly be surprising to learn that the informer, Sheldon Seigel, adopted some of the tactics of those with whom he associated,

> and himself surreptitiously recorded many conversations. . . . It is but another indication of the furtive and devious character of those who engage in these diabolical activities that Seigel himself had participated in the Hurok and Columbia bombings, even while serving as a vital Government informer.

The court then turned to the government's erasure of the wiretap tapes:

> The significance of the destruction of this evidence cannot be understated in this case. To compel a party who objects to the use of evidence obtained as a result of unlawful wiretapping to go forward with a showing of taint, . . . and then to withhold from him the means or tools to meet that burden, is to create an absurdity in the law.

The court held that the erasure of the tapes "compels us to strictly scrutinize the Government's claim" that Seigel's identity and role in the Amtorg bombing were discovered not by the wiretaps, but rather by an "independent source."

The court reviewed the government's account, which Judge Bauman had accepted as true. It observed that Seigel had succeeded in recording at least one conversation with Parola that "reveals a different version of the manner in which the police learned of Sheldon Seigel's identity." Judge Kaufman pointed to the critical and disputed passage: "You know it's [done?] [not?] on wiretaps." We had asked the court of appeals to listen to that part of the tape and to decide for itself whether the actual word was "done" or "not." The court of appeals followed our suggestion and reached its own conclusion:

> We have concluded, without the slightest doubt, ambiguity or uncertainty, that Parola related to Seigel: "You know it's *done* on wiretaps."

This finding (which, in my own view, is somewhat overstated*) led the court of appeals to a puzzling conclusion:

> If the New York City Police Department did learn of Seigel's involvement from a wiretap lead, the contents of those wiretaps, in the hands of Seigel's counsel at the taint hearing, may have dealt a shattering blow to the Government's proof of independent source. For if wiretaps were indeed involved, Parola's in-court testimony on independent

*I have played the tape to several hundred students over the past several years and the vast majority have agreed with the court of appeals. But every year a small number of students—especially those from Brooklyn—hear the word "not." My own "hearing" varies over time.

> source, undermined on this critical point, would clearly have counted for little thereafter.

This conclusion is puzzling because Parola's credibility had *already* been devastated by other unambiguous and undisputed portions of the tape recordings, which conclusively demonstrated that Parola had repeatedly lied about matters central to his task of obtaining information from Seigel and which he could not possibly have forgotten, such as the threats to kill Seigel, and the "deal" about not being advised of his rights. The conversation about wiretaps—even if it had clearly established that Parola had told Seigel that he had been discovered by wiretaps—could easily have been forgotten by Parola, since it had been tangential to his major task.

Why, then, did the court focus on this ambiguous conversation as the straw that would have broken Parola's credibility? My guess is that the appellate judges were seeking to spare Judge Bauman embarrassment: had the court of appeals detailed the contradictions and lies in Parola's testimony, Judge Bauman's reliance on his credibility would have seemed preposterous, if not downright dishonest. This way, by focusing on Judge Bauman's innocent mistake about one particular conversation, the court could avoid casting serious aspersions upon a district judge's findings of fact.

In any event, the court's observation that Parola's testimony "undermined on this critical point, would clearly have counted for little thereafter," led it to a consideration of the appropriate remedy for the government's misconduct. It began with some philosophy:

> Of course, we all suffer when, in Cardozo's classic phrase, the criminal goes free because the constable has blundered. There are those who argue that on occasion illegal methods must be employed to preserve the rule of law. Justice Brandeis responded eloquently to that argument:
> "Our government is the potent, the omnipresent teacher. For good or for ill, it teaches the whole people by its example. Crime is contagious. If the government becomes a lawbreaker, it breeds contempt for law; it invites every man to become a law unto himself."

The court then announced its result:

> [We] conclude, therefore, that under the circumstances of Seigel's case, destruction of the tapes denied to [Seigel] the necessary armaments with which to pursue the adversary encounter. . . . Since the tapes are no longer in existence, remand for further proceedings would be futile.

> Accordingly, the order of civil contempt against Seigel is reversed and vacated.

As if to make its conclusion absolutely unambiguous, the court also stated that Seigel "could not be prosecuted under any circumstances" for the Amtorg or Glen Cove bombings or for possession of the explosives found in his car. Finally, as if in direct response to Judge Bauman's criticism of my cross-examination of Parola, the court of appeals took pains to commend "counsel for Seigel [who] explored complex factual and legal issues competitively yet courteously and always in the pursuit of the truth." We understood this to signify approval, at least by inference, of the cross-examination techniques we had employed.

We explained to an unbelieving Seigel that this meant that he was totally off the hook. He could not be prosecuted and he did not have to testify. After two years of threats, fears, and isolation, Sheldon Seigel was free to leave the courthouse and begin his life anew without fear of prosecution, contempt, Parola, or—presumably—the JDL. He did not have to make the difficult choice between testifying against his friends or facing a long imprisonment.

"Do You Know Who Isn't in Court Today?"

The Hurok trial was not yet over. It had been recessed until the court of appeals had rendered its decision. The morning after the decision, Judge Bauman reconvened the Hurok trial. Seigel was again called to the stand to testify, but this time without the threat of contempt. As expected, he refused. Without Seigel's testimony, the judge was forced to dismiss the Hurok prosecution against all the defendants.

Stuart Cohen, Sheldon Davis, and Sheldon Seigel started to leave the courtroom, congratulating each other and laughing, when Judge Bauman turned to them in anger and said, "Do you know who isn't in court today? Iris Kones." As my thoughts turned to the innocent victim of the Hurok bombing, I heard the judge's voice grow louder and angrier: "Someone has committed a dastardly, vicious, unforgivable, unforgettable crime; someone is frustrating the administration of justice in a case that, in my mind, involves murder. People who deliberately do so will learn the power of the law even if there are those who have literally gotten away with murder." While enunciating these final words, Judge Bauman averted his eyes from the young defendants and focused them directly at me, almost as if to say, "And you are responsible."

His words went through me like a knife. Never had I been so uncomfortable as I was then, with the case over and my client entirely victorious. He was right. In one sense we were responsible; I, Harvey, Jeanne, and the others who had labored on Seigel's behalf. Had we not devised our novel legal arguments—had we not devoted days and nights to his defense—it is entirely possible that the court of appeals might have affirmed Judge Bauman's contempt citation and ordered Seigel to be jailed. And no one will ever know for sure whether Seigel would have broken under the pressure of imprisonment.

I sat in court for a full hour after everyone else had left. I wanted no part of the victory celebration. I could not forget Iris Kones.

Government by Informer

The Seigel case has continued to bother me over the years. I teach it in my criminal law class every year, playing the tapes and reviewing the complex legal and factual issues for my students. Sometimes I invite "Pete" Putzel to present the government's perspective. Sometimes I ask Jeanne and Harvey to join me. The students' reactions vary from year to year. Sometimes Parola emerges as a hero, other times as a villain. Seigel is always despised and pitied. Judge Bauman is generally disliked. My own role is critically questioned, especially my decision to take the case, and sometimes my cross-examination. Of all the *dramatis personae,* the students always empathize most with Jeanne, who was herself a law student while playing an important role in the litigation.

The case provides a superb teaching tool, since it raises profound questions, both legal and moral, about the limits of government intervention to prevent and prosecute the most serious crime. It requires the students to think hard about the role of informers like Seigel. We live in an age of government by informer. Every law enforcement agency has its stable of informers; every organization of any significance—and many of no significance—has been penetrated. Informing has become, if not an honorable trade, a mass occupation. It is impossible to estimate how many informants are currently operating. They move in and out of their roles too quickly to be tagged and counted. They are used promiscuously to obtain information about the most trivial and the most serious of crimes. They manufacture crime in order to sell their product. They lie about crime in order to give their employer what they think he wants to hear.

The tapes of the Parola-Seigel conversations dramatically reveal the kinds of pressures placed on an informer to come up with any information, no matter how speculative or ill-founded. But the selective use of informers may well be indispensable to effective law enforcement. All governments throughout history have used informers, and they will continue to do so. The civil rights movement might well have failed had the FBI not been able to penetrate the Ku Klux Klan, and we would know far less than we do about organized crime without informers.

The JDL case was not a situation where the constable had accidently "blundered," as Judge Kaufman charitably suggested. It was a situation in which the government simply could not have penetrated the JDL—and could not, therefore, have prevented potentially disastrous consequences—without breaking the law. Accordingly, the decision was made—a calculated and deliberate decision at the highest level—to violate the laws, to engage in "civil disobedience" in the interest of a higher cause.

There are many who will argue that the government simply did what it had to do; that it could not responsibly have sat back and remained within the law when to do so would have courted disaster. In litigating this case, I sometimes shared that view, especially when I learned about some of the JDL plans that were aborted by Seigel's information.

But in the last analysis, it was right that the government should have lost its case. It is one thing for the agents of the government, acting under enormous pressure, to take expedient actions deemed necessary to protect important values. It is quite another for the courts, reflectively reviewing such actions in the context of a criminal prosecution, to accord them an air of constitutional legitimacy. As Associate Justice Robert H. Jackson observed in his dissenting opinion in the World War II Japanese relocation cases: when a government official violates the Constitution, "it is an incident." But if the courts then approve his actions, "that passing incident becomes the doctrine of the Constitution. There it has a generative power of its own, and all that it creates will be in its own image."

In the JDL case, too, it may have been necessary for the government to do some of the things it did to prevent disaster; but once the disaster had been averted and the culprits apprehended and exposed, the necessity for securing convictions through unconstitutional means was not as compelling. In one important sense, therefore, I can understand and condone police officer Parola's actions more easily than I can Judge Bauman's attempt to legitimatize those actions.

Government agents will continue to engage in constitutional violations, generally for less compelling reasons than existed here. In most such cases they will have their cake and eat it, too, since the courts will ignore the violations or deem them harmless and sustain the resulting convictions. Every time a court throws out a conviction on constitutional grounds, it makes the cost of constitutional violations a bit higher. In any particular case, especially in one as serious as the Hurok bombing, the cost may seem excessive; but considering how rarely the courts actually impose such costs, every decision like that rendered in the Seigel case must be seen as a victory for the United States Constitution.

EPILOGUE

The Jewish Defense League is now a shadow of its former self. Consisting of several hundred extremists spread around the major northeastern cities, it makes an occasional noisy appearance at a Nazi rally or a Palestinian demonstration. It plants bombs in Communist bookstores. And it harasses Soviet diplomats. When Yasir Arafat came to the United Nations in November of 1974, one of the league's new leaders offered a bounty for his assassination and was arrested. The league no longer remains a significant factor in Soviet-American relations or in domestic American politics. No State Department cables about its activities crisscross the Atlantic these days.

The single most important factor in hastening the demise of the JDL was the death of Iris Kones. That senseless tragedy weakened to the breaking point whatever remaining pillars of support the league enjoyed within the Jewish community. It demonstrated that the JDL had so cheapened the currency of civil disobedience and violence that it had lost whatever meaning and purpose it might have had if selectively and intelligently employed. Even those militants who could justify the use of violence against Soviet or PLO officials were appalled by the bombings directed against Hurok and Columbia, and especially by the death—even if accidental—of a young Jewish woman.

In an ironic way the acquittal—more accurately, the non-conviction—of "the JDL Three" may also have contributed to the demise of the organization. The league's strident denials of complicity in the face of Seigel's incriminating disclosures made its leaders appear unwilling to assume responsibility for their excesses. More important, however, the non-conviction left the JDL with no heroes or martyrs around whom to build a following: if Seigel, Cohen, or Davis had been convicted and sentenced to long prison terms, their status as "political prisoners" would have been exploited by the JDL as a focus of continued protests and militancy. But without such a focus, and in the face of its dwindling support, the Jewish Defense League has become a noisy but impotent relic of the past.

Most of its former officers and activists have returned to the mainstream of American life. Stuart Cohen now runs a travel agency. Sheldon Davis, while still formally associated with the league, devotes most of his time to rabbinical studies at the Jewish Theological Seminary. Bert Zweibon is back to administering estates (and recently told me, employing his characteristic graveside humor, that he was "bored stiff"). Rabbi Kahane is in Israel, leading a group of right-wing Orthodox Jews who want to settle in the West Bank. During one recent demonstration Kahane was arrested by the Israeli police and treated a bit roughly. He complained that even in America he had never been manhandled like that—to which the Israeli policeman responded, "Here in Israel, we don't have to worry about offending the 'Jewish vote.' "

Sheldon Seigel and his wife, Tova, moved to Long Island after the trial, where they opened a furniture stripping and repair shop. Sheldon has stayed away from the JDL and out of trouble since he walked out of the courtroom on that June day in 1973.

Santo Parola still works as a detective. Several years after the close of the Seigel case, I called the New York City Police Department and asked if I might interview him. After some hesitation Parola agreed.

It was a warm June day when I arrived at police headquarters near the Manhattan side of the Brooklyn Bridge. "Counselor," Parola said, extending his hand warmly, "it's nice to see the only lawyer who ever tripped me up on the witness stand in twenty years of testifying." I told him that it was Seigel and not I who had tripped him. "You should tell that dopey kid when you see him next," Parola said, "that he made us change our rules down here." Pointing to a metal detector, he explained, "That's designed to make sure that no one brings a hidden tape recorder into police headquarters. And the new rule, the 'Shelley Seigel Rule,' is that all interviews have to be conducted at police headquarters." After I was frisked for hidden recorders, we proceeded into a small room and began chatting.

The conversation turned to Brooklyn, with Parola saying, "You know, I could never have broken the case without having grown up in Boro Park. I used to see Jewish kids like Shelley all the time when I was growing up. Dopey, punk kids who were envious of us. If you played them right, you could have them eating out of your hands. Shelley was just like that. There was a part of him that wanted to be a tough Italian cop like me. I spotted that right away and played on it. We used to talk tough together—Italian talk, not Jewish talk. About cars, explosives, the Mafia, all that kind of stuff. He ate it up. Gradually, I turned him into an Italian, and then into a cop. I never succeeded completely. But I got a part of him, a good part of him. I never could have done it unless I knew Boro Park, unless I knew what made dopey kids like Shelley tick."

Why had they decided to blow Seigel's cover and use him as a witness?

"It wasn't me who decided that," Parola objected. "I was mad as hell. Shelley was the best goddamn informer I've ever had in twenty years. You know, he could have made a fortune on us. Any other informer I know would have asked for money. He could've gotten twenty-five thousand, maybe fifty thousand for the information he gave us. But he never asked for a nickel. He was a hell of a lot more valuable as a stool than as a witness. But the damn feds decided they needed him. Why, I don't know. Isn't the prevention of bombings more important than putting a few dumb kids in jail for a few years? And look how it came out. We blew our stool *and* we lost our case. The feds screwed it up royally. They went back on their word, and they made me the fall guy. They told me to promise the kid the moon, and I did. Then they made a liar out of me. They broke my promises, and then I had to deny making them."

How could an experienced cop like Parola have been fooled by a "dopey kid" like Sheldon? I asked. "He was good. At least he *became* good. The irony is that *we* created the Frankenstein that did us in. You know, when I think back, I remember being suspicious. Is this kid taping us? I remember thinking. But I guess I got sloppy. He trusted us and we trusted him. We were all damn fools. We all trusted each other too much."

Had it ever occurred to Parola that I had the same advantage over him that he had over Sheldon precisely because I also grew up in Boro Park "with lots of guys like you?" Parola laughed as I continued, "I used to play basketball with kids like you, tough Italian kids who were always flexing their muscles and starting fights. Our strategy was to let them get overconfident. Let them think we were scared. Let them become sloppy and lazy. And then fight back. It worked when we were kids, and it worked with you."

Parola was shaking his head and laughing. "You really are a card, counselor. You certainly did fool me. I remember thinking that you were giving me all kinds of openings during your cross-examination of me, that you were hitting me grounders [a stickball term]. You did get me overconfident and sloppy. And then you dropped the bomb. I was really scared. For the first time in my career I was afraid of the law. I didn't know what the judge or the feds would do to me."

Then he paused and smiled at me as he whispered, "You know how I felt when you finally won that case, counselor? I felt great, really great. Shelley didn't deserve to go to jail."

As I was getting up to leave, Parola turned and put his arm on my shoulder. "Counselor," he said, "this is really an all–Boro Park case. I broke the case and turned Shelley because of what I knew about the old neighborhood. And then you came in from Cambridge and broke me because of what you remembered about the old neighborhood. The only guy who didn't know the old neighborhood was Judge Bauman. And he never really understood the case. He didn't understand Shelley; he didn't understand me; and he didn't even understand you. He thought he understood you because you were both fancy lawyers. What he didn't realize was that you're really a Brooklyn street kid, a street fighter in a three-piece suit. That's why I like you. That's why, if I ever get in trouble, you're gonna get a call from me, counselor. I want a street kid in my corner, even if you were never a two-sewer man. In court, counselor, you're a three-sewer man." That was the ultimate compliment from a fellow Boro Parker.

—2—

"Whatever Else It May Be, It Is Not Murder to Shoot a Dead Body. Man Dies but Once."

A man lies dead. *His enemy comes along and thinks he is asleep,* so he stabs the corpse. [Has] the enemy . . . *attempted* to murder the dead man[?] The law may sometimes be an ass, but it cannot be so asinine as that.—Lord Reid in *Haughton* v. *Smith,* House of Lords (1974).

First-year law school classes are generally conducted by the "Socratic method." The professor plays the role of the all-knowing Socrates, presenting hypothetical cases and directing rapid-fire questions at the bewildered students. As soon as a student seems to have arrived at a correct answer, the professor changes one of the crucial facts of the case and asks the student whether the change affects his answer. The constantly shifting "hypothetical"—the make-believe case with ever-changing facts—is a staple of legal education, designed to sharpen the future lawyer's mind and prepare him for the combat of the courtroom. Some students complain about this "paper chase" method of education, but many seem to enjoy the challenge.

One "hypothetical" that always intrigues and confounds first-year criminal-law students is whether a defendant can be convicted of attempted murder if he shoots at an object that he believes to be a living human being, but that turns out to be a corpse or a dummy.

When I began teaching criminal law, there had been no such actual case reported in the annals of jurisprudence, and so the issue had to be presented through the vehicle of "hypotheticals," or analogous cases.

My favorite case came from the Sherlock Holmes story, *The Adventure of the Empty House.* Holmes is being stalked by Colonel Sebastian Moran, "the best heavy game shot" and "the second most dangerous man in London" (the most dangerous is, of course, Professor James Moriarty, for whom Moran works). In order to lure his pursuer from the bush, Holmes commissions an eminent sculptor to create a wax likeness of the great detective's head. The "bait" is placed in the window of Holmes' Baker Street house and is periodically turned to create the impression of movement. In due course, Colonel Moran appears in an alley across the street and takes aim at "Sherlock Holmes" with his high-powered rifle. He fires and the bullet strikes the sculpture "plumb in the middle of the back of the head and smack through the 'brain.' " Moran is immediately captured and admits that his intent to murder Holmes had been foiled by the detective's clever artifice. As the arresting officer is taking Moran away, Holmes asks, "What charge do you intend to prefer?" Inspector Lestrade replies, "Why, of course, the attempted murder of Mr. Sherlock Holmes." The great detective ponders for a moment and then, shaking his head, offers a dissent: "Not so, Lestrade," proposing instead that Moran be tried for several unsolved murders. Thus, the perplexed reader never learns whether, under English law, a "killer" who shoots the "brains" out of a dummy can be convicted of attempted murder.

An actual dummy case was decided by an American court and was included in several criminal law casebooks. A Missouri hunter shot a "deer" that turned out to be a stuffed carcass set up by park rangers to catch poachers. The issue was whether the hunter could be convicted of attempting to take a deer out of season. The court held that "It is no . . . crime to attempt to do that which is legally impossible to do. For instance, *it is no crime to attempt to murder a corpse because it cannot be murdered.*" [My italics.]

Some scholars disagreed with this dictum, arguing that if the defendant believed the "corpse" to be a live person whom he intended to kill, he could be convicted of attempted murder.

I have been fascinated by the law of attempts since my first year as a law student. One of the earliest cases I studied involved a man named Damms who had taken his wife for a car ride and then brandished a gun; she fled, but he caught up with her and raised the pistol to her head. Slowly, deliberately, he pulled the trigger. It did not fire. He had forgotten to load it! Two police officers witnessed the event and heard Damms exclaim—after he had pulled the trigger of the unloaded gun—"It won't fire. It won't fire." (There was no evidence as to whether the exclamation was made in a tone of assurance, disappointment, surprise, or desperation!) He was convicted of attempted murder, and appealed on the ground that it had been impossible to kill his wife with an unloaded gun. The court upheld the conviction, concluding that

> the fact, that the gun was unloaded when Damms . . . pulled the trigger, did not absolve him of [attempted murder], if he *actually thought* at the time that it was loaded.

I wrote a law journal note on this case in which I analyzed the concept of "impossible attempts," using as my hypothetical illustration the "firing of a gun at an apparently sleeping man who had died of natural causes moments before the shooting." I tried to distinguish between attempts that were impossible because of fortuitous factors that were beyond the control of the individual (such as the mechanical jamming of the gun as it was being fired), and attempts that had failed because the individual exercised some control (such as the rapist who changed his mind when he discovered that his potential victim was pregnant). Citing Sigmund Freud's studies of the unconscious, I speculated that Damms' failure to load the pistol may have reflected unconscious ambivalence on his part about killing his wife. My paper was sophomoric and fraught with all the pitfalls of armchair psychology, but it got me thinking about the law of attempts and the defense of impossibility.

When I began to teach criminal law at Harvard Law School, I devoted a significant portion of the course to untangling the web of criminal attempts. Every year the class would divide into warring factions over the Sherlock Holmes story or the hypothetical case of the "killer" who stabbed his enemy believing him to be alive, only to be saved from a murder charge by his victim's demise moments earlier. Most students began by agreeing with Lord Reid's statement in the House of Lords that the law would indeed be an ass if it were to permit the attempted murder conviction of the corpse–stabber or dummy–shooter. I played the devil's advocate, pressing the students for distinctions between the corpse-stabbing case and other hypotheticals where the students favored attempt convictions.

One such hypothetical involved the novel *The Day of the Jackal,* in which President de Gaulle escapes an unseen assassin's bullet by taking an unexpected bow at the instant the shot is fired. Another involved the man who planted on board an airplane an explosive device, which failed to explode because of a mechanical defect.

By the time the class was over, many of the students had been converted to the position that there really was no principled distinction between the attempts that were impossible (the corpse and dummy) and those foiled by unanticipated circumstances (the bowing president and the defective explosive). In each case, the defendant intended to kill and did everything in his power to bring about that result. Indeed, I even went so far as to argue that in a moral sense there is no valid distinction between the defendant who did everything within his power to kill *but failed* and the defendant who actually succeeded. Why, I asked, should the fortuity of success or failure determine the extent of a defendant's punishment?

These classes were always exciting to me, but there was an air of unreality about the assortment of hypothetical corpses and dummies trotted out to illustrate the complexity of impossible attempts. Indeed, critics of the hypothetical method of law school teaching would cite the "corpse case" to illustrate how unrealistic and bizarre law school hypotheticals could be. Imagine, therefore, how excited I became when, after a decade of teaching, I was asked to argue the first court case involving a defendant who had actually shot a man who turned out to have been a corpse.

A Real Corpse Case

It all began in October of 1975 when an attorney named Jeffrey Cohen asked me whether I would be interested in arguing the appeal for the brother of a friend of his who had been convicted of murder for shooting a corpse.

"You've got to be kidding!" I exclaimed. "Cases like that don't really happen except in the warped minds of law professors."

He assured me that it had really happened. I told him that if the court record of the case actually presented that intriguing issue, I would definitely want to argue it. What an addition it would make to my criminal law course!

Jeff flew up to Cambridge several days later with a box of transcripts and told me the sad story of the people involved in the case. (Law professors, in the excitement of a fascinating fact pattern, sometimes tend to forget the human tragedies that often underlie it.) His friend's brother, a twenty-three-year-old man named Melvin Dlugash, came from a middle-class family in the Bensonhurst section of Brooklyn (the neighborhood adjoining Boro Park). Mel's father and two brothers were accountants; his sister was a premed student at the University of Pennsylvania. Mel, like his brothers and sister, had attended college. On the surface, the family was like many others in their upwardly mobile neighborhood. But Mel was different. He suffered from grand mal epilepsy and experienced periodic seizures, which left him disoriented and confused. Mel had led a troubled life since his adolescence. In 1971, while studying at Syracuse University, he had been arrested for illegal possession of a target pistol. After pleading guilty to a misdemeanor, he was given a probationary sentence. That was his only formal brush with the law during his college years, but after graduation he began to run with a tough crowd.

. . .

On Friday night, December 21, 1973, Mel and two of his friends, Mike Geller and Joe Bush, had gone out drinking and partying. Mike lived in a basement apartment in the Flatbush section of Brooklyn; Joe had been staying with him for several months and was supposed to be sharing the rent and expenses. During the course of the evening, Mike asked Joe several times for his share of the rent. Joe responded angrily that he didn't owe anything and that if Mike persisted in his demands he was "going to get hurt." At about midnight the three returned to Mike's apartment, where they continued to drink. At about three o'clock, the arguments between Joe and Mike escalated. Mike again demanded the rent money—$100—and Joe again threatened to hurt him if he didn't lay off. Mike repeated his demand.

Suddenly Joe drew a long barreled .38-caliber revolver from his pocket and aimed it point-blank at Mike. Mike backed away. But there was no stopping Joe. Joe fired his pistol three times at Mike's heart. Mel watched as Mike fell to the floor, blood cascading from the wounds in his chest.

Joe then turned to Mel, pointed his gun at him, and said, "If you don't shoot him, I'll shoot you." Joe wanted it to appear that they were in it together, so that Mel would not be able to point an accusing finger at Joe. Although Mel had his own gun, it was in his boot, and he was frightened of Joe. After some hesitation, Mel walked over to Mike's prone and motionless body and pulled the trigger of his .22-caliber automatic pistol. Five bullets ripped into Mike's head several minutes after Joe's .38-caliber bullets had penetrated Mike's heart.

By the time Mike's body was discovered early the next morning, Joe and Mel were on their way to upstate New York. They stayed out of town for several days, and Mel, after having several seizures, returned to his parents' house on the day after Christmas.

Mel's Confession

On December 27 Mel's parents were leaving for a vacation. His sister—home from college for Christmas vacation—drove them to the airport. Alone in the house Mel suddenly felt the familiar aura that precedes an epileptic seizure. Within seconds he was writhing on the floor, biting his tongue, and losing consciousness. When his sister returned, she found him lying on a couch in the basement looking dazed and confused. She tried to talk to him, but he couldn't speak coherently. He just grumbled and motioned to her that he had to go to sleep. It was five o'clock in the afternoon.

An hour later there was a knock on the door. A man identifying himself as "Mel's friend" said he was looking for Mel. He was directed to the couch where Mel was resting. The man was not Mel's friend. He was a plainclothes homicide detective named Joseph Carrasquillo, who was in charge of investigating Mike's murder.

Carrasquillo gave the dazed Mel his *Miranda* warnings, advising him of his right to remain silent and to have a lawyer. The detective then asked the required question: "Now that I have advised you of your rights, are you willing to answer questions without an attorney present?" Mel nodded in the affirmative.

Detective Carrasquillo was now free to ask Mel what he knew about Mike's death. Mel responded that he knew nothing about it, since he had been away for four or five days on a trip upstate with his friend Joe Bush. The detective then asked Mel whether he would be willing to go down to the station house for the purpose of identifying some pictures of Joe Bush. Mel agreed. When they arrived at the 69th Precinct—the same precinct I had walked to every week for Police Athletic League meetings during my early teens—they took Mel to the interrogation room. Carrasquillo began by informing Mel that the police had several witnesses who had told them that he owned and carried a pistol.

At this point Mel told the detective that he had just suffered an epileptic seizure. The detective told Mel that he could not get medication until after the interrogation was completed.

Mel then began to tell the detective how Joe had shot Mike after an argument about the rent money and how he "was afraid of Joe Bush." He demonstrated to the detective how he went over to Mike's body and fired into Mike's head with his .22-caliber pistol. Mel said that the amount of time between the shooting by Joe and his shooting was "anywhere from three minutes, maybe five minutes tops." When the detective asked Mel why he had shot at his friend's body, he explained that Mike "was already dead" and that he "feared for his life."

After giving these statements to Detective Carrasquillo, Mel was placed under arrest and charged with murder. An assistant District Attorney, Joseph M. Lauria, and a stenographer were summoned to take a formal confession. The confession, which would constitute the heart of the prosecution's case included the following:

[ASSISTANT D.A. LAURIA]: On December 22nd, at about 3:30 in the morning, were you present at 740 East 52nd Street?

A. Yes.

Q. Was anybody else with you?

A. All I'm sure of was Joe Bush.

Q. Why is it that you are not sure?
A. I had a convulsion between now and then. Whenever I have convulsions—epilepsy convulsions and I—

But the Assistant D.A. cut Mel off in mid-sentence.

Q. What did Joe Bush do?
A. Well, first Joe pulled out the gun and started shooting. He caught me quite a bit off guard. I really didn't think he was going to do it.
Q. [What] happened then?
A. It ended up after Mike had fallen to the floor. This was after Joe had his .38 on him, I started shooting on him. Now, why—

But again the Assistant D.A. would not let Mel finish his sentence.

Q. I'm not interested in why. How many times did you fire on him?
A. About five.
Q. Was Mike doing anything to you at that time?
A. No, Mike was dead.
Q. Did you check for pulse before you fired the shots?
A. No, he didn't move.
MR. LAURIA: I have no further questions.

Mel's sister, who was a friend of Jeffrey Cohen's brother, called Jeff and asked him for help. Jeff agreed, and after preparing the case for trial, got two experienced Brooklyn criminal lawyers to try it.

In the meantime Joe Bush—the man whose shots initially killed Mike—was nowhere to be found. He traveled around the country as a fugitive before eventually returning to New York, where he again got into trouble. He was arrested this time, but the New York City Police failed to identify him as the person wanted in connection with Mike's killing. Even though Joe Bush was in the custody of the New York City Police Department, he remained on record as a fugitive until one day when a remarkable coincidence occurred: Joe Bush and Mel Dlugash ended up in the same prison van. Mel immediately informed his lawyers of this, and Joe Bush was formally charged with Mike's murder along with Mel.

Bush's lawyer eventually struck a plea bargain with the District Attorney's office. Under the terms of the bargain, the murder charge against Bush was dropped in exchange for his plea of guilty to a charge of manslaughter. Bush was sentenced to imprisonment for a term of five to ten years. Mel, convinced that he had neither caused nor intended the death of a living human being, refused to plead guilty to manslaughter and decided to stand trial on the murder charge.

On September 8, 1975, Mel's trial for murder began in the Kings County Supreme Court.* After hearing medical testimony about Mel's epilepsy, the judge ruled that his confessions had been voluntary. The jury would learn what Mel told the detective and the D.A. on the day of his arrest. Indeed, without his confession there would be no case, since Joe Bush was unwilling to talk about what had happened. The prosecution's case would be based mainly on what Mel had told the D.A.

The indictment charged Mel with "acting in concert" with Joe Bush in causing the death of Michael Geller by gunshot wounds. Under this theory, the People—as the prosecution is called in the New York courts—had to prove that Joe and Mel had *jointly* planned to kill Mike. If they could prove such joint planning, it wouldn't matter whose bullets had actually killed Mike. The People would only have to prove that any one of the bullets from either gun, or any combination of these bullets, had caused Mike's death. This is so because when criminals act jointly, each criminal is legally responsible for what *he* does, what the *other* does, and what they do *together.* For example, if two armed bank robbers enter a bank and *one* of them shoots and kills a guard in the course of the holdup, the *other* robber is equally guilty of the murder. If *both* fire at the guard, it wouldn't matter whose bullet hit him first; *each* would be responsible for his death.

But if the People could not establish that Joe and Mel had jointly planned Mike's death—if the evidence showed that Joe's decision to shoot Mike was made independently, without any prior approval by Mel—then the government's burden of proof against Mel would be more difficult: In order for Mel to be convicted of murder, the People would have to prove beyond a reasonable doubt that 1) Mike was *actually* still alive when Mel fired at Mike's head, three to five minutes after Joe had fired into his heart, and that 2) Mel *believed* that Mike was alive and intended to kill him when he fired.

The Battle of the Experts

As soon as the trial began, it became clear that the People could not prove that Joe and Mel had acted jointly. There was no evidence that Mel had any prior agreement with Joe to kill Mike. The only evidence—Mel's confession—was that Joe had acted impulsively and independently in shooting

*Crimes like murder are within the jurisdiction of state, rather than federal, courts, except in special situations.

Mike and that Mel had not done anything until several minutes after Joe had shot Mike. The trial judge, after hearing this evidence, ruled that the People had failed to prove joint action. The People now had to prove that Mike was still alive three to five minutes after Joe shot him. The case became a battle of medical experts, with each side calling leading forensic pathologists to the witness stand.

The principal medical witness for the People was Dr. Francis Melomo, the coroner who had performed the autopsy on Mike's body within hours of its discovery. At that time no one knew who had shot first; all the coroner could determine was that Mike had been shot *both* in the heart and in the head by several bullets of two different calibers. Since autopsies are conducted from the head down, the report concluded that the suspected cause of death was "multiple bullet wounds of head and chest with brain injury and massive bilateral hemothorax [blood in the chest cavity] with penetration of heart; homicidal." Dr. Melomo's direct testimony simply repeated the conclusions of his autopsy report.

On cross-examination he was asked a hypothetical question—a question based on a series of assumptions supported by the evidence. (Ordinary witnesses are not generally permitted to answer hypothetical questions, but expert witnesses are.) The hypothetical question put to Dr. Melomo was this:

> Assuming the deceased were shot [in the chest] with a .38-caliber weapon [Joe's gun]. And further assume that some three to five minutes later the deceased was [shot in the head] with a smaller caliber weapon [Mel's gun]. Doctor, with any degree of medical certainty could you tell this jury whether the deceased was alive at the time that the latter shots were fired into his head?

The jury waited as the doctor pondered his answer. Finally, in a low voice, he replied, "No. I couldn't answer that."

The People's other expert witness was Dr. Dominick DiMaio, the Chief Medical Examiner for the City of New York, who had overseen the autopsy. He testified that one of the .38-caliber bullets—which was shot from Bush's gun—penetrated "the lung and then it crosse[d] through the heart from left to right." He was then asked if that bullet alone would have been fatal. His answer was "Yes."

The trial judge asked whether that meant "the man would die instantly?"

THE WITNESS: No, not necessarily.
THE COURT: That's all I want to know.

The defense attorney then asked:

Q. But you would have no positive way of knowing how long it would take him to die?
A. No.

Finally, Dr. DiMaio was asked the same hypothetical question asked of Dr. Melomo: Could he conclude with any degree of medical certainty whether Geller would still be alive three to five minutes after being shot through the chest? His answer, like Dr. Melomo's, was "No."

The defense team decided to call only one expert witness: Dr. Milton Helpern, who had been New York City's Chief Medical Examiner for twenty years and Chairman of the Department of Forensic Medicine at the New York University School of Medicine. He was regarded throughout the world as the dean of forensic medicine and legal pathology. Dr. Helpern was asked if "anyone [could] say how long it would take for the deceased in this case to expire after receiving [the] wounds [administered by Bush's .38-caliber bullets]?"

Dr. Helpern confirmed the statements of the People's medical experts:

> No. That cannot be stated with any degree of certainty. The deceased could have died from the chest wounds very rapidly. He literally can drop dead in some cases from the wounds. Those wounds can [also] be delayed . . . in the time it would take for death to occur. But . . . in most cases they're rapidly fatal.

To Testify or Not to Testify?

Following all this expert testimony, the defense team had to make a crucial and difficult decision: to leave things as they were, or to take the chance of putting Mel himself on the witness stand. Joe Bush had made it clear that he was unwilling to testify for either side, and neither side wanted to take the chance of subpoenaing him as a reluctant witness.

Whether to call a criminal defendant as a witness in his own behalf is one of the most critical and difficult decisions a trial lawyer must make. Even though every defendant has an absolute constitutional right not to testify at his trial, many experienced trial lawyers believe that juries invariably think that a defendant who fails to testify has something to hide. They are usually right! But often, what he is trying to hide is not his guilt of the crime for which he is on trial; he is trying to hide the fact that he had previously been convicted of other crimes. Under the rules of evidence, a defendant's prior record cannot generally be introduced if he does not testify. But if the defendant elects to take the witness stand, the prosecution is permitted to cross-examine him about his prior record, ostensibly to impeach his credibility as a witness. The jurors are instructed by the judge not to consider the defendant's past record as evidence of his guilt, but only as it bears upon his credibility as a witness. Everybody recognizes this for the fiction that it is. Most defendants and their lawyers fear, and understandably so, that if the jurors find out that the defendant has a criminal record, this will prejudice their consideration of his guilt or innocence. Some jurors may even conclude that the defendant should be convicted and punished because he is a bad or dangerous person, without regard to whether he committed the crime at issue.

On occasion, the defense attorney has little choice because when the prosecution's evidence demands a direct response by the defendant, the defense attorney may have to take the chance of exposing his client's criminal record. The judgment is a complex and subtle one that always depends on the facts of the particular case. (One criminal lawyer I know, who charges $50,000 for a criminal trial, says that $5,000 of the fee is for preparing and trying the case; the remaining $45,000 is for advising the client at the close of the prosecution's case whether to take the witness stand.)

In Mel's case, the question was close. On the one hand, Mel had a prior conviction, but it was for the relatively minor crime he had committed as a college student; on the other hand, the People's case was not very strong. There was the ever-present danger that Mel could strengthen it during the prosecutor's cross-examination of him. How would he explain his bizarre decision to shoot five bullets into the dead body of his friend? Would the jury believe that he was afraid of Joe Bush when Mel himself was armed with a loaded pistol? If he was so terrified, why had he gone upstate with Bush after the crime? There could be some tough questions on cross-examination.

The defense team decided to leave well enough alone and not call Mel. They understood that without his testimony there would be no evidence in the record—other than Mel's comment during his interrogation by Detective Carrasquillo—that he shot the bullets into Mike's head because Joe had ordered him to do so at gunpoint. The law recognizes a defense based on duress or coercion, but it is extremely limited and difficult to establish. The defense decided that the potential risks of having him testify outweighed any realistic benefits.

"The Big Contention"

The case went to the jury on the basis of the medical experts' conflicting opinions. The defense objected to the case being sent to the jury at all, arguing that on the basis of the medical testimony, no juror could conclude beyond a reasonable doubt that Mike was alive when Mel shot him. The judge decided, however, that the jurors should decide "the big contention" in this case—"whether the deceased was alive at the time."

This dispute raises a most profound issue of morality and science: when does life end? Scientists, theologians, philosophers, and lawyers have been debating this conundrum for centuries. Some have argued that life continues until the heart ceases its pumping action. But with the advent of artificial respirators, the heart can be kept pumping long after the other biological functions have irreversibly ended. Accordingly, most doctors have suggested "brain death"—manifested by the cessation of electrical activity from the brain cells—as a more useful criterion for the legal termination of life. (A similar debate rages at the other end of the life spectrum as well: when does life begin?)

The trial judge did not, however, invite the jury to enter into this cosmic discourse. He simply instructed the jury that a

> person is guilty of murder when, with intent to cause the death of another person, he causes such death.

The judge defined "intent" in the context of a murder charge as

> doing of an act deliberately, willfully, knowingly, feloniously, as distinguished from doing an act by mistake or by accident or by negligence or by carelessness.

He then instructed the jury how to go about deciding whether the defendant had the intent required for murder. He explained that "intent is the secret and silent operation of one person's mind. It is not something that can be photographed." But in determining the defendant's intent, the jurors may use what is known as a "presumption":

> under our law, every person is presumed to intend the natural and probable consequences of his acts.

The judge cautioned, however, that "this presumption . . . may be accepted or rejected by you."

Having instructed the jury that it could convict Mel of murder only if it found that Mike was alive when Mel shot him, the judge explained that if the jury did not so find, it could still convict him of *attempted* murder. The judge's charge included an instruction on the thorny dilemma of "impossible attempts."

> Now, ladies and gentlemen, even though it was factually or legally impossible to kill the deceased because of his prior death, you would be warranted in convicting this defendant of *an attempt to murder* if you found beyond a reasonable doubt that . . . the defendant actually intended to kill the deceased, believing in his own mind that the deceased was living, even though he was dead.

The court thus invited the jury to convict Mel of attempted murder for shooting a corpse, but only if it found that Mel *believed* Mike was alive.

After several hours of deliberation, over two days, the jury returned a unanimous verdict: Mel was found guilty of murder. The jurors had concluded that Mike was still alive when Mel shot him. They did not have to confront the secondary issue of whether Mel would have been guilty of attempted murder if Mike had been dead by that time. But that intriguing issue was still lurking in the case, ready to reassert itself.

Several weeks after the trial, Mel was brought back to court and given a mandatory term of fifteen years to life imprisonment for murder. Under this sentence, Mel would have to serve a minimum of eight and a half years in prison; and he might have to spend the rest of his life behind bars. Joe Bush, who admittedly fired the first and lethal shots, but who pleaded guilty to manslaughter, would be eligible for release in five years and could serve no more than ten years. The price of demanding one's constitutional rights to a trial can be costly indeed!

The First State Appeal

It was after Mel's trial and conviction that I met Jeffrey Cohen, who introduced me to the Dlugash family. The family then retained me to prepare the briefs and argue the appeals. My first task was to meet the client. I went to the Men's House of Detention in Brooklyn. The warden directed me to a cell brimming with confined humanity. There were at least seven people peering through the bars of Mel's cell: all were big; most were black; several were loud. In striking contrast stood Mel—just over five feet in height, pale in complexion, and quiet in his stuttering voice. Mel had obviously worked on his short body; it was muscular and powerful—a necessary protection in the violent world of the House of Detention.

We were taken to a conference area where we talked briefly. I told him my plan for the appeal. He expressed little interest. His only question was "when can you get me out of here on bail?" I told him that bail was virtually impossible after a conviction for murder. He asked me to try. I told him that there would be no chance—at least not until after appeal. He expressed dissatisfaction and reluctantly returned to his cell.

I requested an expedited appeal and submitted our brief within a few weeks. Our main contention was that the murder conviction could not stand, since the evidence simply did not establish beyond a reasonable doubt that Mike was alive when Mel shot him. The burden of proving a fact beyond a reasonable doubt means that it is not enough if that fact is likely or even probable; it must be as nearly certain as human limitations permit a fact to be proved—at least in theory.

We argued that it was impossible for a jury to conclude beyond a reasonable doubt that Mike was alive when Mel shot him, since even the People's expert witnesses had acknowledged that *they*—the doctors who were responsible for the autopsy—could not determine "with any degree of medical certainty" if Mike remained alive three to five minutes after Joe shot him. (We never got into the issue of whether "heart death" or "brain death" was the governing criterion. In most disputed cases, brain death precedes heart death. Indeed, one important purpose of defining death by reference to the brain is to permit the termination of life-support systems—or the commencement of organ removal—while the heart is still capable of functioning, but where there is no possibility of renewed consciousness. In this case heart death had obviously preceded brain death, and we did not want to focus the court's attention on the latter concept.)

The People conceded that there was no *direct* evidence that Mike was still alive, but it argued that there was strong "*circumstantial* evidence" supporting this conclusion. The current law is that a criminal case may be based on "circumstantial evidence," but only if "the proven facts . . . exclude to a moral certainty every hypothesis except that of guilt."*

In its brief, the People pointed to the fact that when Mike's body was discovered his chest cavity was filled with blood. Since it may take as long as ten minutes for the cavity to fill and since the heart would remain beating while this was occurring, it was possible that Mike was alive when Mel shot him. But Dr. Melomo had testified that he could only "guess" how long it took for the cavity to fill in this case. "Guesstimates"—even when made by experts—do not constitute proof beyond a reasonable doubt.

Our second major contention in the appellate brief was that the murder conviction could not stand because regardless of whether Mike was *actually* alive when Mel shot him, the evidence did not establish beyond a reasonable doubt that Mel *believed* he was alive. If Mel believed that Mike was already

*The most common example used to explain the difference between "direct" and "circumstantial" evidence is the following: if someone tells you he was just outside and saw it raining, that would be direct evidence that it was raining; but if you saw a group of people coming in with wet umbrellas, that would be circumstantial evidence that it was raining.

dead—whether his belief turned out to be correct or incorrect—he could not have intended to kill him. The only direct evidence on this issue came from Mel's own testimony: in his confession he said he believed Mike was dead when he shot him.

The third point raised in our brief was that Mel's confession to Assistant D.A. Lauria should not have been admitted into evidence because Lauria had improperly cut off Mel's attempt to explain why he had shot Mike. The D.A.'s action gave us an opening to get Mel's "testimony" before the appellate courts without the risk of having him testify before the jury. Jeffrey Cohen prepared an affidavit of what Mel *would have said* to the D.A. had he not been cut off:

> First, I was certain that Michael Geller was dead before I shot him. Second, I was in dread fear of my life [because Bush] was holding a gun on me and telling me, in no uncertain terms, that if I didn't shoot the dead body, I, too, would be killed. This was a threat I had no doubt would be carried out, since I had, just minutes before, watched Bush . . . kill my best friend.

Whichever way this legal issue was resolved, I wanted the judges to read Mel's statement and understand what was going through his mind when he fired the five bullets into his friend's head.

The oral argument took place on February 5, 1976, in the marble courthouse of the Brooklyn Appellate Division, tucked away into a quiet corner of a beautiful residential street in Brooklyn Heights. The panel consisted of five judges, but one judge dominated the entire argument.

Justice Irwin Shapiro was a true son of Brooklyn: a cynical, impatient tone infused his every question. With an unembarrassed Brooklyn accent, he probed every weakness in our case. Many of his questions were rhetorical, designed not so much to elicit a response, but rather to demonstrate that he understood the case in all of its subtleties. He pressed me hard on the blood-filled chest cavity; then on the five bullets: "Wasn't one or two enough to make the point? Why did he have to shoot five? Doesn't that show something?" He seemed satisfied with my answers. As I began to make my final point, he suddenly cut me off (ironically, it was just as I was beginning to make the argument about Mel being cut off by the Assistant D.A., but I resisted the temptation to make any analogy): "We've heard enough from you, Professor. Let's hear what your distinguished adversary from the District Attorney's office has to say."

The D.A.'s office was represented by the chief of its appeals section, a shrewd and scholarly lawyer named Helman R. Brook. Before Brook even reached the lectern, Shapiro was at him: "What's your evidence he was alive? I don't see it."

Brook began to marshal the circumstantial evidence from his brief. "Not good enough. Not good enough," Shapiro kept interjecting. Every time Brook came up with a circumstantial argument, Shapiro came back with an hypothesis of innocence. Justice Shapiro was arguing my case for me.

Within a few minutes Brook began to change his tack. Taking a deep breath he admitted that the evidence that Mike was alive when Mel shot him was a bit "iffy."

Shapiro pressed him: "Does that mean that you concede that the murder conviction cannot stand?"

"We will not press the murder conviction," Brook almost whispered, visibly squirming. "But we do argue there was enough evidence for attempted murder."

Shapiro affected a broad smile as he directed his cynicism at the assistant D.A.: "Are you trying to tell me that a defendant can be convicted of attempted murder for trying to kill a corpse?" The judge's voice became a full octave higher as he enunciated the last word.

Brook stood his ground: "That's exactly what we are arguing, your Honor."

Shapiro shook his head in apparent disbelief. "That certainly is an interesting theory. Haven't heard that one before."

Brook proceeded to argue that the New York state legislature had recently amended the law of attempts to eliminate the defense of "impossibility." Under that old defense, a defendant could win if the crime he had attempted was "legally impossible" to accomplish.

For example, in a much-cited English hypothetical case, Lady Eldon had traveled to France and had purchased some fine lace, which she believed to be French, and thus subject to an import duty. Rather than pay the duty, the not-so-noble lady decided to smuggle the lace past the customs inspector. The inspector discovered it, and the embarrassed lady confessed her "crime." But upon inspection, it was determined that it was the lady who had been cheated rather than the customs authorities: the lace was not French at all; it was a cheap English copy and not subject to duty. Had Lady Eldon *attempted* to evade the duty? She certainly had *intended* to commit the crime. If the facts had been as she believed them to be, she would have been guilty of smuggling. But can a crime be committed by a criminal intent coupled with an innocent act?

(The contemporary version of Lady Eldon's "crime" is committed every day in New York when a tourist is sold a "stolen" expensive brand-name watch for a fraction of its list price. What the tourist ends up with is a cheap imitation manufactured specifically for use in this scam. Is the cheated tourist guilty of attempting to purchase stolen goods because that was his unmistakable intent?)

Most authorities had concluded that Lady Eldon could not be guilty, since what she had attempted to do was "legally impossible": one cannot attempt to evade duty on an article that carries no duty. But some authorities disagreed. The defense of impossibility was in total confusion.

Under the amended New York statute an impossible attempt could be punished if the crime *would* have been possible had the actual circumstances been as the defendant "believed them to be."

Thus, Lady Eldon (and the watch-buying tourist) would be guilty—as would the out-of-season hunter who shot the stuffed deer, and the person who deliberately shot at someone who he erroneously believed was alive.

As Brook was developing his broad argument, Justice Shapiro kept pressing him on the particulars of this case: "But where is your evidence of belief here? How did you prove that *this* defendant mistakenly believed that the deceased was alive when he shot him? Is there any evidence to contradict his own statement that he believed the deceased was dead?"

Brook pointed to the five bullets; the presumption that a person intends the natural consequences of his conduct; the absurdity of shooting into a body believed to be dead; the absence of any convincing explanation.

To each of these arguments, Shapiro responded, "Not enough, not enough."

When Brook completed his argument, I began to rise to give my rebuttal. Justice Shapiro cut me off: "Don't you know when you're ahead?" he asked with a smile. Of course I knew I was ahead *with him;* but I couldn't be certain of what the other judges—who had spoken hardly a word—were thinking. I decided to leave it to Justice Shapiro to convince the others.

We did not have to wait long for the result. On March 1, 1976—just three weeks after the oral argument—a unanimous court reversed the murder conviction. After reviewing the medical evidence, the court concluded that the People had

> failed to prove beyond a reasonable doubt that Geller had been alive at the time he was shot by the defendant.

Having determined that the murder conviction could not stand, the court turned to the People's argument on attempted murder and found that the

> uncontradicted evidence is that the defendant . . . believed [Geller] to be dead, and . . . there is not a scintilla of evidence to contradict his assertion in that regard.

It concluded, therefore, that Mel could not be convicted of attempted murder, since he did not intend to kill the corpse.

Mel was acquitted of all charges and the indictment was ordered dismissed. (The only real surprise contained in the opinion was that it was not written by Justice Shapiro; its author was Justice Martuscello, who had remained silent during the oral argument.)

The *Daily News* ran a lengthy story under the caption: "Didn't 'Slay' A Dead Man, Court Rules." The *New York Times* ran its story under the more subdued heading, "Question of Death of Victim Upsets Murder Conviction."

As soon as the decision was rendered, we immediately arranged to have Mel released. It looked as though Mel's legal ordeal might be over. But a new one was just beginning, since the People is entitled to appeal to the New York Court of Appeals if the defendant prevailed on his appeal to the appellate division.

The *Coup de Grâce* Argument

Review by the New York Court of Appeals involves a two-step process: first, the losing party applies to a single judge of that court; then, if that judge decides that review is appropriate, the case is calendared for oral argument by the entire court. The People brought its application before Chief Judge Charles D. Breitel.

One late afternoon in 1976, I was home cooking dinner when the phone rang. A voice on the other end of the phone said, "This is Charlie Breitel. I want to talk to you about that fascinating corpse-shooting case."

I didn't know how to respond. I had always been taught that *ex parte* communication with a judge was improper. I suggested to Judge Breitel that we should get Helman Brook on the line.

"I've already spoken to Helman," the judge assured me. "I'm familiar with the case and I'm strongly inclined to grant his petition, but I thought I should give you an opportunity to try to talk me out of it, though I doubt you'll be able to, since this is the most interesting criminal case I've seen in a long time. My colleagues on the court would never forgive me if I let this one get away."

I asked Judge Breitel whether he wanted me to make my argument right there over the phone, with no papers in front of me.

"Sure," he said, "all I want to hear is a general argument why we shouldn't take the case. It's all very informal. This is how we do it down here in New York, Professor."

I began to argue that the appellate division's opinion was a narrowly focused review of the evidence that had simply concluded that the People had failed to prove the case. It had no broad significance.

Breitel laughed: "Nice try, but what about the attempt issue? Isn't this the first case of a person shooting a corpse that he believed to be alive?"

"That issue isn't in the case," I replied, "since there was not a scintilla of evidence that the defendant believed the deceased was alive when he shot him."

"But," the judge interjected, "he couldn't have been absolutely certain he was dead. Isn't it reasonable to assume that the defendant was acting like the commanding officer of a firing squad, whose job it is to administer the *coup de grâce*—just to make absolutely sure."

I disagreed, but I could see it was hopeless. Judge Breitel was really into the case; he wasn't going to let go. He ended the conversation by advising me to be prepared to respond to the *coup de grâce* argument.

A week later the formal order was issued: the People would be permitted to appeal. It would be a rare experience for me. I would be appearing in the role of counsel for *appellee,* defending the opinion of the lower court, rather than in my usual role of counsel for the *appellant,* attacking the opinion of the lower court. The appeal focused squarely on the issue that had first seduced me into the case—and that had intrigued Judge Breitel and generations of law students: under what circumstances, if any, can a person be convicted of attempted murder for shooting at a corpse? We all realized that however this issue was decided, the case would become a law school classic. It would replace the wild assortment of hypotheticals that law professors had been driven to concoct in the absence of a real case.

I traveled to Albany to argue in the magnificent chambers of the New York Court of Appeals—a small marble building in the intersecting shadows of the elaborate mall and downtown Albany's pitiful ghetto. The trip to Albany is a reminder of the anachronistic fact that this small town on the Hudson is still the capital of the Empire State. Most of the lawyers in the courtroom that day had made the hundred-and-fifty-mile journey from New York City, as had most of the judges. It is hardly surprising that everyone always seems a bit tired and grumpy in that courthouse—especially near the end of the day when they can be seen shuffling bus and train schedules in anticipation of the trip back to New York's real capital.

The oral argument before the seven judges of the court of appeals was like a septiphonic cacophony. Each had his own points to make. The court was plainly divided on the central issues. One judge insisted that there was more than enough evidence to support a murder charge based on the original theory that Joe and Mel had jointly planned Mike's death. This was a preposterous view—since the record contained no evidence of any planning—but that didn't stop the judge from urging it.

Another judge kept asking how the shooting of a corpse could possibly constitute the crime of attempted murder. A third expressed scepticism about evidence of intent. A fourth wondered aloud about the trial judge's instructions. The remaining judges asked scattered questions about the facts and the law. It was impossible for either side to present a coherent argument for more than a few minutes at a time.

When the decision was finally rendered on May 12, 1977—fourteen months after the appellate division's decision—it bore the unmistakable hallmarks of a compromise. It agreed with the appellate division's decision that the murder conviction must be dismissed because the People had failed to prove that Mike was still alive when Mel shot him. "Whatever else it may be, it is not murder to shoot a corpse," the court said. "Man dies but once." But it held that Mel was guilty of attempted murder, since there was sufficient evidence that he *believed* Mike was alive when he shot him.

The court began its discussion of attempted murder by stating the general rule developed in most American jurisdictions that "legal impossibility is a good defense but factual impossibility is not. . . ." It offered an illustrative array of "legally impossible" attempts, which included:

> defendants who shot at a stuffed deer [or who] . . . attempt to bribe a juror where person bribed was not, in fact, a juror. Lady Eldon and her French lace.

The court then gave examples of "factual" impossibility, which is not a defense:

> [A] man shot into the room in which his target usually slept and, fortuitously, the target was sleeping elsewhere in the house that night. [A] defendant agreed to perform an abortion, then a criminal act, upon a female undercover police investigator who was not, in fact, pregnant. [A man] had sexual intercourse with a woman, with the belief that she was alive and did not consent to the intercourse, . . . when the woman had, in fact, died from an unrelated ailment prior to the acts of intercourse.

This bizarre catalog of impossible attempts demonstrates that the distinction between "legal" and "factual" impossibility is often no more than a semantic after-the-fact justification for reaching a particular result: if the court wants to acquit the defendant, it categorizes the impossibility as "legal"; if it wants to convict the defendant, it calls the impossibility "factual."

The two shooting cases mentioned by the court are good examples: in the first, the defendant shot a stuffed deer and was acquitted on the ground that it is *legally impossible* to take a stuffed deer. In the second, the defendant shot into an empty bed and was convicted because his attempt was merely *factually impossible.* But what possible difference is there between shooting at a dummy, believing it to be alive, and shooting at an empty bed, believing it to contain a living person? What if the empty bed had contained a dummy instead of a pillow? Under the traditional reasoning, that difference might transform the case from the category of factual impossibility to the category of legal impossibility and transform the defendant from a guilty attempted-murderer to an innocent dummy–shooter.

It is no wonder that several states—including New York—had amended their attempt statutes to eliminate the distinction between legal and factual impossibility. Under the amended law, neither legal nor factual impossibility constitutes a valid defense so long as the "crime" that was attempted "could have been committed had the attendant circumstances been as [the defendant] believed them to be." Under this statute, all of the dummy–shooters would be guilty, since their bullets would have killed living objects if the actual circumstances had been as they "believed them to be."

But the new statute would also result in conviction in somewhat more questionable cases, such as the ignorant man who, believing in voodoo, makes a doll in the image of his enemy and sticks pins in it believing that they will kill the enemy. Under the statute he can be convicted of attempted murder, since if the circumstances were as he "believed them to be"—if voodoo really worked—he would have killed his enemy. The tourist who bought the cheap imitation watch that he believes to be stolen would also be guilty (attempting to receive stolen property); as would the man who had intercourse with a twenty-year-old prostitute whom he erroneously believed to be a fifteen-year-old virgin (attempted statutory rape); and so would Lady Eldon, who smuggled the English lace erroneously believing it to be French (attempting to evade duty).

These attempt convictions are understandable if the function of the law of attempts is to punish the "bad" person who intended to achieve a result that he believed to be criminal and who manifested that intent by specific action. And that was precisely what the New York law was supposed to do. As the court of appeals put it:

> The basic premise of the Code provision is that *what was in the actor's own mind* should be the standard for determining his dangerousness to society and, hence, his liability for attempted criminal conduct.

With these considerations in mind, the court concluded that under the amended law "if defendant believed the victim to be alive at the time of the shooting, it is no defense to the charge of attempted murder that the victim may have been dead." In other words, under New York law, it *is* attempted murder to shoot a corpse, if the shooter believes it is alive. What Lord Reid of the House of Lords said would make the law "an ass"—punishing someone for attempting to kill a corpse—thus became the law of New York.

We expected the court to reach this conclusion, since the amended statute contemplated that sort of situation. We argued that because the New York approach placed so much emphasis on what was in "the actor's own mind," it followed that in order for a corpse-shooter to be guilty of attempted murder, the People would have to produce overwhelming evidence that in his "own mind" he believed the body to be alive when he fired the shots. In this case, of course, there was no direct evidence that Mel believed Mike to be alive; indeed, what little evidence there was on the issue of Mel's belief—his own confession—was to the contrary.

But the court of appeals—apparently as part of its compromise—had no difficulty "finding" that there was "ample" evidence from which "the jury was certainly warranted in concluding that the defendant acted in the belief that Geller was yet alive when shot by defendant." But what was this ample evidence? The court gave two examples: first, it pointed to the fact that

> . . . defendant admitted firing five shots at a most vital part of the victim's anatomy from virtually point blank range. [The jury could thus] conclude that the defendant's purpose and intention was to administer the coup de grâce.

But of what relevance is the fact that Mel fired *five* shots instead of *one,* or that he fired them into the victim's head rather than his leg? If the victim had been walking around when Mel shot him and the issue was whether Mel intended to kill or merely *wound* a live person, then the number of bullets and their location would be relevant in proving that the intent was to kill. But where the sole issue was whether the defendant believed the prone body was alive or dead at the time of the shooting, little light is shed on that dispute by the number or location of the bullets. Indeed, the traditional *coup de grâce* is generally administered by means of a single bullet rather than a fusillade.

The court next pointed to the fact that

> . . . not only did defendant not come forward with his story immediately, but when the police arrived at his house, he related a false

version designed to conceal his and Bush's complicity in the murder. All of these facts indicate a consciousness of guilt which defendant would not have had if he had truly believed that Geller was dead when he shot him.

This argument is not particularly compelling. Of course Mel felt "a consciousness of guilt." Whether he had shot a dead body *or* a live one, he had done something terrible. His initial evasions and falsehoods do not prove that he believed that Mike was alive when he shot him. They simply prove that he was nervous and frightened about his complicity—whatever it may have been—in the killing of his friend. They certainly fall short of proving "beyond a reasonable doubt" that Mel believed that Mike was alive.

In any event, there was still a long step to be taken before the court could conclude that Mel was guilty of attempted murder. It was not enough that there may have been sufficient evidence from which a jury *"could* conclude" that Mel was guilty of attempted murder; the court of appeals had to be certain that the jury that had erroneously convicted Mel of murder *did,* in fact, conclude that he was also guilty of attempted murder.

It is reasonable to speculate, of course, that since the jurors unanimously concluded that Mel was guilty of murder, they could in all likelihood have also found him gulity of the lesser crime of attempted murder—*if* they had ever reached that issue. Indeed, there is a concept in the law known as the doctrine of "lesser included offenses" that reflects this likelihood. The doctrine permits an appellate court to conclude that if a jury convicted the defendant of a greater crime, such as *armed* robbery, it also would have convicted that defendant of the lesser included crime of *unarmed* robbery. Thus, in a case where a defendant had been convicted of armed robbery, and where the appellate court had concluded that there was insufficient proof that he was actually armed, under the doctrine of "lesser included offenses" there would be no need for the appellate court to send the case back for a new jury trial on the crime of unarmed robbery: it could simply conclude—on its own, and without the need for a new jury verdict—that the defendant was guilty of unarmed robbery.

But the other side of the coin is that if there are any elements of the lesser crime that are *not* included in the greater crime, the constitutional right to trial by jury requires that there be a new jury trial, since no appellate court may "find" facts that have not been found by a jury. The constitutional right to trial by jury includes the right to have a jury—rather than a judge or even several judges—resolve each and every disputed factual issue.

The People was resting its argument on the claim that attempted murder is a lesser offense included within the crime of murder. And, on the surface, that appeared to be correct. In both crimes the defendant must intend to kill the victim: it is murder if he succeeds; and it is attempted murder if he fails. In order for the jurors to convict Mel of murder—as they did in our case—they had to make two findings: 1) that Mel had *intended* to kill Mike; and 2) that he had *succeeded* in doing so. The court of appeals had concluded that there was insufficient evidence that Mel had succeeded (because there was a reasonable doubt whether Mike was still alive when Mel shot him.). Thus, the murder conviction could not stand. But it would seem to follow that the court of appeals could rely on the jury's conclusion that Mel had *intended* to kill Mike; and it could hold—without the need for a new jury trial—that Mel was guilty of attempted murder. The analogy to armed and unarmed robbery seemed compelling. The logic seemed airtight. But there was a subtle flaw in the People's argument.

Although it is true that murder and attempted murder both require that the defendant "intend" to kill the victim, the *method* by which the jury may find the necessary intent differs dramatically for the two crimes: for the crime of murder, once the jury concludes that the defendant did, in fact, kill the victim, it is permitted to *presume* his intent from the act of killing. Indeed, in this case the trial judge had expressly invited the jury to employ this presumption, if it chose to do so, in considering the crime of *murder:* "under our law every person is presumed to intend the natural and probable consequences of his acts." But the law of attempt, especially in New York, focuses very heavily on the "actor's mental frame of reference"—on what was in his "own mind." Thus, in an attempt case the jury is not permitted to presume intent from the act. It must conclude—independently of the act —that the defendant specifically intended to achieve the result.

In a case like ours, this means that the jury must decide, without the benefit of any presumption, that when Mel shot Mike, he actually intended to kill him, believing him to be alive at the time. Indeed, the trial judge, in instructing the jurors about intent for the crime of attempted murder, did not invite them to employ any such presumption. He instructed them that in order to convict Mel of *attempted murder* they would have to find that "the defendant actually intended to kill the deceased, believing *in his own mind* that the deceased was living."

We argued that the crime of attempted murder—at least in the case of "impossible attempts"—was not a lesser included offense to the crime of murder. Certainly, we contended, it was not a lesser included offense in the specific context of this case, where the trial judge had given such different intent instructions for murder and attempted murder.

The court of appeals simply ignored our argument; the judges pretended that we had not made it—as courts are prone to do when it is difficult to answer an argument. The court applied a syllogism, without any recognition of its subtle—yet by now obvious—flaw. It reasoned as follows:

> . . . The jury convicted the defendant of murder. Necessarily, they found that defendant intended to kill a live human being. Subsumed within this finding is the conclusion that defendant acted in the belief that Geller was alive. Thus, there is no need for additional fact findings by a jury.

The court of appeals thus ordered the defendant to be found guilty of attempted murder and to be sentenced for that crime.

This time, the *New York Times* headline read: "Corpse Can Be Shot But Not Murdered." The story continued: "The New York State Court of Appeals, the state's highest tribunal, has ruled that a person cannot murder a dead man, but that it still may be a crime to try to do so."

The court of appeals compromise decision—holding that Mel was innocent of murder but guilty of attempted murder—was a practical victory. The maximum sentence for attempted murder was fifteen years to life; and the minimum was one year. If Mel received the minimum—which was possible—he could be released in several months, since he would get credit for some of the time he had served in jail before his reversal by the appellate division.

Shopping for a Judge

There is a story about a criminal defendant whose case was being argued by one of the great criminal lawyers of the day. After losing in the highest court, the defendant turned to him and asked plaintively, "Where do we go from here?" The lawyer looked him straight in the eye and responded, "What do you mean *we? You* go to prison. *I* go back to my office."

I was not satisfied with that result. By this time, Mel—who had been out of jail for more than a year—had settled down. He was living at home and working at a steady job in Manhattan. He desperately wanted to avoid going back to jail—even for a few months. If he went back, he would lose his job, his new friends, and his new life; he would have to start all over again when he got out, and he wasn't sure he could make it.

Mel's family was upset with me after the court of appeals decision. They felt that I had been too academic in my argument; that I had neglected the emotional aspects of the case. I disagreed, believing that the emotional aspects of the case were against us, and that we could win the case—if at all—only by developing a rigorous intellectual argument. I was disappointed, of course, that many of our arguments had been ignored by the court of appeals. I was committed to getting the decision reversed; and I was determined that Mel would never spend another day in the miserable hellhole of a prison where I had visited him.

I have to admit that my ego was on the line as well. I knew that the decision of the court of appeals would become a standard case for criminal-law classes and casebooks. I did not want to be immortalized as the loser —or even partial loser—of a classic case. I was convinced that it had been wrongly decided: that there had to be a new jury trial on the issue of attempted murder. I was eager to try the attempted murder case before a jury if we got a new trial. I could almost hear the resounding speech I would make to the jury about the absurdity of convicting a man of attempted murder for shooting a corpse that he knew was dead. ("The law may sometimes be an ass, but it cannot be so asinine as that.")

But I am getting ahead of myself. The court of appeals decision was the law, and we had to get it reversed. I decided that our best hope was to seek a writ of habeas corpus in the federal district court in Brooklyn. Habeas corpus—the "Great Writ" of common law—empowers the federal courts to inquire into constitutional defects in state court convictions. The federal court in the district where a conviction was obtained may grant such writs when the defendant can show that he is being confined—or threatened with imminent confinement—on the basis of an unconstitutionally obtained conviction. Habeas corpus has roots deep in Anglo—American law. The Supreme Court has declared that "there is no higher duty than to maintain it unimpaired," because of its central role in "the unceasing contest between personal liberty and government oppression." But the Great Writ is praised in theory far more often than it is employed in practice. Federal judges rarely grant writs of habeas corpus, though they are frequently sought by desperate defendants. In this case, I thought we had a chance—if we drew the right judge.

Before we could seek a writ of habeas corpus in the federal court, we were required by law to exhaust all of our state court remedies. Accordingly, we made a halfhearted effort to get the appellate division to order a jury trial, but it said it was without power to do so, remanding the case to the trial court so that Mel could be resentenced for attempted murder. This next stage was crucial for several reasons: First, it would determine what sentence Mel would receive; he could receive any term between one year and fifteen years. Second, it would determine whether Mel would have to return to jail right away or whether he could remain out on bail until we had exhausted our legal remedies. This would affect our strategy for the remainder of the case. If Mel were remanded to prison, he could serve his entire sentence—especially if it were near the low end of the permissible range—before we ever got to the federal courts. Even if we were then to win in the federal courts, the victory would be a Pyrrhic one.

Knowing how important this sentencing stage could be, we were relieved to learn that the original trial judge who had presided over Mel's trial had retired. A new judge, we reasoned, would be less committed to the results of the original trial and more open to viewing the case from the current perspective of a rehabilitated and employed defendant. We also felt that a new judge would be more sympathetic to our request for a stay of Mel's sentence to permit us to level another attack on the original decision.

With that in mind, we "shopped around"—as lawyers should always do —for the best state judge we could get. (In the state court a lawyer has some ability to "shop" for his judge in certain situations; in the federal courts such "judge shopping" is almost impossible because all judges are randomly pulled out of a wheel.) We canvassed the available judges and came up with several who, we thought, were sufficiently intelligent and motivated to understand our relatively subtle argument. (It is amazing how many judges —especially, but not exclusively, state judges—lack the basic intelligence to understand a moderately complex legal argument. Some are just plain stupid; others lack the necessary legal education; still others are lazy or impatient.)

One afternoon, Jeff Cohen called me and said in an excited tone of voice: "Judge Brownstein is sitting this week." Judge J. Irwin Brownstein was exactly the kind of judge we wanted: clever, independent, compassionate, well educated, and experienced. I was worried that he might even be a bit too smart. He would not only understand our argument but he might also be able to see its soft points. But I'm always happier with a smart judge, and Brownstein was as smart as they come.

Jeff and I decided to take direct action. After alerting Helman Brook, we went to Judge Brownstein's courtroom to explain the bizarre history of the case and ask him to take jurisdiction over it. We were counting on hooking him by the inherent fascination of the issues. He was duly fascinated. Instead of assigning the case to another judge—as he could have done—he decided to keep it himself. He set it down for sentencing on August 2, 1978.

But we were not ready for sentencing quite yet. We wanted to take one more shot at getting a new jury trial. We prepared a brief for Judge Brownstein arguing that regardless of what the highest court of New York had said, no judge could constitutionally impose a sentence on Mel for attempted murder without a jury verdict on that crime.

When Judge Brownstein received our brief, he invited both sides to a conference in his chambers. Helman Brook, Jeff Cohen, and I arrived in his office and began to discuss the case informally.

"This is one hell of a crazy case," the judge began. "I've been studying the papers, and I think the defendant may have something, but I'm not sure I can do anything about it. I've seen the probation report, and this kid doesn't belong back in jail, but my hands are tied by the court of appeals."

Our best hope was to persuade Judge Brownstein to impose a short sentence and then to grant Mel a stay, to enable us to pursue our remedies elsewhere. I also urged him to state for the record that he thought we had a strong legal argument. I anticipated that this might help in the federal court, since judges generally give more weight to the arguments of other judges than they do to the adversary presentations of lawyers. Much to my surprise, he placed on the record his belief that the court of appeals had "*made a finding of fact" that should be made by a jury, and that this* constituted a "deprivation of due process" that should "be reviewed." Judge Brownstein had given our constitutional argument the imprimatur of judicial acceptance.

He then sentenced Mel to the minimum allowable term of one year, and stayed the execution of the sentence until thirty days after we exhausted all our state remedies. We had requested this thirty-day grace period in order to permit us to file our petition for habeas corpus in the federal court before Mel began serving his sentence. A state court judge has no power to grant a stay pending federal review, but by scheduling Mel's surrender thirty days after we exhausted our last state remedy, the judge was, in effect, giving us a chance to go to the federal court and begin our habeas corpus litigation there while Mel was still out on bail.

Litigating a criminal case with the defendant out on the street gives a defense lawyer an enormous psychological advantage: many judges—often conservative by nature—are reluctant to change the status quo. They are even more reluctant to make a decision that frees an imprisoned defendant than to make a decision allowing a free man to remain at liberty.

We proceeded immediately to lay the foundation for our federal habeas petition. We had to "exhaust" our remedies—as well as ourselves and the courts—and so we went through the paces of appealing through the New York court system again. But our eyes were pointed clearly in the direction of the federal courts, where we knew our only real hope of relief lay.

The Student Solution

While we were maneuvering our way through the labyrinths of state court proceedings, I was teaching my usual first-year criminal-law class at Harvard. As we approached the section of the casebook dealing with the law of attempts, it occurred to me that it might be useful—both for me and the students—to use Mel's case as a vehicle for studying the law of impossible attempts. I assigned two students to argue Mel's side, two students to argue the People's side, and three to serve as judges. The rest of the class was to ask questions of the participants. An aura of excitement filled the classroom on the day of the oral argument. The student advocates were committed to their positions and they performed as well—or better—than most lawyers with years of experience. The student judges were far better prepared than most of their real-life counterparts, and asked extremely probing questions.

One of the questions a student judge put to the student prosecutor was rather simple, indeed obvious, but I had never thought of putting it quite the way she did:

> Assume, Mr. Prosecutor, that the defendant had *originally* been charged with attempted murder, rather than murder, and that the trial judge in the attempted murder trial had given the jury the instruction that "under our law every person is presumed to intend the natural and probable consequences of his acts." If the defendant had been convicted of attempted murder on the basis of that instruction, could the conviction stand?

The student prosecutor—one of the ablest students in the class—tried her best to argue that an attempted murder conviction based on the "presumed intent" instruction could stand, but in the end she had to admit that the law was against her.

Suddenly I had a solution to my dilemma. I told the class that the exchange had given me an idea for how to frame my argument to the federal district court.

In our brief to the district court, I borrowed heavily from the classroom exchange, putting the argument exactly as the student had put it.*

I intended to present the point in a similar fashion at the oral argument. But the federal district judge we had drawn conducted the oral argument in a rather atypical manner. The judge was Eugene H. Nickerson, who had been the County Executive of Nassau County and a senior partner of a prestigious law firm before being appointed to the bench.

Judge Nickerson presided over his courtroom the way an experienced law professor presides over an advanced seminar. He did not encourage performances by the attorneys. He told each side which aspects of their arguments he agreed with, which he disagreed with, and which ones required clarifica-

*Assume that [Mel] had *originally* been charged only with attempted murder (rather than murder); assume that at the *attempted murder trial,* the trial judge had given the [presumed intent] instruction; assume that the jury had convicted the defendant of attempted murder *on the basis of this instruction.* Could this court sustain that conviction of *attempted murder* on the basis of that intent instruction? Unless the answer to the question is "yes," this court must vacate the attempted murder conviction in this case.

tion. You could see that he was not predisposed toward a particular result and that he was genuinely trying to be fair (a characteristic altogether too rare among judges). He kept the "seminar" in session for about an hour and then proceeded to tell us that he had never granted a writ of habeas corpus and wasn't even certain he actually knew how to do it in the approved way. He told us, without disclosing which way he was leaning, that he wanted us to know that this was the most interesting criminal case ever to come before him. That's all I wanted to hear! I knew that once it caught his attention, we were halfway home. He adjourned the court, indicating that he would have a written decision before too long.

As Judge Nickerson was leaving the bench, he came over to me and said, "I notice that your father is here, Professor," pointing to an elderly man sitting in the spectator section of the courtroom.

"Yes," I replied, "he often comes to watch my brother or me in court. But how did you know it was my father?" I asked out of curiosity.

The judge replied, "Oh, I remember him being on a jury panel a few months ago, but the prosecutor threw him off the jury because his children are defense lawyers."

By this time my father had approached the bench and joined the conversation: "Those prosecutors, they never let me serve on a jury because of my kids. I don't understand it. I would be very tough on criminals. I'm not like my kids."

Judge Nickerson looked at my father compassionately and said, "Isn't that always the problem. Parents are held responsible for the sins of their children." After that cryptic comment, we all left the courtroom to await his decision.

A few days later, Judge Nickerson issued his opinion. For the first time in his judicial career, he granted a writ of habeas corpus ordering Mel's freedom unless the state accorded him a new trial.

Judge Nickerson held that the "Due Process" clause of the United States Constitution entitled Mel to a new jury trial for the crime of attempted murder—unless the state could show that the old jury had found that when Mel fired he believed Geller was alive and intended to kill him. He held further that any such findings would have to be based on instructions that appropriately described "the intellectual process whereby the jurors might make the finding." He then concluded that the jurors, in Mel's first trial for murder, may well have found Mel's intent by following the instruction that "every person is presumed to intend the natural and probable consequences of his acts." Since such a presumption would not be proper in an attempted murder case "the conviction cannot stand under the due process clause."

The decision was a total victory. Mel would get a new trial—the remedy we had asked for. And much to my personal satisfaction—and that of the student participants in our moot court—our legal arguments had prevailed in the end. But the case was not yet over. The state has the right to appeal the granting of a writ of habeas corpus by a federal district judge. The appeal would be to the United States Court of Appeals for the Second Circuit—across the East River in lower Manhattan. If the state again lost in the Second Circuit, it could apply to the Supreme Court for a writ of certiorari. And the rate of success of *governments* in obtaining Supreme Court review in criminal cases—especially under Chief Justice Burger—has been astronomically higher than the rate of success by defense lawyers. We were concerned, therefore, that what we won in a lower court might again be taken away from us by a higher court.

Plea Bargaining After the Appeal

I decided, therefore, to write a letter to the District Attorney in an effort to dissuade him from appealing Judge Nickerson's order, and urging him instead to enter into a plea bargain under which Mel would plead guilty to a lesser crime that would assure him his continued freedom. In the letter I pointed out that the crime had occurred about six years earlier and that Mel had been at liberty and working for more than three and a half years, after having served eight months in confinement. If the state was to appeal, "the case would necessarily drag on for another two years," with proceedings before the United States Court of Appeals, the United States Supreme Court, and the district court:

> What conceivable purpose would be served by sending him back to prison at that point? The man who would go to prison would be a different person from the one who is alleged to have participated in the tragic events [many years earlier]. It would truly be triumph of form over substance, of technicality over justice.

Several days after receiving the letter, Helman Brook called me. The District Attorney, Eugene Gold, had asked the advice of his four chief aides: they had deadlocked, two in favor of accepting a plea bargain, and two in favor of litigating the case all the way up to the Supreme Court. The District Attorney himself had cast the deciding vote: the People would not appeal, provided that Mel would plead guilty to the most serious crime under which he could avoid returning to prison. We had an agreement—at least in principle. Now came the time to do some hard bargaining about details.

The District Attorney's office proposed that Mel plead guilty to manslaughter. We objected because such a plea would constitute an acknowledgment that Mel had killed Mike, and Mel just couldn't admit to that because he didn't believe it.

We countered with a proposal that Mel plead guilty to unlawful possession of a gun. The D.A.'s office rejected our proposal. Helman laughed: "The next crime you're going to suggest is desecration of a corpse." We were at loggerheads. There was no crime on the books serious enough to satisfy the D.A. that at the same time would permit the judge to grant a probationary sentence.

Finally, I suggested, half jokingly, "Why don't we make up a crime?" Helman asked what I meant.

"Well," I offered, "why can't we come up with a crime that fits the peculiar facts of this case—say, something like attempted manslaughter."

Helman seemed interested. Although there is no such crime on the New York statute books, it did make some logical sense. Manslaughter is the *negligent* killing of a human being. Mel was certainly negligent. Had Mike still been alive when Mel shot him—even if Mel erroneously believed he was dead—Mel would probably have been guilty of manslaughter. Since Mike was dead, it would follow that he was guilty of something like attempted manslaughter. Pleading to this "crime" would allow the judge to impose a probationary sentence, and would allow the D.A. to claim that Mel had pleaded guilty to a serious crime involving a grave threat to human life. We agreed on a plea bargain.

On December 4, 1979—six years after the tragic events—Mel went back to the Supreme Court in Brooklyn and pleaded guilty to "attempted manslaughter in the second degree." When Judge Brownstein tried to explain the "crime" to Mel, he had difficulty:

> In order for you to be guilty of the crime of attempted manslaughter in the second degree it would have been necessary that you on December 22, 1973, in the County of Kings, did recklessly—did attempt to recklessly—*it's incredible*—did recklessly attempt to cause the death of Michael Geller by means of a deadly weapon, to wit, a loaded firearm.

But an agreement had finally been reached to resolve this case, and a small dose of incredibility was not going to stop it now. Judge Brownstein sentenced Mel to five years of probation, and Mel walked out of the courtroom a relatively free man. He would have to behave himself for five years, and he was certainly prepared to do that.

That case of the twice-killed corpse was finally over. It would live on in law school casebooks and classrooms around the country, intriguing and confounding generations of law students.

— 3 —

"Would You Represent 'The Meanest Man in New York'?" The Case of Bernard Bergman

The question I am most often asked—by students, lecture audiences, friends, and even my parents—is how can you defend a client when you *know* he is guilty of a despicable crime? It is a question criminal lawyers always ask themselves, since the vast majority of defendants they represent are plainly guilty. Some criminal lawyers claim to represent only innocent clients. Don't believe them! It's a ploy! No full-time criminal lawyer represents a significant number of innocent clients. Attorney William Kunstler (whom I once helped represent) claims that he will defend only people he "loves," but even he tends to fall in love with clients who are guilty as hell. The Perry Mason image of the criminal lawyer saving his innocent client by uncovering the real culprit is television fiction; it rarely happens in real life. Almost all criminal defendants—including most of my clients—are factually guity of the crimes they have been charged with. The criminal lawyer's job, for the most part, is to represent the *guilty,* and—if possible—to get them off. How can we do it and still sleep at night?

Some of the answers come easily:

- It isn't the lawyer's job to determine the guilt or innocence of his client—that's for the jury or the judge to decide.
- Even the guiltiest defendant is entitled to an adequate defense.
- It's important for lawyers to challenge the government in order to keep it honest.
- The alternative is a legal system like that of countries such as the Soviet Union, where lawyers will represent only defendants "entitled" to a defense!

- The lawyer's function goes beyond defending the innocence of his client: it includes plea bargaining and obtaining the shortest possible sentence.

None of these arguments—compelling as they may be—really tells the whole story of why defense lawyers represent guilty defendants. Defense lawyers are an egotistical lot—and the challenge of "getting off" an obviously guilty defendant is a great ego trip. It is also a great source of future clients; and clients mean money; and money means the good life that so many defense lawyers crave.

Many lawyers don't have the stomach to represent guilty criminals; they should stick to other areas of the law. There simply aren't enough innocent defendants to keep more than a handful of criminal lawyers in business. Nobody should become a criminal defense lawyer without being prepared to devote the vast majority of time to representing *guilty* clients.

Not all guilty defendants are universally despised. Draft evaders, Klansmen, members of the JDL, urban rioters, all have their champions. Some defendants, however, are both guilty *and* universally despised. These clients focus the dilemma of the criminal defense attorney most sharply.

In the summer of 1977 an old friend asked me to become involved in a case that tested the principle that every defendant—no matter how unpopular—is entitled to a lawyer. The defendant was a rabbi named Bernard Bergman, who allegedly controlled dozens of substandard nursing homes in New York. At this time Bergman was one of the most hated and vilified people in New York. Although he stood formally charged with only two rather technical crimes, he had been accused by the press of numerous serious crimes. The public wanted him behind bars. My friend asked me to try to keep that from happening.

Well before Bergman was indicted in 1975, the press and some politicians had tried and convicted him of almost every crime and sin imaginable: of hastening the death of old nursing-home patients; of billing Medicaid for dead patients; of sadism toward and contempt for old people; of running rat-infested homes with the smell of urine and feces in the air; of using his homes to launder funds for the Joseph Colombo organized-crime family; of corrupting public officials at the highest levels of government; of billing Medicaid for expensive household items and for the interest on personal loans; of defrauding and cheating the federal and state governments of countless millions of dollars; and of secretly controlling more than a hundred nursing homes and hundreds of millions of dollars in nursing home properties and related assets.

The Media Blitz

The media blitz had begun with a series of exposés by the *New York Times* and the *Village Voice.* Within three months the *Times* alone had run *sixty-two* articles about Bergman. In January and February there were televised news reports about Bergman nearly every day. It is fair to say that virtually everyone within range of the New York media had seen the image of the bearded, yarmulke-wearing rabbi, juxtaposed with charges of patient abuse, organized crime connections, massive fraud, political corruption, and religious hypocrisy.

Columnist Pete Hamill called him a "rat bastard." Another columnist, Jeff Kamen, quoted his ninety-three-year-old grandmother's description of Bergman as "that awful, horrible man who tried to hide his crimes under his yarmulke and now he is the shame of all of us Jews." The *Daily News* characterized him as "the czar of a $200 million national conglomerate of Medicaid nursing homes where the aged are dumped to die." Judge Louis Kaplan, who had headed an earlier investigation into nursing homes, concluded that if what he had read about Bergman was true, he "wouldn't consider him a human being." John Hess, a *New York Times* reporter responsible for some of the earliest charges, wrote a letter to a Jewish newspaper accusing the "Bergman clan" of fostering anti-Semitism by "using religion as a shield" and suggesting that it was "high time that the Jewish community spit out from its ranks those who blacken its name." Even the *National Lampoon* ran a two-page caricature of a bearded (and beaked) nursing home operator named "Rabbi Birdman," gleefully watching an old patient wallowing in urine and then getting hit on the head by a falling concrete reproduction of the Ten Commandments.

Jack Newfield, a writer for the *Village Voice,* wrote in a front-page article that

> In my lifetime in this city, I have never encountered anyone as rotten as Bernard Bergman.
>
> I have seen slumlords who gouged welfare tenants out of a few extra dollars of rent. I have seen muggers who hurt blind newsdealers and then stole their seeing-eye dogs. I have seen judges who are corrupt and bigoted.
>
> But Bernard Bergman, in a certain sense, is the worst. He is the worst because he is the most respectable.
>
> The fact is that the Bergmans of this world are one cause of anti-Semitism.

The *Village Voice* article was entitled "Is This the Meanest Man in New York?" The question was meant to be rhetorical.

When the press discovers—or creates—a villain, the politicians cannot be far behind. A young Manhattan assemblyman named Andrew Stein, with high political ambitions, made a career out of attacking Bergman. He called him "one of the worst men that we've ever read [about] or investigated" and accused him of heading "a fraudulent empire of pain." Congressman Edward Koch—later elected Mayor of New York—tried to outdo Stein. Others, including United States senators, joined in the attack. Committee hearings were held and televised, showing Bergman being interrogated about alleged connections with Meyer Lansky and Joe Colombo. The image of Bernard Bergman—a prayer book in his hand, a yarmulke on his head—became familiar to every New Yorker.

By the time I was asked to enter the Bergman case, two and a half years had elapsed since the beginning of these exposés. But the public vilification had still not abated.

Bergman had pleaded guilty—pursuant to a plea bargain—to a federal indictment charging him with Medicare violations and to a state indictment charging him with offering a bribe. These were relatively minor crimes compared with the charges that had been leveled against him by the press and politicians. The federal sentencing judge, Marvin Frankel, had sentenced Bergman to four-months imprisonment for the federal crimes. This sentence had produced banner headlines and instant outrage throughout the country. I recalled reading about Judge Frankel's sentence and being outraged myself at what seemed to be a judicial slap on the wrist. The media heaped abuse upon Judge Frankel for his softheartedness. Jack Newfield's headline read "How the Fixer Fooled the Dumb Smart Judge." Assemblyman Stein called on all New Yorkers to write letters to the state sentencing judge urging "the harshest sentence legally permissible." Congressman Koch warned that "there will be anti-Semitism flowing from the fact" that the judge and the defendant were both Jewish. And Special State Nursing Home Prosecutor Charles J. Hynes convened a press conference at which he blasted the four-month sentence as "insubstantial" and as reflecting "special justice for the privileged." Judge Frankel's sentence became the center of the storm—with calls for investigation and even impeachment of the judge.

The Special State Nursing Home Prosecutor, Charles Hynes, was especially incensed by the four-month sentence, because as part of the joint federal-state plea bargain, he had agreed to recommend to the state sentencing judge that he should impose *the same sentence* that Judge Frankel had imposed, and that the sentences should run concurrently. If the state judge was to follow that recommendation—as judges generally do—Bergman would receive two sentences of four months, both to be served at the same time. With credit for good behavior, he could be home in less than a hundred days.

But the public's thirst for vengeance was somewhat quenched when Judge Aloysius Melia, the state sentencing judge, refused to accept the Special Prosecutor's half-hearted recommendation and sentenced Bergman to an additional year in state prison—to be served *after* he completed his four-month federal term. Judge Melia's sentence was greeted warmly by the press, and the Bergman case seemed over as the prison doors closed behind the old rabbi.

But the fight was just beginning. While Bergman went off to serve his four-month federal sentence in the Federal Penitentiary at Allenwood, Pennsylvania—the "Country Club," as the press characterized it—his lawyers began to raise legal challenges to the additional year of imprisonment imposed by the state sentencing judge. Jack Litman, a former student of mine, had been retained by Bergman to challenge Judge Melia's sentence in the New York State Courts. Litman had been an assistant District Attorney in Frank Hogan's office, where he had successfully prosecuted scores of murderers. Now he was in private practice defending those charged with crime. He was regarded as one of the best criminal defense lawyers in New York, with an excellent reputation for tough, energetic advocacy. But the New York courts refused to hear his pleas on behalf of Bergman. So sensitive was this case that all three levels in the New York judiciary had rejected Litman's formidable legal arguments without so much as a written opinion.

When I was asked to enter the Bergman case all of the state remedies had been exhausted. He was scheduled to surrender within the week at Rikers Island to begin serving his one-year state sentence. The press was clamoring for his return to prison. Photographers stalked his residence. It was rumored that he might surrender a few days early to avoid the massive publicity.

"In a Few Minutes You'll be Getting a Call . . ."

The inital request for me to become Bergman's lawyer came not from Bergman himself, but from an old and dear friend of mine named Bernard Fischman. Fischman, a senior practicing attorney in a large New York law firm, has devoted much of his life to civil liberties and civil rights causes. One of the founders of the original National Lawyer's Guild and a long-time activist in the American Civil Liberties Union, Fischman—who was by then in his early sixties—had been a guiding spirit for me throughout my career.

He told me in his gentle, halting voice that he was going to ask me to consider doing something that I wouldn't want to do. But he urged me not to say no until I heard the whole story and gave it some thought. His words came slowly: "In a few minutes you'll be getting a call from Rabbi Bernard Bergman. He wants you to represent him. He's scheduled to begin serving his state prison sentence in a few days and wants you to try to keep him out. I know—and he knows—that there is almost no chance. He has lost up and down in the state courts. Maybe you can get a stay of surrender from the Supreme Court. He's desperate! He doesn't think he can survive another year in prison—especially at Rikers Island. Please give it your most serious consideration."

I began to answer, but my old friend cut me off. "I know what you've read in the papers. I've read it too. That's part of the problem. The judges have also read the papers and seen the TV. Please, don't believe what you've read until you've heard the other side. Alan, I can assure you as my friend that there *is* another side." Fischman said he would send me the sentencing memorandum that had been prepared by Bergman's lawyers and the sentencing decision that had been rendered by Judge Frankel. He asked me to read them before I made up my mind.

Fischman ended his call with a challenge: "Alan, he's not going to be an easy client and this is not going to be an easy or pleasant case. But please, please think hard about it."

Within minutes of my conversation with Fischman, Rabbi Bergman called. His sons, Stanley and Meyer, and his son-in-law Avram Kass, a graduate of Columbia Law School, were all on the line with him. Dr. Bergman introduced himself by telling me that he knew my family and my reputation as a defender of the underdog. "There's no greater underdog in the world today than me. I need your help. I'm a broken, ruined, and sick man. I cannot possibly survive any more imprisonment. It's a death sentence." I agreed to read the sentencing material. He said he would send it to me in Cambridge that day by messenger.

I spent that night going through the sentencing memorandum. I was not surprised that it was a persuasive and meticulous document. But I was astounded at its approach in attempting to persuade Judge Frankel not to imprison Bergman. Most sentencing memoranda try to make the defendant sound like an untarnished angel. This one was different. It began by reminding the sentencing judge of all the accusations that had been leveled at Bergman by the press and the politicians; indeed, it presented the judge with Xeroxed copies of the media attacks on Bergman. At first glance, it looked like a document that might have been prepared by the prosecutors—if not by Assemblyman Stein! Then, it went through each accusation point by point, documenting its genesis, its snowballing, and its denouement. For example, the charge that Bergman was linked to organized crime was discussed as follows:

> On December 25, 1974, the *New York Times* printed the following story by John Hess:
>
> - Investigations turned yesterday to *allegations* of underworld ties and political protection, and the *report* that an alleged associate of Joseph A. Colombo Sr., the reputed underworld figure, had lived in the penthouse of a nursing home for the indigent.
> - The issue *was raised* by Senator Charles H. Percy . . . following *allegations* by Representative Edward I. Koch. . . .
> - . . . Referring to *reports* that underworld interests were using the nursing-home industry to launder funds, [Assemblyman Stein] declared: "It is *our information* that there are connections between the Bernard Bergman empire and organized crime."
>
> A careful reading of these excerpts indicates that this "twister" was created by the following chain of events:
>
> - The *Village Voice* reported a relationship between Mr. Scarfone and a Bergman nursing home.
> - Representative Edward I. Koch picked up the story and it is transformed into "allegations" by the Congressman.
> - Following these "allegations," the "issue is raised" by Senator Percy.
> - Andrew Stein . . . responded by holding a news conference in which he said, "It is our information that there are connections between the Bernard Bergman empire and organized crime."
> - John Hess wrote a story in the *New York Times.*
>
> In fact, every single allegation in that story concerning Dr. Bergman was totally false [as proved by] Rocco Scarfone's testimony.

Each of the other charges was similarly unraveled. It turned out that Bergman controlled only a handful of nursing homes, not the 117 attributed to him by the press; that the allegations of patient abuse were based on a report about conditions in nursing homes *in general* some *eighteen years earlier;* that the Special Prosecutor—after an extensive investigation—was "unable to produce even a single current allegation against Dr. Bergman involving patient care"; and that the amounts actually overcharged or mischarged were paltry when compared with the press allegations and with what other nursing-home operators charged.

The sentencing memorandum was a devastating attack on trial by press and politicians. An entirely different picture of Bergman—and of his attackers—emerged; not of a totally innocent Bergman, but certainly of a man far less culpable than he was portrayed by the media.

It was obvious that Judge Frankel had studied the sentencing memorandum. His opinion found that

> The media (and people desiring to be featured in the media) have vilified him for many kinds of evildoing of which he has in fact been innocent.
>
> . . . Although there are serious crimes, they are moderate in comparison to the full panoply of the offenses originally charged. There was certainly nothing about whether the Bergman nursing homes had given good or bad nursing care.

After reading Judge Frankel's opinion I was persuaded that the press and the politicians had attacked Bergman unfairly. These attacks had succeeded in persuading virtually everyone—including me—that Bergman was the worst kind of scoundrel. The *New York Times* was *almost* correct in describing Bernard Bergman as the individual who had "come to personify the charges of abuse and scandal" in the nursing home industry. In the public mind Bergman did "personify" all the evils of the industry; but he had not "come to" that personification by accident; it had been the press and the politicians that had created the false, but journalistically and politically salable, image of the bearded and yarmulke-wearing rabbi as the personification of all the collective evils of a corrupt industry.

This is not to say that Bergman's homes were models of cleanliness and compassion, or that Bergman's accounting methods were above criticism. But it was demonstrably true that other nursing home operators—with more homes and greater abuses—received few headlines.

Bergman had been tried and convicted by the press and by ambitious politicians of an assortment of crimes of which he was neither legally nor factually guilty. If that could happen to the rich and powerful Bernard Bergman, it could happen to others as well. I decided to take the case because I believed, and still believe, that Bernard Bergman was being made a scapegoat for an entire industry—and indeed for the entire guilt-producing process by which busy Americans dispose of their aging parents and grandparents. I believed that his ostentatious Jewishness—his rabbinical degree, his organizational affiliations, his beard, and his yarmulke—had contributed to this scapegoating by Jews and non-Jews alike. I believed that the legal system had been distorted, perverted, and abused in order to *get* Bergman. I still believe that some of the prosecutors, and especially some of the judges, were caught up in a vigilante atmosphere and lacked the courage to decide this case on neutral principles of law. If the legal system could not resist the lynch mob in a case like this, how could it be counted on to resist even more intense pressures that would inevitably confront it during times of crisis?

I took the case with my eyes open. I realized that we would probably lose. I knew I would be maligned. But I had no idea how bitter the criticism would be.

Of all the notorious cases I have been associated with—cases including alleged Mafiosi, pornographers, members of the Nazi party, and murderers on death row—not one has provoked more intense and personal attacks against me from every segment of society: radicals called me a sellout; civil libertarians warned that I would be endangering my credibility as a fighter for underdog causes; members of my own family refused to talk to me; a dinner date got up from the table and walked out when I told her whom I was defending; my students openly hissed me in class when I mentioned the case in a discussion of plea bargaining. Even a Justice of the United States Supreme Court—a man known for his liberalism—complained to a mutual friend: "I don't understand how Alan can be representing that shit. I thought he was a civil libertarian."

Having decided to take the case I arranged to meet with my client in his midtown Manhattan office. The walls of the reception area were an eerie reminder of a bygone age: the plaques, citations, and photographs were hanging as if nothing had changed. In this office Rabbi Doctor Bernard Bergman was still a man to be honored. After a brief wait Rabbi Bergman emerged with his family entourage. He was shorter and thinner than I expected. His face was drawn and he looked fatigued, but there was still a twinkle in his eyes and enthusiasm in his voice. He greeted me effusively: "Sholem aleichem," he said, extending both hands toward mine. "How is your family?" he asked, reminding me that he had known my grandfather and several of my uncles. Without waiting for an answer, he took out a large sheaf of documents and began to show them to me. "You mustn't believe what you've read in the paper about me. Take a look at these." One by one he placed before me testimonial letters from patients and relatives of patients at his nursing homes attesting to their excellence. "We don't have our patients just sitting around and doing nothing. We have classes in Bible and Talmud. We have synagogue services. We have many, many activities.

Here, look at this letter," he said, showing me one that praised him for the personal interest he had taken in a particularly difficult patient.

As I was looking through the letters, Rabbi Bergman started to tell me about his background. From the humblest of origins in Hungary, he had emigrated to the United States in 1929. He started his career in the nursing-home business as a chaplain in a small home. By 1974, when his troubles began, he was among the most influential Orthodox Jews in America—perhaps in the world. Reputed to be worth more than $100 million, he had held the presidency of numerous Jewish philanthropic, religious, and educational organizations. Rabbi Bergman showed me a dog-eared copy of the Congressional Record of May 15, 1967, which reproduced the testimonials bestowed upon him at a dinner held in his honor. Among the letters and speeches were tributes from President Lyndon Johnson ("His exceptional service to the public trust . . . sets an example that is worthy of the nation he has served so long and so well"); from the president of Israel ("His soul responds to all cries, for his heart is good and receptive to the concept of Judaism and humanism—because of this his friends are legion and his admirers many"); from the president of Yeshiva University ("Dr. Bergman has occuped, with distinction, many important posts of leadership . . . in the total Jewish community"); and from an assortment of governors, senators, and other respected public officials.

He paused at each plaque hanging on the wall and explained its significance. Some had been awarded to him for his philanthropy. Others had been given to his nursing homes for their "high standards of patient care."

It was an extraordinary display, designed to impress me not so much with his legal innocence but rather with his high qualities as a person. But it was too well-rehearsed, too packaged, too predictable. What I was being shown was obviously a rerun of many past performances for others. I took it all in with equanimity. I knew that it was as easy to receive tributes from politicians if you are respected (and wealthy) as it is to incur condemnation when you are despised. I did not believe the glowing accounts of the nursing homes, since I knew some people whose relatives had been patients in them.

I explained to Rabbi Bergman that this was all very interesting, but that it was not my job to assess him as a person, or even as an operator of nursing homes. My job was to present the constitutional challenges to the additional sentence that had been imposed upon him by Judge Melia. I asked his son-in-law Avram Kass, the lawyer, to tell me the facts giving rise to the constitutional issues.

Kass outlined the legal issues, while Stanley and Meyer Bergman added facts about the nursing home business. The rabbi remained in the background, occasionally interjecting a comment. The legal issues seemed relatively straightforward. They raised important constitutional questions about the obligations of a prosecutor in implementing a plea bargain. It seemed to me, as I listened, that if the defendant's name had been anything but Bergman, the legal result would have been a foregone conclusion. The courts would almost certainly have held that the Special Prosecutor had breached the terms of the plea bargain when he publicly attacked the sentence he had agreed to recommend to the state sentencing judge, and that the resulting one-year state sentence—imposed in addition to the four-month federal sentence—was invalid.

But the public mood against Bergman was ugly. Legal pundits were surmising that Judge Frankel, by calling it honestly and fairly and without regard to the public mood, had ruined his promising judicial career. In the face of a decade of brilliant opinions, books, and articles, he would always be remembered as the judge who "let Bergman off" with four months. It took an enormous amount of courage for a judge to do that. Would other judges be willing to take similar risks by ruling *for* Bergman—especially after they saw what the press had done to Judge Frankel?

The Legal Issues

The legal story begins with the media blitz of late 1974 and early 1975. By the spring of 1975 the pressure on state and federal prosecutors to put Bergman in jail had become intense. In response to the press disclosures about Bergman, the New York State legislature had created a new office of Special Prosecutor for Health and Special Services with a staff of nearly a hundred and an annual budget in excess of $7 million. Its primary goal, as far as the public was concerned, was to get Bergman. A massive investigation of the Bergman family began. The United States Attorney's office for the Southern District of New York had also started its own investigation.

These prosecutors were soon to learn, however, that it is far more difficult to prove a case in court than it is to make allegations in the press or in a legislative committee. Columnist Jack Newfield, for example, relied heavily on an anonymous letter from a man who claimed to have known Bergman when he first came to the United States; the letter included numerous allegations that were demonstrably false, but Newfield reprinted it in its entirety. Such an anonymous letter could not, of course, be used in court. Despite massive investigatory efforts—the subpoenaing of thousands of documents and hundreds of witnesses—neither the Special State Prosecutor nor the Federal United States Attorney's office could prove (or even responsibly allege) most of the charges that had been made in the press. There was no evidence that patients had been abused; no proof that Bergman secretly controlled hundreds of nursing homes; no organized crime connections. All that the state and federal prosecutors were able to establish to the satisfaction of grand juries was that Bernard Bergman and his son had violated certain technical accounting disclosure regulations in filing Medicare and Medicaid forms.

The resulting state and federal indictments—announced by prearrangement on the same day and charging virtually identical conduct—were a disappointment bordering on embarrassment, especially for the Special State Prosecutor. After all the media hoopla, the public believed that Bergman was surely guilty of far more extensive crimes. They expected more serious indictments.

But even these meager charges could not easily be proved by the prosecutors. Bergman's chief counsel—the exceptionally able Washington lawyer Nathan Lewin—advised his client to "go to trial" and fight the case. There was no proof that the allegedly false statements made in the Medicare forms had been deliberate, and the prosecutors would have a tough time making their case. Indeed, the records disclosed that the accounting violations—"overaccruals," to use the technical term—had occurred only in the Bergman homes for which *one particular accountant* had been responsible; there had been no overaccruals in Bergman homes not served by him; and there had been similar overaccruals in other homes not owned by Bergman for which that accountant had been responsible. (To my family's embarrassment, and to the confusion of several media people, the accountant was named Dachowitz.) Bergman blamed the accountant for the overaccruals and denied all knowledge that they had occurred. To back up his denials, he voluntarily underwent a lie detector test, the results of which supported his contentions. The prosecutors apparently realized that Bergman's guilt would be difficult to prove and feared even further embarrassment if they were to lose their highly publicized—and enormously expensive—cases.

The prosecutors—particularly the Special State Prosecutor—faced another serious problem. Since both the federal and the state indictments charged virtually identical criminal conduct, it seemed clear that Bergman could not be tried both by the federal and state authorities. The Fifth Amendment to the Constitution provides that no person may "be subject for the same offense to be twice put in jeopardy of life or limb"; and the courts had recently held that once a defendant had been tried by either the federal or state government, he could not be tried by the other branch for substantially the same conduct. Thus, the Special State Prosecutor was concerned that if the federal authorities brought Bergman to trial first, the state would be shut out—much to his embarrassment.

In order to assure a conviction against Bergman for which the Special

State Prosecutor could receive some credit, a representative of that office approached Bergman's lawyers and proposed that both the federal and state charges against Bergman be resolved by a plea bargain, jointly agreed upon by the Special State Prosecutor, the United States Attorney's office, and the Bergman family.

What Is a Plea Bargain?

There is nothing very mysterious about a plea bargain. (A television interviewer once asked me whether I "believed" in plea bargaining; recalling the joke about the religious skeptic who was asked whether he believed in Baptism, I replied, "Believe in it? Why, I've actually seen it done!") A plea bargain is nothing more than a contract whereby the bargaining parties exchange promises. It is like other contracts—such as for food, cars, rent—except that the stakes are different. In a plea bargain, the defendant gives up his constitutional right to a trial in exchange for a lesser prison sentence. Sometimes, the stakes are even higher: a defendant facing the death penalty may be bargaining for his life. Plea bargaining is reminiscent of the devil's contract with Faust, except that it is regarded as entirely valid and is enforceable by the courts.

Theoretically, it may be difficult to justify a bargain involving constitutional rights: no court would tolerate a prosecutor's offer of *money* to a defendant to give up his rights. Imagine a sign at the courtroom door saying: "$100 reward to any defendant willing to waive his right to a lawyer; $200 reward for waiving his privilege against self-incrimination; $500 reward for waiving a jury trial." But the Supreme Court has officially sanctioned—indeed encouraged—prosecutors to offer the defendant a consideration far more valuable than money, namely his freedom, in exchange for his constitutional rights. The sign that implicitly hangs on many courtroom doors today—painted by no less a scribe than the Supreme Court—says, Reward of so many months, years, and life itself for defendants who give up their right to trial. More accurately, the sign often says, *Punishment* of so many months, years, or death for defendants who invoke their constitutional right to trial.

Plea bargaining, as sanctioned by the Supreme Court, has become the primary mode of resolving criminal cases in the United States today. Approximately three-quarters of all criminal cases are now resolved by some kind of plea bargain rather than by a trial.

The plea bargain offered by the Special Prosecutor in the Bergman case was that Bernard Bergman would plead guilty to several counts of the federal indictment and also to a new state indictment, but that he would receive only *one sentence:* whatever term of imprisonment the federal judge imposed on him would be *the* term he would serve; the state judge would then impose the identical state sentence to be served concurrently with the federal one. Thus, if Judge Frankel—the federal judge—was to impose, say, one year, the state judge would also impose one year to be served in the federal penitentiary at the same time the federal term was being served. (Since a human being has only one body, a concurrent, identical sentence is the functional equivalent—for most purposes—of no sentence at all.)

The state indictment to which Bergman would plead would be a new one charging him with having offered a bribe to a state assemblyman. (Bergman could not plead to the original indictment—which was identical to the federal indictment—because of double jeopardy.) The assemblyman was Albert Blumenthal, the well-known liberal minority leader of the State Assembly. The charge was that Bergman had asked his assemblyman to see what could be done about certain delays in obtaining a license for one of his nursing homes. Blumenthal agreed to look into the problem, but made a request in return. He told Bergman that there was a federally funded minority job-training program in his district, and requested Bergman to permit members of the program to receive job training at the home if it was going to open. It seemed a perfectly reasonable request and Bergman agreed to it. But what Blumenthal failed to tell Bergman—and no one claims that Bergman knew it—was that Blumenthal, in addition to being a state assemblyman, was also a private *attorney* for the job-training program. Blumenthal's request could thus be construed as the solicitation of a bribe, and Bergman's agreement as an offer of a bribe.

During the course of the investigation, Bergman had informed the Special State Prosecutor that he had information that might incriminate Assemblyman Blumenthal. Under New York law Bergman could not be required to disclose that information unless he was given total immunity from prosecution—called "transactional immunity"—for any crime about which he was to testify. The Special Prosecutor wanted the information about the assemblyman, but didn't want to give Bergman total immunity. He was afraid—as Assistant U.S. Attorney Pattison had been afraid in the JDL case—that if Blumenthal's lawyers learned that Bergman had been given total immunity in exchange for his testimony, they could have a field day attacking Bergman's motives and credibility in testifying against Blumenthal. The prosecutor was willing to settle, therefore, for a plea of guilty by Bergman with no additional sentence. The Bergman family was offered an additional incentive to accept the plea bargain: if Bernard Bergman pleaded guilty, his son Stanley—who had also been indicted—would be "cut loose," and all charges against him would be dropped.

Why Lawyers Bargain

Why would the prosecutors, in a situation like the *Bergman* case, propose a plea bargain? After all, they had already persuaded two grand juries that there was enough evidence to warrant both federal and state indictments against Bergman and his son. Each carried the potential for long prison sentences. What does a prosecutor *gain* by allowing the defendant to plead guilty to a small portion of the indictment under which he can receive a fraction of the sentence possible under the original indictment? Prosecutors are not a magnanimous breed. They will propose—or accept—plea bargains only when they see benefits to *themselves* in the arrangement. And the perceived benefits may take a variety of forms—some less noble than others. The principal advantage to a prosecutor of a plea bargain in this kind of case is *certainty:* by tying down a plea bargain, under which the defendant pleads guilty to something, the prosecutor guarantees a conviction. Without the plea bargain, he is exposed to the uncertainties and vagaries of a jury, a judge, and the appellate courts.

Certainty is an extraordinarily important factor to many prosecutors who believe that statistics are as important to their careers as to a ballplayer's. A plea bargain enhances their won and lost record. A win is defined as a conviction, even if it is for a lesser crime than that contained in the original indictment; and a loss is defined as any case in which a conviction is not obtained, even if it was in a difficult or impossible case. The won and lost record of a prosecutor—and of a defense lawyer as well—is a meaningless statistic, but it is bandied around as an important criterion of success and competence.

A plea bargained case, with its predetermined result, also protects a prosecutor against the criticism that might result from losing a highly publicized case—and any prosecutor who lost the Bergman case would be charged by the press with incompetence, or worse. After all, if the press had been able to convince the public of his guilt, why hadn't the prosecutor been able to persuade a jury of it? Prosecutors' careers can be ruined—or at least damaged—by an acquittal in a highly publicized case.

Plea bargains are also arranged to induce a defendant's cooperation against another person targeted for prosecution. In this case, the Special Prosecutor's interest in convicting Assemblyman Blumenthal played a role in his willingness to bargain with Bergman.

At a simpler level, a plea bargain means less work—fewer long nights and weekends, more time with family and friends—for overworked prosecutors (who are not paid by the hour, but rather by the year).

In the *Bergman* case, the motivation of the prosecutors in proposing a plea bargain was the desire for certainty. Their cases against Bergman were weak, and the public expectation of a conviction was great. The prosecutions were complicated by the fact that although the federal and state governments had indicted Bergman for the same conduct, only one government could try him for it. The risks to the prosecutors were too great to warrant trials. A plea bargain—though not ideal from the prosecutors' point of view—was the best option under the circumstances.

If the prosecutors would benefit from a plea bargain then why would a defendant consider accepting the offered deal? Why, under the circumstances of this case, would Bernard Bergman have considered pleading guilty to crimes of which he believed himself innocent and of which his lawyers thought he might be acquitted? The simple answer is that it can sometimes be in the interest of *both* the prosecutor *and* the defendant to resolve their disputes by a plea bargain rather than run the risks of a jury trial. In the end, a plea bargain—like any other bargain—often splits the difference: neither side gets everything it wanted; both give up something and gain something. Both sides get what they often want most: *certainty.* *

After all, even innocent defendants—rare as they may be—are sometimes convicted. Once a case goes before a jury the result is unpredictable. And defendants, like prosecutors, often prefer certainty—even if it means the certainty of a short sentence. Moreover, trials are enormously expensive. Had Bergman gone to trial, the legal fees would certainly have been in the hundreds of thousands of dollars. This may not have been the reason why Bergman bargained, but it is the reason for many less affluent defendants, particularly middle-class ones who are ineligible for free legal assistance but who cannot afford the legal fees of a long trial and appeal.

Sometimes a criminal defendant is encouraged to plea bargain by his defense attorney under circumstances when it is probably not in the defendant's best interest to do so. It is the lawyer who stands to benefit from the plea bargain. Criminal lawyers often receive a flat fee for a case—say $2,500. That may be all the defendant can raise. The lawyer receives that sum—and only that sum—no matter how long it takes to resolve the case. In that situation it may be to the lawyer's advantage to plea bargain as many cases as possible, since it takes far less time to bargain a case than to try it. The more cases he can bargain, the more flat fees he can earn. His hourly rate for plea bargained cases will thus be far higher than for litigated cases: if it takes ten hours to bargain a case, then the lawyer who received $2,500 is earning $250 dollars an hour; if it takes a hundred hours to try the same

*Lenny Bruce used to say, "In the Halls of Justice, the only justice is in the halls."

case, then he is making only $25 an hour—hardly enough to pay the overhead.

Lawyers rarely speak of the issue this way; they tend to rationalize their plea bargaining by thinking that they are benefiting their clients. Sometimes they are, but sometimes they are not. I'd be suspicious of lawyers who *always* bargain. They generally get the worst deals for their clients, since the prosecutors know that they are bluffing when they threaten to go to trial. The best deals are generally secured by those lawyers who rarely bargain; by those lawyers who litigate and win many of their cases. Those are the lawyers whom the prosecutors most fear; and those are the lawyers to whom they are prepared to give the most to eliminate the risk of being beaten.

Nathan Lewin, Bergman's chief counsel, was one of the most feared lawyers in the United States. He tried most of his cases and won a large percentage of them. The Bergman prosecutors knew whom they were up against when they proposed their plea bargain

Lewin originally recommended against a plea bargain; he wanted to fight and he thought he could win. He was later to write that

> Facing enormous lawyer's bills, critical health considerations, and the prospect of a trial before a jury inflamed by the public clamor, [Bergman] rejected his lawyer's advice that he go to trial, entered a plea bargain.

Primary among the considerations motivating Bergman to consider the proposed bargain was concern for his son Stanley. He did not want his son to suffer for sins attributed to him by the press and politicians. Prosecutors often play on this kind of familial fealty.* Bernard Bergman, as the patriarch, could not bear the thought of his son's conviction. Despite his belief in his own and his son's innocence, and his lawyer's recommendation against accepting a plea bargain, Bergman directed Lewin to try to work out the best possible deal that would result in a single sentence for himself and for the dropping of all charges against his son.

Weeks of tough bargaining ensued. It was like a Persian bazaar: there was haggling over every item; both sides pretended to want to terminate the negotiations; but eventually there was a narrowing of disagreement.

*In another case I was involved in, a prosecutor—in the U.S. Attorney's office for the Southern District of New York—threatened to indict my client's innocent son (who had just graduated law school), his eighty-year-old father, his sister, and his wife— unless my client became an informant. We filed a complaint with the United States Attorney, and he promised not to authorize an indictment of the son unless he was personally convinced of the boy's guilt; the son was never indicted.

Since the proposed bargain was designed to *guarantee* that Bergman would receive only one sentence, it required the state judge to agree in advance that he would not impose any sentence in addition to the one imposed by the federal judge. Accordingly, the original text of the proposed plea bargain, drafted by the Special State Prosecutor's office, included the following paragraph: "The judge of the New York State Supreme Court who will sentence Bernard Bergman on his plea of guilty to bribing Albert Blumenthal will agree to impose no sentence additional to that imposed by the United States District judge on the federal indictment."

The parties to the proposed plea bargain approached the state judge assigned to the case to solicit his approval of the deal—a commonplace and entirely acceptable procedure, so long as all of the parties are present. The Special State Prosecutor asked the state judge to agree not to impose any sentence in addition to that imposed by the federal judge. Had the state judge agreed to this request—as it was expected he would—the matter would have been resolved to everybody's satisfaction. But the state judge refused to be formally bound by the federal judge's sentence. "I'm not going to buy a pig in a poke," he said. This created a dilemma for the bargainers.

After considerable bickering, a substitute agreement was finally hammered out. It was designed to achieve the same goal—one sentence to be determined by the federal judge—but without requiring the state judge formally to tie his own hands in advance.

The substitute agreement was that the Special State Prosecutor would *recommend* to the state sentencing judge that he should impose no sentence in addition to that imposed by the federal judge; and that the state sentence would be imposed immediately following the federal sentence. The reason this was seen as the functional equivalent of an agreement by the state judge to impose no additional sentence was that state judges in New York ordinarily accept the prosecutor's recommendation. The provision for having the state sentence immediately follow the federal sentence was to prevent pressure on the state judge—by press, politicians, or others—that might follow from a low federal sentence.

Indeed, Judge Aloysius Melia—the state sentencing judge—expressly informed Bergman that he had "told your counsel and the Special Prosecutor that ordinarily I accept the recommendation of the prosecutor for a lesser sentence, and I also told him that I see no reason at this point in time to believe that I would not do so here . . ." He then went on to give the required caution to Bergman that under the law he could be sentenced to serve the maximum term "regardless of what sentence is imposed by the federal court." But despite this boiler-plate caution, the message to all concerned was clear: Bergman would receive a single sentence—the one imposed by federal Judge Frankel. The deal was signed, sealed, and delivered.

The Federal Sentencing

Under the terms of the plea bargain, Bernard Bergman pleaded guilty in both federal and state courts on the same day, confident that he would serve only one sentence.

Shortly thereafter, the already insignificant state guilty plea was diminished even further when Judge Melia dismissed the bribery indictment against Assemblyman Blumenthal. He concluded that no crime had been committed, since Blumenthal—by agreeing to try to expedite the licensing of a Bergman nursing home in exchange for having a minority job-training program located at the home—"did not receive or demand any unlawful emolument or promise of compensation for this." If Blumenthal, who had *initiated* the request, was not guilty of a crime, it would seem to follow that Bergman, who had merely acceded to it, could not be sentenced to an additional term for his part in this non-crime.

The responsibility was now squarely on Judge Frankel. He would be the sentencing judge for both the federal and state crimes. It was *his* sentence that Bernard Bergman would serve. Indeed, Judge Frankel expressly recognized his unique sentencing function when he stated that "as part of the detailed plea agreements it is expected that the prison sentence imposed by this Court will comprise the total covering the state as well as the federal convictions."

On June 17, 1976, in a courtroom packed with politicians, the press, and attorneys for both sides, Judge Frankel announced that Bernard Bergman was sentenced to four months of imprisonment.

The outcry was deafening: the newspapers, radio, and television stations condemned the sentence; politicians attacked it; and members of the public decried it.

The Special State Nursing Home Prosecutor, Charles Hynes, was worried that the press might hold him responsible for having agreed to recommend that no additional sentence be imposed by the state judge. Accordingly, he instructed his press secretary to convene a press conference at the Special Prosecutor's office.

Special Prosecutor Hynes then went to the state court and requested a postponement of the state sentencing, ostensibly on the ground that there was still a dispute about the amount of money Bergman owed the state. The postponement was granted. The Special Prosecutor was thus able to avoid, at least for the moment, the embarrassment of standing up in court and making the recommendation he was obliged to make to the state sentencing judge, namely, that he should not impose any sentence in addition to the four-month sentence just imposed by Judge Frankel.

An army of reporters carrying TV cameras and tape recorders then followed Special Prosecutor Hynes back to his office for the press conference. Speaking in an angry tone, Hynes said that he was "extraordinarily disappointed" by the "insubstantial sentence" that Judge Frankel had imposed upon Bergman. He wondered whether it reflected "essential justice" or "special justice for the privileged." And he complained that "our continued investigation into the nursing home industry may, I fear, be adversely affected by this sentence." Special Prosecutor Hynes' statement was quoted in its entirety by the *New York Times;* headlined in other papers; played on the radio; and shown on most of the TV news programs.

It is not surprising that when Hynes finally appeared before Judge Melia to make his agreed-upon "recommendation," it was taken by most observers with more than a grain of salt. Hynes acknowledged that Bergman had lived up to his part of the bargain and that now

> I have the obligation to fulfill my commitment [and] would recommend that whatever sentence you impose be a concurrent one with the Federal sentence imposed on June 17, 1976.

Hynes made it clear that he was not happy with his role. "I make the recommendation I was required to make," he stated. With these words Hynes was asking the judge to impose a sentence that he had previously characterized as "disappointing," "special justice," and "insubstantial." The judge obviously understood that the "recommendation" was intended by the Special Prosecutor to be no more than a formal compliance with his legal obligation set out in the plea bargain.

The pressure was intense on Judge Melia to impose a sentence in excess of that imposed by Judge Frankel. Assemblyman Andrew Stein had visited Judge Melia and urged him to impose the harshest sentence possible. Stein also orchestrated a campaign of letter writing directed at Judge Melia. He arranged a "vigil," "picket line," and a "march" outside—and inside—of Judge Melia's chambers on the day of the state sentencing, co-sponsored by numerous elected officials. It is not surprising, therefore, that Judge Melia departed from his ordinary practice and "rejected" the prosecutor's "recommendation." Instead, he sentenced Bernard Bergman to a year in prison *in addition* to the sentence that had been imposed by Judge Frankel.

Melia justified his departure from practice by pointing to the seriousness of the charge—a charge that he had previously dismissed against Assemblyman Blumenthal on the ground that it was not a crime at all—and to Bergman's "shilly-shally on the amount of money owed to the People of the State."

The Special Prosecutor was relieved and pleased; the politicians and the press were satisfied. Judge Melia became the hero of the hour. Bergman, who had agreed to plead guilty on the basis of an assurance that he would receive only one sentence—the one imposed by the federal sentencing judge—found himself faced with *two* sentences totaling four times the amount to which he had been sentenced by the federal judge. He had not gotten what he had bargained for. He had bartered away his valuable constitutional rights for a mess of pottage—to be served in a jail cell for sixteen months.

Bergman immediately began to challenge the additional state sentence on the ground that the prosecutor's conduct—his press conference coupled with his recommendation to Judge Melia—constituted a violation of the plea bargain. His lawyers submitted briefs to the New York State Supreme Court, the appellate division, and the court of appeals. Each court rejected the arguments without any written opinions. It was at this point that I entered the case.

Seeking a Stay of Surrender

My first task was to try to get a stay of Bergman's surrender. He was scheduled to begin serving his one year state sentence at Rikers Island within the week. We had to find a way of keeping him out of prison while we presented his claims to the federal courts. Any victory we might achieve would be hollow if Bergman had already completed service of his entire invalid sentence. Even the Supreme Court cannot order the restoration of a year of a sixty-five-year-old person's life. It was essential, therefore, that we obtain a stay from one of the federal courts. But federal courts are extremely reluctant to interfere with the implementation of state sentences, and stays are rarely granted. The notoriety of this case—indeed, the overt press clamor for Bergman's immediate surrender—made it even more difficult than usual. But we had to try.

My first effort was directed at United States Supreme Court Justice Thurgood Marshall. Each of the Supreme Court Justices is assigned one of the judicial circuits for purposes of considering emergency applications, such as a request for a stay. Since Justice Marshall had served on the United States Court of Appeals for the Second Circuit—New York, Connecticut, and Vermont—he was assigned that circuit. Marshall was regarded as a liberal, but his record on granting stays was not promising. On several occasions, he had granted a stay only to be overruled by the other Justices. He was now reputed to be a bit reticent about granting such applications.

Within days of agreeing to enter the case I submitted an application to Justice Marshall requesting a stay. Marshall asked the Special Prosecutor's office to respond. That was a good sign, since the majority of stay applications are denied without such a response. But after several days he denied our application. It was now Friday afternoon. Bergman was scheduled to surrender the following Tuesday at ten in the morning. We had one last hope: the federal district court in New York. I worked frantically over the weekend preparing a petition for a writ of habeas corpus and a stay application. I completed the documents at four o'clock on Monday morning and brought them to the clerk's office at the federal courthouse in New York at nine.

By midmorning, we were ready to make our pitch for an emergency stay. In the federal court, there is always one judge assigned to hear emergency motions of this kind. The judge that day was Robert J. Ward.

I walked into Judge Ward's courtroom and waited for a break in the proceedings. He was hearing an extremely technical motion in a complex financial case. He seemed bored by it. When a recess was called I approached the bench and told the judge that I had an emergency application. As soon as I introduced myself, Judge Ward went out of his way to welcome me to his court "all the way from Cambridge." I was at once pleased and somewhat embarrassed that he knew who I was and that he was being so effusive in his welcome. He announced that his court was always open for emergency applications and he asked me for the name of the case.

"*Bergman* versus *New York,*" I responded, and began to describe the motion.

"Bergman," Judge Ward yelled, "you mean Bernard Bergman?"

"Yes," I replied, "Bernard Bergman."

The judge could not hold back his fury. "That man should be in jail. What are you doing here in federal court? That's a state court case. How dare you interrupt these proceedings with that case. The case I'm hearing now is very important. We have lawyers down from all over the country."

I informed the judge that Berman was scheduled to begin serving his sentence in less than twenty-four hours and that this was an "emergency" within the rules.

Judge Ward cut me off: "Let Bergman go to jail and I'll consider his motion when I'm through with this case in a few days."

"But, your Honor," I responded, "the constitutional issue in this case is a very serious one and it will become moot if the defendant begins to serve his sentence."

The judge was not impressed. "This man will not get any special justice in my courtroom. Most habeas corpus defendants litigate their cases while they're in jail. That's just what Bergman should do. I have no sympathy for him whatsoever."

I thought I saw my opening in the judge's last comment and I responded, raising my own voice just a bit.

"We're not asking for sympathy and we're not asking for special justice. The problem is precisely that Bergman has been getting special justice. The prosecutor in this case deliberately violated his plea bargain. Yet the state courts haven't even had the courage to write an opinion. This case poses a real challenge to the ability of the federal judiciary to resist trial by newspaper and politicians. I am confident that this court will meet that challenge."

Suddenly the tone of the entire proceeding changed. Judge Ward assured me that his sympathies would not affect his decision and that the case would be decided on its merits. Almost as if to prove it, he began to express agreement with our legal contentions. He gave me an opportunity to spell out my argument in detail and then turned to the lawyer from the Special Prosecutor's office—a young man named Arthur G. Weinstein—and began to question him about the statement made by the Special Prosecutor following Judge Frankel's imposition of the four-month sentence:

JUDGE WARD: I recall that the prosecutor, the state's Special Prosecutor, had some critical remarks.

MR. WEINSTEIN: It expressed his dissatisfaction with the sentence, your Honor.

THE COURT: And was that reported in the media prior to the sentencing by the state court judge?

MR. WEINSTEIN: Yes.

THE COURT: You defend that?

MR. WEINSTEIN: [N]one of this material was in the record.

THE COURT: Well, let us make a record, then. That is what these proceedings are for.

MR. WEINSTEIN: Your Honor, I will tell you what was said to the best of my recollection. I don't have a copy of the press statement with me. (Paper handed to Mr. Weinstein by Mr. Dershowitz.)

MR. WEINSTEIN: I am handed a copy from the *New York Times.* Mr. Hynes criticized the sentence that was imposed by Judge Frankel.

THE COURT: I want one more thing clearly on the record. He then got up in state court and made what statement?

MR. WEINSTEIN: He recommended that whatever sentence *you, the Judge,* impose be a concurrent one with that in the federal court.

THE COURT: He made that with a straight face?

MR. WEINSTEIN: Your Honor, I was not present. I don't know what the facial characteristics were.

THE COURT: Counsel, it simply comes down to this: Was there a bargain, and if so, was it kept?

When the arguments had concluded, Judge Ward returned to his chambers, promising a decision "very shortly." It was sweating time: we were sixteen hours from surrender hour. It was too late in the day to appeal an adverse decision by Judge Ward, and the court of appeals did not open for busines the next morning until ten-thirty—half an hour after Bergman had to surrender. We thought we had turned Judge Ward around during the argument, but it was always possible that he could be turned again.

After about thirty minutes—which seemed like thirty hours—Judge Ward emerged from his chambers and slowly read his decision:

> Although the Attorney General has indicated that the facts here are similar to those presented every day, this Court cannot agree. The publicity surrounding this case is not what can be said to be ordinary publicity. The case has received and, I would note, is receiving this afternoon substantial media attention.
>
> [S]ufficient arguments have been presented for this Court to conclude that there are serious constitutional questions involved in the state's execution of the plea bargain.
>
> Further, . . . the sentence which the petitioner is scheduled to begin serving tomorrow could well be served and his claim mooted were a stay denied . . .
>
> Accordingly, the Court will grant a stay pending the hearing of this motion, and sets the matter down for a hearing before the Honorable Gerard L. Goettel. . . .

"Bergman Wins 11th Hour Stay of Jail Term," read the next morning's headlines. The *Daily News* editorial—entitled "Justice Delayed"—included the following:

> Justice delayed is justice denied, and once again Bernard Bergman, the gross symbol of all that was wrong in nursing home care, has made a mockery of justice.

Jack Newfield quipped: "By the time Bergman goes to prison, *I* may be in a nursing home."

The Special Prosecutor's office—embarrassed by the press criticism and by their inability to put Bergman behind bars—appealed Judge Ward's order. But the court of appeals affirmed the order and continued the stay. The stage was now set for the evidentiary hearing before Judge Goettel. Bergman was reprieved—at least for the time being.

The hearing began in the summer heat of late July. Judge Gerard Goettel, the judge to whom the case had been assigned by lot, was a quiet and serious man. Before his appointment as a federal district judge, Goettel had been a United States magistrate in the same courthouse.

Both sides were extensively represented at the hearing: Bergman's legal team, in addition to me, consisted of Jack Litman and his partner Lewis Friedman; the Special Prosecutor's legal team included half a dozen lawyers. The hearing room was packed with assistant United States Attorneys, other lawyers, the usual courtroom observers, and the ever-present media army, including television artists in the courtroom and cameras in the hallway.

Judge Goettel began the proceedings by disclosing that his "maternal grandmother was named Mary Hynes" and that it was conceivable that he was related to Special Prosecutor Charles Hynes. He asked whether either party wished to pursue that matter. We declined to move for his disqualification on so flimsy a basis.

The basic issue at the hearing—the issue around which all the testimony revolved—was whether the Special Prosecutor had broken the plea bargain. The leading case on this issue was a Supreme Court decision entitled *Santobello* v. *New York*, decided in 1971. In *Santobello*, the defendant had been charged with two state felony counts relating to gambling. His attorney negotiated a plea bargain pursuant to which he would plead guilty to a lesser offense, a misdemeanor carrying a maximum penalty of one year in prison. Part of the deal was that the state prosecutor "agreed to make no recommendation as to the sentence." When the case came on for sentencing, the particular prosecutor who had agreed to the plea bargain had been replaced. The new prosecutor, apparently ignorant of his predecessor's agreement, recommended to the sentencing judge that he impose the maximum sentence of one year. The defense counsel objected to the prosecutor's recommendation. But the judge, while denying that he was influenced by the prosecutor's recommendations, sentenced Santobello to a year in prison.

Appealing his one-year sentence, Santobello claimed that the prosecutor had broken the plea bargain. Like Bergman, the defendant got nowhere within the New York State Court system and sought a stay of his imprisonment from the Supreme Court. Unlike Bergman, he received the stay from a Supreme Court Justice and the case was argued before the entire Supreme Court. The decision was rendered by Chief Justice Warren Burger, who ruled that the prosecutor, by making his recommendation, had broken the plea bargain.

The basic questions to be resolved at the Bergman hearing—questions derived directly from the *Santobello* decision—were whether the Special Prosecutor had violated the plea bargain by his public criticism of Judge Frankel's sentence, and whether the sentencing judge was aware of this criticism.

Evidentiary hearings do not normally produce many surprises: the basic facts are generally *known* to both sides; they are *established* for the record at the hearing. But this hearing was full of surprises—even some bombshells.

We knew, of course, that Special Prosecutor Hynes had held a press conference at which he attacked Judge Frankel's sentence; the text of the statement had been published in the *New York Times.* The statement seemed relatively spontaneous, as if it had been drafted on the run, between the courthouse and his office. But there was something about it that left us in doubt. At first I couldn't put my finger on it, but then I noticed that the statement never mentioned the precise length of the sentence—four months. This seemed strange, since it was the four months that had generated so much criticism. I began to suspect that perhaps the statement had been drafted in advance of Judge Frankel's sentence—in anticipation of a sentence that might prove embarrassing to the Special Prosecutor. We decided to call Special Prosecutor Hynes to the witness stand to find out whether our suspicions were accurate. Litman examined him.

Hynes was a cagey and reluctant witness. At first he denied that he had even called a "press conference":

> [I]t was not a press conference . . . I responded to a series of questions put to me by the press.

Indeed his initial testimony was that "the first time" he "decided to discuss the matter with the press was following" the close of court proceedings, after the imposition of the federal sentence by Judge Frankel. When pressed, he acknowledged that he had made up his mind to give a prepared statement to the press about the Frankel sentence "the day before" the sentence was imposed. Again pressed, he then said he had begun working on a draft of the press statement "two days before the date of the sentence." Within a few moments Hynes was saying, "I was in error"—it was "three days" prior to the date of sentence.

Hynes eventually admitted that *several* days before the sentencing he called an old friend in Washington who was then working as a press secretary on Capitol Hill and asked him to draft a press release about the light sentence he anticipated from Judge Frankel. The friend, a former *Washington Post* reporter named David Jewell, was subpoenaed into court and testified that he came to New York to confer with Hynes about a press statement to be issued after the federal sentence: it could have been "a week before the sentence." Hynes' own press secretary, who wrote the first draft of the statement, confirmed that she began working on it—at Hynes' direction—about a week before the federal sentencing date.

The purpose of the statement, according to the press people, was to keep Special Prosecutor Hynes from being "pilloried" by the media and to preserve "his public image." Jewell testified that he had advised Hynes that "the sentencing of Bergman was the single most important critical aspect of the investigation to date; that this is what it was all about." He urged Hynes to issue a strong public statement "because you just can't go the old lawyer route of hiding in a closet. . . . These are post-Watergate days and we can't do that anymore." The entire staff "discussed the question of whether or not this statement could be construed as being in opposition to the plea bargaining," Jewell testified. There was pressure from the lawyers on Hynes' staff not to issue any statement: "lawyers don't want to do that sort of thing." But the press advisors insisted that for Hynes to remain silent would be a disaster: "We had a classic press relations, lawyer-type confrontation," Jewell recalled.

Apparently more concerned with his image than with his obligations under the plea bargain, Special Prosecutor Hynes sided with his press advisors and decided to issue a public statement critical of any "light" sentence that Frankel might impose. Although he was aware that this might undercut the plea bargain into which he had entered with Bergman's defense attorneys, Hynes decided not to notify the defense attorneys of his intention to issue the statement.

The hearing had uncovered precisely what we had suspected, and even more: the decision to criticize the Frankel sentence was not a spur-of-the-moment reaction; it was the result of a deliberate and premeditated plan to preserve the Special Prosecutor's "image," even at the cost of undercutting the plea bargain. Judge Goettel, when he learned about the advance planning, observed that "several rather unexpected aspects" had developed.

Another unexpected development was Judge Melia's denial that he had ever read or heard the statement made by Special Prosecutor Hynes about the Frankel statement. This testimony created a real dilemma for us. We were certain that the judge could not be telling the truth: there was hardly a person in the city of New York who had not heard or read the statement. Yet Judge Melia—who was intimately involved in the case—claimed ignorance. We checked and discovered that he had been in New York that evening, that he generally watched the evening news, and that he always read the *New York Law Journal* and the *New York Times.* But he persisted in denying the obvious. (It was so obvious that everyone was familiar with the Special Prosecutor's statement that even Judge Goettel acknowledged it. At one point during the hearing—when I suggested that Bergman be sentenced by another judge who had not read the Special Prosecutor's statement—Judge Goettel observed: "I don't think you can find a judge in the state of New York who hasn't got some awareness of [the Special Prosecutor's statement]." I couldn't resist responding, cynically, "Except, perhaps, Judge Melia.")

It is difficult enough to cross-examine a judge: most lawyers simply won't do it; they prefer to leave his testimony intact rather than incur the wrath of the witness-judge or of other judges. But here the usual difficulty was even greater. We had to go beyond conventional cross-examination; we had to get him to change his testimony 180 degrees; we wanted him—in effect—to admit that he was not telling the truth. But we had no choice. His denial was devastating to our case. If he had not, in fact, learned about the Special Prosecutor's statement, then that statement—improper as it may have been—was "harmless error"; it could not possibly have had any impact on his sentence. We had to cross-examine him vigorously and get him to change his testimony.

The defense team decided that I would assume this delicate task even though I lacked Litman's experience and talent as a cross-examiner. I reasoned that Litman and his firm had to practice in the New York criminal courts on a daily basis; they appeared before Judge Melia frequently, and they might understandably be reluctant to alienate him any more than necessary. I would probably never appear before him, so the professional risks to me were not as great.

I decided to conduct the cross-examination as if I was attempting to impeach the testimony of any lying witness; I would pay no special deference to the fact that the witness was a judge. I suspected that Judge Melia would expect to be handled with kid gloves. I decided that the element of surprise might shake loose the truth and so I began my cross-examination on an unusually aggressive and challenging note:

Q. Is it not a fact, Justice Melia, that you had written out in advance of the date of sentencing your entire text of the sentencing remarks including the final sentence of one-year-consecutive prior to the day in which you imposed sentence? Yes or no.
A. No.

Q. Is it a fact—again yes or no—that you had written out a draft of that statement prior to the day of sentencing?
A. I wrote out a rather—
Q. Yes or no.
A. Yes.
Q. May we have a copy of that draft? Do you have it with you?
A. I don't know. I might say it is in the—
Q. Please don't respond to any question other than the one I asked, your Honor.

I then turned to the heart of the cross-examination and established that Judge Melia subscribed to the *New York Law Journal* and the *New York Times* on a daily basis. I also got the judge to acknowledge that he had kept a collection of newspaper clippings relating to the Bergman case. Obviously realizing how unlikely it was that he would have skipped front-page stories about the biggest case in his judicial career, Judge Melia began to vacillate in his denials and then to admit that he had read about the Frankel sentencing:

Q. On the day following the imposition of the sentence by Judge Frankel on Dr. Bergman, there appeared a story on the front page of the *New York Times* involving that sentencing.
Is it fair to say as you sit here now that it is *certain* that you would have read the story?
A. Yes.
Q. Is it fair to say as you sit here now that it is certain that you would have read the story that appeared on the front page of the *Law Journal* involving the Bergman sentence the next day?
A. I don't know. It is probable.
Q. It is probable?
A. It is probable. I know I read the *Times*.
Q. Did you read the entire story in the *New York Times* involving the Bergman sentencing?
A. I think so.
Q. I would like to show your Honor a Xerox copy of a front-page story that appeared in the *New York Law Journal* and ask you whether it refreshes your recollection. The headline reads, "Bergman State Sentence Stayed; United States Court Gives Him Four Months."
Is it possible that you, who subscribe to the *New York Law Journal* and read it every day, could not have read a story which begins by stating, "Bergman State Sentence Stayed?"
MR. WEINSTEIN: Objection.
THE COURT: Sustained.

Q. Does the viewing of the top part of the headline, "Bergman State Sentence Stayed," refresh your recollection as to whether you in fact read the *New York Law Journal* story that day?
A. No.
Q. It is your testimony here that you might not have read that *New York Law Journal* story?
A. My testimony is that I do not know . . .
THE COURT: It would be . . . appropriate to let him look at it for a moment.
(Pause)
A. Thank you.
(Pause)
A. Yes, counsel, I think I did read this.
Q. Your answer then, I take it, is that your recollection has been refreshed and it is now your testimony you did read this article?
A. Yes, sir.

Having gotten him to change his tune about the newspapers, I turned to television and asked him whether he had watched the eleven o'clock news on Channel 4 on the day of the Special Prosecutor's conference. When I advised him that an artist's rendition of his face had appeared on the Channel 4 eleven o'clock news that night along with extensive coverage of the Special Prosecutor's press conference, he equivocated.

Finally, I asked Judge Melia what we regarded as the key question:

Q. When you read or learned that the Special Prosecutor was extraordinarily disappointed in the federal sentence, were you aware at that time that the Special Prosecutor was obligated to recommend to you that you would impose that very same sentence that he indicated he was extraordinarily disappointed in?

This time the judge did not equivocate:

A. The answer is yes.

We had done what we had set out to do. The record was now clear that Judge Melia *had* read that the Special Prosecutor was "extraordinarily disappointed in the federal sentence"; it was also clear that when Judge Melia read it he was aware that the Special Prosecutor was obliged to recommend that he impose the identical sentence. There could be no dispute, therefore, that the Special Prosecutor had effectively communicated to Judge Melia his true feelings about the sentence he was formally obliged to recommend. The Special Prosecutor could thus come before Judge Melia and—with a straight face—recommend that he also impose a four-month concurrent sentence, comfortable in the knowledge that Judge Melia was aware that his true view was that if the judge accepted his "recommendation," the Special Prosecutor would be "extraordinarily disappointed."

The remainder of the hearing proceeded along predictable lines, with few surprises. The press coverage was intense, with drawings of the participants appearing on the TV news each night. Toward the end of the hearing, a column written by Robert Lipsyte appeared in the *New York Post* that confirmed my family's worst fears. It included the following comments:

> Bernard Bergman, the Medicaid looter, was not in jail yesterday. In fact, he wasn't even in court . . . Jack Litman was there, Jack, the tough former Assistant DA who prosecuted Rap Brown, who nailed William Phillips so hard the rogue cop screamed out in court "You are the scum of the earth." And Alan Dershowitz was there, Professor Dershowitz of the Harvard Law School, defender of "I Am Curious (Yellow)" and "Deep Throat." Dershowitz has written about the obligation of government to assess [actions] in terms of their "human rights impact." But yesterday he was with Bergman, too. This is a very lawyerly kind of trial, no broad strokes about right or wrong, no parade of aged cripples left to rot in Bergman nursing homes, no damaging evidence about bribes or fraud. Strictly motions, feints, obscure precedents, Dershowitz asking to see some documents the judge is holding because "the adversary eye sees things differently from the judicial eye." The young state Attorneys General worked hard, and seemed to sweat, because Litman and Dershowitz are tough, experienced law-slingers who come high. During a recess, [Andrew] Stein wondered how such eminent lawyers could defend such a bad man. "It's a big score for them," he said. "Think how many Russian poets Dershowitz can spring with Bergman's money." How can those guys go back and lecture about ethics and write textbooks, and what do they say to those kids at Harvard?

The hearing was soon over and the case was in Judge Goettel's hands. Generally, a lawyer has some sense of how a judge is going to decide a case after a lengthy hearing, but Judge Goettel was extremely guarded. He dropped few clues. He was plainly troubled. Indeed, it took him nearly two months to write his decision. When it was finally rendered, it was forty pages long and reflected his doubts and uncertainties.

After reviewing the facts developed at the hearing, Judge Goettel made a crucial finding in our favor concerning the Special Prosecutor's press statement:

> Hynes' statement attacking the federal sentence was clearly and totally unwarranted and improper [and] manifestly contrary to state law. [It] violated the New York Code of Professional Conduct which prohibits prosecutorial statements prior to sentencing that are "reasonably likely to affect the imposition of sentence."

In support of his conclusion that Special Prosecutor Hynes had engaged in professional misconduct, Judge Goettel cited an ethical rule prohibiting statements by prosecutors "designed to sway or influence public opinion to gain political advantage . . . or to attempt to influence or intimidate the judiciary." The Special Prosecutor's statement had certainly been designed "to gain political advantage" by enhancing "his public image," and to influence Judge Melia's sentencing decision.

Having made these crucial findings, it would ordinarily follow that a judge would rule in our favor. But this was no ordinary case and Judge Goettel proceeded to make some extraordinary leaps of logic.

First, he reasoned that the Special Prosecutor's statement—improper and unlawful as it was—did not violate "the *letter* of the [plea bargain] agreement." The judge acknowledged that the plea agreement did expressly prohibit "press statements *following the plea*"; but he focused on the fact that "no mention was made of press statements following *the sentencing.*" (He neglected the obvious fact that since the sentence necessarily had to *follow* the plea, there was no need for an additional and redundant prohibition.) By invoking this bit of pettifoggery, the judge was able to conclude that the Special Prosecutor's statement did not constitute a technical violation of *Santobello.*

Next, Judge Goettel turned to the actual sentencing recommendation made in court by the Special Prosecutor. He made a finding favorable to us on this issue as well:

> There is no doubt that the Special Prosecutor's recommendation of no additional sentence was tepidly offered. It did not literally comply with the plea agreement, . . .

Again, the ordinary consequence of such a finding—that the plea bargain had not been literally complied with—would have been a ruling in our favor. This was especially true, since the judge had focused so heavily on literal compliance in holding that the Special Prosecutor's improper and unlawful statement had not technically violated the plea bargain. But this time Judge Goettel did a complete about-face and downplayed literal compliance:

> Had the Special Prosecutor attempted a glowing endorsement of the sentence recommended . . . it would have been rank hypocrisy.

Thus, in an artful act of verbal gymnastics, Judge Goettel found that the Special Prosecutor's improper and unlawful statement critical of the federal sentence did not require judgment on Bergman's behalf because it *did not* literally violate the terms of the plea bargain; and he found that the Special Prosecutor's "tepidly offered" sentencing recommendation, which *did* literally violate the terms of the plea bargain, did not require judgment for Bergman because it would have been "rank hypocrisy" for Hynes to comply with the terms of the plea bargain. Heads, the Special Prosecutor wins, and tails, the defendant loses—especially if his name is Bernard Bergman!

The opinion suggested that Judge Goettel simply lacked the guts to free Bernard Bergman, even though he found most of the essential facts in his favor. As I reread the opinion, I felt compassion for Judge Goettel: basically an intellectually honest judge—an all-too-rare phenomenon—he was compelled to find the facts in our favor. But he simply could not bring himself to issue the writ of habeas corpus and incur the media and political wrath that would predictably follow. I believe that he decided—consciously or unconsciously—to split the difference; to make findings of fact that would enable us to present a powerful case to the court of appeals. If *that* court was prepared to take these facts to their legal conclusion, then *it* could order his release. Judge Goettel would thus be performing his duty, as the finder of fact, without incurring the wrath of the press. A three-judge appeals court is better able to withstand that kind of pressure than a single newly appointed judge.

The strongest clue to Judge Goettel's unwillingness to take the responsibility for freeing Bergman appeared in the final paragraph of his opinion discussing Bergman's application for bail pending appeal. Throughout the opinion Goettel had acknowledged that this was a close and difficult case. But he simply refused to decide Bergman's application for bail.

There was no basis in law for such abdication of responsibility. Indeed, when we went before the court of appeals to request bail, the judges were openly upset at Judge Goettel for shifting the responsibility to them for a bail decision that, under the law, must be made by the district judge. Again, there was nothing ordinary about the case of Bernard Bergman. The specter of the media hung over the courtroom, and Judge Goettel—though holding life tenure as a judge—had become a judicial prisoner of the press.

The bail panel of the court of appeals had no difficulty deciding that Bergman should be permitted to remain at liberty pending the decision of the court of appeals. Chief Judge Irving Kaufman—the judge who had ruled in our favor in the JDL case—declared from the bench that "there are some very serious questions" and that there certainly is "a chance that Bergman may prevail."

But when the appeal was argued on its merits several months later, the three judges—none of whom had been on the bail panel—seemed to dismiss our arguments out-of-hand.

Judges Walter Mansfield and Henry Friendly began to attack my legal contentions as soon as I approached the lectern. At times the attack seemed almost personally directed at me for representing Bergman; I felt as if *I* were the subject of the appeal. There was hardly a word of criticism directed at the Special Prosecutor whose conduct had been found by Judge Goettel to be improper and unlawful. We left the courthouse discouraged, but wondering how the court of appeals could write an opinion rejecting our contentions on the basis of the facts found by Judge Goettel and the law established by the Supreme Court.

The opinion was rendered just before Christmas of 1977. A unanimous panel ruled against Bergman. The opinion was written by Judge Friendly, and it was quite remarkable, especially for him. Friendly was generally a stickler for the rule prohibiting the court of appeals from substituting its own findings of fact for those made by the district judge. The opinion in the *Bergman* case, however, bore little relationship to the facts found by Judge Goettel.

Judge Friendly's opinion made no mention of Judge Goettel's finding that the deliberate and well-planned issuance of the press statement was improper, unethical, and unlawful; instead, Friendly made it appear that it was Bergman who was asking the court of appeals to overrule a conclusion by the district court that the press statement had been proper. No mention was made of Judge Goettel's finding that the Special Prosecutor's in-court recommendation to Judge Melia "did not literally comply with the plea agreement"; indeed Judge Friendly—inexplicably and without support in the record—concluded that "*admittedly* Hynes made the recommendation he had promised to make." There is nothing more galling to a lawyer—or more intellectually dishonest—than when a judge rejects an argument the lawyer has repeatedly and forcefully made by using the words "admittedly" or "concededly." We had never admitted anything of the sort. We had contended—and Judge Goettel had agreed—that the Special Prosecutor had *not* "made the recommendation he had promised to make." Now Judge Friendly was not only rejecting our argument; he was not only disputing Judge Goettel's finding; but he was doing all this by pretending that we had *admitted* something we were vigorously disputing.

The rest of the opinion followed predictable lines. The court found nothing wrong with Hynes' press statements nor with his "tepidly" offered recommendation. A plea bargain is not broken merely because "of lack of adequate gusto in a prosecutor's recommendation." A tepid recommendation by a prosecutor is perfectly permissible "unless something in his facial expression or his tone indicated to the judge that he would prefer not to have his recommendation accepted." This last "unless" was quite remarkable in light of the record in this case. It was clear to everyone—as Judge Goettel had remarked repeatedly throughout the hearing—that the Special Prosecutor did, in fact, *prefer* not to have his recommendation accepted. He did not need to communicate that preference nonverbally through "facial expression" or "tone." He had already communicated it directly and verbally by his press statement. But, since the Special Prosecutor had not made any funny faces in the courtroom, the press statement did not constitute a communication of his obvious preference that the sentencing judge not follow his recommendation.

The court held that "the Special Prosecutor committed no breach of the plea bargain" and that Bergman would have to go to prison to serve his one-year state sentence.

Our petition for rehearing drew forth another barrage of criticism from the press: "Bergman played the American legal system like a pinball machine, and he is still playing it," complained Jack Newfield. Newfield criticized me personally and professionally for pursuing all available legal remedies.

All of our last minute efforts failed, and on February 6, 1978, Bernard Bergman surrendered to state authorities on Rikers Island.

EPILOGUE

Bernard Bergman survived his imprisonment on Rikers Island. He was popular among the inmates, whom he helped in numerous ways. He is now back at home and engaged in scholarly writings about Talmudic law. He is out of the nursing home business, but much of his time is still taken up with remnants of his past activities. His dispute with the Special Prosecutor's office over the money he owes the state is still not completely resolved. "Four Years After Nursing Home Trial, Bergman's Affairs Remain a Tangle of Litigation," read a *New York Times* headline in 1980. The story cataloged several dozen lawsuits and other legal matters that were still pending. I am not involved in any of this litigation, but I still continue to receive criticism for my representation of Bergman in the federal proceeding.

Charles Hynes was appointed Fire Commissioner of New York City.

Andrew Stein was elected Borough President of Manhattan, primarily on the strength of his role in the Bergman investigations. His campaign slogan reminded the voters that it was he who was responsible for putting "animals" like Bernard Bergman in prison.

Marvin Frankel—the judge who sentenced Bergman to four months—resigned from the bench shortly after the termination of the Bergman case. Many observers attributed his decision, at least in part, to the public and political reaction to his Bergman sentence. Had his chances for promotion to the court of appeals not been dashed by the Bergman episode, he might well have remained on the bench and distinguished himself as one of the great appellate judges on the federal bench.

His sentencing statement in the Bergman case is now recognized as a classic judicial opinion. It appears in several criminal law casebooks and is studied by law students around the country.

Two

DISTURBING THE PEACE

—4—

Defending Pornography from Fundamentalist and Feminist Censors: Deep Throat and the First Amendment

The Harvard Law School parking lot was nearly empty on that Sunday morning in May of 1976. I was there to meet a potential new client named Harry Reems. Although his face—and body—had been seen by millions of Americans, I didn't know what he looked like. I had not seen him in his role as the doctor in *Deep Throat,* nor in any of the dozens of other roles that had earned him the title "undisputed king of the porno actors." I didn't think I would have any trouble recognizing him, however, since I had seen a few skin flicks and had an image of what a porno star would look like.

The only other person in the lot was a young man, unmistakably identifiable as a law student by his three-piece suit and leather attaché case—the unofficial uniform of Harvard Law School. I was wearing jeans and a sweat shirt, having jogged to my office several hours earlier, not expecting to meet anyone.

I felt a little uncomfortable about greeting a potential client in my jogging clothes. But I thought, a bit disdainfully, who is he—a porn actor who appears naked on the screen—to complain about my attire. In any event, he was coming on short notice, having called that morning to ask if he could see me right away. I told him that my office building was locked on Sunday and we arranged to meet in the parking lot at eleven-thirty.

At the appointed time, I went out to the parking lot and looked around. No Harry Reems. I waited another fifteen minutes, expecting a cab to pull up and an overgrown stud to saunter out. No cab arrived. Finally, I turned to the slightly built young man, who also seemed to be waiting for someone, and asked whether he had seen anyone arrive in a cab before I had come out.

"Other than me, no one's gotten out of a cab."

I asked him if he was waiting for the library to open.

"No, I'm waiting for Professor Dershowitz."

I looked at him with surprise and said, "I'm Alan Dershowitz, who are you?"

Responding with equal surprise, he said, "*You're* Professor Dershowitz? My God! I expected some gray-haired eminence in a pinstripe suit. I'm Harry Reems."

"*You're* Harry Reems?" I exclaimed. "I expected some sex symbol wearing a shirt opened to the belly button." We each had a good laugh, both feeling a bit foolish about our stereotypes.

We went to my office and began to talk about his legal problems.

"I'm in serious trouble for what I did in *Deep Throat,*" Reems said.

Deep Throat was the most famous pornographic film ever made, having grossed in excess of $60 million. Its female lead, Linda Lovelace, had captured the imagination of the media with her unique oral skills. The film had become the first of its genre—hard-core pornography—to achieve a modicum of social acceptability. Respected members of the community attended performances without the usual dark glasses and raincoats; comedians referred to it on TV; Woodward and Bernstein code-named their key Watergate informant after it. More than ten million Americans had seen it at least once. It had played for nearly 400 consecutive weeks in some theaters. *Time* magazine reported that on the CIA-operated ship *Glomar Explorer,* the "most popular flick" shown to the crew (at United States government expense) was *Deep Throat.* Vice President Spiro Agnew had seen a videotape of it at a party at Frank Sinatra's estate. It had become a part of the pop culture of America.

"I was just an actor in the movie," Reems went on, "but a federal jury in Memphis, Tennessee, convicted me of a felony last week. I'm facing five years in prison for being a male sex symbol, and I'm looking for a lawyer to handle the appeal."

Harry Reems was no mere sex symbol. He was an extremely intelligent young man. "A nice Jewish boy earning his livelihood by doing what lots of people would *pay* to do"—as he described himself. He was born in Scarsdale, New York, with the name Herbert Streicker, attended the University of Pittsburgh, dropped out, joined the Marines, and later set out to become a stage actor. He had performed with the La Mama troupe, the New York Theater Ensemble, and the National Shakespeare Company in New York City. He had even done a Wheaties commercial. During Christmas of 1969, "when things got rough and there was no work around . . . , a fellow said he knew where I could make $75 doing a stag film." Never even having seen such a movie, he nervously accepted and reported for work. His two female costars, both doctoral students in sociology at NYU, put him at ease, and he completed several "loops." Streicker was an instant success, not so much because of his looks, but because of his extraordinary ability to perform repeatedly on cue. In a business where time is money and the major cause of delay is male incapacity, a porno actor capable of filming several sequences in one day's shooting is understandably in demand.

Streicker told me how he ended up as the male lead in *Deep Throat.* He had been hired—at $150 a day—as a sound and lighting technician for a sex film being shot near Miami, Florida, in January of 1972. When the original male lead failed to appear, the director, Gerard Damiano, asked Streicker to fill in—at a $50 cut in salary. Since it took only one day to shoot the film's half a dozen sex shots (they were later edited into 18 different scenes), he earned only $100 for his performance. His contract did not call for any royalties. When the shooting was finished, Streicker's role in the enterprise ended: he participated neither in the editing nor distribution of the film—not to mention its enormous profits. He didn't even control his own name: the director selected the stage name "Harry Reems"—with some vague sexual allusion in mind—without even consulting Streicker. He was pleased, of course, that the film was well-received and widely shown. He retained "Harry Reems" as his professional name, and performed in several other sex films. But his role in *Deep Throat* was over, or so he thought.

More than two years later, on the morning of July 7, 1974, Streicker was awakened at five o'clock by a knock on the door of his Greenwich Village apartment. An FBI agent greeted the sleepy and disheveled actor and handed him a warrant requiring his presence in Memphis, Tennessee, a city that Streicker had never even visited. Herbert Streicker—alias "Harry Reems"—had been indicted by a federal grand jury in Memphis for participation in a nationwide conspiracy to transport an obscene film in interstate commerce. He was the first actor in American history to face a federal indictment for his role in a motion picture.

The case attracted national attention. Indeed, that appeared to be the prosecutor's purpose in indicting an actor. Prosecuting producers and distributors of porno films was familiar ground and hardly anyone took notice. The indictment of an actor was certain to capture the attention of the public. The prosecuting attorney was a bright young Bible Belt fundamentalist named Larry Parrish. (The names of all the participants sounded like adolescent puns: Reems, Streicker, Lovelace, Parrish.) Parrish, a native of Nashville, was dubbed by the press as "Mr. Clean," "The Memphis Heat," and "The Memphis Smut Raker." A born-again Christian, and an elder in the First Evangelical Church, Parrish genuinely believed that pornography was the bane of modern America. He once told a reporter, "I'd rather see dope on the streets than these movies," explaining that drugs could be cleansed from the body, but pornography's damage was "permanent." When asked why he became a prosecutor, Parrish cited the warning to evildoers in Romans 13:4, that God had appointed ministers on earth to carry out his wrath against them. He believed it was his mission to conduct "search and destroy" operations against the porno industry. As a prosecutor of pornography, he had few peers, having already secured more than forty convictions.

Many observers saw the decision to bring Reems to trial as evidence of Parrish's prosecutorial creativity. As one Memphis lawyer, familiar with Parrish's tactics, put it: "Parrish figured that putting an actor on trial was the way to get publicity [and] a man is less likely to pick up public sympathy than a woman." Parrish himself acknowledged that his purpose in prosecuting Reems was to spread the word that no one involved with a porno film was immune from prosecution:

> Until *Deep Throat,* actors and actresses in this sort of film were unknowns. But in *Deep Throat,* [they] created a star. It all comes down to the lick log. Where your daddy took you when you were bad, bent you over and gave you a couple of licks. Well, if Mr. Streicker gets off easy, with all that publicity and all, his career could just take off. But if he gets a couple of licks [the adolescent puns continue] maybe he'll think it isn't worth it after all.

"The buckle of the Bible Belt"—as Streicker called Memphis—was an ideal setting for Parrish's modern morality play.

The Memphis Trial

The judge selected to preside at the trial was Harry Wellford, a former member of the Tennessee Republican Executive Committee. "If it weren't for people like Harry Reems," Judge Wellford said in open court, "we wouldn't have movies like *Deep Throat*. . . . Ain't no actors; ain't no film." Judge Wellford, a short, cantankerous conservative, instructed Reems' Memphis attorney that he would "not hear of any such nonsense as a First Amendment defense." He warned the lawyer that if he dared to argue to the jury "that your client's conduct is protected by the First Amendment, I am going to charge the jury that [this] is not a First Amendment case." With a prosecutor like Parrish and a judge like Wellford, it is easy to understand why the government selected Memphis as the ideal location for its prosecution of Harry Reems.

Since the film was being distributed from New York, and since most of the defendants lived there, the Southern District of New York would have been the natural locus of any investigation, indictment, and trial. But it is difficult to offend a New Yorker. One can find any possible combination of sexes and species entangled in lustful embrace on the screens of Times Square movie houses. And the proliferation of massage parlors, health spas, and encounter studios—or whatever euphemism brothels are masquerading under these days—caters to all tastes, no matter how bizarre or anatomically inconceivable. There was a considerable risk that a jury, exposed to this diet of degeneracy every day, would return a ho-hum verdict of not guilty by reason of boredom. So the government brought the case in Memphis. But there was one problem. The Sixth Amendment to the United States Constitution provides that "the accused shall enjoy the right [to a trial in] the State and district wherein the crime shall have been committed." The film *Deep Throat* had not been made in Memphis, nor had it ever been shown there. Moreover, Harry Reems had never set foot in that city before the legal proceedings had begun. How could it be argued that Reems had committed any crime in that state or district? The answer required imaginative legal thinking, and Parrish was up to the challenge.

The indictment, cleverly drafted by Parrish, charged 117 persons and corporations with a nationwide conspiracy to create an obscene film and to distribute it *throughout the United States.* The crime had thus been committed in each and every district where the film *could have* been shown. Under the theory of this indictment, any local United States Attorney could decide the most appropriate district in which to prosecute. This raised the specter of the federal government's dragging black militant publishers from Harlem to Mississippi, and labor organizers from Michigan down to North Carolina, in order to have them tried before maximally hostile jurors. It also gave the federal government the power to impose the most parochial standards of obscenity on films or magazines designed for the most sophisticated audiences.

Among those named as part of the conspiracy were technicians, distributors, the New York advertising agency that had prepared layouts for the movie—virtually everyone who had anything to do with the film's creation, distribution, or exhibition. Parrish later acknowledged that there "were probably 500 co-conspirators," but that "we weren't going to prosecute people like the ticket sellers or popcorn machine guys or projectionists."

Of the 117 individuals and corporations named in the indictment, only 18 were actually prosecuted. The remaining 99 were given the status of "unindicted co-conspirators." An unindicted co-conspirator is someone who the grand jury—in reality the prosecutor who controls the grand jury

—believes is guilty but has decided, for any of a number of reasons, not to indict. (President Nixon was named by the grand jury as an unindicted co-conspirator in the Watergate cover-up.) Among the unindicted co-conspirators was Linda Traynor, alias Linda Lovelace, the female star of *Deep Throat.* Lovelace had previously testified before a federal grand jury in Brooklyn under a grant of immunity, and there was some question whether she could be prosecuted in the Memphis case. Instead, she was subpoenaed to testify against Reems, but she disappeared and the FBI was unable to track her down. (Some courtroom observers referred to the missing witness as "Sore Throat.")

The indictment charged 77 "overt acts" by the co-conspirators. An overt act is any conduct—no matter how innocent—that is performed as part of the conspiracy. Of the 77 overt acts charged, only one mentioned Herbert Streicker: "Between Jan. 10, 1972 and Jan. 19, 1972, . . . Linda Traynor [alias Lovelace], Charles Traynor, Gerard Damiano . . . and Herbert Streicker [alias Reems] traveled from New York, New York to Miami, Florida." Although there is nothing illegal about such travel, the trip was allegedly made in furtherance of the overall conspiracy. Under this theory, Streicker could have been indicted even if he had never acted in the film —so long as he went along on the ride.

The trial began on March 1, 1976. Ninety witnesses were called—77 by the Government, 13 by the defense. The film was shown in the public courtroom, the only place in Memphis where the public could see it—and without charge. The case received widespread coverage in the press, especially when the defense attempted to call actors Jack Nicholson and Warren Beatty as expert witnesses to testify on the limited role played by actors in the creation and distribution of a film. Judge Wellford refused to allow their testimony. Little of the evidence had anything to do with Reems' role in the alleged conspiracy. Most of it concerned events that occurred before and after the filming. The conspiracy, according to the indictment, began in February of 1971 (a year before Reems' involvement), and continued at least through June of 1975 (three and a half years after Reems' role ended). Under the open-ended law of conspiracy, testimony relating to the entire period of the crime was admissible against each of the co-conspirators, regardless of how limited his or her individual role may have been.

Assistant United States Attorney Parrish did not deny that Reems' role in the conspiracy was extremely limited. He told the jury that Reems

> made the movie, he got his money for making the movie . . . and he is out, he doesn't do anything else . . . he got out early.

This concession by Parrish was crucial to Reems' defense. Reems claimed that under the law in effect at the time he appeared in front of the cameras in January of 1972, *Deep Throat* would not have been deemed obscene. Under the Supreme Court decisions in force at that time, a sexually explicit film was constitutionally protected if, taken as a whole, it possessed "redeeming social value." Regardless of how explicit a particular scene might be, the film was protected under the First Amendment unless: "(a) the dominant theme of the material taken as a whole appeals to a prurient interest in sex" (whatever that means!); "(b) the material is patently offensive because it affronts contemporary community standards . . ."; "(c) the material is *utterly without redeeming social value.*" The Supreme Court, in a series of decisions culminating in a 1966 case involving the book *Fanny Hill,* had ruled that no book or film could be banned unless all three of these elements "coalesced." That had been interpreted to mean that no matter how dirty a film or book was, it could not be prosecuted so long as it had any socially redeeming value—a message, a few laughs, or even useful information about sexual technique.

Under this permissive test, *Deep Throat* was probably entitled to the protection of the First Amendment. The film was—according to at least a few reviewers—somewhat humorous; and it was said to be better than the typical stag film in its cinematic technique. Reems and his trial lawyer believed that he could not be convicted of any crime under the obscentiy standards in existence in January of 1972.

But Parrish was not prosecuting Reems under *those* standards. He was prosecuting him under very different standards that had been established by the Supreme Court in June 1973—a year and a half *after* Reems had completed his role in the film. Under the new standards—announced by Chief Justice Warren Burger in *Miller* v. *California*—a film could be prosecuted even if it contained some "redeeming social value." Under the *Miller* test, a sexually explicit film was entitled to the protection of the First Amendment only if, taken as a whole, it possessed "serious literary, artistic, political, or scientific merit." (The acronym for this test soon became SLAPS.) There is a significant difference between the old and new tests. For example, under the new test, a slapstick sexual comedy could probably be prosecuted: while it would not be "utterly without redeeming social value," it might still lack "serious literary, artistic, political, or scientific merit."*

*The *Miller* test raises the intriguing issue of whether explicit sex can be used to increase the readership of a magazine that is, at least in significant part, political. It is a fact of life that sex sells magazines, and magazines that sell more have greater political influence. It cannot be doubted that magazines such as *Penthouse, Playboy, Esquire,* and *Cosmopolitan* exercise considerable political influence in this country. Nor can it be doubted that their circulation,

In the *Reems* case, Judge Wellford instructed the jury that in order for a sexually explicit film to be constitutionally protected it must contain "serious literary, artistic, political or social value." Reems' trial lawyer vehemently objected, requesting the pre-1973 instruction that limited obscenity prosecutions to those films that were "utterly without redeeming social value." The objection was overruled.

Harry Reems was not being tried under the law as it existed at the time he acted in *Deep Throat,* but rather under a new set of standards that had come into existence a year and a half after it had been completed. The general rule is that a defendant must be tried under the law that was applicable *at the time he committed his alleged criminal conduct.* But Parrish persuaded Judge Wellford that "the conspiracy" itself continued past the date of the *Miller* decision in 1973; that it continued as long as the distribution of *Deep Throat* continued. (Under this theory, Reems' *crime* continues to this day, since *Deep Throat* is still being distributed.) According to the prosecutor's argument, he could thus be judged by a standard that came into existence after his own *role* ended, but while his *crime* continued.

As Parrish himself rhetorically asked: "[Reems] made the film, got his money and got out back in 1972, that is, he didn't do anything else as a part of the conspiracy, he didn't do any more overt acts, he didn't participate any further, and the question arises why in the thunder does he wind up being charged [with acts that took place] four years later?" His answer was that "once a person joins a conspiracy, he is liable for *everything* that happens in that conspiracy until it is ended." (Reems once asked me whether he would have been guilty of *murder* under the prosecutor's theory, if some strong-arm techniques used by the distributors had resulted in someone's death many years after the film had been completed. I told him that—under Parrish's theory—he could be guilty of that crime.)

In order to get out of the conspiracy, according to Parrish, Reems was obliged "to take up affirmative actions to defeat and destroy the conspiracy." But what could Reems have done? He could not have "exposed" the crime, as one might expose a secret conspiracy, since it was universally known that the film *Deep Throat* was being distributed in interstate commerce. He could not legally have prevented the distribution and exhibition of the film, since he retained no legal rights to it. Did the prosecutor expect him to go out and physically destroy all existing prints of *Deep Throat?*

---

and hence their influence, would be diminished significantly if they were not permitted to appeal "to the prurient interest" of their readership. I have written about this subject in the context of the prosecution against *Screw* magazine. See "Screwing Around with the First Amendment" in the January 1977 issue of *Penthouse* magazine.

The jury was left to speculate about these questions as it considered its verdict. After reviewing the evidence for several hours, it deliberated for only minutes before voting unanimously to convict all the defendants on all the charges. Sentencing was deferred pending submission of motions for a new trial. And Reems went off in search of an appellate lawyer.

It was now just a few days after the jury verdict. "It's great to be out of Memphis," Reems told me. "If you hang around that town too long, you begin to believe they may be right. I really dread having to go back there for sentencing. What do you think Wellford will give me? How do you think my chances are on appeal? Do you want to take the case?"

I knew I wanted to take the case the minute I heard about it. Two of the areas of law I was most interested in were the First Amendment and conspiracy. This case combined both in a fascinating context.

Streicker told me the reason he had come to me was that he had heard that I had successfully defended the film *I Am Curious (Yellow).* That film, made in Sweden, had been the first commercially distributed motion picture to show explicit sex.

The *"I Am Curious (Yellow)"* Case

"This is not the *I Am Curious* case," I told him, "and I don't think we should litigate this case the way we litigated that one." I explained that in the *I Am Curious* case, we had argued that it was none of the court's—or the government's—business what went on behind the closed doors of an adult movie theater. As long as children were not permitted into the theater or offensive material was not displayed outside, it was entirely up to the adult film-goer to decide whether or not to enter and view the film. I strongly believed, and still do, that this is the proper constitutional rule. The First Amendment says that Congress shall pass "no law . . . abridging the freedom of speech," but the Supreme Court had ruled that books and films determined to be obscene by the courts were not protected by the First Amendment. This required the courts to view individual films and decide, on a film-by-film basis, whether the sex was graphic enough to make it obscene or whether the literary value was serious enough to outweigh its offensiveness. This process required the courts to become censors of private morality and tastes.

There can never be objective standards of obscenity. Obscenity is truly in the eye of the beholder, or—as Justice Douglas once quipped—"in the crotch of the beholder." One person's obscenity is another's art, and yet another's comedy.

Former Justice Potter Stewart of the United States Supreme Court once admitted that he could not define obscenity, but he assured us that "I know it when I see it." But other judges, who also claim to know it, see it quite differently. Each Justice has his or her own personal definition of obscenity, which is rarely written into opinions. Justice Byron White's law clerks say that their boss looks for a sufficient degree of erection and penetration before he classifies a film as obscene; they refer to this as "the angle of the dangle" rule. Justice Brennan's clerks label his criterion, which permits anything short of a full erection, the "limp dick" standard. The late Chief Justice Earl Warren used to regard the portrayal of "normal" sex—no matter how graphic—as constitutionally protected; but when "abnormal" sex was even hinted at, he would fly into a rage. "Would my daughters be offended?" was his personal test. The late Justice Hugo Black believed that dirty pictures were absolutely protected by the First Amendment, but that dirty words—such as "Fuck the Draft"—were not. Justice John Paul Stevens, on the other hand, believes that dirty words deserve more protection than dirty pictures. Every Justice has his own standards, and they are just as likely to reflect individual tastes, hang-ups, and upbringing as they do constitutional doctrine or precedent.

The bottom line is that obscenity is what five Justices of the Supreme Court say it is at any given time. This demeans the Supreme Court's role as guardian of the First Amendment and empowers the Justices to impose their own tastes upon the nation. It gives little guidance to filmmakers, actors, and others whose work brings them close to the border between protected speech and impermissible pornography.

In the *I Am Curious (Yellow)* case, we decided to launch a direct attack against this judicial approach to the regulation of obscenity. When the film was banned in Boston, we brought a lawsuit in federal court. We refused to exhibit *I Am Curious* to the curious judges, in order to dramatize our contention that the content of a film was none of the government's business so long as it was being shown behind the closed doors of an adult movie theater.

During the course of the argument, one judge referred to his grandmother, who had accidently wandered into a French movie believing it to be a travelogue, only to be shocked by its sexual content. He wondered how we could assure that his grandmother would be protected. I told him that the theater could put up explicit warnings, but he was concerned that the warnings could themselves be so explicit as to be offensive. As we were engaged in this dialogue, I was reminded of an old story of the Jewish traveler who noticed that his watch had stopped working; seeing a store with watches and clocks in the window, he entered and asked the owner to fix his watch. "Fix your watch?" he asked in surprise. "I don't fix watches; I'm a mohel, I perform circumcisions." "You perform circumcisions?" the customer asked. "Then why do you have clocks and watches in your window?" The owner answered without hesitation, "What do you *want* I should put in my window?"

It is possible, I reminded the judge, to devise symbols that are not necessarily so explicit as to offend, and yet clear enough to provide adequate warning. He seemed satisfied.

The federal court eventually issued an opinion that was to become—for a brief time—a landmark in the law of obscenity. It held, in a 2 to 1 decision, that no movie theater could be prohibited from showing the film so long as it is not ". . . advertised in a manner pandering to a prurient interest in sex . . ., shown to an audience not warned of its possibly offensive character, or . . . shown to children under the age of 18 years."

This decision promised to get the government out of the business of judging the content of each film and into the business of setting general external standards for the regulation of movie theaters.

Not surprisingly, the Attorney General of Massachusetts appealed this precedent-setting decision; he was joined by the federal government (which, under President Nixon, had ranked obscenity prosecutions as among the five highest law-enforcement priorities). The Supreme Court granted review and I was asked to argue the case for Grove Press, which distributed the film in America.

Burger and Bear-Baiting

The *I Am Curious (Yellow)* case was to be my first argument before the High Court, and I was somewhat nervous as I entered the hushed marble and mahogany courtroom. I had prepared extensively for my fifteen-minute presentation—but I could not anticipate what awaited me. I had hardly reached the lectern to begin my argument, when Chief Justice Warren Burger asked if he could "interrupt" to inquire whether I thought a state had the power to prohibit a "bear-baiting contest." I didn't have the slightest idea what a bear-baiting contest was—we don't have many bears in Brooklyn or Cambridge—but I guessed that it must involve sadistic cruelty to animals. I told the Chief Justice that I did not think the act of bear-baiting was protected by the Constitution, since the states have the power "to protect the interest of animals."

I tried to get the argument back on track: "I think the example would be better if it were a *film* of bear-baiting." But the Chief Justice interrupted me once again: "Let's stay on the live." I drew a distinction between an act that harmed another being and a film of consensual lovemaking that did not intrude upon the sensibilities of those who chose to view it. The Chief Justice shot back:

> [Y]ou are saying that it's all right to kill one bear and five dogs in the filming process, but it isn't right to kill many more of them in live showings, is that a distinction . . .

I tried again:

> No. I would say a state would have the right to prohibit the killing of dogs and bears whether for film or for other purposes.

The Chief Justice persisted in what was becoming increasingly a filibuster, as he simply would not let me get on to the issues in the case:

> Let's say 14 states didn't have any statutes against bear-baiting, and 4½ million had watched bear-baiting or the filming of bear-baiting. Would that have the slightest relevance in your judgment on whether the showing of bear-baiting in Boston, Massachusetts, could or could not be stopped . . . ?

I thought this finally gave me an opening to get back to the case, as I directed my answer away from bear-baiting and to the issue of whether the Constitution permitted a consenting adult to view an arguably obscene film in the privacy of a discreet movie theater:

> No, the First Amendment protects the individual's right to receive information necessary to satisfy his emotional and intellectual needs. The fact that some other people in the United States have seen it is not necessarily relevant. The thrust of our [position would take prosecutors] from [inside] the theater—that is only attended by people who want to go—and would put them outside the theater to protect you and me from the intrusion on our sensibilities that would occur if movies . . . thrust advertisements or pictures on unwilling viewers.

But the Chief Justice would still not be diverted. Though I had never mentioned a bear in my answer, he challenged me:

> Are you suggesting that it is a universal rule that everybody is offended by bear-baiting, for example?

Every time I tried to change the subject, he brought us back:

> [H]ow about moving the bear-baiting into a theater and charging $5 admission for it?
>
> I don't want to overwork you on the bear-baiting, but in order to

have a film of bear-baiting, you've got to go through an unlawful process in the first instance.

Finally—less than a minute before my time had expired—the Chief Justice asked whether *I* thought the analogy to the bear-baiting contest was "valid." I told the Chief Justice what I thought:

> I think the analogy of bear-baiting is not valid [because it] is an illegal act which hurts animals. It is different from [lovemaking] presented on a screen to a public which has chosen to view it.

By this point my time was nearly up. I barely—excuse the pun—had an opportunity to summarize my argument that under a functional definition of privacy

> a theater with its curtains drawn down deserves [at least as much] constitutional protection [as] a home with its shades drawn up.

The Chief Justice had monopolized the entire argument with his bear-baiting analogy. The other eight justices were unable to ask questions, though several of them seemed anxious to probe certain points. Some of them seemed embarrassed by their Chief's performance. By the end of the argument, I finally understood what a bear-baiting contest must feel like to the bear.

Several months later the Supreme Court rendered a 5 to 3 decision in the *I Am Curious (Yellow)* case that did not reach the broad issue decided by the district court (nor did it mention bear baiting); instead, it decided the case on a narrow procedural ground. We eventually settled the case to the advantage of the defendants. The earlier opinion, suggesting that all censorship of the content of movies exhibited to adults in discreet settings was unconstitutional, remained the only court decision on that issue until June of 1973 when the Supreme Court changed the definition of obscenity in *Miller* and a series of companion decisions.

In these cases Chief Justice Burger, writing for the majority, rejected the approach I had argued in the *I Am Curious (Yellow)* case.

> We categorically disapprove the theory . . . that obscene, pornographic films acquire constitutional immunity from state regulation simply because they are exhibited for consenting adults only . . . The States have a long-recognized legitimate interest in the quality of life and the total community environment, the tone of commerce in the great city centers, and, possibly, the public safety itself.

I explained to Reems that we could no longer expect to convince any court to accept our broad constitutional attack on movie censorship. Chief Justice Burger had put that argument to rest—at least for the present.

The Press Presents Our Case

I concluded that our best line of legal defense in the *Reems* case was to try to turn the newly decided Supreme Court cases to our advantage. Since these cases changed the law of obscenity, we could argue that the Memphis judge and jury should not have tried Reems under these new standards for conduct because the old standards were in effect when he was filming *Deep Throat.*

Parrish would argue, on appeal, as he had successfully argued to Judge Wellford, that since the conspiracy continued after the Supreme Court's decision in *Miller,* it was perfectly proper for the jury to apply the *Miller* standard.

As I laid out the arguments pro and con, it became clear that a decision on this issue could go either way; there were plausible arguments on each side. In the prevailing mood against obscenity, I could not afford to place all my reliance on a technical, legal argument. We had to persuade the media, the public, and the courts that the conviction of Harry Reems was an outrage. Before this case could be won in court, it first had to be won in the public mind.

This posed a dilemma for me. I do not like to see cases tried in the press. The dangers of media hype are obvious. I am constantly appalled at the way prosecutors leak stories to friendly journalists in a calculated effort to poison the atmosphere against certain criminal defendants. The Bergman case had been a prime example of the hysteria that can be generated by the press and politicians. Moreover, there are legal and ethical prohibitions against a lawyer using the media to affect the outcome of a pending case. I certainly didn't want to run afoul of these prohibitions.

I told Reems about my reservations. "This has been a media case from beginning to end," he said. "I can't enter this battle with one-and-a-half hands tied behind my back. Parrish has used the media to the hilt. He's been featured in *Time* and *Newsweek.* He's been on every TV talk show. He's become the darling of the law-and-order crowd. Can't we fight fire with fire?"

"Why can't *you* take him on?" I asked Reems. "I'll stay in the background and help you with the information and legal arguments."

"That won't work," Reems said. "He gets a lot of credibility from being a lawyer. He can always dredge up a case or a statute that I've never heard of. There has to be a lawyer in the ring with him, and I want that lawyer to be you."

I agreed finally, but told Reems where I would draw the line. I would not seek media coverage, but would respond to press inquiries. I would not become involved in organizing rallies or demonstrations, but I would speak about the constitutional dangers of this kind of prosecution. Reems cautioned me that the media would hound me and that the story would get bigger now that I was in the case. "You're going to give me credibility," he said. "Before you, it was a Mr. Clean versus a porno actor. Now it's also a battle of legal heavyweights."

Reems' media instincts were on target. As soon as he announced to the press that he had retained me as his lawyer, my phone didn't stop ringing. Story after story appeared in dozens of newspapers and magazines. Reems and I were invited to appear on TV and radio talk shows. The media were writing and distributing our briefs for us.

The initial story appeared in the *New York Times*. It told how the Reems prosecution was first seen "as a joke," but is now being understood "as a very serious issue":

> With Mr. Dershowitz as the lead lawyer and the American Civil Liberties Union and other prominent groups and individuals prepared to help, Mr. Reems has some of the country's most impressive legal talent working on his appeal.
>
> He also has the support of some of the country's best-known entertainers: Colleen Dewhurst, Ben Gazzara, Mike Nichols, Stephen Sondheim . . . Warren Beatty, Jack Nicholson and Gregory Peck.
>
> As Mr. Dershowitz interprets the *Deep Throat* case, "Any person who participates in any way in the creation, production, editing or distribution of a sexually explicit film, newspaper, book, painting or magazine can be hauled into a Federal court anywhere in the United States and charged with participating in a national conspiracy."

Soon, a long front-page analysis by Nat Hentoff of the *Village Voice* appeared. It was subsequently used by other writers as the basis for dozens of additional stories. Hentoff began by warning his readers of the consequences of a defeat in the *Reems* case.

> Alan Dershowitz, a Harvard Law School professor and one of the nation's preeminent constitutional lawyers, has never been known as an apocalyptic civil libertarian. Accordingly, when Professor Dershowitz speaks of the recent criminal convictions in a porno-film case as

> being so chilling as to ultimately also freeze the printed word, the warning is weightier than if it had come from those who habitually clamor that the constitutional sky is falling . . .
>
> Should the verdict against Harry Reems be sustained, obscenity indictments throughout the country will pyramid.

Hentoff explained that the implications of the Reems prosecution go well beyond obscenity. If a conspiracy charge like this one was to be upheld on appeal, the government could make dangerous use of that precedent in political cases involving, for example, antiwar activists. He then turned to the legal arguments we were preparing, and he summarized them in terms easily understandable to a general audience:

> One has to do with Reems being convicted for a crime that was not a crime when he "committed" it.
>
> "That's one of the many outrages in this case," says . . . Dershowitz. "[H]ere was an actor who, on the one day he worked on *Deep Throat,* had no idea what the ultimate film was going to look like. He knew it was a sex film, but he had not seen any script in advance. There was no way he could know whether it was going to be soft core or hard core. And, in fact, Harry never even saw the film before it was released. Yet he's convicted of a conspiracy to move the film, in the form it finally took, across state lines."

The Hentoff article had enormous impact. Hundreds of readers came forward and volunteered their assistance. It was our best possible brief. It also generated numerous other stories—presenting our side of the case in a positive manner—in hundreds of newspapers and magazines. The headline-writers invoked every adolescent pun their imaginations could generate:

KING OF THE PORNO ACTORS FINDS HIMSELF IN DEEP THROES
IN TROUBLE UP TO HIS THROAT
HOW HARRY GOT REAMED
DEEP THREAT
PORN'S DEEP GOAT
REEMS SHAFTED IN BIBLE BELT

Our speaking appearances were widely covered by the media. The *New York Times* described a joint appearance at the Harvard Law Forum:

> Harry stood with a portrait of Supreme Court Justice Felix Frankfurter beaming down on him. Beside him sat Alan Dershowitz, look-

ing like a tweedy Marx Brother with his wild nimbus of ash-blond hair, saying that he felt Harry Reems' trial was the most significant First Amendment conspiracy case since Dr. Spock.

Dershowitz acted as a sort of kibitzer for Harry. He noted that the crew of the *Glomar Explorer,* [which] had been shown a videotape of *Deep Throat,* had more to do with transporting obscene material in interstate commerce than Harry Reems did. Would Larry Parrish prosecute *them?* When I asked Parrish, he said: "They're not insulated against prosecution."

Before our joint apperance on the Tom Snyder Show, an assistant producer got us confused. (Harry was wearing his three-piece lawyer's suit.) We went along with the mistake for a few minutes, with Reems expounding on habeas corpus and me describing Linda Lovelace. But then Snyder emerged and recognized us.

Not all the stories were flattering. Mike Royko complained in a syndicated article how depressing it was that after two hundred years of men like Jefferson, Paine, Debs, and Darrow, "we are now asked to fight for the right of Harry Reems to be a public creep . . . Anybody who contributes to his defense fund," Royko concluded, "is a mental moonbeam."

If Herb Streicker had not become an actor, he would have been a first-rate press agent. Every time a story appeared, he placed it in his press kit and sent copies to other journalists. This had a snowball effect. The Reems case became a good story because it was a good story. Everyone was reporting it, and so everyone should report it. It was almost impossible to pick up a newspaper or magazine, or turn on a TV or radio talk show without coming across some reference to the Reems case. Reems had become an overnight celebrity; and even I was occasionally recognized by strangers who would come up to me with good—and sometimes not so good—wishes for the case.

More important, however, the publicity was having its intended effect on the public, on the Justice Department, and on the courts. We began to get the message that the Reems conviction was an embarrassment. This was exactly what we had hoped would happen.

How The Justice Department Gagged on *Deep Throat*

The first sign that the strategy was working came when Solicitor General Robert H. Bork filed a brief in another case admitting that a federal judge had erred in using the *Miller* standard to obtain the conviction of a Kentucky theater owner who had shown *Deep Throat* before the *Miller* decision was handed down but was prosecuted afterward.

The federal authorities in Memphis lost no time in registering their displeasure at Bork's action. Even before he had seen a copy of Bork's brief, Parrish's boss, Thomas F. Turley, Jr., the U.S. Attorney in Memphis, attacked the Solicitor General as "corrupt" and "remote," charging that he "divines from the Georgetown cocktail circuit and discussions in and around the faculty lounges [of] New Haven and Cambridge what he thinks the law ought to be." Nor was the prosecutor alone in his disapproval of the Solicitor General's action. Judge Harry Wellford, who presided over the Memphis *Deep Throat* trial, stated publicly that he was "shaken considerably" by the Solicitor General's action, since it seemed as though Bork was "just plain throwing in the sponge in this case."

Judge Wellford's outburst against the Solicitor General was nothing compared to the bizarre tactic he employed in a flagrant attempt to influence the Supreme Court's decision in the case of the Kentucky theater owner. In a move without any basis in accepted judicial practice, the judge sent a letter to the Clerk of the Supreme Court telling of his personal concern with the issues raised in the Kentucky case and included with it a copy of a sixty-page "brief" dealing with those issues. The brief—which was written by none other than Larry Parrish—argued that the Solicitor General's position should be rejected.

As soon as I read about Judge Wellford's action—he did not have the courtesy to notify us formally—I contacted the Solicitor General's office and the Clerk of the Supreme Court. I reminded them that judges are not supposed to take sides in pending cases. The Solicitor General's office, as appalled by the action as I had been, promised to file a motion to strike the brief and letter. This episode ended with the Supreme Court Clerk's office returning Judge Wellford's package unopened—in effect, treating it as the "crank letter" it was.

Over the next few months, as we waited for the Kentucky decision to be handed down by the Supreme Court, Reems crisscrossed the country in an attempt to raise funds to defray his considerable legal expenses. Although I was handling his appeal for a nominal fee, Reems had incurred considerable expenses at his trial in federal district court.

The trial, the fund-raising, and the uncertainty of the outcome of the ordeal had all taken their toll on Harry. He told one reporter of the frustration of having to "run around in a situation where I have to rely on the generosity of others rather than on my own independent spirit." Before the *Deep Throat* prosecution began, he had begun developing a reputation as an actor in legitimate films in Europe. Now he was broke and unable to work. He complained that the publicity from the trial, instead of adding to his reputation as an actor, had turned him into a curiosity. He was learning how powerful the force of the government can be when it is unleashed against an individual—even one with prominent and vigorous supporters.

On March 1, 1977, the Supreme Court handed down its opinion in the Kentucky case. A unanimous court reversed the convictions, holding that the defendants, "engaged in the dicey business of marketing films," had no fair warning that their movies might be subjected to new standards. The Court stressed that the issue of fair warning was of paramount importance in cases where First Amendment values are at stake.

All the defendants in the Memphis *Deep Throat* case immediately filed motions asking Judge Wellford to reconsider his earlier holdings in light of the Supreme Court's new decision.

While the new decision had changed the law, national events had changed the political climate. In January, 1976, Jimmy Carter had taken office. He soon replaced Turley, a conservative Republican, with Mike Cody, a liberal Democrat who had supported blacks for political office in the South, had once headed the local ACLU branch, and had even defended theater owners charged with showing obscene movies. This was too much for Larry Parrish, and in early March of 1977, he announced he would resign and enter private practice. There was an angry reaction among his many supporters, and eventually a deal was worked out whereby Parrish retained a consulting role in the appeals of "his" old cases.

Shortly after the changeover in the Memphis U.S. Attorney's office, Judge Wellford ruled on the defense motions for new trials in the *Deep Throat* case. There was a critical difference between the Kentucky case and ours: the Kentucky defendants had been charged with committing acts that ended on a specified day prior to *Miller.* The Memphis defendants, on the other hand, had been charged with participating in an ongoing conspiracy, which allegedly had not yet ended, since the film was still being distributed. Judge Wellford seized on that point, and denied the new trial motions of all Reems' co-defendants on the grounds that activities engaged in *after Miller* were subject to the standards announced in that case. Further, he said, there was adequate evidence of continued criminal conduct after *Miller* by each of those defendants.

But Judge Wellford's decision treated Harry Reems differently. In one terse sentence, the judge stated that since all of Reem's activities had taken place prior to *Miller,* he alone was entitled to a new trial. It was widely assumed that Wellford had gone out of his way to treat Reems differently because he wanted to placate the press and de-escalate the media war against him. Legally, the case against Reems was not that much different from the case against some of his co-conspirators: if Reems had remained part of the conspiracy after the Miller decision—as the prosecution contended—then he too could be judged by post-*Miller* standards. The real difference between Reems and the other defendants—and the difference that we believed prompted the judge's decision—was that Reems had become the subject of sympathetic national attention, while the other defendants had not. Because of this Reems would remain free, while his co-defendants would be sentenced to prison.

A few days after Wellford handed down the order granting Reems a new trial, the Justice Department announced that it would dismiss the indictment against Reems. Reems was now a free—if tired—man. We had won the case in court and in the Justice Department. I had not won it just with technical legal briefs; Harry Reems had won it by masterfully employing the media to communicate his story to the public.

The Case of the Wayward Greyhound

Harry Reems got out of the porn business and Larry Parrish eventually left the government. But the Parrish approach to prosecuting pornography—picking a location for a trial on the basis of prosecutorial advantage, regardless of where the acts occurred—continued to pose dangers to our civil liberties. A few years after the Reems case, I became the defense attorney in another obscenity prosecution illustrating these dangers.

The case involved a sexually explicit film entitled *Belinda,* which was distributed by Terry Levene, an entirely legitimate producer of motion pictures and concerts. The film was a box-office disaster. But there was at least one very interested viewer—an FBI agent who had been sent to a nearly empty Buffalo theater to see it and take notes. He described *Belinda:*

> The color, sound film . . . begins with a group of people . . . looking at . . . a corpse in the identification room of a hospital. The scene shifts to . . . an individual identified as MILLER who is dragging and shoving BELINDA across a snow-covered hill . . . MILLER throws her down and rubs his hands over her clothing and BELINDA's boyfriend, DOUG, who has been watching, jumps MILLER and they begin to fight. The next scene shows DOUG with a woman who is enticing him in what is an infra-red type scene with all red lighting. The woman performs fellatio on DOUG. The next scene shows MILLER in bed with *the* black woman after which time he gets out of bed, goes to the door, knocks, and asks for WILLIAM. He then enters the room, which apparently is a bathroom as there is a female sitting on a toilet stool when he enters the room. The female then performs fellatio on MILLER who is standing in front of her.

We vigorously disputed the accuracy of that description, characterizing it as nothing more than an anatomical road map of the characters' sexual exploits. In our brief, we offered a very different description:

> *Belinda* . . . is a full-length motion picture with a plot, with character development, with serious camera work and editing, with interesting musical background. [I]t employs different cinematographic techniques to convey its point of view. In scenes depicting non-exploitive sexual relationships, the film employs a process known to cinematographers as solarization. This process imposes a muted and filtered quality upon the action, thus distancing the viewer from the details of the lovemaking—which makes the sexual conduct much less graphic and explicit to the viewer—and conveying an overall sense of the fluidity of the act. This process has been used extensively by such film makers as Fellini and was recently employed by the award-winning film *Looking for Mr. Goodbar.* [T]his is intended to be contrasted with the brutal and exploitive sexual conduct involving William Miller, the pimp, and his two prostitutes. In order to convey this striking contrast visually, the filmmaker photographed the exploitive sexual scene with a far more graphic, explicit and genital focus.

These very different descriptions of the identical sixty minutes of celluloid only go to show that the perceived value of a film is indeed in the eyes of the beholder—or that a lawyer can try to make a silk purse out of a sow's ear.

The major issue in the case did not center, however, on whether the film was obscene, but rather on whether it had passed through the state of New Jersey on its journey from New York City to Buffalo. In January of 1972, *Belinda* had been booked for a showing in Buffalo, and it was shipped from a Manhattan warehouse. The Buffalo United States Attorney—who was engaged in an anti-obscenity campaign—indicted Terry Levene for transporting an obscene film in interstate commerce.

When the indictment was issued, Levene's first reaction was to say that the United States Attorney in Buffalo had a lot to learn about geography, since New York City and Buffalo are in the same state. To his chagrin he soon learned that the U.S. Attorney was an expert not only in geography but in the subtleties of the law of interstate transportation. Unbeknownst to Levene, the warehousing company that stored *Belinda* had decided to leave the driving to Greyhound. The usual Greyhound route between Manhattan and Buffalo was through the Lincoln Tunnel and onto the New York State Thruway. This route included a brief pass through the town of Paramus, New Jersey. According to the government's theory, the film—

encased in a locked steel box—had spent several minutes in the state of New Jersey while stored in the baggage compartment of a speeding bus. This happenstance, so the argument went, converted an *intra*state trip into an *inter*state trip, thus giving the federal government jurisdiction over the matter and turning Levene into a federal defendant. After a jury trial he was convicted. Although he received a suspended sentence, the felony conviction—if it was to stand—could ruin his career. I was retained to prepare and argue his appeal.

When I heard about the facts of the case, I recalled my teenage years as a frequent Greyhound bus traveler. A girl friend had lived in New Jersey; several summer camps and hotels where I had worked had been located in the Catskills; and on a few occasions high-school classmates and I would make a pilgrimage to Union City, New Jersey, the nearest locale that permitted burlesque dancers to peform their art. I recalled the bus trip out of the Port of New York Authority terminal at Fortieth Street and Eighth Avenue, through the Lincoln Tunnel. What stuck in my mind were the long delays and the incessant traffic. I remembered the many occasions when the bus driver would change his route because of traffic. "We're bypassing the tunnel, folks, and trying the bridge," he would announce. Then he would drive up the city streets and across the George Washington Bridge, or, on occasion, the Tappan Zee Bridge in Westchester.

Then it struck me! While the exits from the Lincoln Tunnel and the George Washington Bridge are in New Jersey, the other side of the Tappan Zee Bridge is just above the New Jersey border *in New York.* If the bus carrying *Belinda* took the Tappan Zee route, it would not have passed through New Jersey. The encased film would have remained safely within the geographical bounds of New York State during its entire journey, and there would be no interstate transportation, no federal jurisdiction, and no federal crime. My client's conviction would have to be reversed.

I began my research not in the library but at the local bus terminal. I discovered that one of the several authorized routes between New York City and Buffalo—an indirect one, to be sure—took the bus over the Tappan Zee Bridge, up to Albany, and on to Buffalo. I also learned that the Interstate Commerce Commission permits buses to deviate from their authorized routes in order to avoid weather and traffic delays. A call to the weather bureau proved discouraging, since there had been neither rain nor snow on that January day. But still, it was *possible* that heavy traffic conditions had caused the bus to deviate from its authorized route and to remain within the borders of New York.

At the trial the government had not been able to specify the *precise* Greyhound bus on which the film had traveled; all it could establish was the *date* of the shipment. And it was undisputed that several Greyhound buses had made the Manhattan to Buffalo trip on that day.

As I was doing this research I couldn't help thinking about the absurdity of the law that made my client's guilt—indeed his reputation and career—turn on the fortuity of whether a particular bus happened to take one route or another on a particular day. *He* had no idea on which bus the film would be shipped—or even that it was going to be shipped by bus. Federal jurisdiction often turns on such minutiae—for example, whether a phone call or a letter went from one state to another. But the law is a series of technicalities, and cases are won or lost on the basis of who can best turn them to a client's advantage. I can still recall the oral argument in this case, during which each of the appellate judges and both of the lawyers were immersed in the fine print of Greyhound timetables rather than in the broad issues of legality and morality.

In the end we won the case in a hotly divided 2 to 1 decision. Judge James Oakes—who sometimes took the bus from his home in Vermont to the courthouse in Manhattan and who seemed most interested in the "wayward Greyhound" issue—concluded that no jury could reasonably infer from the evidence "that a shipment between two points in one state would pass through another state, especially when it is not at all obvious from a road map that there is any more direct route from New York City to Buffalo than the New York State Thruway which does not cross any state line." Judge John R. Bartels never reached that issue, deciding instead that the conviction had to be reversed because there was undue delay between the indictment and the trial—an issue we had "thrown in" to the brief just to be safe, but one on which we had no realistic expectation of winning.

The third judge on the panel, Walter Mansfield, wrote a blistering dissent. Without viewing the film himself, he concluded that it was "hard, explicit pornography." He appended to his opinion the entire text of the FBI agent's description of the film—the anatomical road map of Belinda's sexual adventures. What purpose that appendix could possibly serve—except to titillate generations of lawyers and law students who can now turn to page 392 of volume 600 of the Federal Reporter (2nd series) for amusement—was not explained in the opinion.

That seemed to be the end of the matter, since the assistant U.S. Attorney in charge of the case told me that the government would probably "let sleeping Greyhounds lie" and not seek further review. But two weeks after the government's time to appeal had expired, the United States Attorney's office filed an extraordinary application before the court of appeals, seeking a *retroactive* extension of its time to file a petition for rehearing before the entire bench of the court of appeals—all nine active judges. Almost immediately, Judge Mansfield granted it. I decided the time had come for some unusual action on our part. I wrote a six-page letter to the Justice Department urging it to overrule the United States Attorney's office—and, in effect, Judge Mansfield—and to drop the case. Only the Solicitor General of the United States can grant permission for the government to seek rehearing of, or appeal from, a case it has lost in the court of appeals. In my letter, I outlined the background of the case and urged the Solicitor General to deny the prosecutor's request to appeal. Ultimately he refused to grant permission and the case finally ended.

Deep Throat and the Feminist Censors

Until the spring of 1980 all of my encounters with the banning of obscenity had been with censors from the political right. In addition to the three cases I've described, which had been prosecuted by conservatives out to impose their morality on everyone, I had been involved in a series of debates about obscenity with William F. Buckley, one of the country's leading conservative spokespersons, and an intellectual whom I admire. These debates—which took place in theaters, on television, and in the press—were seen as unambiguous clashes between classic liberalism, which has always advocated virtually unrestricted speech, and conservatism, which has generally encouraged some degree of censorship in the interest of preserving morality.

In a debate in Sander's Theater at Harvard, Buckley took the position that we, as a people, must not be prepared "to lay down any sense of responsibility for ourselves and for our children." As part of that responsibility it was entirely appropriate, indeed mandatory, that we "resist corporately" certain degrading displays: "Anyone who sees *Deep Throat* cannot believe the proposition that the divinity of the individual can in any sense survive an experience that debasing. This is a common loss."

I did not rest my anticensorship argument on the claim that pornography is without its costs, acknowledging that its proliferation may well

> coarsen sensibilities; it may well degrade women; it may even have subtler and more pervasive effects on the quality of life. I believe that expression really does matter; that ideas do have impact.

But I pointed out that if this was allowed to serve as a justification for banning all expression that produces "undesirable" effects, the door would be open to a broad regime of censorship:

> Books like *Fear of Flying;* magazines like *Playboy, Cosmopolitan* and *High Times;* movies like *Last Tango in Paris;* and singers like Bob Dylan—these are the "Marxes" and "Lenins" of the sexual revolution. Banning junk like *Deep Throat* and sleazy porn magazines while permitting other, far more influential purveyors of the message of the sexual revolution is an exercise in self-satisfied futility. Spiro Agnew had the "right" idea. In order to even begin being successful at influencing promiscuity and other "evils," you have to censor radio, TV, songs, universities, the press, best-sellers, Hollywood movies—the popular media.

I ended by asking Mr. Buckley whether censoring only hard-core pornography would do any good, or whether it would be necessary "to institute a regime of censorship whereby the government decides what is good and what is bad for consenting adults."

Buckley responded that he was not prepared "to codify a general position." But he was prepared "to say it is a legitimate concern of a community how people treat each other."

He concluded with a characteristic Buckleyism:

> If we approved of Dershowitz's Schemata [we would be] moving towards the day when it is perfectly all right for a 16-year-old to commit fornication on a public stage so long as he's paid the minimum wage.

In debates of this kind, nobody ever really wins, since members of the audience have generally made up their minds and are there to support their champions. Until a few years ago, the sides were clearly drawn in the debate over obscenity: men and women of liberal political persuasion generally opposed censorship of obscenity, while men and women of conservative persuasion often supported such censorship. Over the past several years, however, a new dimension has been added to the debate. Many feminists, some with deep attachments to liberal causes, have argued that the evil of pornography cannot be ignored. They believe that pornography promotes sexist attitudes and violence against women. Some have proposed boycotts. Others have called for government censorship. Civil libertarians, most of them supporters of feminism, continue to oppose censorship of pornography, regardless of its alleged evils.

Deep Throat Comes to Harvard

In the spring of 1980 this controversy was played out in a dramatic confrontation at Harvard University, and I was at the center of the storm.

It all began with adolescent foolishness by some drunken Harvard College students. While viewing the film *Animal House,* they had tossed beer cans at the screen and damaged it. The Quincy House Film Society, the student group that had sponsored the event, was responsible for the screen. In order to raise the several hundred dollars needed for repair, they decided to show *Deep Throat,* and scheduled four performances during a May weekend.

This decision produced an immediate protest from some of the women students who lived in Quincy House. "This is our home," one of the women complained. "We shouldn't have to be subjected to abuse and degradation right in our own living room."

The uproar had caught the men of Quincy House by surprise. The showing of *Deep Throat* had become an exam-time tradition at many colleges. It was seen as a lark, an escape from the tensions of the tests. But the feminists were beginning to take pornographic movies, especially *Deep Throat,* quite seriously.

Several weeks before the proposed showing, Gloria Steinem had written a provocative article in *Ms.* magazine about *Deep Throat* and the exploitation of its female lead, Linda Lovelace. Pointing to the $60 million allegedly made on the film—not counting "the subindustry of sequels, cassettes, t-shirts, bumper stickers, and sexual aids that it inspired"—Steinem characterized *Deep Throat* as a cheap feature that had been turned into "a national and international profit center and dirty joke." At the heart of the dirty joke, according to Steinem, was Linda Lovelace "whose innocent face offered movie-goers the titillating thought that even the girl-next-door might be the object of porn-style sex." But it was a joke with widely felt consequences: "Literally millions seem to have been taken to *Deep Throat* by their boyfriends or husbands (not to mention prostitutes by pimps) so that each one might learn what a woman could do to please a man if she really wanted to."

Moreover, Linda Lovelace was now claiming that her innocent face had been a mask covering up the agony of a battered wife who had been imprisoned by her husband-pimp. Several years after the completion of *Deep Throat,* Lovelace wrote an autobiography entitled *Ordeal,* in which she told a sordid story of how she had been made to perform her "sexual sword-swallower trick" at gunpoint. She had obtained no enjoyment from her public sexual exploits and had indeed suffered serious physical and psychological damage.

After reading Linda Lovelace's account I called Harry Reems and asked him whether his recollections of the filming of *Deep Throat* corroborated her claims that she had been forced into performing by her husband. Harry, who was then working off-Broadway in a stage play, laughed and said, "Are you kidding? Sure her husband, Chuck, was an asshole, but he was hardly around during the filming. Damiano sent him away because he would get jealous of how much she was enjoying the sex. She was really into it. We had a good relationship before and during the filming."

I told Harry that Lovelace had written that when "she saw how upset Chuck was, [she] decided [she] would *pretend* to enjoy it with Harry." I asked whether it was possible that she was only acting.

"Linda Lovelace acting?" Harry exclaimed. "Have you ever seen her in a film? She couldn't even pretend to be acting. Somebody wrote the book for her. It's a rip-off."

Whether true, false, or somewhere in between, Linda Lovelace's account struck a responsive chord among many feminists. Gloria Steinem's widely read article presented a sympathetic portrait of Linda Lovelace as the victim of everything the "sleazy pornocrats" had come to represent. Using Lovelace's ordeal as the symbol of sexist repression, many feminists—led by Steinem, Susan Brownmiller and others—declared all-out war against pornography. The movie *Deep Throat* came to symbolize the antiwoman evils of the commercial sex industry.

The organization through which Gloria Steinem spoke—Women Against Pornography—emphasized education, sensitization, and boycotts as its primary weapons in the war on porn.

Although boycotts are themselves protected by the constitutional right of free expression, civil libertarians are appropriately concerned about the effect of overly broad boycotts, such as those directed against general bookstores. We remember the uses to which boycotts had been put during the McCarthy period. The threat to boycott motion-picture studios and television stations that employed "red," "pink," or "suspect" actors, directors, or technicians, led to the notorious "black lists." In an interview in *Playboy* magazine, I had expressed some of those concerns:

> Take what [some of these] women are now doing and ask yourself the question, Would you favor it if their objection were to books about atheism or communism instead of pronography? If you would not, then it seems to me that you can't be in favor of a boycott against stores that sell *Playboy* and *Penthouse,* because they're equally protected.

The growing dispute between civil libertarians and feminists had split the ranks of some liberals, and the issue was achieving some notoriety in the press. I had, perhaps, added some fuel to the fire by my criticism of the "new feminist censors" in several articles and speeches. I did not deny that some pornography is degrading to women, but I argued that it is precisely the function of the First Amendment to protect those whose speech offends and degrades.

I pointed out that some of the most strident opponents of pornography inadvertently provide the most compelling arguments for its constitutional protection by characterizing it as "Fascist propaganda." (The Fascists, not surprisingly, used to call it "Communist propaganda.") All propaganda is within the central core of the First Amendment. Nor did I dispute the claim that some pornography may contribute to an atmosphere of violence against women. We simply don't know for sure. But speech often causes undesirable consequences—political violence, riots, even revolutions. That should not, I argued, be a reason for suppressing speech itself.

A few days before the scheduled showing of *Deep Throat* at Quincy House, I attended a dinner meeting at which Gloria Steinem was the guest speaker. I knew her casually from some earlier political wars during which we had been on the same side of the barricades. Now, it appeared, we were championing different causes in the emerging battle between feminists and civil libertarians. I asked whether this divisive confrontation between traditional allies was really necessary. She responded that there need be no conflict, because most feminists were opposed to government censorship. "We remember that the same federal statute—the Comstock Act—that prohibits the mailing of obscene materials also prohibits the mailing of birth-control and abortion information." She told me that she believed in education and private boycotts rather than censorship. We discussed the potential misuses of generalized boycotts, and she acknowledged that my concerns were legitimate, as I had acknowledged the importance of her concerns. I left our meeting convinced that a feminist antipornography position need not be inconsistent with the First Amendment. Indeed, it is the First Amendment right of feminists to protest pornography as vehemently as they protest any other perceived evil—so long as no effort is made to censor it.

But some of the women of Quincy House who were opposed to *Deep Throat* were not content to protest. First they tried to cancel the showing by calling for a vote of the students who lived in the dormitory. They lost by a margin of three to one. Forty-nine percent of the women who voted opposed the showing; and forty-eight percent favored seeing *Deep Throat.* Next they tried to get the Harvard University administration to forbid the scheduled showing. The Dean of Students wrote a letter to the Quincy House Film Society urging it not to show *Deep Throat,* but he would not ban it. The members of the film society, caught up in the adversary challenge by the feminists, voted to go forward with the event.

The Quincy House women, with the assistance of other feminists, decided to picket the performances and to use the occasion to sensitize students to the evils of pornography. Pamphlets were prepared presenting the feminist perspective on pornography. A slide show, graphically depicting the exploitive and sexist nature of pornography, was scheduled for presentation in an adjoining room an hour before the first showing of *Deep Throat.* Several prominent local feminist speakers had been asked to address the hundreds of protesters expected in front of Quincy House on the evening of the first scheduled performance.

I had heard about the anticipated confrontation, but had taken little interest in it. The First Amendment seemed to be in full bloom that spring at Harvard. No one was being prevented from expressing his or her views. The Quincy House Film Society was going to show *Deep Throat;* the Harvard administration was expressing but not imposing its views; the feminists were preparing pamphlets, slide shows, and speakers to present theirs; and everyone was free to see and listen to all or none of these expressions.

The feminists seemed to be making their point quite effectively: more students were expected on the picket lines and and at the slide show than at the movie itself. Many in the Harvard community, while supporting the *right* of the Quincy House Film Society to show *Deep Throat,* now believed that the society had been insensitive to the feelings of their feminist housemates by exhibiting an offensive film in the dormitory that was home to them all. I shared that view.

The Attempt to Get an Injunction

Suddenly everything changed. A few days before the scheduled showing, two women residents of Quincy House, not satisfied to protest and picket, called the local District Attorney's office and asked the police to stop the showing of *Deep Throat.*

The District Attorney of Middlesex County, where Harvard is situated, was an elderly politician named John Droney, who had repeatedly won reelection on an uncompromising law-and-order platform. He not only became apoplectic when he heard about the obscenity issue but he had no love for Harvard students. When Droney learned that the twin evils of obscenity and Harvard might merge on that fateful Friday night in May, he dispatched an assistant to court in an effort to secure an injunction against the scheduled showing.

If there is anything more obnoxious to a civil libertarian than the punishment of speech *after* it has taken place, it is the issuance of a *prior* injunction to prevent speech in the first place. Prior restraint—as an injunction against speech has come to be known—is the purest form of censorship. It seeks to prevent the speech from ever reaching the public. When the Nixon Administration learned that the *New York Times* was planning to publish the Pentagon Papers, it sought an injunction. My teacher and dear friend, the late Alexander Bickel, had argued for the *Times* against the injunction. The Supreme Court, in denying the government's request, had said that prior restraint is anathema to the First Amendment, even where national security interests are alleged. Now, almost ten years later, the District Attorney of Middlesex County was seeking an injunction to prevent the showing of a dirty movie to a small group of students in a college dormitory at Harvard.

It was noontime Friday, only hours before the scheduled performance, when Carl Stork and Nathan J. Hagen—the co-presidents of the Quincy House Film Society—received telephone calls from the D.A.'s office directing them to be in Judge Charles R. Alberti's courtroom at two o'clock for a hearing on the injunction. Stork and Hagen, Harvard College juniors at the time, tried to call me in my office. But I was at lunch, and my secretary couldn't locate me. Stork and Hagen told her the story and requested that I come to the court to assist them as soon as possible. I returned from lunch at two-fifteen, to learn that I was expected in court—fifteen minutes earlier!

Once again, as when I met Harry Reems, I was out of uniform: this time in a pair of chino pants and a sport shirt. Quickly, I borrowed a colleague's ill-fitting jacket, dug an old brown tie out of my desk drawer, and drove off to the courthouse in downtown Cambridge.

Within minutes, and still out of breath, I found myself before Judge Alberti, arguing against the injunction. With no books, cases, or statutes in my possession, I had to wing it. The judge was most understanding, asking Assistant District Attorney Lawrence Hardoon to let me look over his shoulder at the relevant statute and cases.

After a few minutes of argument, the judge granted a short recess in order to allow me to confer with my clients whom I had not yet met or even spoken to. We introduced ourselves and I asked Carl to fill me in on the background of the case. It was then I learned for the first time that the complaint that had led to the D.A.'s request for an injunction had been made by two fellow students at Quincy House.

This revelation did not change the legal situation: it was the District Attorney, John Droney, who was seeking the injunction, even though the original complaint had been submitted by private citizens. He was seeking the injunction under a Massachusetts statute, enacted several years earlier, that empowered the courts to prevent the showing of films found to be obscene.

The Civil Liberties Union had, of course, opposed the legislation on constitutional grounds, but the Massachusetts courts had upheld it. The D.A. had two weapons in his arsenal against pornography: he could seek an injunction *before* the film was shown; and/or he could seek criminal prosecution *after* the film was shown. Droney began by seeking an injunction.

Now I was in court, representing Stork and Hagen on behalf of the Civil Liberties Union of Massachusetts, arguing against the issuance of the injunction that would prevent the scheduled showing of *Deep Throat* at eight o'clock that night.

After some legal argument, Judge Alberti declared that he was ready to see *Deep Throat* to decide whether it was obscene. I argued that the judge need not view the film: no matter what its content, I said, it would be unconstitutional for him to enjoin the showing of any film. If the D.A. thought the film was obscene, he could wait until it was exhibited and then arrest those responsible for its being shown. Judge Alberti insisted, however, on having *Deep Throat* screened for him. As the equipment was being wheeled into the courtroom, I informed the judge that I had no intention of watching the film.

I was preserving an important point for any jury trial that my clients might face in the future. I would tell the jurors that I had never seen *Deep Throat* because I had chosen not to, and that they had never seen *Deep Throat* because they had chosen not to. I would argue that the right to choose not to see a film is just as important as the right to choose to see a film. Indeed, most countries that *prevent* their citizens from seeing certain films also *require* their citizens to see other films. I would remind the jurors that it was the District Attorney who was *making* them see a film they had chosen not to see, in order to have them decide whether other people, who have also chosen not to see it, would be offended if they were to see it. I hoped, by this argument, to point out the absurd nature of the jurors' task in an obscenity prosecution, and to get them to focus on the important issue—namely, whether the outside of the movie theater, the only thing that the unwilling public may have to endure, is offensive to those who cannot avoid it.

Judge Alberti excused me from watching *Deep Throat*—I have still not seen it to this day—and Stork, Hagen, and I left the courtroom while the judge, half a dozen assistant D.A.'s, and a few courthouse personnel watched Linda Lovelace and Harry Reems on a small video-cassette machine.

After about forty minutes Judge Alberti abruptly had the videotape machine shut off and summoned us back into court. "I've seen enough," he declared with a disgusted look on his face. Then, turning to me, he said, "You're the lucky one. I had to sit through that trash." The judge then rendered his decision: he declined to issue an injunction against the scheduled showing of *Deep Throat,* because although he regarded it degrading both to men and women, he found that it was not obscene under the relevant Massachusetts standards.

The effect of this ruling was to deny the District Attorney's office the legal power to prevent the showing of the film. Under the terms of the statute, it was still open to that office to arrest and prosecute those responsible for the exhibition of an obscene film *after* the event. But, since Judge Alberti had premised his ruling on a finding that *Deep Throat* was not obscene, it was questionable whether the District Attorney could arrest Stork and Hagen on the premise that it was.

Upon leaving the courtroom that afternoon, I told Assistant District Attorney Lawrence Hardoon that I hoped Judge Alberti's finding of nonobscenity ended the matter, and that there would be no criminal charges brought against any students for showing the film that night. Hardoon said that he could not tell me what the D.A.'s office would do.

I advised Stork and Hagen that although I had taken every possible precaution, there was no guarantee that showing the film that night would not result in their arrest. I cautioned against martyrdom; the inside of a jail cell is a lonely place after the cheering crowds have gone home. The decision to go ahead with the screening, however, had to be their own. They told me that they would take the risk and show the film.

"Free the Quincy House Two"

When I arrived at Quincy House shortly before eight o'clock, a circus atmosphere prevailed. Hundreds of pickets marched outside urging potential viewers to stay away. There was some pushing and shoving. Slogans were shouted: "Freedom of the Press is not Freedom to Molest." "Pornography is an incitement to violence."

I walked past the pickets and spoke to the assembled viewers and protesters:

> Whether you folks like it or not, you are part of a rather important political event . . . I am not here to either encourage or discourage the students who decided to see this film . . . Were I not involved in this lawsuit, I would be out there defending the rights of those picketers to . . . persuade you not to see this film.

I then went on to condemn, in what now appears to me as overly harsh terms, the students who had complained to the District Attorney:

> It is a serious matter when the law is invoked to arrest and prosecute and censor. Those two women who brought this complaint join the tradition of the Saudi Arabian government that tried to censor the *Death of a Princess* film, and Richard Nixon who tried to censor the Pentagon Papers. If those women want to be a part of that tradition they ought to at least know what they have embraced. Feminist fascists are no better than any other kinds of fascists.

Two members of the audience stood apart from the protesters and the raucous, adolescent crowd of beer-drinking viewers. They were Massachusetts state detectives Thomas Spartichino and William Flynn. Dressed in coats and ties, they sat quietly in the corner of the dining room—waiting patiently for the movie to begin and end.

The District Attorney had decided to arrest Stork and Hagen despite Judge Alberti's ruling that *Deep Throat* was not obscene. The *Deep Throat* case was so important to Droney that he pulled state detective Thomas Spartichino off a murder investigation to watch the film and make the arrest.

I tried to secure a federal injunction against the arrest of my clients, by telephoning the emergency judge. But in the midst of our conference the first show ended and the officers arrested Stork and Hagen, confiscated the film, and seized the money the society had collected for the tickets. By confiscating the film, Droney had done precisely what Judge Alberti had said he could not do: he prevented the three other scheduled showings of *Deep Throat* on the ground that it was obscene.

Amidst shouts of "Free the Quincy House Two," Stork and Hagen were taken to Cambridge Police Headquarters and booked on charges of disseminating matter they knew to be obscene. A band of students marched behind them and protested the arrest on the steps of the police station. Among the protesting students were some of the same women who earlier had organized the feminist demonstration. As I later described this irony:

> . . . the minute the kids were arrested, the minute the law was invoked, everything changed—the women became the goats, the kids became the heroes. One lesson that we all learned was that the least effective way of delegitimizing this kind of speech is to invoke the law; it has the opposite effect. You get all the good people on the side of the bad acts.

Several days after the arrest, the Civil Liberties Union of Massachusetts filed a civil rights action in Boston Federal Court charging District Attorney Droney with violating the rights of Stork and Hagen, as well as those of the audience members who were denied the right to attend the three scheduled showings that had to be canceled after the film was seized. Jeanne Baker, who was then serving as general counsel to the Civil Liberties Union, was in charge of that lawsuit. I remained responsible for defending Stork and Hagen against the criminal charges they were facing in state court—felonies punishable by five years in prison.

In law, as in some sports, the best defense is often a good offense. We decided, therefore, that filing a federal civil rights action against the District Attorney would be an important part of our defense strategy. It would put him on the defensive—literally make him the defendant—before a federal judge, and require him to justify his conduct in arresting Stork and Hagen and in seizing the film in the face of Judge Alberti's finding that it was not obscene. Even more important, from a practical point of view, the filing of a federal lawsuit would empower us—the plaintiffs in that suit—to subject the District Attorney to "discovery" proceedings. Discovery proceedings are mechanisms for compelling the parties to a lawsuit to answer questions by the opposing lawyers under oath before trial. They are designed to speed up the trial itself by encouraging the lawyers to do the hard work of discovering the facts and limiting the issues before it begins. Discovery is not generally available in criminal cases, and so Stork and Hagen could not compel District Attorney Droney to answer their questions in the criminal case. But discovery is available as part of a federal civil-rights action, and so Jeanne Baker and I—working in tandem—would be able to use discovery in the federal civil rights lawsuit to help prepare our defense to the state criminal charges.

We immediately scheduled a deposition—an oral interrogation under oath—of District Attorney John Droney. Since the deposition was part of the federal suit, it was conducted by Jeanne Baker. I was seated next to her, taking notes of anything that might prove helpful in the criminal case.

She first established that Droney had been willing to take the law into his own hands:

BAKER: [T]he fact that . . . Judge Alberti had found the film not to be obscene, did not deter you from your purpose to stop the showing of the film?

DRONEY: Obviously.

BAKER: And you feel that you can make a determination that criminal arrests should occur after a Superior Court Judge has found the film to be not obscene?

DRONEY: That's right.

BAKER: You feel that you can prevent the showing of a film that a Superior Court Judge has ruled not to be obscene?

DRONEY: We did it.

BAKKER: You effectively acted as censor in this case?

DRONEY: That's right.

Having gotten Droney to admit—indeed proclaim—that he had acted as a censor, Baker's next goal was to try to box him into a corner from which he could escape only by dropping the prosecution against Stork and Hagen. We knew that Droney believed that all pornography is connected to organized crime, so Baker asked him whether he thought the showing of *Deep Throat* at Quincy House was in any way connected to that evil. Droney took the bait:

DRONEY: I believe any showing of this film is connected with organized crime.

BAKER: Was there any evidence in this case involving Messrs. Hagen and Stork, of organized crime involvement?

DRONEY: Someone had to furnish the film.

Upon further questioning, Droney said that given the choice between prosecuting the supplier of the film or the students, "there would not be any question, I would prosecute the supplier." Droney tried to excuse his failure to investigate the supplier by pointing to a personnel shortage—"I would like to investigate them but I have a limited amount of men, you know." This excuse soon became implausible in the face of Baker's questions:

BAKER: Have you ever directed that Messrs. Hagen or Stork be approached through their defense counsel by an Assistant District Attorney to determine whether [they would provide] information to your office with respect to the source of the film . . . ?

DRONEY: No.

BAKER: Have you ever made any inquiry . . . as to the physical location of the supplier of the film to the Quincy House Film Society?

DRONEY: No.

At this point in the deposition, Droney's attorney requested a short recess. I took advantage of this opportunity to look at the cannister of the film, which the D.A.'s office had seized at Quincy House.

When the deposition resumed, Baker asked Droney whether he would drop all charges against Stork and Hagen if they would give him the name of the company that supplied *Deep Throat* to the students. Droney had little choice, since he had stated under oath that he would much prefer to prosecute the supplier than the students. He agreed.

We satisfied our part of the bargain by pointing to the shipping label on the front of the film cannister, which had been in the custody of the District Attorney's office since its seizure at Quincy House. Clearly marked in bold print was the name "S.R.O. Entertainment" and a New York City address. S.R.O. is a large distribution company that publishes a catalog of films available for rentals to colleges and universities throughout the country.

All charges against Stork and Hagen were dropped. Neither S.R.O. nor anyone else was ever prosecuted for the events at Quincy House. Eventually, the Civil Liberties Union of Massachusetts dropped its lawsuit against District Attorney Droney. The *Deep Throat* case at Harvard was over. Stork is now a technical assistant to the president of a computer software firm in Seattle, and Hagen is now working in Boston, and plans to go to law school in the near future. (Harry Reems—having tried the off-Broadway stage for several years without financial success—has again returned to starring in pornographic films.)

The Continuing Debate Over Pornography

But the controversy between those who would censor pornography and those who would not continues. I recently participated in two debates on the subject that illustrate the adage about politics making strange bedfellows.

The first was with Andrea Dworkin, a radical feminist who believes in "direct action"—including violence if necessary—to destroy all pornography. Dworkin has written a book entitled *Pornography: Men Possessing Women.* She characterizes her writing as "revolutionary," and sprinkles it generously with four-letter words and long, explicit excerpts to illustrate the evils of pornography.

The debate was billed as "an intellectual car crash between absolutists," and like most car crashes it produced a great deal of noise and little forward progress. Among the several hundred in attendance were a few dozen women who tried to shout me down. "Down with the pornocrats," they shouted, whenever it was my turn to speak. "We don't want to hear from people who support porn." These women wanted to censor not only pornography itself but those who would defend it on First Amendment grounds. A smaller group—calling themselves "Dykes on Bikes" and carrying chains —threatened violence. The woman who reported the story in the *Boston Globe* described the event as follows: "What these . . . men and women saw

—and some of them created—was an ugly collision between about forty enraged radical feminists in the audience and Dershowitz, who defended free speech and became a symbol for the entire American legal system."

In the course of our debate, Dworkin called for the total destruction of all pornography: "We will know that we are free when the pornography no longer exists." She urged her followers to use the law when possible to end the tyranny of pornography and to take the law into their own hands when necessary—to destroy the pornographic presses.

When my turn came I tried to explain—over the booing and hissing—that what I support is freedom of choice about pornography. I informed the audience that a recent law in Iran prohibiting pornography also required all women to keep their faces covered. I reminded them that efforts by the Moral Majority to "clean up" television included feminist programs within the definition of pornography. I told them that the same District Attorney who had attempted to ban *Deep Throat* had *succeeded* in censoring a beautiful film about lesbianism, by invoking the same anti-pornography statute. I quoted Gloria Steinhem to the effect that "the long history of anti-obscenity laws makes it clear that such laws are most often invoked against political and life-style dissidents." I cautioned that if any group of Americans could succeed in taking the law into its own hands, it would be the Moral Majority who far outnumber the radical feminists. They would destroy the presses that publish books they deem offensive: books advocating birth control, abortion, and sex outside of marriage. "Among the first books they would want to ban," I warned, "are the writings of Andrea Dworkin." Dworkin scoffed.

The other debate was with the Reverend Tom Michel, leader of the Moral Majority in New England, who called for vigorous government censorship of pornography. When asked how he felt about joining forces with radical feminists like Andrea Dworkin in the common goal of eliminating pornography, Reverend Michel said that he was willing to accept the help of all who would join his crusade. I then asked whether his organization would, if it had the power, ban Andrea Dworkin's writings. He answered without hesitation: "We would most certainly ban such ungodly writings. It is not necessary," he reasoned, "to use pornography to illustrate its evils. It is only necessary to read the Bible." I reminded the Reverend Michel that the Bible has been among the most censored books in the history of the world.

Everybody Wants to Censor Something

Once the door is opened to censorship on grounds of offensiveness—whether by feminists or fundamentalists—it will be difficult to control. Deep down, everyone would like to censor something. Many Jews believe that swastika-wearing Nazis should be prevented from marching through neighborhoods of concentration-camp survivors. Some blacks would ban books, such as *Little Black Sambo* and *Huckleberry Finn,* which present offensive racial stereotypes. Gays disapprove of films that project a negative image of homosexuality. There is no objective basis for comparing degrees of offensiveness. If obscenity is in the eye of the beholder, then offensiveness lies deep in the history and psyche of those who feel it. Can anyone—especially a government—make a comparative assessment of the offensiveness felt by a concentration-camp survivor seeing a swastika, a descendant of a slave seeing a burning cross, a woman who has been raped seeing a portrayal of sexual brutalization? If the government is to ban one, it must ban all. If it is to refuse to ban any, it must refuse to ban all.

If feminists succeeded in banning material offensive to them, then fundamentalists would surely succeed in banning material offensive to them. The choice is between a society in which everyone must tolerate some offensiveness at the price of diversity, or a society that permits only expression that is offensive to no one.

Recently at Harvard, a feminist instructor tried to have *Playboy* removed from the library because she was offended by it. Imagine what a university library would be if every instructor could remove every book or magazine he or she deemed offensive. The library building could be converted to squash courts, and the few remaining books and magazines stored in some file cabinets.

It is no victory when the left succeeds in banning something conservative in reaction to the right's success in banning something liberal.* Every time either the right or the left achieves this kind of "victory," the First Amendment is the loser. And when the First Amendment loses, we all lose the power to choose. To advocate censorship is to choose not to be able to choose at all.

*The State Department recently demonstrated its "evenhandedness" over Northern Ireland by refusing to grant visas for American speaking tours to "extremists" from both sides. The losers were the American citizens who were "protected" from hearing both views.

5

How I Spent My Summer Vacation: Nudity and Environmentalism on the Cape Cod Beach

The dunes of lower Cape Cod are among the most beautiful sights in the world. Towering above the white sands of the Atlantic beach, they rise and fall in subtle patterns shaped by winds, tides, and other mysterious forces. During the summers I spend as many days as I can in a small rented cabin nestled among those dunes in the town of Truro. Many of my briefs and articles were drafted at the beach or on the deck (as I am sometimes nostalgically reminded during the cold winter when grains of sand dribble out of a file). I have shared the house with two other civil liberties lawyers, inspiring one friend to post a sign near the entranceway that reads, "Warning: Defense lawyers' hideaway; Prosecutors will be violated."

About a quarter mile from our house stands the tallest and most majestic of the Cape's dunes. Called "High Dune," it rises more than a hundred and fifty feet above the ocean. It then falls steeply into a small shrub-coated valley called "Brush Hollow," which is the lowest point in the dune profile. The contrast provides a strikingly beautiful asymmetrical landscape of sand, shrubs, ocean, and sky. For generations this beautiful area has marked the informal location of a nude beach, where Cape Codders have felt free to discard their swim suits in quest of the total tan. Over the years High Dune has reportedly looked down upon the naked bodies of such literati as Eugene O'Neill, Margaret Sanger, John Reed and his wife Louise Bryant. It was all very chic, quite informal, and completely unpublicized. Small groups of local bare-bathers would congregate at discreet distances from one another. Gawkers were rare, and when a bathing-suited wanderer from the town beach would stroll the mile south to High Dune, the accepted rules of beach etiquette required him to pretend that he did not notice that his neighbors were sunning themselves in the altogether.

In the late 1960s and early 1970s, with the popularization of body freedom, nudity became a cause, and thousands of serious young people decided that it was morally wrong to hide one's body. Bare became beautiful, and the beach below High Dune became a gathering point for the beautiful and not-so-beautiful from all over the Northeast. By the summer of 1974 the informal nude beach had extended to nearly a mile, and on any Sunday in August more than a thousand bare bodies could be seen on that glorious stretch of sand. The nature of the beach changed. There was no longer room for discreet distances, or pretense. Voyeurs abounded, especially motorcyclists who perched atop the dunes, equipped with binoculars and cameras. A commercial shuttle bus ferried both gawkers and gawkees from the town center to the beach. Peddlers, performers—and even a few pushers—created a carnival atmosphere. It was no longer the elite literary gathering of O'Neill's days, but it was good clean fun and everybody seemed to enjoy it.

Everybody but the residents and town fathers of Truro! Truro, with its winter population of 700 and its summer influx of 3,000, is part of the Cape Cod National Seashore. Before the nude beach gained its newfound popularity, Truro was a quiet summer resort, with a handful of small restaurants, few motels, and almost no commercialism. The winding country roads are narrow, picturesque, and sparsely traveled. Bicyclists, strollers, joggers, and dune-buggiers were more numerous than cars. The town's summer residents consist largely of lawyers, academics, and doctors (especially psychiatrists); politically, it is decidedly liberal; its ethnic composition is primarily WASP and Jewish.

Suddenly Truro became a "with it" town, as guitar-carrying, long-haired beach kids rolled in from all over the Northeast. At first many liberal lawyers and psychiatrists loved it, with several joining the flower children on the beach, doffing their expensive French swim suits in an uncomfortable but self-righteous display of liberation, not to mention flab.

I recall one incident during August in which a group of naked young women were sitting on a blanket as an older, distinguished-looking man strolled into view. As he came closer you could almost tell, despite his total lack of attire, that he was a psychiatrist: bearded and pipe-smoking, he carried all the hallmarks of the stereotypical shrink. Suddenly one of the women shrieked and dived under the blanket saying, "Oh, my God, that's Doctor Cohen, my analyst!" Dr. Cohen walked by without losing his cool or making any effort to cover up, but we all wondered what the next several analytic sessions would be like.

Soon the crowds became too much for the homeowners of Truro. Local residents had trouble parking. During an eighteen-day period in August of 1974, the Park Service counted a total of 1,248 cars illegally parked on the sides of the road. Shortcuts were discovered—more often created—over private property and fragile dunes. Most important of all, the residents of Truro just plain disliked the kinds of people who were now attracted to the area by the popularity of the nude beach. The newcomers were louder, cruder, freer, druggier, and dirtier than the regulars. There were rumors of sexual goings-on. A gay nude beach materialized a short way down from High Dune. The quality of life and leisure in Truro was being altered—imperceptibly at first, and then noticeably.

Meetings were convened. Angry debates took place. Some town residents didn't want to interfere. Others—even some who themselves had indulged in the town's most popular spectator sport—proposed a total ban on all beach nudity. Still others suggested regulations designed to keep the crowds down and the abuses under control. Everybody disavowed objecting to nudity per se, though it was clear that some of the townspeople had always been opposed to allowing skinny-dipping, and were using the external problems as an excuse to ban nudity. (At one point a proponent of the ban argued that the nudists were damaging the delicate dunes; an opponent cynically challenged him to run down the dune fully clothed, while he ran down the same dune stark naked—to find out which dune-climber caused more damage.) Eventually those who advocated a total ban on nudity prevailed and the Truro Neighborhood Association decided to try to persuade the federal government to prohibit nudity throughout the national seashore.

The Right to Bare Arms

During the summer of 1974 several of the most committed nudists came to our house for legal counsel. Their leaders were Steve Williams, a bronzed beach-lover who lived in Truro all year long and had been elected its beach commissioner, and Lee Baxandall, a scholar of Marxist esthetics who headed an organization called "Free Beaches." Several other men and women, most of them academics and professionals, also came along to plead the cause of free beaches. At first we treated their constitutional claim as a joke. "Of course, there's a constitutional right to go nude," I assured them. "It's in the Bill of Rights, in the Second Amendment: 'the right to "bare arms." ' " But they were serious. They wanted me to bring a court challenge to any federal regulation that prohibited nudity on isolated portions of the seashore traditionally used for that activity. I advised them that it would be difficult to persuade a court that there was a constitutional right to cavort in the nude on a federal beach, and I also told them that I didn't regard their desire to go naked as the most pressing legal issue of the day. But I did believe that a total ban on nudity—extending even to isolated stretches of the national seashore—would go too far.

The issue, to my mind, was similar to the right of adults to view movies behind the closed doors of a theater. Here there were no doors, but the isolation of the beach served the same function. The government should have the power to regulate the externalities—the numbers, the parking, the trespassing, the damage to dunes, the sensibilities of those who don't want to be exposed to nudity—but it should not have the power to prohibit consenting adults from nude sunbathing in isolated areas. I agreed to ask the Civil Liberties Union, on whose national board I then served, to become involved in the case if the government enacted a total prohibition on nudity. The Massachusetts Civil Liberties Union agreed to represent the nudists on the condition that I become their counsel and agree to do the work. We put together a team including Jeanne Baker, with whom I had worked on the JDL case; Judith Mizner, a recent law school graduate then working as a civil liberties volunteer; and John Reinstein, the staff attorney for the Civil Liberties Union. We set up our "law office" for the case on the deck of our Cape Cod house and began to develop a strategy to defend the constitutional rights of our clients to sunbathe in the nude at High Dune.

We decided to approach the problem in two different ways: first, to go on the offensive and bring a lawsuit challenging the constitutionality of any federal nudity ban as soon as one was enacted; and second, to go on the defensive by waiting until one of our clients was arrested in the buff, and defending his case on constitutional grounds. In that way, as Baker put it, "we would have both flanks covered." (As with the pornography cases, it became almost impossible not to fall into adolescent double entendres at every turn: some of the worst involved "bare allegations," "non-suiting" our opponents, and "debriefing" our clients.)

We did not have to wait long for the federal government to act. During the winter of 1974–1975 the United States Park Service promulgated the following regulation:

> Public nudity, including public nude bathing, . . . is prohibited. Public nudity is a person's intentional failure to cover with a fully opaque covering that person's own genitals, pubic areas, rectal area, or female breast below a point immediately above the top of the areola when in a public place. This regulation shall not apply to a person under 10 years of age.

The Superintendent of the Cape Cod National Seashore, Lawrence C. Hadley, announced that as of May 19, 1975, all public nudity would be prohibited on the Cape Cod National Seashore and that first-time violators would be punished by a $25 fine. (The regulations permitted a maximum punishment of six months imprisonment and a $500 fine.) The government, anticipating massive civil disobedience, arranged for helicopter surveillance, horse-mounted park ranger patrols, and oversand vehicle strike-forces dispatched by dunetop radio surveillance teams. There were even informers in "plainclothes" (who, naturally enough, were soon referred to as "uncover cops"). Dozens of new park rangers were hired and trained especially for this assignment. The rangers were divided into teams consisting of one male and one female, and rules were drafted requiring the arresting officer to be of the same gender as the arrestee. (Whether this rule was to be employed on the gay beach was a matter of avid speculation.) A federal magistrate was summoned to the Cape from Boston for special nudity duty during the summer. The federal government was gearing up for a massive display of power. The nudists were gearing up for an equally massive display of skin. The issues were met, and a stark confrontation seemed unavoidable.

On the day the regulation went into effect we filed our lawsuit in federal court. The plaintiffs were eight men and four women who had frequented the nude beach and who wished to continue to do so without risk of arrest. The plaintiffs were either homeowners in Truro or long-time residents. One was a prominent Boston lawyer; another was a science teacher at Milton Academy, a private boarding school near Boston; a third was an ordained Methodist minister.

Steve Williams, the chairman of Truro Beach Commission, set out his recollections of the nude beach in an affidavit:

> As a child with my family, I walked toward the least-occupied area of beach available. Invariably approaching families and other groups of nude bathers, it was customary to courteously skirt their presence and to leave a polite distance between us before disrobing.

Edmund and Susan Cabot set out their experiences:

> . . . I am 39 years old, my wife is 36. We have four children, ages 4 to 9. I am a science teacher at Milton Academy; my wife is a housewife and elected Town Meeting member in Milton. We own two houses, in Milton and Truro. We started using the "free beach" at Brush Hollow this past summer after having looked at it with mixed feelings from the neighboring Ballston Beach for two years previously. Nude bathing with a number of strangers was a completely new experience

> for all of us. At first, we were anxious about our own reactions and everybody else's, but it was immediately obvious that everyone at Brush Hollow was there to enjoy themselves in the water and in the sunshine, without pretenses. It was good seeing our own children losing their giggly obsession with certain parts of the body and begin to gain a better acceptance of human variety and of themselves as a part of this.

We argued that the regulation violated the plaintiffs' right to freedom of expression under the First Amendment and their right to privacy under the Fourth Amendment. Acknowledging that the crowds had created problems, we contended that they could adequately be handled by discreet regulations less restrictive of constitutional rights than a total ban on nudity. We suggested that in order to prevent damage to the dunes, the Park Service could assign a few rangers atop the most frequently traversed dunes; to solve the parking problem, the rangers could vigorously enforce the no-parking rules; to reduce the crowds, the Service could impose numerical limitations on the beach population. It would take fewer resources—less money and a smaller number of rangers—to police these externals than it would to enforce the total prohibition on nudity.

We petitioned the court to issue an injunction prohibiting the enforcement of the nudity ban at isolated stretches of the seashore traditionally used by nude bathers. Judge Frank Freedman, who was assigned to hear the case, set it down for a hearing, but proposed that we first take a "view" of the "scene of the crime"—the nude beach at High Dune.

On a bright, cool June day, a large group of overdressed lawyers—the judge, his clerks, and the various attorneys for the nudists, the town, and the government, most uniformed in three-piece suits—boarded a small fleet of single-engine planes for the brief flight over Cape Cod Bay. We were met at the Provincetown Airport by an armada of jeeps and beach buggies, and driven—over the fragile dunes—to the site of the nude beach. To everybody's obvious disappointment, there were no skinny-dippers—or any other kind of dippers—on the beach that crisp day. The judge had to content himself with viewing the naked sand, leaving to his judicial imagination the impact of multitudes of nude bodies upon the beaches and dunes.

The "view" having been completed, the hearing was convened on a sultry day later in the month when everybody would rather have been on the beach. I called as my first key witness, Lawrence Hadley, the Superintendent of the Cape Cod National Seashore and a proponent of the ban on nudity. I elicited from him the nature of the complaints that had led to the enactment of the prohibition:

Q: Would it be fair to characterize these complaints [trespass of private property owner's rights, damage to the resources, mainly dunes and beach grass, increasing littering along the town roadsides] as all going to problems relating to over-use of the facility and [not] to whether the users do or do not wear bathing suits on the beaches?
A: I believe [the] answer to that is yes.
Q: [T]he problem cannot fairly be characterized as "nudity per se"?
A: Yes.

I then asked Hadley if the problems would be the same if some other group—nonnudists—had been attracted to the beach at Brush Hollow in large numbers.

Q: [A]ssume that . . . it became known that this was a wonderful beach for [blacks] to get together, . . . and suddenly you discovered that there were twelve hundred black families fully attired in bathing suits who would come on a Sunday and use the beach. Would the problem be any different than it is now?
A: I suspect that problems would be identical.

I proceeded to take Mr. Hadley over each of the specific problems of overcrowding and to ask him whether they could be solved by means short of a total ban on nudity:

Q: [Could] the problem of over-parking be substantially reduced by means other than the total ban on nudity?
A: Yes.
Q: [W]e were told about the problem of destruction to the dune by people walking down that dune. Is there presently a federal prohibition against people walking down that dune?
A: No, sir.
Q: Is the problem of over-use a general problem throughout the United States in the National Parks [such as] Yellowstone Park and Yosemite?
A: Yes.
Q: Is it not true that there has been some restriction on the use of hiking paths . . . as a result of the over-use of the National Park System?
A: . . . I am aware of the management plans which are directed to the regulation of use in the Parks, varying kinds of use.

Having established that there were alternative methods of dealing with at least some of the problems of overcrowding, I introduced into evidence a document prepared by the Park Service, which had cataloged several options for dealing with the nude beach at Truro:

Q: [D]o I understand [one alternative to] mean that nude bathing would continue to be allowed at Brush Hollow but there would be a limitation on the number of people who would be allowed to use the beach at Brush Hollow?

A: Yes, sir.

Q: Is it not the fact that . . . the enforcement costs for allowing nude bathing at Brush Hollow, consistent with numerical limitations . . . would be the same as for a total ban on nudity?

A: Correct.

Hadley admitted that the average daily population at the nude beach—approximately 340—was not in excess of what the beach would support; nor was the average Saturday or Sunday population of 600; indeed, even the high of 1,200 bathers on a Sunday in August was manageable. The real problem was projected *future* populations if use of the nude beach continued to double each year as it had over the previous several years. He also admitted that beach populations, whether of clothed or nude bathers, could be controlled by means other than a total ban on nudity. (As a New Yorker who had been introduced to ocean bathing at the crowded beaches of Coney Island and Rockaway, I couldn't identify with the idea that even 5,000 bathers on the long stretch of beach beneath High Dune might constitute "overcrowding.")

The lawyer for the Truro Neighborhood Association then questioned several residents who were opposed to the nude beach. One homeowner testified that the fishing had gotten worse since all those nudists scared the bass away. Another began to say that the financial value of his house had diminished over the past several years, but he quickly backed off when he saw me take out my checkbook in preparation to making him an offer on his property. (All houses in Truro had nearly doubled in value over the previous several years, and I was indeed prepared to offer to buy his house from him for what he had paid for it six years earlier.)

The hearing was soon over. We anticipated that Judge Freedman would render his decision before the Fourth of July weekend. But no decision was announced, and the legal status of skinny-dipping remained in limbo for several weeks. During the beginning of that period an uneasy truce prevailed between the "nudity rangers" and the "nudity buffs." The traditional nude beach beneath High Dune looked like a staging area for a Marine assault: beach buggies carrying radio-equipped rangers surrounded the area, blocking every access route; binocular-gazing rangers were visible for miles atop the dunes; helicopters flew overhead with telephoto cameras. All was in readiness for the expected confrontation with thousands of determined nudists whose only weapons were their naked bodies. ("No fear of hidden arms from that crowd," I heard one ranger quip.) But no one showed up. The beautiful beach remained barren, as the nudists dispersed in quest of isolation and solitude along the miles of empty beaches stretching from Wellfleet to Provincetown. New patches of nude mini-beaches emerged along the coast. A dozen naked bodies here, a few couples there, a family elsewhere. It could have stayed that way with little trouble. There were no longer any parking problems, dune damage, or crowds.

The Nudity Cops

But the rangers had their mandate—a total ban on *all* nudity—and they were determined to enforce it to the hilt regardless of the costs. They dispatched airborne and dune-top scouting patrols, scanning the terrain for an exposed breast or bare bottom. They imported quiet motorized beach-cycles capable of sneaking up on a nude couple and catching them before they could slip back into their suits. At first it took on the quality of a game. For every tactic adopted by the rangers, the nudists adopted a counter tactic. Equipping *themselves* with binoculars and whistles, groups of nudists would occupy an isolated area and post garbed lookouts whose task was to blow a warning blast that sent the uncovered assemblage scurrying for cover. Soon the beach patrols increased in numbers and frequency. Before long the entire twenty-mile stretch of beach from Wellfleet to Provincetown was covered with vehicle tracks. Even garbed beachgoers were approached by rangers, suspicious that they had just slipped into their suits to avoid arrest. "What are you wearing under that robe," asked a zealous ranger of an overdressed woman. The nudity patrols—visible everywhere, in the sky, on the beach, atop the dunes, even at sea in boats—had come to disturb the serenity of the seashore.

There were inevitable confrontations: nudists—uniquely unsuited to carry identification—gave the rangers false names. Our lead plaintiff, Steve Williams, was arrested for stealing a sign warning that "nudity is prohibited"; confident that we would win our case, he was planning to change the "is" to "was" and to present it to us as a victory gift. Some naked offenders tried to outrun or outswim the arresting officers. Others tried to out-talk or out-quip the rangers: one swimmer who was caught with his suit draped around his arm, offered the defense that he "didn't know his ass from his elbow." Another, who was found floating naked in an inner tube, claimed that he was "properly a*tired.*" Many cursed and some even threw a few punches. Soon the rangers—most of whom were college kids—were equipped with guns. (One ranger, who had frequented the nude beach herself the previous year, was regarded as "unsuited" for nudity duty.)

Several of the town residents who had favored the ban on nudity soon came to believe that they had created a Frankenstein. It was clear that far more environmental damage was done by the beach buggies, the dunetop patrols, and the helicopters than by the nudists. Even the *Cape Codder,* the conservative local newspaper that had campaigned vigorously for the ban on nudity, began to wonder about its enforcement. An editorial, aptly entitled "Nudity: Turning the Other Cheek," included the following comments:

> [N]o federal case is created by those who go off by themselves, solitarily or nearly so, and take off their bathing suits to enjoy sun and surf. All that is required is the gentle touch. And it seems to us that this could be attained by the Seashore's suspending its jeep patrols along the beach in Wellfleet and Truro and giving its rangers the more healthful task of foot patrol. It wouldn't hurt to leave the binoculars back at headquarters, either.

"The Issue Is Not a Moral One . . ."

The massive display of federal power continued beyond the Fourth of July weekend and then increased after Judge Freedman rendered his decision in mid-July. In that decision the judge reviewed the evidence—which had not included the actual enforcement of the ban by the park rangers—and arrived at some interesting conclusions. He began by observing that "the issue is not a moral one and . . . it is not nudity per se but the attraction of the nude beach . . ." The court then addressed "the threshold inquiry"—"the extent of protection, if any, that the Constitution affords nude bathers who congregate on a semi-isolated stretch of federal beach land used traditionally for such purposes." He concluded, quite reasonably in my view, that the free speech claims of nude bathers is "akin to that of the student-plaintiff . . . who asserted a First Amendment right to wear his hair long." He then went on to consider our claim of personal liberty, which I regarded as the essence of the case:

> Although it matters little where this substantive right is found in the Constitution, I hold that it does exist and find its base in the concept of liberty as protected by the Due Process Clause of the Fifth Amendment. Such liberty is simply the right of the ". . . people to be let alone in the governance of those activities which may be deemed uniquely personal."
>
> Personal liberty is not composed simply and only of freedoms held

Steve Schapiro/Black Star

Rabbi Meir Kahane, leader of the JDL, leads his followers in an anti-Soviet demonstration.

Wide World

Four members of the JDL are charged with the 1971 bombing of the Soviet Trade Agency (Amtorg). Sheldon Seigel is on the left, Sheldon Cohen on the right, next to a television reporter.

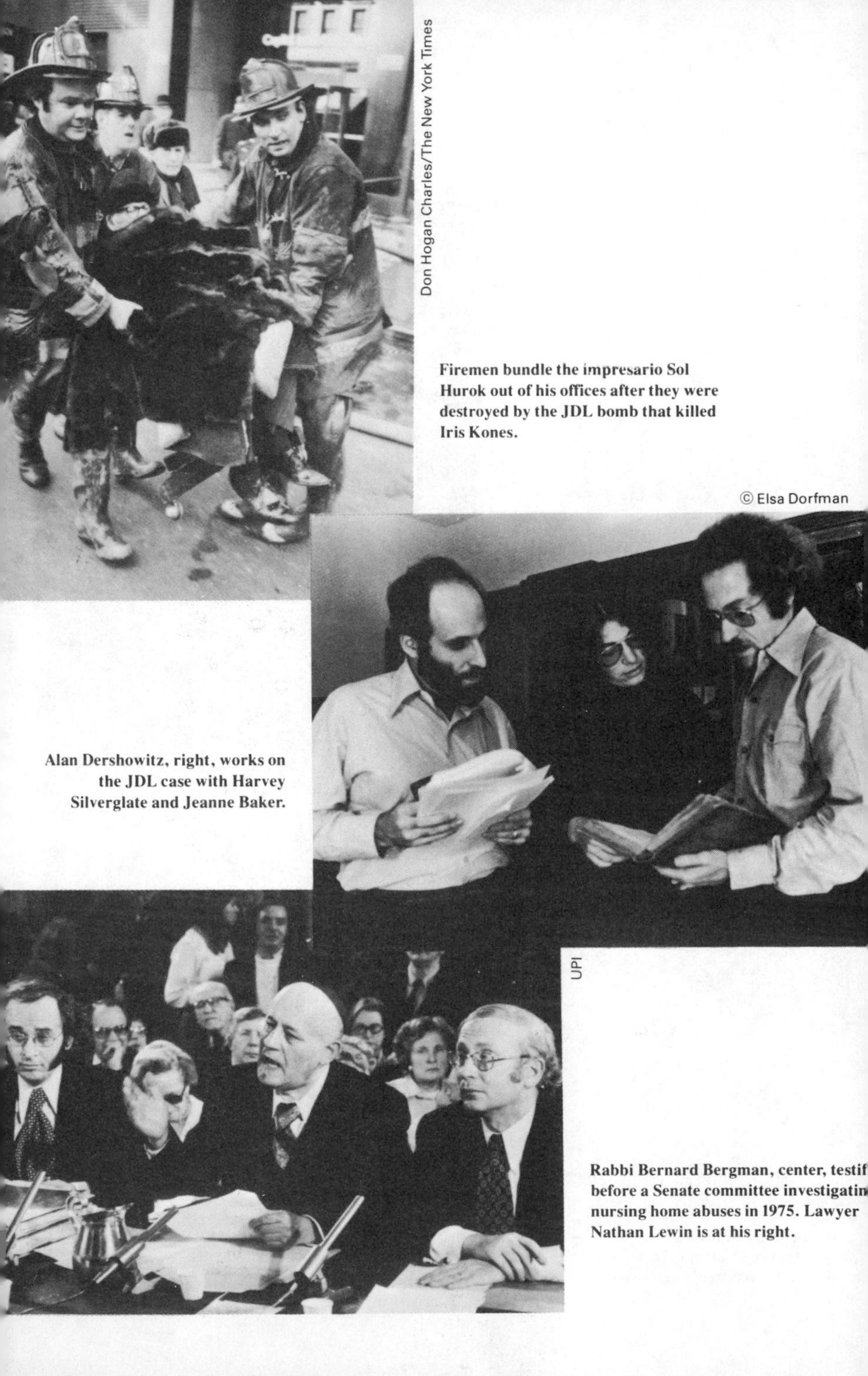

Firemen bundle the impresario Sol Hurok out of his offices after they were destroyed by the JDL bomb that killed Iris Kones.

Alan Dershowitz, right, works on the JDL case with Harvey Silverglate and Jeanne Baker.

Rabbi Bernard Bergman, center, testif before a Senate committee investigatin nursing home abuses in 1975. Lawyer Nathan Lewin is at his right.

James J. Kriegsmann

This inscribed photo of porn star Harry Reems hangs in Alan Dershowitz's office.

Rick Stafford

William F. Buckley and Alan Dershowitz debate the Harry Reems case at Harvard's Sanders Theatre.

Anthea Letsou

Feminists protest the showing of *Deep Throat* by the Harvard Quincy House Film Society in the spring of 1980. At center (in shirtsleeves), John Reinstein of the Massachusetts Civil Liberties Union talks to Dean Archie Epps of Harvard College.

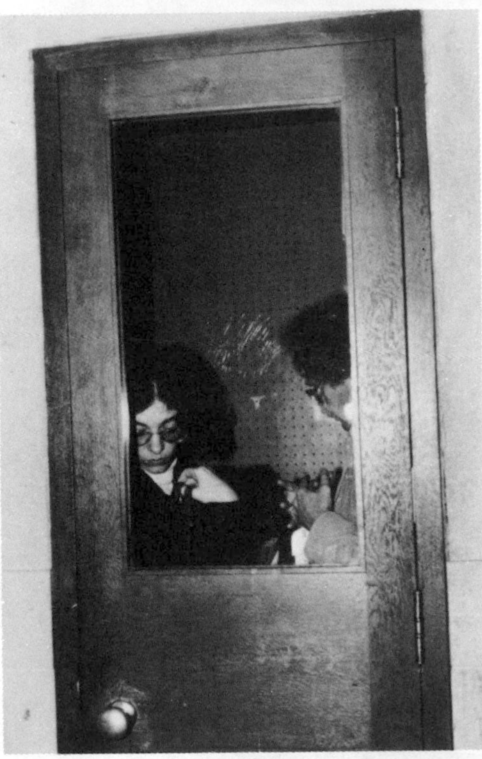

Anthea Letsou

Alan Dershowitz and Jeanne Baker huddle in a telephone booth as they attempt to secure a federal injunction against the arrest of the Harvard students for showing *Deep Throat*.

Anti-pornography activist Andrea Dworkin directs an obscene gesture at Alan Dershowitz during their debate at Harvard in 1981.

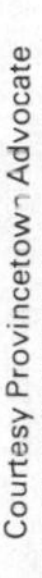
Courtesy Provincetown Advocate

Two rangers observe the "evidence" at the nude beach demonstration in the summer of 1975.

Sam Falk/The New York Times

Stanford professor H. Bruce Franklin in his Venceremos office.

Wide World

Former CIA agent Frank Snepp leaves federal court after a district court ruled that he must surrender all of his earnings from his book *Decent Interval*.

Yuma Daily Sun

Ricky and Raymond Tison on death row.

Wide World

Soviet dissident Anatoly Shcharansky shortly before his 1978 arrest on the charge of being an American spy.

Pamela Craig/National Law Journal

Edmund Rosner, after his release from prison.

UPI

Robert Leuci (right) and Treat Williams, who portrayed him in the film *Prince of the City*.

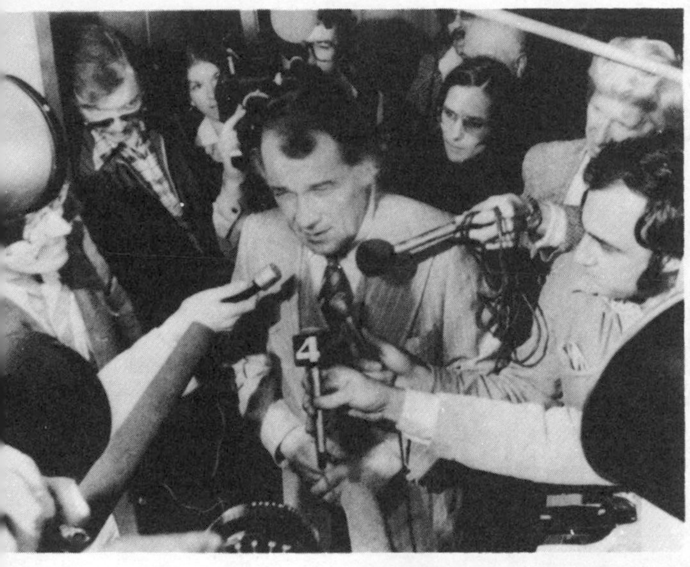

F. Lee Bailey, surrounded by reporters on his arrival at the Federal Building in San Francisco during the Patty Hearst trial in 1976.

Philip W. Smith/Courtesy New Jersey Network

Alan Dershowitz arguing before a panel of state chief justices in favor of the televising of all criminal trials.

> to be fundamental but includes the freedom to make and act on less significant personal decisions without arbitrary government interference.
>
> I have concluded that while it is a novel claim some measure of constitutional protection must be afforded the traditional practice of nude bathing at Brush Hollow.

Up to this point, the opinion was a victory. Judge Freedman was the first federal judge to hold that the right to go nude on an isolated beach was deserving of some constitutional protection. Acknowledging that this "would appear to be the furthest extension that this doctrine has heretofore seen," Judge Freedman then went on to balance the rights of the nudists against the power of the government to regulate the seashore.

He first discussed the nature of the crowding, parking, and environmental problems to which the challenged regulation was purportedly addressed. As we expected—indeed as we had acknowledged—he found them to be serious. He then considered the question of whether these problems could be solved by means short of a total ban on nudity, such as dune control and parking regulations. Judge Freedman agreed with our assessment:

> The Court agrees with plaintiffs that it may well be that each of the problems created by nude bathing could have been separately handled and perhaps successfully so.

Under our legal analysis, this would have required that he strike down the nudity ban as unconstitutional. After all, he had found that nudity in isolated areas was deserving of "some measure of constitutional protection," and he had also found that each of the external problems associated with the nude beach at High Dune "could have been separately handled" by regulations less restrictive than a total ban on nudity. But he then went on to weigh the importance of the liberty asserted—the right to go nude—against the problems that had been and would continue to be generated by allowing the activity to continue. He concluded that

> [w]hile the Court found some protection for the right asserted by plaintiffs, it appears clear that this narrow liberty has been outweighed by the considerations which led defendants to adopt the regulations.

The total ban on nudity was thus upheld in the context of compelling environmental and crowding problems. The decision was a loss for the nude bathers at Truro, but a victory—we were assured by the "movement" leaders—for the "free beach movement." Judge Freedman had written a

Magna Charta for skinny-dippers. By holding that nude bathing in isolated areas is entitled to some constitutional protection and that the government could prohibit it only by demonstrating external problems, the court had confirmed the legitimacy of nude bathing as such. The government could no longer ban it simply on moral grounds; it had to find other, external, justifications that outweighed the measure of constitutional protection to which nude bathing was entitled. We were assured that the decision would have substantial impact on the rights of nude bathers in uncrowded areas of national parks and on beaches, rivers, and streams in other parts of the country.

Naked Defiance

As news of the decision spread across the Cape, the nudity rangers escalated their enforcement. During the rest of the summer of 1975 there were numerous small confrontations and one major one. The leaders of the "free beach" committee spent most of the summer—apparently indoors—planning a massive "nude-in" demonstration for a Sunday in late August. Nostalgic veterans of the civil disobedience of Vietnam war days, they spent hundreds of hours on the logistics of this naked defiance.

I disagreed with the tactic, believing that civil disobedience should be reserved for the most compelling moral issues. But the Civil Liberties Union agreed to provide observers to protect against police abuses. (The number of volunteers for this observation duty exceeded that for any other demonstration in the fifty-year history of the Civil Liberties Union.) In the end there were no police abuses, as the Park Service wisely decided to let the demonstrators be. Several hundred committed nudists—accompanied by several dozen equally committed voyeurs and a few observers—descended upon the beach, careful to avoid trespassing or illegal parking. Some of the leaders, eager to avoid arrest, wore skin-tone bathing suits on which they painted pictures of their genitals. (Pictures, the courts have held, are more entitled to First Amendment protection than the real thing.) One of the men asked my advice about whether he could be charged with obscenity because of the painting on his suit. Upon viewing the size of the genitals he had painted, I advised him that obscenity was no problem, but he might get into trouble for fraud or false advertising. After a full day of undisturbed frolicking, several of the leaders who had dispensed with their suits were arrested in the parking lot by undercover rangers who had observed them in the buff. We defended them—some successfully on technicalities—but most of their cases were settled by paying the $25 fine.

During the spring of 1976 we prepared our appeal of Judge Freedman's order to the United States Court of Appeals for the First Circuit. I argued it on April 7, and in late July—after another half-summer of "hide-and-go-seek" and confrontations between rangers and nudists—the court of appeals rendered its decision. It echoed the conclusions of the district court in somewhat muted tones:

> We may assume for purposes of this case that appellants' interest in continuity in engaging in a pleasurable activity on public property must be afforded some measure of substantive constitutional protection.
>
> . . . Given this assumption, however, we have no doubt that the evidence presented below supports the district court's conclusion that the [government's] action was sufficiently justified . . .

We decided that the recent trend of Supreme Court opinions gave us little hope for success in that Court and refrained from seeking review. The legal battle for nudity on Cape Cod was over, and we had lost. But the guerrilla wars continued as committed nudists persisted in their defiance of the ban in increasingly ingenious ways.

The current status of nudity on the beaches of Truro can best be summarized by recalling a story from the 1920s. A British journalist asked an American what he thought about "prohibition." The American's answer expressed the attitude of many of his countrymen: "It's a hell of a lot better than no liquor at all." The total prohibition against nudity remains on the books and in force on the beaches of Truro. But to the many who continue to doff their suits, it's a hell of a lot better than no nudity at all.

6

The First Amendment and the Vietnam War: The Cases of the Stanford Stalinist and the CIA Whistle-Blower

If hard cases make bad law, as Oliver Wendell Holmes once said, then wars make even worse law. Some of the most dangerous precedents restricting basic freedoms have grown out of governmental efforts to curb opposition to wars. During the Civil War, President Lincoln suspended the writ of habeas corpus; during World World I, President Wilson authorized massive prosecution of peaceful draft opponents and political radicals; and during World War II, President Roosevelt ordered the roundup and detention of 110,000 Americans of Japanese descent. One of the terrible legacies of the Vietnam war—and one that may live beyond the painful memories of the war itself—is the toll it took on our First Amendment freedoms.

I was involved in several of the important First Amendment cases growing out of our disastrous experience in Vietnam, and I observed at close range the ravages of war on freedom of speech at home.

The first major Vietnam case was the conspiracy prosecution against Dr. Benjamin Spock, the Reverend William Sloan Coffin, and several other antiwar leaders. I played a consulting role in the defense of Dr. Spock and eventually wrote an article for the *New York Times* about the case.

The most publicized and notorious of Vietnam protest cases was the conspiracy prosecution against the "Chicago 7" growing out of demonstrations in Chicago during the 1968 Democratic Convention. After the trial of that case, the lead defense lawyer—William Kunstler—was held in contempt of court and sentenced to four years imprisonment. I was part of the legal team assembled to prepare the appeal of that contempt order.

Another major prosecution was against the Berrigan brothers and other radical leaders of the draft resistance movement. I was asked to work on the defense of that case, but was "fired" by one of the more militant defendants when he learned that I was a Zionist.

The release and publication of the Pentagon Papers in 1971 was perhaps the single most important event in turning American public opinion against the war. While the *New York Times* and the *Washington Post* were fighting in court to continue publishing portions of the Papers, Senator Mike Gravel of Alaska was taking more direct action: he convened an emergency night-time meeting of his subcommittee on Buildings and Grounds and placed the Papers in the public record. The "Gravel Edition" of the Pentagon Papers was then published by Beacon Press of Boston. I represented Beacon Press and, subsequently, Senator Gravel in litigation that eventually went to the United States Supreme Court.

The bitterness of the Vietnam war spread rapidly over college and university campuses. What began as peaceful teach-ins and protests soon turned to confrontation and violence. The Harvard strike of 1969 was followed by three years of continuous turmoil on that venerable campus, culminating in violent confrontations. These unhappy events led the university to attempt to suspend or dismiss numerous students. I represented several of these students against the university.

At Stanford University the leader of the antiwar group was a professor of English literature named Bruce Franklin. He was a Maoist, a Stalinist, and an advocate and practitioner of direct action. As a result of several speeches he gave and activities in which he participated, the Stanford administration decided to strip him of tenure and fire him. It was the first political firing of a tenured professor by a major university since the terrible days of McCarthyism. I took his case on behalf of the American Civil Liberties Union.

Finally, as the war was winding down and the United States was deciding to withdraw from Vietnam, the CIA was given a major role in overseeing the American evacuation. One of the highest ranking CIA agents in charge of the operation was Frank Snepp. Snepp wrote an uncensored account of his experiences—taking care, however, not to disclose any classified material. He refused to submit his manuscript for prior "approval" by the CIA, as required in his employment contract. When his book entitled *Decent Interval* was published the CIA sued him, and the case eventually was decided by the Supreme Court. I was one of his lawyers throughout the litigation.

The Vietnam war cases, many of which were decided against the claims of free speech, all raised troubling issues concerning the conflict between First Amendment values and the alleged demands of "national security" during a wartime situation. These issues are far more difficult than the First

Amendment issues raised by pornography and nude beaches. The stakes on both sides are considerably higher: political speech—such as opposition to the war or the draft—is closer to the core of the First Amendment than the kind of "sexual speech" typically involved in porn or nudity cases (though the line is sometimes fuzzy); and the demands of national security—such as the secrecy of agents or war plans—are more compelling than the claims of privacy, autonomy, and "morality" at stake in porn and nudity cases. It is not surprising, therefore, that these wartime First Amendment cases are among the hardest—and the most destructive of First Amendment liberties—that confront our courts.

This chapter tells the story of two of these cases: Stanford's firing of Bruce Franklin and the CIA's lawsuit against Frank Snepp. I have selected these because they raise the most fundamental issues of free speech in unusual contexts that have not been much discussed, and also because I was most deeply involved in them.

"This Is a Really Bad Guy . . ."

When I first began teaching at Harvard Law School in 1964, the Harvard campus was a sedate and somewhat insulated place. Most law school students lacked political fervor and passion. Neatly outfitted and conservative in their appearances, they seemed more interested in their clubs, sports, and careers than in the burning issues of the day.

By the late 1960s everything had changed. There was ferment in the air, especially over the escalating American involvement in Vietnam. In early April of 1969 the Harvard student strike took place. Beginning as a demonstration of opposition to ROTC at Harvard, it quickly spread into a generalized protest against the university's "complicity" in the war effort. Radical students seized University Hall—the main administrative center of the university—and were cleared by club-wielding police summoned by President Nathan Pusey. The campus was never the same after that.

Hostility and distrust were in evidence in the classroom; the threat of violence—or at least incivility—was ever present. The faculty was badly divided. The spirit of open-minded inquiry was absent. Political positions hardened on all sides. Harvard University was not a pleasant place to work or study. This is not to deny that the climate was electric and exciting. But it was also diverting. My memory of those years is filled with countless faculty meetings debating the appropriateness of various responses to the invasion of our sanctified tranquillity. Deans became arbitrators; university presidents became police chiefs; professors became prosecutors and defense attorneys.

My home phone was constantly ringing: a student was being arrested or disciplined; a professor was being shouted down in class; a dean was threatening inappropriate discipline. While throwing myself into the drama of these unfolding events, I sometimes longed nostalgically for the tranquil—if somewhat boring—atmosphere of my first few semesters at Harvard.

While all this was going on I received word that I had been recommended for a one-year fellowship at the Center for Advanced Study in the Behavioral Sciences, on the Stanford University campus in Palo Alto, California. No place could have seemed more distant—both in the location and atmosphere—from the frenzy of the Harvard campus. Situated atop a lovely hill overlooking Lake Lagunitas, the "Stanford Think Tank"—as it was sometimes called—consisted of a series of interconnected wood-frame bungalows. Each fellow got a room with a serene view, some secretarial and research assistance, and a great deal of privacy and isolation. Telephones were not permitted in the rooms, and outside activities were discouraged. The purpose of the fellowship was to stimulate reflection, research, writing, and intellectual exchange among the fellows. Forty are selected each year from a large pool of applicants and recommendees. The "class" of 1971–1972 included such distinguished academics as psychoanalyst Bruno Bettelheim, sociologist Nathan Glazer, philosopher Robert Nozick, psychologist Gardner Linzey, educator Lawrence Cremin, and political theorist Michael Walzer. Generally one law professor is included every year, and I was thrilled to be the one selected for that class. I looked forward to the splendid isolation of a telephoneless, studentless, and clientless year of intellectualizing and volleyball (the recreational pastime of the fellows).

I arrived in Palo Alto on a Sunday night in early September of 1971. I didn't set my alarm clock for the next morning: sleeping a bit late was to be one of my sabbatical luxuries. But at seven-thirty I was awakened by the ringing of my telephone. The shrill voice on the other end of the phone—not at all what I expected from the stereotypical "mellowed out" Californian—declared: "I have to talk to you about the Franklin case." The last thing I wanted to talk to anybody about, especially at that hour of the morning, was another case. Wasn't I entitled to ignore—for just one year—the often exaggerated claims of "injustice" about which every litigant moans? And what better place to pretend that all was well with the world than in the hills of Palo Alto.

"What case? Who's Bruce Franklin and what is he charged with?" I asked, vaguely recalling the name, but associating it with one of the numerous city plus number combinations in the news every day. (The Seattle 7, the Chicago 7, the Cantonsville 9, and other such combinations had become so much a part of the current vocabulary that when I heard a passing reference to the Indianapolis 500, the first image conjured up was of a massive conspiracy rather than of an auto race.)

"You mean you don't know about the Franklin case? He's the Stanford English professor—with tenure—who's being fired. We need help, and Leonard Boudin told us that you might be willing to assist us, and so we are calling you immediately."

They sure did. I hadn't even been to my new office yet. I explained that this was my sabbatical year and I just couldn't get involved. "Why don't you call some of the professors at the Stanford Law School," I suggested hopefully, pointing out that a number of them were famous for their involvement in civil liberties and academic freedom causes.

The caller—who described herself as a member of the faculty political-action group—laughed. "They're the enemy. We can't get any help from the law school. President Lyman's got them all sewed up. The few young teachers who agree with us are scared to speak up."

"Why don't you have Franklin's lawyer call me," I proposed—hoping to get off the hook. "I'll be happy to discuss the issues with him."

"That's just the problem," she responded. "Franklin doesn't have a lawyer. He had a lawyer earlier, but now he's run out of money and the university won't pay for one. He tried to get a law professor to help but there aren't any volunteers."

I told her that I could not believe that Stanford would actually subject a tenured faculty member to dismissal without making some provision for counsel—or, at the very least, without some faculty member of the law school volunteering to serve as his advocate.

She replied, "You really are new here. After a few days nothing will surprise you about the Franklin case."

I agreed to have lunch with her and two other members of her group, after again making it quite clear that I could not be counted on for anything beyond that meeting.

The Franklin case came up again in conversation the next day. I ran into a new neighbor who was a former colleague on the Stanford law faculty—I had taught there for the summer term five years earlier—and I asked him about the case. "You have to understand, this isn't a civil liberties case; it doesn't really involve academic freedom. This is a really bad guy who trains Chicanos in the hills to shoot guns. He's the head of an organization called Venceremos that plants bombs on campus. Why, just a few weeks ago a bomb went off right near here"—pointing a few blocks away—"in the faculty ghetto." (The "faculty ghetto" is the name given to the area of the campus where faculty and administrators live in lovely houses built on land leased to them by Stanford.) "Franklin's turned this place into a jungle. He also uses his classroom for political purposes," my friend continued. "You know what the students call his course in Melville and Hawthorne?" Without waiting for me to guess, my friend answered his own question. " 'Maoville and Ho-thorne.' He's not a professor. He's a political organizer and a terrorist."

"Well, that's certainly different from what I was led to believe by that woman who called me," I said. "He definitely should be fired if they can prove he did those things, especially the violence."

"He's not exactly charged with those things," my friend said, a bit apologetically. "He's very careful never to get caught doing anything violent. He sneaks around the campus giving orders to kids and local Chicanos over a walkie-talkie; he's never there when the violence takes place. But we've finally got him. He made a couple of speeches inciting violence and we can prove that. He also tried to shout down Henry Cabot Lodge when he spoke at Dinklespeil Auditorium."

"Then it really is a free-speech case," I countered. "The only actual charges against him relate to speeches he gave and some shouting."

"That's true," the Stanford professor acknowledged, "if you look at the case in its narrow sense."

"What about the counsel issue?" I asked.

My friend responded: "He doesn't want a lawyer. He wants to represent himself so he can make political speeches at the hearing. If he wanted a lawyer he could get a dozen without any problem."

It came as something of a surprise, therefore, when Bruce Franklin called me on the phone a few days later and asked me whether I would be willing to represent him at the hearings. He told me that he did want to make a political defense, but that he also wanted a lawyer to present the First Amendment and other legal arguments. I told him that my commitment to the Center precluded me from being his lawyer. He said he understood, but asked me if I would agree to meet with him for an hour to discuss the counsel issue. I went to his house accompanied by Joel Klein, now a prominent Washington lawyer, but then a young man who had just graduated from Harvard Law School and was spending the year at the Center as my research assistant. We spent half an hour looking for Franklin's house on a dark street of small lower-middle-class bungalows near downtown Palo Alto. (There was no address plate on his house, we later learned, because he had been subjected to harassment by his neighbors.) When we finally found the house and rang the bell we could hear a number of locks being opened. Franklin appeared in the open door dressed in a blue workers' shirt. He looked around suspiciously, let us in, and quickly locked the door.

"Never know when the pigs"—he pronounced it with a stereotyped black accent that made it sound like "peegs"—"are gonna try and bust in again. We almost had a shoot-out a few weeks ago."

My feeling of fear quickly gave way to one of disgust when I saw a large poster of Stalin hanging in his living room. (Anybody who works in a university has seen posters of Mao Tse-tung, Lenin, and Marx, but I had never seen a poster of Stalin before. In my naïveté I had not even realized that there were any remaining Stalinists around.)

I started the conversation—rudely, I guess—by announcing that next to Hitler I regarded Stalin as the most evil person who had walked the earth during my lifetime. Franklin accused me of being brainwashed into believing those lies that had been spread about Stalin in the American press, and he assured me that before he was through with me I, too, would be a Stalinist. I advised him not to waste his time and to get down to the subject of our meeting. We talked for about fifteen minutes. He played me some tapes of the speeches that formed the basis for the charges against him, and we briefly discussed whether those speeches might be protected under the First Amendment. He then asked again whether I would represent him. I reiterated that I could not, and we went back to debating the merits and demerits of Stalinism for another fifteen minutes. The discussion ended with neither of us changing our views. As I left he handed me two books—the red book of Chairman Mao's quotations and the collected writings of Lin Piao. He asked me for a couple of dollars for the books, whereupon I returned them. He then told me I could have them as the "fee" for my consultation.

Klein drove me home. I later learned that he returned to Franklin's house and continued to discuss the problem of obtaining a lawyer. After some consideration of alternatives, Klein—who was not yet a member of the bar—agreed that he would assist Franklin in preparing legal arguments and briefs before the hearing committee. That was the closest Franklin would come to getting a lawyer to help him defend against the charges brought by Stanford.

I started my research at the Center, and the experience proved to be all that it had promised. In the adjoining cabin was Bruno Bettelheim, the brilliant student of Freud, who had revolutionized the psychoanalytic treatment of autistic children and had written several classics in the field. During his year at the Center, Bruno was writing a book about his school for emotionally disturbed children, which was published under the title *A Home for the Heart.* Since I had done considerable work on the legal issues growing out of hospitalization of the mentally ill, we conferred often on his book and on my work. Bruno and his charming wife brought a bit of prewar Vienna with them wherever they went: at four o'clock on most days, Mrs.

Bettelheim would arrive at Bruno's cabin at the Center with a silver tea service and an assortment of cakes and crumpets. Frequently they would invite me to join them in their repast and reminiscences.

I was working on a long study of the origins of preventative detention —confining people on the basis of predictions of what they might do in the future—in English and American law. Every day I would come to my cabin, look out on the scenery, read for several hours, confer with my research assistant, eat lunch with my colleagues, play a few games of volleyball (social scientists versus "real" scientists was the usual division), and write for a few more hours. Then I would go for a swim, either in the ocean at nearby Santa Cruz or in the pool that came with my house. It was idyllic and even productive.

But I couldn't escape the Franklin case. Bruce would drop in on me at the Center; his supporters would be waiting for me when I got home; outsiders from around the country called and wrote me about the threat to academic freedom that was raised by the proposed firing. The case was in the papers every day, and the debate was becoming more and more acrimonious and polemical.

Bruce Franklin had genuinely shaken the tranquil atmosphere of Stanford. In the eyes of every administrator and most faculty members, he had come to symbolize the difficult years that Stanford—along with other universities—had experienced in the late sixties and early seventies. Stanford, like most rural universities, was unprepared for the radicalism of this period, since radicalism had not had any real history on the immaculately manicured lawns and palm groves of this most beautiful of American campuses. "The Harvard of the West," Stanford University had been a symbol of wealthy California conservatism. Until World War II, it had been a bastion of racism, but then it had opened up and recruited a superb faculty from around the country, especially from Ivy League schools. In order to entice that faculty, it had offered unparalleled material inducements in the form of free land and subsidized housing on the lovely campus. As a result of this cozy arrangement the private and professional lives of the faculty were closely merged with the university. When there were protests, demonstrations, or trashings directed against Stanford, they were felt directly, and personally, by the faculty—especially by the large number of senior faculty who lived on the campus.

Between 1967 and 1971 the Stanford campus experienced what one professor characterized as "something like a reign of terror." Trashing had produced $250,000 worth of damage; arson had destroyed irreplaceable documents; fire bombs and bullets had marred the tranquillity and safety of the faculty haven. The invisible specter of Bruce Franklin—campus revolutionary—was ever present. He was regarded as the moving spirit behind the violence, though he could never be placed at the scene of any crimes. He was Beelzebub incarnate in the devil theory that many invoked to explain this phenomenon, so uncharacteristic of the Stanford campus.

I thoroughly disagreed with Bruce Franklin's politics and disapproved of his methods. I also disliked him as a person, despite (perhaps because of) our common background. We were about the same age and we were both from lower-middle-class Brooklyn families. He, like me, was the first member of his family to finish college. Having enrolled in ROTC as an Amherst student, he enlisted in the Air Force and served for three years as a squadron intelligence officer in the Strategic Air Command. (The incongruous image of Bruce flying a nuclear bomber while reading the works of Mao and Stalin still occasionally pops into my head.) Following that stint he attended graduate school at Stanford, where he received a Ph.D. in English and was asked to remain as an assistant professor. His politics at that time were liberal and democratic; he supported Adlai Stevenson and Lyndon Johnson.

Like many other liberal academics Franklin became radicalized by the Vietnam war. The process was intensified by a year in Paris, where he came under the influence of some Viet Cong intellectuals. He returned to Stanford as a full-fledged revolutionary committed to the armed struggle. He and his equally radical wife, Jane, founded an organization they named The Peninsula Red Guard; it eventually merged with an offshoot of a radical Chicano organization called the Brown Berets, and became the Venceremos ("we shall overcome"). The Venceremos was a violent revolutionary organization, whose official manifesto called for armed struggle and required its members to keep weapons (M-1 rifles were recommended).

Franklin vehemently denied any personal participation in violent activities, but he proudly boasted of his membership on the central committee of Venceremos and of his ownership of several weapons. His involvement —indeed his leadership role—in armed revolutionary organizations caused him to be feared and despised by his academic colleagues, especially since one of the favorite targets of the revolutionaries was Stanford University. As the Vietnam War escalated so did Franklin's activities. When Henry Cabot Lodge came to speak at Stanford in January of 1971, he was shouted down with cries of "pig" and "war criminal," and then drowned out by continuous chanting and clapping. Eventually, the program had to be canceled (just as a similar program had been canceled several years earlier at Harvard). Franklin participated in the shouting but denied complicity in the chanting and clapping that brought the program to an untimely end.

Following this incident, Franklin received a letter from Stanford President Richard Lyman informing him that he would be suspended for one quarter without pay. Franklin's response to President Lyman began as follows:

> To the Chief Designated Agent of the Board of Trustees of Leland Stanford Junior University, Heirs of the Family Who Stole This Land and the Labor of Those Who Built Their Railroad, War Profiteers and Rulers of the U.S. Empire.

It was signed:

> In the spirit of Nguyen Van Troi/Power to the people!/Bruce Franklin/Central Committee/Venceremos.

(Nguyen Van Troi was a Viet Cong guerrilla who had attempted to assassinate Defense Secretary McNamara in Saigon during the Kennedy administration.)

Several weeks later Franklin spoke at an antiwar rally directed against the Stanford Computation Center, which was involved in war-related research. His speech included the following: "[W]hat we're asking is for people to make that little tiny gesture to show that we're willing to inconvenience ourselves a little bit and to begin to shut down the most obvious machinery of war, such as—and I think it is a good target—that Computation Center." Following shouts of "Right on," a group of listeners marched on the Computation Center and physically shut it down, causing some damage. Franklin did not join the demonstrators himself; he watched from a safe and discreet distance. The police eventually cleared the building and ordered the demonstrators to disperse. At this point Franklin joined the crowd and protested the order. He walked up to the police, argued with them that the dispersal order was illegal, and urged the crowd to remain. Many did, and the police used force to effect their order. Minor injuries were sustained by some demonstrators.

Later that night a rally was held on the campus at which Franklin gave the closing speech. In it he advocated "the methods of people's war." There was some dispute about whether he explained what he meant by this term. He claimed that he told the demonstrators that "people's war meant that they should go back to the dormitories, organize people into small groups, and talk with them, or play football, or whatever, as late into the night as possible." Within a few hours of Franklin's speech there was more violence and this time several people were seriously hurt.

The next day President Lyman announced that Professor Franklin would be fired from his tenured position on grounds of "substantial and manifest neglect of duty and a substantial impairment of his appropriate functions within the University community."

Franklin demanded a formal hearing, and a faculty advisory committee of seven full professors was convened to consider the charges and recommend an appropriate sanction. It was difficult to find seven professors who did not despise Franklin—and with good cause.

Though charming in a superficial way, Bruce Franklin was, in my view, an obnoxious and closed-minded fanatic for whom the world was neatly divided into good and evil. Everything capitalistic or American was evil, and everything Marxist, Stalinist, or Maoist was good. He refused to criticize the Soviets or the Chinese for their suppression of dissent or for their barbaric judicial systems. He refused to acknowledge any virtues in the American system—even including those constitutional safeguards on which he was relying for his defense.

Franklin's total commitment to the party line can perhaps be illustrated by an incident that took place a few months after he presented me with the little red volumes of the wisdom of Mao Tse-tung and Lin Piao. Franklin appeared at my door demanding the return of the latter volume: "Lin Piao has been officially discredited. I am under instructions to retrieve and destroy all volumes of his work."

I laughed and said that I wouldn't participate in any book burnings; the volume was now mine and I intended to keep it. I joked that if he succeeded in retrieving and burning the other remaining copies then mine might someday become a valuable collector's item.

Bruce did not laugh: "I must retrieve the volume," he insisted.

"I'm sorry," I replied, equally adamant, "you can't have back my copy."

Bruce grew intense: "I will get it back, even if I have to take it from you."

At this point, anxious to avoid a confrontation, I told Bruce that I couldn't find it and that it probably had been thrown out. That seemed to satisfy him.

"This Isn't a Civil Liberties Case at All"

My serene days at the Center continued for several weeks after my arrival. I really wanted to stay out of the case, especially in light of my dislike for Franklin and his methods. I was hoping that the university would come up with hard evidence that Franklin had personally engaged in violence so that he could be fired without relying on his speeches and statements. But as time went on two facts became disturbingly clear: Franklin was being fired for his speeches; and Franklin could not get a lawyer from the Stanford community—or anywhere else, for that matter—to defend him at the hearing.

Having just completed three tense years at Harvard during which numerous agitators and radicals had been disciplined, I reflected on the differences between Harvard and Stanford. At Harvard, the administration made scrupulous efforts to assure that students were represented. To be sure, I had been criticized by a few colleagues for providing some of that representation, but I was allowed to assume that role. At Stanford, not a single law professor was prepared to become Franklin's advocate. The university hired a team of first-rate outside lawyers at enormous expense to prosecute Franklin. But it refused Franklin's request for a modest sum of money to enable him to retain an outside lawyer. I was disturbed at the prospect of a tenured professor being prosecuted for his speeches by a team of well-paid lawyers and being denied the means to have a single lawyer or law professor assist him in the complex issues of fact and constitutional law presented by his case.

The requests for me to represent Franklin persisted, as did my refusals. Finally, in a desperate attempt to pass the case off to someone else, I called the American Civil Liberties Union in San Francisco and told them about the case. They had been aware of it but had not gotten involved. I sensed some reluctance to take on Stanford, and that got me even angrier. I had served on the National Board of Directors of the ACLU for several years before coming to Stanford, and I believed strongly in the principles for which that organization stood. The former president of the San Francisco chapter of the ACLU was a Stanford law professor and he had lobbied hard to keep the organization out of the Franklin case. I called the professor and he gave me his views: "This isn't a civil liberties case at all. It's a contract case. Franklin broke his contract."

I asked him which provision of his contract denied him the right to make First Amendment speeches.

He responded that the speeches were not protected by the First Amendment and he threw out a challenge: "I was president of the ACLU chapter and I know its philosophy. I bet there aren't two people on the board of that organization who believe that this is a civil liberties case."

I accepted his challenge: "Let's debate it in front of the board members and let them decide."

He agreed and a meeting was convened in San Francisco. After each of us presented our views the board voted: all but one member agreed with me that it was a civil liberties case and that the speeches were protected by the First Amendment. I was asked to file a brief with the faculty committee setting out the ACLU's views on the legal issues. I decided that I could perform that function consistent with my commitment to the Center and I secured permission of the Director of the Center to file the brief.

Word quickly spread around the Stanford campus that I had gotten the ACLU into the case. I was criticized for my intrusion into the affairs of my host university. President Lyman went on the radio to attack me:

> It is a myth that all speech is constitutionally protected. No constitutional lawyer in the land—no, not even Mr. Dershowitz, the Harvard law professor come to Stanford to save us all from sin—not even Mr. Dershowitz could make such a sweeping claim.

I responded with my own statement in the *Stanford Daily:*

> There are important civil liberties issues at stake in the Franklin firing. If Dr. Lyman wants to challenge my views of the Constitution or civil liberties—and those of the American Civil Liberties Union—I invite that challenge, on its merits.

Lyman rejected my invitation to debate and continued to attack me—both personally and through his surrogates—in highly personal terms. The hostility toward me and toward the ACLU spread quickly among the established faculty. Not surprisingly, it soon reached the Faculty Committee that was considering the Franklin case.

Initially, the Committee refused to accept any input from the ACLU, either in the form of an oral presentation or a brief. Eventually, it permitted us to file a brief, amicus curiae (or more accurately "friend of the committee"). I assumed the responsibility for writing it. Much to their credit, two Stanford law professors—John Kaplan and Paul Brest—eventually joined me in signing the brief. The brief that we wrote was anything but a radical document. It began by presenting the ACLU's traditional position on "fair warning": "No person should be subject to discipline for having engaged in conduct, unless that conduct was proscribed by clear rules available to him at the time he engaged in it." It emphasized that fair warning is particularly important in speech cases:

> [W]here a speech component is involved, a calculating person has the right to go . . . up the line; and he must be told—in advance of his conduct—precisely where that line is. The line may not be drawn—or discovered—after the activity has been completed.

The brief then proceeded to analyze each of the charges against Franklin. It began with the shouting down of Henry Cabot Lodge. Not surprisingly, the ACLU vigorously disagreed with Franklin's contention that there is a "right" to silence a speaker who is deemed to be a "war criminal":

> [I]f the Board concludes that Professor Franklin intentionally engaged in concerted activity designed to silence Ambassador Lodge—that is, to prevent him from speaking at all—then it is the Civil Liberties Union's position that some discipline would be appropriate.

It defended, however, Franklin's right to heckle, boo, and express displeasure at the speaker or disagreement with his views. If members of the audience may cheer and applaud approval, they must also have a coextensive right to demonstrate disapproval:

> The rule of thumb [is] that the speaker's entire address must be allowed to be heard, but it may be frequently interrupted, so long as he is permitted to continue a short time after each interruption. This rule does not make for the most comfortable or effective oratory, but the American Civil Liberties Union believes it to be the constitutionally required balance . . .

Turning to Franklin's speeches prior to the afternoon occupation of the Computation Center and the evening violence on the campus, the ACLU argued that the speeches themselves were protected by the First Amendment, since they did not urge immediate, violent action.

Finally, the brief considered Franklin's actions and statements in front of the Computation Center after the police had ordered the crowd to disperse: it argued that a speaker has a constitutional right to argue with a policeman about his order to disperse. He also has the right to urge others to disobey the order if he—in good faith—believes that the order was unlawful. The only exception would be a situation where the speaker's urging "creates a clear and present danger of serious bodily harm." We concluded therefore that only if

> the evidence establishes that Franklin incited persons to immediate violence against the persons of the police, then such incitement could well constitute a clear and present danger.

The brief was anything but a radical document; it simply articulated the traditional positions of the ACLU and asked the Committee to apply them to the facts of the Franklin case. It also urged the university to apply the standards of the First Amendment and not hide behind the defense that because Stanford is a private university, the Constitution has no applicability to its actions. It took no position on the facts. Nor did it advocate a particular result.

The hearing itself followed predictable lines. The university's team of excellent attorneys presented its case in a low-keyed, lawyerlike manner. Franklin used the hearing as a platform for his politics and for polemics. As the attorney for the ACLU, I attended several of the hearing sessions. There was one table for Franklin's side and one table for Stanford's side. Franklin had decorated his table with posters of various revolutionary leaders, including Stalin. Since the ACLU was on Franklin's side, Bruce invited me to sit at his table. I told him that I would be uncomfortable sitting at a table with a poster of Stalin. He wouldn't take it down so I sat apart from him at my own table. One day I brought two of my own posters and set them up at my table before the hearing began. My posters also bore the last names of his revolutionary heroes, but their first names and faces were different: my Marx was Groucho and my Lennon was John. Of course I had no intention of keeping these innocuous pictures on my desk during the hearing; I had brought them as an attempt at humor. But Bruce didn't find my pictures funny at all. He castigated me for mocking his heroes and warned me that my conduct would never be tolerated in a true socialist democracy.

Within a few weeks after the close of the hearings, the Advisory Board rendered its one-hundred-and-sixty-eight-page decision. It followed the ACLU's guidelines in assessing Franklin's role in the shouting down of Henry Cabot Lodge and concluded that there was no evidence that Franklin had prevented Lodge from speaking.

Moving to Franklin's speech prior to the occupation of the Computation Center, the Board found that

> Professor Franklin did intentionally incite and urge persons at the White Plaza rally to occupy the Computation Center illegally.

The Board also sustained the charges relating to the police dispersal order, finding that

> Franklin did intentionally urge and incite others to disobey the order to disperse, thereby increasing the danger of arrest or injury to those present.

Finally, the Board rejected the ACLU position in regard to the evening speeches:

> The Board is strongly persuaded that Professor Franklin intentionally urged and incited his audience to engage in conduct which would disrupt activities of the University community and threaten injury to individuals and property, . . .

Then, in a move that surprised a great many observers, the Board, in a 5 to 2 vote, concluded that Franklin should be fired immediately. It had been widely believed, even by Franklin's most vociferous critics, that some form of compromise sanction—suspension, probation, or deprivation of some salary—would be proposed. But the Board rejected these lesser sanctions. President Lyman and the Stanford Trustees immediately implemented the Board's decision and Franklin was sent packing.

"The Franklin Era Is Over"

But that was not the last of Bruce Franklin at Stanford. His response to his firing was predictable. He convened a press conference at Venceremos headquarters in Palo Alto. As he spoke, his wife stood beside him carrying an M-1 carbine. Bruce rejected the verdict of the "liberal fascists" on the Board and called for a violent response: "I don't think anything would be going too far. I certainly don't think the people on the Advisory Board should be allowed to keep teaching their classes." Franklin vowed to continue the fight against the Stanford "fascists" from outside, threatening to employ the techniques of guerrilla warfare.

But effective guerrilla warfare requires support from within, and Franklin could not have been encouraged by the reaction to his firing among Stanford students and faculty. The mood on the campus was described by the *New York Times* as "apathetic" and "mild." There was one small rally and some threats of trashing, but the students and professors returned to their studies without incident. Bruce Franklin's influence on the Stanford campus—whatever it might have been earlier—had diminished to insignificance. In the words of one Stanford professor:

> The Franklin era at Stanford is over. The apologist for violence at the University is gone . . . The memory of that era, with its trashing, its arson, and its physical injury will remain in the minds of Stanford faculty members.

Following the Franklin firing I gave a lecture on the implications of the case. I predicted that Franklin himself would soon be forgotten because his message would be rejected in the free marketplace of ideas. But the Committee's decision would be long remembered as a leading precedent in the jurisprudence of universities. I criticized the decision for failing to draw the critical distinctions between "advocacy," which is protected under the First Amendment, and "incitement," which may not be. I explained that

> Advocacy is the communication of ideas; it is directed at intellect; it affords the listener an opportunity to reflect on it. Incitement, on the other hand, . . . is a spur to automatic action, intended to bypass the rational thought processes. It is against this oversimplified background that the classic case of shouting fire in a crowded theater can best be understood. Shouting the word "fire" is not the communication of an idea designed for reflective thought; it is precisely the same as if a fire *bell* were intentionally rung. It is intended to spur an automatic series of responses.

The Board, I argued, confused these concepts by defining incitement to include advocacy.

I concluded my lecture by pointing an accusing finger at some of the faculty who pretended that the Franklin case raised no important civil liberties issues:

> How often have I heard the absurd remark that Franklin is being fired for what he "did," not for what he "said," without a recognition that this quibble doesn't hide the fact what he "did" was to make speeches. How often I have heard the statement that this case does not involve "academic freedom," it is simply an employer firing an employee for disloyalty—as if a requirement of loyalty and academic freedom were compatible. [T]he true test of a genuine civil libertarian is how he responds to a crisis close at hand.

The Franklin case—or at least this phase of it—was over. Other phases continued, including a lawsuit brought by Franklin in the California courts. (As of this writing—more than a decade after the firing—that suit has still not been resolved.) I continued my work at the Center and paid little attention to the daily concerns of the Stanford campus. One issue did, however, attract my attention.

"Such a Course Will Never be Taught at Stanford"

Among Stanford's faculty was an extremely controversial professor named William Shockley, who had won a Nobel Prize in Physics in 1956 for his work on transistors. For several years Shockley had been doing research and writing in the area of genetics. He had published several controversial articles claiming that blacks tended to be less intelligent than whites. Not surprisingly these obnoxious conclusions were greeted with derision and refutation by most respected geneticists. They were also met with calls for censorship by some scientists and by many students. The radical left at Stanford—including Bruce Franklin—took the position that Shockley's views should not be heard on the Stanford campus. Shockley's lectures on genetics were frequently interrupted and canceled, and even his classes on physics were occasionally disrupted by hostile students.

During my year at the Center the issue came to a head. Shockley proposed to offer a special graduate elective on "Dysgenics: New Research Methodology on Human Behavioral Genetics and Racial Differences." The campus immediately erupted. "Such a course will never be taught at Stanford," said a student leader of the radical left.

After much controversy a five-member faculty advisory committee was assigned the task of recommending whether Shockley's course should be permitted to be taught at Stanford University. They studied the issues for three months and advised that the course be authorized on a one-shot basis and without credit. Despite this, the Dean of the Graduate School refused to authorize the course.

Many of the Stanford left, which had been critical of Franklin's firing, were delighted at the Shockley decision. Some of the Stanford right, which had welcomed the Franklin firing, were upset at the Shockley decision. Most centrists supported the university on both decisions. Almost nobody was critical of both decisions.

I viewed the Dean's decision in the Shockley case as the opposite side of the Franklin coin: each had denied academic freedom to a controversial and extremist advocate of obnoxious views.

At first I decided to remain silent on the Shockley issue. My involvement in the Franklin case had been disruptive to my work and had created real tensions between me and my former colleagues at the Stanford Law School. I followed the controversy with interest, but said nothing publicly about it. But after the Dean's decision to overrule the faculty committee—and after no public criticism of it—I wrote an article for the *Stanford Daily* arguing that the university had completed the cycle of repression by denying academic freedom to a reactionary just a few months after denying academic freedom to a radical:

> I suppose there are some who regard this as somehow symmetrical and as proving that Stanford is indeed neutral on the pressing issues of the day. I regard the twin decisions in the Shockley and Franklin cases as a sad commentary on the state of free speech and academic freedom at Stanford. . . . It has once again taken the easy way out, in the Shockley case by capitulating to the censors of the radical left just as it capitulated to the censors of the moderate middle and the reactionary right in the Franklin case. The real tragedy is that at Stanford there seems to be no pressure group for freedom

> of speech and academic inquiry for those of all spheres of political opinion.

The reaction to my letter was swift. The first voices to be heard were the ever-present defenders of the university. Donald Kennedy, the chairman of the faculty committee that disciplined Franklin, echoed President Lyman's *ad hominem* attacks on me, instead of addressing the merits:

> The latest sermon from Professor Dershowitz convinces one that President Lyman understated the matter when he described the author as having been "sent from Harvard to save us from sin." [P]oor Dershowitz, peering owlishly down from his balcony at the Center, has mistaken Lake Lagunitas for the Sea of Galilee.
>
> [Dershowitz] should return [to Harvard] and offer courses in a department outside the Law School. . . . I first considered the Department of Philosophy, but decided that Dershowitz' colleagues there might find his view of Ethics a little foreign. So I have decided to recommend that Professor Dershowitz offer instruction in thoracic surgery at the Harvard Medical School. Dershowitz—whatever the state of his medical knowledge—is surely well prepared for the malpractice suits that will follow.

I said that I would respond to Kennedy when and if he addressed the issues instead of engaging in *ad hominem* attacks on me. But I couldn't resist pointing out that I had, in fact, been teaching seminars at Harvard Medical School—without a medical degree and without any malpractice suits.

A far better answer came from Robert Nozick, a professor of philosophy at Harvard, who was also at the Center that year:

> Donald Kennedy, in his heavy-handed attempt to ridicule Alan Dershowitz, says that if Prof. Dershowitz proposed to give a course on ethics under general university auspices, his colleagues in the Philosophy Department at Harvard who teach ethics would protest. We wouldn't.

Nozick argued that Shockley's alleged lack of credentials was merely a pretense to justify censorship of the conclusions he was supporting: if a professor with identical credentials had wanted to teach a course espousing the intellectual *equality* of the races—Nozick asked—would he not be allowed to do so? Finally Nozick pointed out that

> the general nastiness of the public Stanford reaction to Prof. Dershowitz's statements on the Franklin and Shockley cases does little to

refute his charge that Stanford is inhospitable to serious dissent from its general consensus.

I had succeeded, at least, in generating some debate among the complacent Stanford faculty about the Shockley case. For the next several weeks the pages of the *Stanford Daily* were full of discussion, letters, and statements about the case. But to no avail. Neither Shockley nor Franklin was able to present his controversial views in the Stanford classroom, at least while I was there. Stanford returned to its tranquil past as disrupters, dissidents, and disloyalists—of the right, the left, and even the civil liberties centrists—were made to feel unwelcome among its gently swaying palms.

Toward the close of my year at the Center, a reporter for the *Stanford Daily* wrote an article about the Franklin and Shockley cases that concluded with a characterization of which I was proud:

> But through his spirited, albeit controversial defenses of Franklin and Prof. William Shockley and his well-publicized exchanges with Lyman and his advisers, Dershowitz has filled a position that has seldom been occupied at Stanford in recent years—University Gadfly.

At the conclusion of the 1972 academic year I returned to Harvard. Since my return I have taken on the Harvard administration in many controversies, but I have never been as personally attacked as I was at Stanford.

Bruce Franklin continued his revolutionary ways and eventually was arrested for harboring a fugitive sought for murder. He is now teaching literature at Rutgers University in New Brunswick, New Jersey. Professor Shockley is still preaching his divisive gospel of racial inferiority. Richard Lyman has left the Presidency of Stanford and has taken over as head of the Rockefeller Foundation. Lyman's replacement at Stanford, not surprisingly, is Donald Kennedy.

The Suing (and Screwing) of the CIA Whistle-Blower

On November 20, 1977, millions of Americans watched Mike Wallace interview former CIA agent Frank Snepp on *60 Minutes*. The interview was extraordinary for several reasons: it had been conducted at a secret location protected by considerable security; there had been no advance public announcement of it; and the interview comprised two-thirds of the entire program, rather than just a segment.

During the program Snepp told of his transformation from a loyal CIA agent to an internal critic of the agency and then to a public exposer of CIA corruption, treachery, ineptitude, and ingratitude. He described how the

CIA had abandoned its friends in its rush to "bug out" of a dangerous situation:

SNEPP: We left behind on the tarmac or outside the walls of the Embassy 400 to 500 members of the Saigon Special Police Force. We had trained them; they were in imminent jeopardy from the Communists. We also left behind about 400 to 1,200 members of the CIO—the Central Intelligence Organization. We'd also trained them. We also left behind about 30,000 people who had worked for the Phoenix Program.

WALLACE: The Phoenix Program being—?

SNEPP: [T]he counter-terrorist operation mounted against the Communists during the mid-1960s under CIA direction.

WALLACE: You describe all of this leaving behind [as] a "callous act of betrayal on the part of the CIA"?

SNEPP: In some cases betrayal was involved. We saved the people in the white skin. We left behind the Vietnamese.

WALLACE: You say in your book that [intelligence] files . . . were left behind.

SNEPP: That's correct. When the North Vietnamese rolled into Saigon [they] found these files intact. If an experienced counter-intelligence operative . . . put all this data together, he could begin to develop a picture of how the United States operates in a crisis—and this is strategic intelligence any way you cut it.

WALLACE: What you are painting, Mr. Snepp, is a picture of an absolute CIA botch at the end in Vietnam.

SNEPP: It was a failure of leadership.

Wallace questioned Snepp about his "oath" not to reveal any information he had obtained as a CIA agent without prior clearance from the agency:

WALLACE: You signed an oath that you would not go public.

SNEPP: That's right.

WALLACE: Do you really think the CIA does not know how far this has gone, and the fact that you are talking to us?

SNEPP: I think if they did, Mike, I would have been enjoined. I think that they would have gotten a court order to silence me. [I]f the agency were operating in its bad old ways, monitoring telephones, surveilling people illegally, I wouldn't have gotten this far.

The CIA was furious with Snepp for having defied its authority by writing and speaking about his observations in Vietnam without prior clearance. There was talk that he might be prosecuted.

A few weeks after the *60 Minutes* interview Frank Snepp asked me whether I would consider representing him. There was no case yet, but that is often when a person most needs legal counsel. I agreed and we arranged to meet.

When we met a few days later at his publisher's office, I was surprised at Frank Snepp's appearance. He looked like a model for a CIA recruitment poster: quietly handsome in a West Point way, polite almost to a fault (he even called *me* "sir"), fiercely loyal to his country, and discreetly careful not to reveal too much. What was his sin? He hadn't published or otherwise disclosed any classified material that had not already been released or leaked. His criticisms of "The Company" were far from radical. Indeed, his book *Decent Interval* was like its author in several ways: graceful; low-keyed; brimming with information; cautious in its revelations—and, on the whole, a bit boring.

But in publishing his book Snepp had not gone by their book: he had deliberately refused to submit his manuscript to the agency for prior approval and possible censorship. This brought down the wrath of the CIA on his head. The CIA took the position that no individual agent could determine whether specific information might safely be released. Only the agency could make that determination after reviewing everything the agent intended to publish. Accordingly, each agent was required to sign a secrecy oath obliging him to submit all such material for prior censorship.

Although the CIA is supposed to excise only material whose disclosure would endanger the national security, it employs its power of censorship to protect the agency from political embarrassment. For example, it censored the following from a book published in 1974: "[the] otherwise flawless performance [of CIA Director Richard Helms] was marred only by his mispronunciation of Malagasy when referring to the young republic [which used to be called Madagascar]." It also censored such "secrets" as the following: "The Chilean election was scheduled for the following September, and Allende, a declared Marxist, was one of the principal candidates." "Henry Kissinger [was] the single most powerful man at the 40 Committee meeting on Chile." These are only a few examples that have come to light. Other censored "secrets" still remain under wraps.

Snepp was aware of the CIA policy of censoring embarrassing material whose disclosure would not endanger the national defense. Though his book contained nothing classified that had not already been made public, he feared that the censors would suppress his embarrassing evaluation of the CIA's inept performance during the evacuation of Saigon. He refused, therefore, to submit the book for clearance.

Eventually, after some internal disagreement within the Justice Department during the Carter Administration, the government decided not to prosecute Snepp criminally but rather to sue him in order to prevent him from publishing further material about the CIA without prior approval, and to force him to turn over to the government all the money he had earned from *Decent Interval.* Since Frank had worked full time on the book for eighteen months, that meant that if the government were to win, the former CIA agent would be deprived of all the money he had worked for over this period. The total came to more than $100,000.

My role in the case was to be Frank's personal lawyer: to make sure that his interests were not subordinated to the important First Amendment interests presented by the case. (As it turned out, it was Frank who constantly urged his lawyers to place the civil liberties concerns above his personal ones, even though he was threatened with literal impoverishment.) The case was defended in court by an excellent team of American Civil Liberties Union lawyers, headed by Mark Lynch. A Washington lawyer and an expert in national security law, Lynch assumed primary responsibility for the gathering of evidence and for the courtroom presentations. I helped write the briefs and advised the defense.

The case was tried in the Virginia Federal Court—the district in which the CIA is headquartered—before a crotchety old judge named Oren Lewis. (We had demanded a jury trial, but he had denied it.) "Roarin' Oren," as he was called by the local Virginia lawyers, was ranked by lawyers interviewed for the *American Lawyer* as the worst federal judge in the entire Fourth Circuit in which he sits. Lewis' verdict was a foregone conclusion. At the beginning of the trial he told Snepp's lawyers that he was certain they would be appealing his decision. "I won't disappoint you," he quipped, and then proceeded to describe the route to the court of appeals. "If you don't know how to get down to Richmond, I–95, go south." The trial itself was a mockery. When Mark Lynch respectfully sought to introduce evidence showing that the CIA had not sued other CIA officials who had published *favorable* books about the agency disclosing classified material without prior clearance, Judge Lewis asked incredulously, "You're not serious?" and then ruled that "this is not a First Amendment case." On more than twenty occasions when Lynch asked government witnesses questions, the judge ruled "objection sustained." The only problem was that nobody—neither the government lawyers nor the witness—had *made* any objection. Judge Lewis was sustaining his own objections!

After a heated trial Lewis ruled that Snepp had violated his fiduciary obligation to the CIA by deliberately publishing his book without submitting it for prior censorship. The government was entitled, therefore, to all of the author's earnings on the book. Judge Lewis also issued an injunction against any further violation of the secrecy agreement and required—on pain of criminal contempt—that Snepp submit all further manuscripts to the CIA for prior censorship.

Snepp did appeal to the Fourth Circuit in Richmond and won a partial victory. The court of appeals ruled that it was improper for the district court to take away all of the author's earnings, since it had not been proved that he had "breached a fiduciary duty." If the government wanted to collect any damages in excess of nominal damages—if it sought compensatory or punitive ones—then there would have to be a jury trial.

The situation thus remained in an uncomfortable limbo: the government had won its major theoretical point, since the court of appeals ruled that the CIA contract prevailed over Snepp's First Amendment right to publish a book without submitting it for prior censorship; but Snepp had won an important practical victory, since he could not be forced to give up his earnings unless the government was prepared to go through the cumbersome process of a jury trial.

Frank Snepp was faced with an existential dilemma of the first order. If he was to seek Supreme Court review he risked upsetting this compromise and losing everything. If he decided to forego Supreme Court review he could probably keep his earnings, but he would be giving up the civil liberties principle for which he had risked so much—the right to publish without prior submission. (We were given to believe that if Frank did not seek Supreme Court review the government would also forego such review and would probably not undertake a jury trial.) Prudence dictated accepting the uncomfortable compromise. Principle dictated seeking Supreme Court review. I outlined all the risks to Snepp. It was a decision only he could make.

Snepp, who by this time had become a world-class amateur constitutional lawyer, understood everything. He did not have to ponder long. He decided to go for broke (quite literally), and to seek Supreme Court review of the court of appeals' compromise.

Now the story becomes truly bizarre—if a bit complicated. We submitted a petition for certiorari, seeking discretionary review by the Supreme Court. In our petition we challenged the decisions of both lower courts that the CIA's requirement of prior censorship was lawful. We urged the Supreme Court to review these decisions and to reject the view that the CIA contract requiring prior submission of all manuscripts by ex-agents (a contract which had never even been authorized by Congress) prevailed over a citizen's First Amendment right to publish without prior censorship. This important issue had never been squarely faced by the Supreme Court, and we felt that this was a good case to present to the Justices, since the government had conceded that Snepp had not published any classified or secret information.

In accordance with the Supreme Court rules and practices we submitted a very short petition for certiorari—15 pages. Its purpose was simply to advise the Court of the importance of the issues and to ask it to permit us to file briefs and present oral arguments on the merits of our contentions. Since it was clear that the First Amendment issues were important—indeed fundamental—there was no need to belabor the obvious. There would be sufficient opportunity to present our arguments on the merits of the case if and when the Supreme Court granted certiorari, thus accepting the case for full review.

The government took an interesting tack in response to our petition. It filed two separate documents. The first was a brief *in opposition* to our request for review. In it the government argued that the court of appeals' decision was essentially correct and that no further review was required. The second document was a *conditional* cross-petition for certiorari by the government. In this rather unusual document the government reiterated its primary contention that the Supreme Court should deny further review of the court of appeals' decision because—in its words—"the contract remedy provided by the court of appeals appears to be sufficient in this case to protect the agency's interest." But, it argued, if Snepp's petition for review *was to be granted,* then the government would *also* seek review of the court of appeals' decision and would argue that the court of appeals had erred in reversing the district court decision awarding the government all of Snepp's earnings from the book.

While these petitions and conditional cross-petitions were pending before the Supreme Court, another publishing event was occurring that would—according to many observers—have a decisive impact on the Supreme Court's attitude toward the Snepp case.

In December of 1979 Bob Woodward and Scott Armstrong published an exposé of the Supreme Court entitled *The Brethren.* The main sources for this embarrassing revelation—embarrassing particularly to the Chief Justice who was characterized as stupid, corrupt, malicious, and inept—were the law clerks. By tradition, if not by implicit contract, they were thought to owe an obligation of discretion and confidentiality to the Justices for whom they worked. The Chief Justice was reportedly in a rage about this breach of trust. The publication of *The Brethren* was the talk of the legal profession and—not surprisingly—of the Supreme Court at precisely the time when the Justices were considering the applications for review in the Snepp case. The unprecedented manner in which they handled the Snepp petitions can only be understood against this background.

Every Monday—Monday is the usual decision day in the Supreme Court—we would call the clerk's office to inquire whether the Justices had decided to grant our petition and hear the case. We kept being told that no decision had yet been reached. And then on Tuesday, February 19, 1980 (Monday had been Washington's Birthday), we received the startling news that the Supreme Court had decided not to hear the case or permit us to file briefs—but that it had *decided the case on its merits, without argument or briefing.* Moreover, it had granted the government's conditional cross-petition for certiorari and had reversed the decision of the court of appeals on the money issue. Thus, without giving us a chance to argue or present briefs, the Supreme Court had ruled—in a 6 to 3 decision—that Snepp must turn over to the government all of his earnings on *Decent Interval.*

The Court's unsigned majority opinion was as cryptic as it was vague. It cited no legal precedents in its nine pages of text (and only a few cases in its eleven footnotes). It relegated our First Amendment argument to a footnote, saying that "even in the absence of an express agreement—the CIA could have acted to protect substantial governmental interests by imposing reasonable restrictions on employee activities that in other contexts might be protected by the First Amendment." It decided that the remedy given to the agency by the court of appeals—the remedy that the government in its petition had said was "sufficient to protect the agency's interest"—was not sufficient. In other words, the Supreme Court gave the government *more* than it said it needed. The government had been satisfied with half a loaf, but the Supreme Court had given it a loaf and a half.

No case better illustrates the hypocrisy of "conservative" judges who claim to be adherents of "judicial restraint" and opponents of "judicial activism." The Snepp case is a paradigm of judicial activism: Congress had declined to enact a statute prohibiting the kind of disclosure at issue in the Snepp case or granting the government the power to seize the earnings of an author who had made such disclosures. Moreover, the government was satisfied with the court of appeals' decision denying it the remedy of a constructive trust. Notwithstanding this, the Supreme Court—led by the "conservative" adherents of "judicial restraint"—reached out and gave the government more than Congress had given it and more than it had requested. So much for judicial restraint!

The bottom line was that Frank would have to turn over to the government all of his earnings on *Decent Interval* even though he had not published any classified information or revealed any CIA secrets that had not previously been disclosed by other "authorized" sources. Other former government employees who had written *favorable* books about their agencies or departments—such as Henry Kissinger—would be allowed to keep their profits even though they had revealed classified or secret material and had not submitted their manuscripts for review.* Moreover, Snepp was now under a lifelong injunction—enforceable by contempt—to submit all future writings of whatever kind to the CIA for pre-publication review and censorship. All in all, it was among the most dangerous, far-reaching, and important decisions ever rendered by the Supreme Court in the area of free speech—and it was done without the benefit of briefs or oral arguments. Snepp's name has become part of the legal lexicon: lawyers now characterize a litigant who has gotten short shrift from the Supreme Court as having been "snepped."

The public reaction to the Snepp decision was quick and critical. Anthony Lewis of the *New York Times* wrote that the Supreme Court's constructive trust theory was so far-reaching that it could apply to hundreds of thousands of government employees. "[T]here is genuine reason for alarm," he concluded, "when the Court hands down a decision as uninformed and unconsidered as that in *Snepp* v. *United States* . . . ." Nat Hentoff observed that "no court decision in American history has so imperiled whistle-blowers and, thereby, the ability of all citizens to find out about rampant ineptitude and corruption in agencies purportedly serving them."

Shortly after the decision a symposium was held in New York on its implications. The panelists were Mike Wallace; Anthony Lapham, the former General Counsel of the CIA; and me. Wallace observed that:

> Frank is a friend of mine but I disagree with him on his breaking of the contract. It seems to me a contract is binding and [if] you engage in an act of civil disobedience, then you pay the penalty for engaging in an act of civil disobedience.
>
> Of course, Martin Luther King didn't have to serve a life sentence for his act of civil disobedience. Frank Snepp . . . had every dollar he made from the book taken away from him.

Lapham presented the CIA perspective:

> These obligations—not to disclose classified information acquired in the course of employment, and to give the CIA an opportunity to review the manuscripts in advance of publication—come with the turf. Were they not to exist, the CIA would be out of business. . . .

*The CIA recently took the position that its former director, William Colby, had breached the agreement inadvertently by neglecting to omit certain censored material from the French edition of his book.

This decision may to some modest degree cut down the access of the press to former government employees who are willing to trade national secrets for dollars. That's no great loss in my opinion.

I suggested how the Supreme Court's reasoning might have applied several years earlier when Woodward and Bernstein were writing their books about the Nixon Administration:

If the secret informant "Deep Throat" was a government employee in a position of trust (as he obviously must have been), and if Woodward and Bernstein knew this (as they obviously must have), then the government might be entitled to the profits of Woodward and Bernstein, the *Washington Post,* the motion picture company that made the film, etc., etc., etc.

During the course of the discussion, in attempting to present the "parade of horribles" that could conceivably flow from the Supreme Court decision, I raised the hypothetical example of "a poem written by Frank Snepp—an ode to the trees in Vietnam" and wondered out loud whether the injunction would apply to works of fiction. Before long, that hypothetical came to pass.

After the decision Frank began work on a novel about the assassination of President Kennedy (Snepp was twenty years old when that tragedy occurred). The CIA took the position that even this kind of fictional work had to be submitted to censorship. Under the CIA interpretation of the agreement, Snepp could not show a rough draft of his novel to his own editor without first submitting it to the CIA. Frank was appalled, but he had no choice. He did, however, have the right to express his feelings in the uncensored letter he sent accompanying his fictional manuscript:

Who would have imagined it could happen in this country? Certainly not the framers of our Constitution who conceived the First Amendment as a bulwark against the . . . pre-licensing that had been used to suppress unpopular speech and writing in seventeenth-century England. In those days the benighted writer had but one way to circumvent the strictures the government imposed on him. He wrote in parables. . . . But you have done the British censors of yesteryear one better. You in effect are claiming the right to screen and eviscerate *even* the parables. How far we've come. . . .

[Y]ou are dealing with a novel here. The only "irreparable harm" it could possibly do is to inflict boredom on a reader who has the right to expect better for the tariff.

The CIA rejected Snepp's position and had the novel read by its censor. Eventually it was cleared with no changes.

"The Fatigue of Supporting Freedom"

The conflict between national security and free expression is a real one. It must be confronted and resolved by every society committed to civil liberties yet concerned for its safety. In this respect, the situation is different from the alleged conflicts that motivate the censorship of supposedly obscene material: in most obscenity cases, the "conflict" is contrived and need not exist at all. There is ample room in a diverse and free society for accommodating the desires of those who get pleasure from porn and those who feel the need to be protected from the intrusion of offensive material. The guiding principle that "your right to swing your fist ends at the tip of my nose" suggests a workable approach to the regulation of merely offensive material. But there is no simple rule for the accommodation of free expression and national security, where the expression may expose our security to real danger.

There are, however, some useful guidelines. In the first place, the vast majority of *claims* that the national security will be endangered by free expression are simply not true; most such claims are probably not even believed by the government officials who assert them. The talismanic phrase "national security" is often invoked as a transparent cover for convenience, for political advantage, and for protection from personal or political embarrassment. Every claim of national security—or "corporate security" or "university security" or the security of any institution—should be subject to rigorous challenge, in an effort to separate the contrived from the authentic. But this will not eliminate all conflict. There will be some cases of real and intractable conflict between security and freedom. Our Constitution purports to resolve doubts in favor of freedom, but there are cases where even that presumption will not resolve the problem: where the authentic claims of national security will seem to outweigh the presumption of free expression.

In those cases we need to develop adequate mechanisms for resolving the dispute. Resolution cannot be left entirely in the hands of those responsible for security, such as the executive or the military. Our experience in delegating decision-making authority to these institutions in times of crisis is discouraging.

It has been indeed fortunate for the survival of our liberties that there have always been some Americans—often only a small group and sometimes not those directly affected—willing to challenge governmental high-handedness, even during periods of crisis. Under our constitutional system, it takes only a single person challenging the government to create a case or controversy suitable for judicial resolution.

This is not to suggest that justice should remain blind to the existence of a real emergency endangering the survival of the nation. As former Justice Arthur Goldberg once wrote: "While the Constitution protects against the invasion of individual rights, it is not a suicide pact." But it is precisely during times of crisis, when the balance between momentary expediency and enduring safeguards often goes askew, that courts can perform their most critical function: to preserve or restore a sense of perspective.

In the eternal struggle between liberty and security we have come to expect the executive and legislative branches to champion the latter. The judiciary—with its lifetime tenure, its tradition of independence, and its unique stewardship over our irrepealable rights—is the institution most able to resist the passing fears and passions of a dangerous moment.

But liberty is not a commodity that can be obtained once and for all, and then passively held on to. The battle for civil liberties, as Roger Baldwin, the late founder of the ACLU, liked to say, "never stays won." It must be endured by every new generation and in each new crisis. What Thomas Paine taught us on the eve of our own Revolution remains true today: "Those who expect to reap the blessings of freedom must . . . undergo the fatigue of supporting it."

—7—

An American Lawyer in the Soviet Court System

During the early stages of the Jewish Defense League murder case, in the fall of 1972, the defense lawyers and defendants frequently went to lunch together at New York's famous kosher delicatessen Shmulka Bernstein's. Shmulka must have been sympathetic to the defendants because I don't remember ever seeing a check for the meals. While attempting to digest the peppery Rumanian pastrami, we would be harangued by JDL zealots, including their leader Meir Kahane and his deputy Bert Zweibon, about the plight of Jews in the Soviet Union: "They're being annihilated, spiritually and physically. And what are you fancy liberals doing about it? Nothing, that's what! You're no different from the American Jews who stood by silently while six million of your brothers and sisters were being gassed by the Nazis."

It was hard enough to digest Shmulka's pastrami without those incessant lectures—but with them, I suffered from continuous afternoon heartburn during the case. Maybe that's why I tended to become more contentious during the afternoon sessions. Buddy Hackett, who had also lived in Boro Park, once joked that it was only after eating bland army food for several weeks that he realized that the constant fire in his stomach was not a natural and permanent condition.

These lectures began to have an effect on more than my stomach; they reached my gut. Some of my own family—like many American-Jewish families—had emigrated from what is currently the Soviet Union. I wondered what I would now be doing if they had not had the foresight to leave. Would I be a dissident follower of Andrei Sakharov? Would I be a "refusenik" Jew, seeking to emigrate to Israel or the United States? Or would I be one of the silent millions? As I thought about these alternatives I began to feel a bond with Soviet dissidents. There but for the grace of God, and the foresight of my great-grandparents, go I.

But I also realized that the Jewish Defense League's way was not my way. I abhor violence, especially against innocent targets. Bullets for balalaikas, bombs for ballerinas, ammonia cans for pianists, and a horrible, if unintended, death for Iris Kones—these were as abhorrent to me as the Soviet repression of its citizens. There had to be another way. As I listened to Rabbi Meir Kahane's sermons on Jewish violence, I began to consider alternate approaches to defending Jewish rights in the Soviet Union. I began to talk to some lawyer friends about creating a legal project to defend Soviet dissidents.

A case that had attracted worldwide attention and was the focal point of JDL protest had grown out of the futile attempt by fourteen Jews and two non-Jews who had been refused permission to emigrate to commandeer a small commercial airplane and fly it to Sweden. The plot was discovered by Soviet authorities and the group was arrested, tried, and convicted. Although no one was hurt, two of the Jewish leaders were sentenced to death. An international uproar ensued.

The Soviet Jewry Legal Defense Project

As we were discussing legal tactics to defend these Soviet prisoners, another group of New York lawyers was considering a similar idea. We soon joined forces and established a Soviet Jewry Legal Defense Project, whose purpose was to provide legal assistance for these prisoners of conscience.

It was one thing to write briefs and make arguments, but quite another to get the Soviet authorities to read them and listen to us. I was reminded of the old joke about the Soviet loyalist who brags to his skeptical friend that the Communist Party's scientists have developed a miraculous technique for talking to a dead person. "Sure," responds the skeptic, "they can *talk* to him, but will he *listen?*"

We decided to try to enlist the assistance of an American lawyer whom we believed the Soviet legal authorities would listen to: Professor Telford Taylor of the Columbia Law School. Before becoming a distinguished professor of constitutional and criminal law, Taylor had been the American chief counsel for war crimes at Nuremberg. In prosecuting Nazi war criminals, he had worked closely with two Soviet lawyers: Roman A. Rudenko, who was the Soviet Chief Prosecutor, and Lev N. Smirnov, who had been a senior member of Rudenko's staff. Rudenko had then become Procurator General of the Soviet Union (the equivalent of our Attorney General) and a member of the Politburo. Smirnov had become the President of the Soviet

Supreme Court. Taylor's Soviet associates had emerged as two of the most influential lawyers in the Soviet legal system.

After Nuremberg, Telford Taylor had also achieved renown and distinction, but of a different kind. He had become the conscience of the American legal community. Active in every facet of the human rights and civil liberties movements, he personified the highest tradition of even-handedness and compliance with the international rule of law. During the American involvement in Vietnam he had written an influential book entitled *Nuremberg and Vietnam: An American Tragedy.* He was respected and beloved throughout the civilized world.

I met Telford Taylor while I was a student at Yale Law School, where he was teaching several seminars. He became a role model for me. I took all of his courses and I hoped that someday I could work for him or with him. Now the opportunity to become colleagues was at hand. Taylor agreed to become the head of our Soviet legal project, provided that I would agree to supervise the legal research and brief-writing.

Our first step would be to obtain as much background information as we could from the available witnesses. We learned that many—including the spouses and children of several of the defendants—had emigrated to Israel, so we decided to go there to see them.

In the course of an intensive week of interviewing in several Israeli cities, we managed to question most of the relatives and friends of the imprisoned Soviet defendants, as well as six former Soviet prisoners who had been tried, convicted, and imprisoned with our defendants.

The interviews were emotional, often tearful, as we were told about midnight arrests, closed trials, and abusive prison conditions. It was difficult to comprehend the desperation that would drive men and women to take the actions they did, actions that almost ensured their arrest and long imprisonment. Relatives of the defendants and some of the "conspirators" themselves—wives and daughters who had not been tried—told of the events that led up to the futile attempt to commandeer the airplane at Leningrad in June of 1970.

"We Have an Experienced Pilot"

The story began in 1969 when a forty-two-year-old Jewish pilot named Mark Dymshitz met a thirty-eight-year-old Jewish activist named Hillel Butman. Dymshitz, a member of the Communist Party, was employed as an engineer in Leningrad, having been unable to work as a pilot because he was Jewish. Butman, a lawyer and engineer, was a leading figure in the Leningrad Jewish community, conducting classes in Jewish history, language, and culture. Dymshitz desperately wanted to live in Israel, where he could be a pilot. But he could not get an emigration permit from the Soviet authorities. Butman was also anxious to emigrate, but his efforts, too, had been unsuccessful. Hundreds of other Jews had applied for visas and had also been refused. These Jews were collectively referred to as "refuseniks."

Dymshitz began to concoct a series of harebrained schemes to get out of Russia. He thought about constructing a hot-air balloon or a glider to carry him over the border. Then he decided it would be more feasible to try to hijack a Soviet TU-124 airliner along its route between Leningrad and Murmansk, and to pilot it to Sweden, where he could seek asylum and eventual transit to Israel. Dymshitz proposed this idea to Butman and two other Jewish activists from Leningrad. Their first response—quite understandably—was enthusiasm born of the frustration of repeated failures to achieve their goal by lawful means. It seemed the only way out.

Butman knew several members of another group of Jewish refuseniks from the Latvian coastal city of Riga. This group included Eduard Kuznetsov and his recent bride Silva Zalmanson. Kuznetsov, an intense intellectual, had a long history of dissident activities dating back to his school years. He had helped to edit three of the earliest *samizdat* (underground) publications of the democratic movement in the early 1960s: *Syntax, Boomerang,* and *Phoenix.* By the age of twenty-two, Kuznetsov had become actively involved in criticism of the Soviet regime. This landed him in prison for seven years on charges of "anti-Soviet activities." While in prison, he experienced repeated difficulties for his "attitude." His early confrontations with the law had nothing to do with Jewish issues. Indeed, his passport did not even list him as a Jew, since his mother was a non-Jew and changed the family name from the Jewish "Gerson" to the Russian "Kuznetsov" after Eduard's father had died. It was not until two months before his release from his first imprisonment that he applied to the prison governor to be registered as a Jew. It was the first time the authorities recalled being asked by a half-Jew to change his status *from* Russian *to* Jewish; they were used to the opposite request, and he was turned down.

After his marriage to Silva Zalmanson, Eduard's involvement in Jewish causes increased. The young couple, and several of Silva's relatives, all sought permission to emigrate to Israel. Not only were they denied permission but they were subjected to continuous harassment, humiliation, and provocation. Eduard described some of what he experienced in his prison diary:

> Someone will say the word "Israel" and make an obscene gesture. How people split their sides whenever they hear the old joke, "Jews

> leaving for Israel, your train will depart from the *northern station*!" [the direction of Siberia.]
>
> What do you do when you are everywhere so blatantly humiliated? You can wait year after year—which many people do—living in your suitcase and . . . then receive answers [informing you that] you have no grounds for permission to emigrate.

This was the plight of the refusenik, a person without a homeland, living in suspended animation, waiting for some denouement—either exodus or imprisonment.

It was Hillel Butman who first broached the idea of escape to Kuznetsov and his wife. They were walking together through the forest in Rumbula, where the Nazis, aided by local anti-Semites, murdered 25,000 Jewish citizens of Riga in 1941. They approached the modest stone placed on the execution site by several young Jewish militants in 1963. The Jews of Riga often took the bus to Rumbula just to walk among its tragic memories and reflect. The discussion between Butman and Kuznetsov turned to the futility of making further applications to emigrate. They agreed that there was no chance that the Jewish emigration movement could succeed unless something dramatic took place. Butman proposed a mass hunger strike, one that would go on for a year. Kuznetsov, always the cynic, countered that "we could always burn our dearly beloved mothers-in-law in Red Square as a sign of protest."

Something different was needed—something that would express the deep despair of the refuseniks. It would have to be a dramatic action by a group of people united in desperation and prepared to suffer greatly in order to "break the dam through which many others will pass." They walked on, looking around to make sure they were alone, and then Butman whispered, "We have an experienced pilot." Eduard and Silva could hardly believe what they were hearing. Butman filled in the details. Kuznetsov raised questions: "How many in the group?" "Can they all be trusted?"

They looked back in the direction of the forest beneath which rested thousands of Jewish martyrs who had not escaped. "Here of all places," Kuznetsov said softly, realizing the fateful decision had been made. As soon as Eduard and Silva glimpsed the possibility of a future in a land free from the slavery of anti-Semitism, there was no turning back. They accepted Butman's offer to join the group, and then Eduard invited two non-Jewish dissident friends, Alexei Murzhenko and Yuri Fedorov, who had served prison sentences with him for anti-Soviet activities, to accompany them. The plan was code-named "Wedding," since the group boarding the plane would pretend to be traveling to a friend's marriage ceremony.

But soon Butman and the Leningrad group began to have second thoughts about Dymshitz's plan. They decided to seek the opinion of Israeli authorities. A coded letter was written and addressed to a Soviet emigrant who had recently arrived in Israel. The Israeli authorities disapproved the plan. A phone call was made from Tel Aviv to Butman with the following message: "Hillel, I visited your uncle Dr. Shimon Butman, and consulted him. He gave the following prescription: 'The medicine can do harm.' " (The initials of Butman's fictional "uncle"—S.B.—are the initials of the Israeli intelligence service, the Shin Bet.) After learning of the Israeli disapproval, the Leningrad contingent backed out of the plot and tried to convince the others to call it off, fearing that it might endanger the cause of Jewish emigration.

Dymshitz told Butman that the hijack plan would be canceled. And it was. After riding in the cockpit of a TU-124, Dymshitz decided that it was too large and complicated an aircraft for him to pilot alone. He decided, therefore, to call off the plan. Butman and his Leningrad friends were pleased to hear of the cancellation and went back to their business of Jewish education.

But Dymshitz concocted another escape plan about which he did not tell the Leningrad group. It involved a smaller, more manageable airplane and it did not include any midair hijacking. Instead, it contemplated commandeering a small twelve-passenger AN-2 aircraft. The plan was for the Kuznetsov group to purchase all twelve tickets on the Leningrad-Priozersk flight. When the plane landed at Priozersk—a small city forty miles from the Finnish border—the passengers were to subdue the two-man crew with a fake pistol and a homemade "knuckleduster" and leave them on the ground without endangering their lives. No one would be injured, so the Soviets would have no excuse to demand extradition of the escapees. (Only political crimes, not crimes of violence, are exempt from extradition under the Swedish-Soviet treaty.) After picking up four additional passengers on the tarmac of the Priozersk Airport, the overweight plane, piloted by Dymshitz, would be flown over the Finnish border and on to Sweden. There the emigrants would request asylum (and ask that the plane be returned to the Soviet Union).

One of the passengers, Josif Mendelevich, drafted a "last will and testament" to be made public only if all the plotters died. Since they had estimated their chances of success at less than five percent, it was, in effect, a suicide note. It began by quoting an appropriate verse from the prophet Zechariah: ". . . flee from the land of the north . . . escape, daughter of Zion dwelling in Babylon." Then it continued:

> By our action we want to draw the attention of the leaders of the Soviet government to . . . the endless tragic situation of Jews in the USSR, and to declare to them that it is in their own interests to let our people go home.
>
> Jews of the world! It is your holy duty to struggle for the freedom of your brothers in the USSR. Know that, to a great extent, the fate of the Jews of Russia—to be or not to be—depends on you.

Unbeknownst to the plotters, the Soviet authorities were aware of the plan. On June 15, 1970—the day of the escape—the KGB conducted a well-coordinated roundup of Jewish activists. Those who had bought the twelve seats for the flight were picked up before they boarded the airplane; those who were to board at Priozersk were arrested even earlier. Butman, who was not even aware of the most recent plot, was arrested while vacationing at a seaside resort with his four-year-old daughter; several other Jewish leaders were seized in Leningrad. On the same day, the KGB conducted searches of Jewish homes in Leningrad, Moscow, Riga, and elsewhere. A legal pogrom had begun. It would spread to other cities and towns over the next few days, as KGB agents burst into the homes of virtually every Jewish leader in Russia, Moldavia, the Ukraine, and Latvia. The entire Jewish leadership of several major cities was arrested, held incommunicado, and charged with a Zionist conspiracy.

"They Should All Be Hanged"

The first Leningrad trial—involving those caught in the act—might have been a straightforward, conventional, criminal prosecution: the defendants would surely have been convicted of unlawfully attempting to leave the country and of improper use of state property—crimes punishable by relatively short sentences. Instead, most were charged with treason and theft of valuable government property—crimes that carried the maximum punishment of *execution.*

The trial was theater: the prosecutors, judges, and defense attorneys reading from their scripts; the defendants making ringing pronouncements of their faith and hopes. Most of the three hundred seats in the courtroom were packed with KGB cheerleaders who, on cue, would shout "They should all be hanged!" and similar epithets. Several of the defendants' relatives were allowed in the courtroom, and one surreptitiously recorded some of the trial.

Since Soviet defendants are held incommunicado during the pretrial investigation, there was no opportunity for them to confer and plan a coordinated defense. Each of the defendants (with one exception) testified so as to place the blame primarily on himself or herself. All of them denied any treasonous intention of harming the Soviet Union; their sole motivation was to emigrate and establish new lives elsewhere. They also said they had no intention to steal the airplane, but were expecting it to be returned to the Soviet Union by the Swedish authorities.

Much of the cross-examination by the procurator—that's what they call the prosecutor—dealt with political issues:

PROCURATOR: Do you not think that anti-Semitism is caused by Zionism?
KUZNETSOV: Zionism has existed only in the twentieth century, but there has always been anti-Semitism.
PROCURATOR: Have you ever read any Zionist literature?
KUZNETSOV: In the way you understand Zionism—no.
PROCURATOR: There is only one way of understanding Zionism—that is the Marxist-Leninist way.
KUZNETSOV: Zionism's your scapegoat.

When several of the defendants attempted to catalog the anti-Semitic experiences to which they had been subjected—for example, a bus driver shouting at Dymshitz, "Hitler didn't kill enough of you!"—the procurator interrupted with the reminder that the Soviet people are "incapable of anti-Semitism."

In his closing speech the procurator made repeated references to "the intrigues of international Zionism" and denied that this was "a trial against Jews." As if to underline his point, he then asked the court to impose the death penalty on one Jew and one "non-Jew": the Jew selected was Dymshitz; the "non-Jew" was Kuznetsov ("I do not consider Kuznetsov a Jew; I think he is a Russian," announced the procurator).

The defendants' closing speeches provided them with their only opportunity to explain their actions. Silva Zalmanson spoke for all the defendants when she said:

> I am completely overwhelmed . . . If the court [imposes the death penalty] then such outstanding men as Dymshitz and Kuznetsov will perish. I do not think that Soviet law can possibly regard someone's intention to live in another country as treason . . . Several of us did not believe that our undertaking would be successful . . . Even when we were at the Finland Station we noticed we were being followed. But it was too late to turn back—to return to the past, to continue to wait and to live in our suitcases. Not even now do I doubt for one moment that I will one day live in Israel whatever happens. This

> dream of mine, consecrated by 2000 years of waiting and hoping, will never desert me. Next year in Jerusalem!!

Silva then began to cry as she spoke in broken Hebrew the words she had so carefully rehearsed: "*Im eskacheck Yerushalayim . . .*" ("If I forget thee, O Jerusalem . . ."). But the procurator stopped her, ordering her not to speak in an alien tongue.

"Death on the Installment Plan"

The judges then retired to consider their verdicts and sentences. (There is an old Soviet saying: "Marriages may be made in heaven, but sentences are made in the Kremlin.") The defendants were all found guilty. Kuznetsov and Dymshitz were sentenced to be shot. The rest were given prison terms ranging from four to fifteen years. The death sentences were greeted with loud applause.

But the applause for the death sentences did not extend to the rest of the world. The Pope expressed his hope that the lives of the two condemned men would be spared as a humanitarian gesture. Western Communist parties demanded commutation. (The American Communist Party, as usual, remained silent.) Andrei Sakharov dispatched simultaneous letters to President Nixon and to Soviet President Nikolai V. Podgorny: the letter to Nixon was in support of the young American Communist Angela Davis, who was facing a long prison term for allegedly providing weapons to revolutionaries; the letter to Podgorny was in support of Kuznetsov and Dymshitz. Another request came from a group of Soviet academics who called on the right-wing Spanish government to commute the death sentences of several Basques and on the Soviet government to show mercy to the two Jews facing death.

The day before the Soviet appeals court was to hear the petitions for commutation, General Franco spared the lives of the Basques. The eyes of the world were now riveted on the Kremlin. On December 31, 1970, the court announced that it would commute the Kuznetsov and Dymshitz sentences to fifteen years of "special regime"—the harshest form of imprisonment.

"Death on the installment plan," quipped a friend of Kuznetsov's, when informed about the commutation. "He'll never survive fifteen years of special regime." Indeed, a special-regime prisoner's diet is not sufficient to sustain life for more than a few years. Yet many do survive, supplementing their meager diet by a number of expedients—and a good deal of sustaining fortitude.

"The International Zionist Conspiracy"

The Dymshitz-Kuznetsov trial was followed in quick succession by a series of trials against individuals in each of the major Jewish population centers. The second Leningrad trial was a classic political-conspiracy prosecution directed against the entire Jewish leadership of that city, both those who had been and those who had not been aware of the various hijacking plans. The indictment itself is remarkable for its undisguised political tone:

> International Zionism is conducting . . . ideological sabotage against the USSR and the other socialist countries by propagating slanderous articles and by sending tourists. These activities have induced [some persons] to set up a Zionist organization in Leningrad. [M]embers of the organization maintained close contacts with Zionist circles in Israel, [and] have been fomenting [among Jews] sentiments supporting emigration to Israel. For these purposes they used anti Soviet Zionist literature, and even works published in the capitalist countries.

The indictment added, almost as an afterthought: "Existing facts irrefutably prove the direct involvement of the Zionist centers with the events in Hungary in 1956 and with the activation of the counterrevolutionary forces in Poland and Czechoslovakia in 1968." (The fact that some of the defendants were less than ten years old at the time of the Hungarian uprising did not, apparently, diminish their collective guilt.)

The literature referred to in the indictment included Leon Uris' *Exodus* (which became the all-time *samizdat* best seller among Soviet Jews*), Howard Fast's *My Glorious Brothers* (which my high school had banned on the ground that it was Communist propaganda), Chaim Bialik's poems, and Randolph S. Churchill's *The Six Day War*.

These conspiracy and literature trials were followed by individual prosecutions against ordinary workers and trades people who had sought to emigrate. Some were charged with "hooliganism" or "parasitism." One was accused of spying for England and Israel. Another was arrested for "knocking a birthday cake out of a woman's hands." All were convicted and received prison terms.

This rhythm of Soviet prosecution—alternating mass prosecutions with

*The mentality of censorship is apparently contagious. When the refuseniks translated *Exodus*, there were battles about which portions should be censored from the *samizdat* version. For example, all references to the interreligious romance between Ari Ben Canaan and Kitty Fremont were excised.

individual arrests—had been described several years earlier by Aleksandr I. Solzhenitsyn in *The Gulag Archipelago:*

> The history of this sewage system is the history of an endless swallow and flow, flood alternating with ebb and ebb again with flood; waves pouring in, some big, some small; brooks and rivulets flowing in from all sides; trickles oozing in through gutters; and then just plain individually scooped-up droplets.

One of the "droplets" was a one-legged carpenter from the city of Derbent named Pinkhas Pinkhasov. He had never been politically minded, but he wanted to emigrate to Israel. His family—himself, his wife, and their six children—was the first in the area to request an exit visa. It was granted in the summer of 1973, but authorities tried desperately to dissuade the Pinkhasovs from leaving, fearing that their departure might encourage others. When he persisted he was arrested and charged with overpricing his services as a carpenter. His family was allowed to leave, but he was sentenced to five years in prison.

"Nazi Brigadiers"

The former prisoners whom we interviewed told us of the conditions they had endured. Some had served with the Kuznetsov-Dymshitz group, and they were able to provide us with details of their confinement. In addition to descriptions of the horrendous physical conditions, the most disturbing information we learned was that the prison camps to which our clients had been assigned were dominated by former Nazi collaborators, many of whom remained unreconstructed anti-Semites. A former inmate gave us the following account of the prison population at one camp that had eight Jews among its four hundred and fifty inmates:

> The other[s] had all been convicted of crimes committed as collaborators when the German Nazi forces invaded the Soviet Union. [They] were serving long sentences [for] one or more murders.
>
> The Jewish prisoners were given the hardest and most unpleasant work. Meanwhile, the Nazi collaborators were given jobs as clerks, security guards, etc., and some of them were referred to as "Brigadiers."

One of the former prisoners told us about the special problems faced by the youngest of the Kuznetsov group, a devoutly Orthodox Jew named Josif Mendelevich. His beard was shaved, his yarmulke removed, and he was forced to eat pork or starve. A particularly poignant story I was told by one of Mendelevich's former camp-mates took place on Passover. Mendelevich secretly conducted a Seder, using a small piece of a dried flower for matzoh. When the time came for making the traditional sandwich of matzoh and bitter herbs, there were, of course, no bitter herbs. But that did not stop Mendelevich, who recited: "The bitter herb is a symbol commemorating Jewish suffering. Here we need no symbol. We swallow the reality of our suffering every day."

The Smuggled-Out Diary

Some of the prisoners who had served with Kuznetsov told us that he was keeping a detailed diary of his prison experiences. They doubted it would ever see the light, however, since prison authorities periodically conducted search-and-destroy operations against all writings. The only chance to smuggle out anything is provided by the day-long private visits—usually in a cabin—that prisoners are permitted at rare intervals with their wives or parents. But before the prisoner and the visitor are allowed into the cabin, both are strip-searched and every orifice of their bodies is examined.

The former prisoners were wrong: Kuznetsov, desperate to have his story told and doubtful that he would ever be free to tell it, worked out an ingenious method for getting his diary out. He learned how to write in a microscopic script that enabled him to squeeze thousands of words onto tiny strips of tissue paper. He would then roll his valuable scrolls into small balls and cover them with a paraffin mixture smuggled out of the camp pharmacy. Before each cabin visit, he would swallow several balls. When he was searched, nothing was found. During the cabin visit, he would excrete the paraffin-coated balls, remove them from his stools, and clean them. His visitor would then swallow the balls, pass the exit search, and excrete them after getting home. The paraffin would be removed, the scrolls unrolled, and the writing typed. In this way Kuznetsov managed to smuggle out prison diaries containing more than 100,000 words.

The first volume, published in Russian, French, and English, under the title *Prison Diaries,* provides an up-to-date account of the post-Solzhenitsyn Gulag. Parts of it read like Dante's *Inferno:*

> I have seen convicts swallow huge numbers of nails, quantities of barbed wire, mercury thermometers, . . . chess pieces, dominoes, needles, ground glass, spoons, knives, and many other similar objects; I have seen convicts sew up their mouths and eyes with thread or wire; sew rows of buttons to their bodies; or nail their testicles to a bed, swallow a nail bent like a hook, and then attach this hook to the door by way of a thread so that the door cannot be opened without pulling

> the "fish" inside out. I have seen convicts cut open the skin on their arms and legs and peel it off as if it were a stocking; or cut out lumps of flesh (from their stomach or their legs), roast them and eat them; or let the blood drip from slit vein into a tureen, crumble bread crumbs into it, and then gulp it down like a bowl of soup; or cover themselves with paper and set fire to themselves; or cut off their fingers, or their nose, or ears, or penis . . .

Other parts of the diary read like a satire from *Krokodil* (the Soviet journal of humor):

> Received my third reprimand for not attending political study classes. The last class I went to, Lieutenant Bezzubov gave us the priceless information that "In China the Zionists and the Red Guards are on the rampage." The academic level of these lectures is truly breathtaking!

We received advance copies of the Kuznetsov diary shortly after it reached the West. We were now armed with the information we needed: eyewitness accounts, affidavits, documents, diaries, and physical evidence. Telford Taylor was given a power of attorney by the closest relative of each of the prisoners, authorizing him to act on behalf of the prisoner in all legal proceedings. But there were some lingering doubts. Would the Soviet authorities permit American attorneys to argue on behalf of Soviet nationals? Did the prisoners themselves want us to file briefs? How would the other Soviet refuseniks—the ones still in Moscow, Leningrad, and Kiev—feel about our intervention? The only way to resolve these doubts was to travel to Moscow and speak to the Soviet authorities and to the refuseniks. This would be no easy task. It was one thing to go to Israel on our legal business. It was quite another to secure a visa to enter the Soviet Union for the purpose of representing Soviet prisoners convicted of treason. It had never been done before. My public involvement in the Jewish Defense League bombing cases—cases discussed repeatedly in the pages of *Pravda* and *Izvestia*—had brought me to the attention of Soviet authorities. "It will be almost as hard for you to get *into* the Soviet Union," I was advised by a knowledgeable source, "as it has been for your clients to get *out.*"

We decided to request Soviet visas in two separate groups. Telford Taylor and Professor George P. Fletcher—a UCLA Law School professor who is fluent in Russian and an expert in Soviet law—applied together, indicating on their application that they were going on legal business. Taylor also wrote personal letters to Procurator General Rudenko and Judge Smirnov, telling them that he was "hoping to travel to the Soviet Union in the near future." He added: "It is many years since we worked together at the Nuremberg War Crimes trials, and I would be very grateful for the opportunity to meet with you while I am in Moscow, to renew our acquaintance and discuss questions of mutual interest professionally." It would be Taylor's job, assisted by Fletcher, to make all formal contacts with the Soviet authorities and to secure their permission for us to represent the prisoners and to file briefs on their behalf.

We decided that I should apply separately in order not to taint Taylor and Fletcher with my JDL associations. I had originally intended to travel alone, as a tourist. But the lawyers' group decided that this might be too risky and that it would be better to travel with someone. I decided to take my twelve-year-old son Elon with me. We applied as tourists interested in learning about the Soviet legal system. It would be my job, if our visa applications were approved, to meet with the refuseniks and to get a sense of their attitude toward our proposed intervention, as well as additional information about the condition of the prisoners.

"Record Everything, Record . . ."

To our surprise, all four visa applications were approved. We traveled to Moscow in separate groups, having agreed to rendezvous at the main dining room of the National Hotel.

Elon and I arrived at the appointed hour and waited. No sign of Taylor or Fletcher. The waiter filled my glass with vodka several times—and Elon's with Pepsi—as we waited nervously. Anything could have happened. We had no backup plan, and there was virtually no way to locate a fellow American in Moscow, since Intourist assigns visitors to particular hotels only after they have arrived in the Soviet Union.

Finally, after two hours, I heard Fletcher's distinct and animated voice. They had been delayed, but finally we were all together. We exchanged our local hotel addresses and telephone numbers, agreed on meeting times and places, and had dinner, talking little about our business.

The next morning was Saturday, and I decided to try to find Moscow's only synagogue. It was the one place, I had been told, where I might meet some refuseniks. The synagogue was not easy to find. It was a long walk from my hotel, and cab drivers would not take you there. But we had a map provided by previous visitors, and finally we found Arkhipova Street and an old building that looked like the synagogues on the Lower East Side of New York. We entered and sat near the back. The *chazzen* (cantor) was chanting in Hebrew; the congregants were whispering in Yiddish; and the sexton was speaking Russian. About an hour after our arrival we were approached by a young man named Yuli, who whispered in perfect English, "Why don't you come outside and meet the real Jews." I asked him what he meant, and he said, "Come on out, and you'll see." When we reached the street it was buzzing with young Moscovites. Yuli introduced us to his friends and we spent the remainder of the morning in intense discussion with several refuseniks.

That night I made some notes of my impressions of the Moscow synagogue:

The drama of the synagogue unfolds on two levels. Inside is the past: the bearded rabbi delivering an approved-in-advance sermon in Yiddish to a throng of frightened and resigned septuagenarians whose children and grandchildren will never enter the synagogue. The whispered Yiddish conversations concern the upcoming holiday: Will there be enough matzoh? Will the KGB limit the number of worshipers as in past years? Will there be American tourists bearing prayer books and *grises* (messages) from relatives abroad?

Outside the synagogue is the future: those not resigned to a life of second-class citizenship; those who aspire to live a Jewish, a free, life outside of the Soviet Union. They gather by the dozens—sometimes by the hundreds—in front of the synagogue toward the end of the service. They used to gather in a small field across the way, between the hoops of a makeshift basketball court, until the authorities fenced it off and closed it on Saturdays. Now they stand in the street, sometimes inadvertently slowing down traffic and providing the police with an excuse to disperse the crowds, as they do on major holidays or when foreign visitors begin to mingle.

The outsiders refuse to enter what they regard as the official Soviet showcase designed to contain, and slowly destroy, Jewish culture. They speak in broken Hebrew and English, languages that reflect their aspirations rather than their reality. Their most prized possessions are contraband copies of *Elef Millim,* an elementary Hebrew reader banned in the Soviet Union as "nationalistic," and out-of-date copies of *Time,* which they get from American tourists. Around their necks are smuggled pendants of the Star of David with such inscriptions as *Zion* and *Am Yisrael Chai* (the Jewish People Live). In their hearts is one thought—Exodus.

Most of those outside the synagogue are outside the system as well. They have made the existential decision: they have applied for exit visas. Once a Soviet Jew has applied for an exit visa there are but two alternatives. If he is lucky he may be permitted to renounce his citizenship and leave. If his application is denied, or simply not acted upon, he faces a series of dilemmas, most leading to prison.

Why, then, do so many choose to risk so much for the slim chance to emigrate? The answer is simple: it is impossible to live as a Jew in the Soviet Union. Discrimination is rampant: certain departments of the leading universities are completely barred to Jews, even to those Jews who have not applied to leave. Everywhere Jewish values and aspirations are downgraded. The Soviet authorities claim that there is no Jewish problem; that is true, except if you happen to be a Jew.

Yuli Wexler, the young man who had approached us in the synagogue, faced imminent imprisonment himself for refusal to serve in the Soviet army. He became our unofficial guide. Among the people he introduced me to was Ida Nudel, who was referred to as the "guardian angel" of the prisoners of conscience. We met on a park bench not far from the ornate steeples of St. Basil's. A short, plump woman in her forties, Ida was the image of a warm Jewish mother. She had assumed the responsibility for keeping tabs on each of the prisoners of conscience. She knew everything there was to know about them: the camps they were in; the date of their last visit; the conditions of their physical and mental health; the medications they needed; the work tasks to which they had been assigned; the legal appeals available to them; and a hundred other important details of their prison lives. She kept a small book filled with the information.

I asked her why she was doing this. "When the Nazis killed our people the world heard only about the numbers, not the people. You can't generate support for numbers. The world has to know *everything* about our prisoners: what they look like [as she said this, she pulled out a file of crumpled pictures of the prisoners]; what they feel like; even what jokes they tell among themselves." With tears in her eyes she began to tell me some prisoners' jokes:

"There was a prisoner who had been tried for calling Khrushchev an idiot. He was not charged, however, with slander, but rather with revealing a state secret."

"A guard asked a prisoner how much time he was serving. 'Ten years,' the prisoner replied. 'What did you do to deserve ten years?' the guard asked. 'Nothing-at-all,' said the prisoner. The guard looked at the prisoner skeptically and said, 'I don't believe you; for nothing-at-all they give you just five years, not ten.' "

I asked Ida, as I had asked all the refuseniks, whether it would be useful to get American lawyers involved in the prisoners' cases. "Definitely, most definitely," she replied and repeated what I had heard a dozen times: "Outside intervention is what is needed. The Soviet authorities must be told that this is not merely a local problem. They must understand that the world cares about our prisoners. American lawyers, politicians, businessmen, should all express interest."

"But could it backfire?" I asked. "Could our intervention hurt the prisoners?"

"We are all future prisoners," she said quietly, "and we have spent many hours discussing tactics. There is one point we all agree on: there must be publicity and outside concern; that is our lifeline." She then reminded me of the final words of the great Jewish historian Simon Dubnov as he was being dragged off to Rumbula to be executed by the Nazis: "The greatest crime is silence . . . Record everything, record . . ."

In the remaining days I met with many members of the refusenik community. We met on trains, in churches, in parks, and—in a few notable instances—in their apartments. There were no substantive discussions in the apartments, since everybody assumed they were bugged. There were disagreements among the refuseniks over a number of issues, such as the propriety of an emigrant going to a country other than Israel if an exit visa was obtained. But there was universal agreement on the need for outside legal help for the prisoners. "If there is one thing the Soviet Union is afraid of, it's the truth." Several Moscow lawyers also told me that the Soviet legal establishment wanted to be recognized by the West and did not want to be viewed as the primitive and lawless system it had become under Stalin. Perhaps, they suggested, if Western lawyers took the Soviet legal system seriously enough to file briefs, the Soviet authorities might be flattered enough to read them.

"So an American Lawyer Comes to Moscow . . ."

While I was meeting with the dissidents, Telford Taylor and George Fletcher were in their hotel rooms awaiting a call from General Rudenko. When the call didn't come, they went to the office of the Procuracy and to the Supreme Court. They were told that Rudenko was on vacation and that Smirnov had suddenly taken ill. It was not clear whether either would be able to visit with the Americans. The two were instructed to return to their rooms and wait for a call. Tuesday, Wednesday, and Thursday went by without a call. Friday was to be our last day in Moscow. By four o'clock in the afternoon there had still been no call, and Taylor and Fletcher began to pack and prepare to leave. Fletcher was unwilling to return home completely empty-handed, so he decided to walk to a nearby bookstore and buy some Russian books. No sooner had he left than the phone rang. (Were Fletcher's movements being watched?) It was the First Deputy Procurator General, M.P. Malyarov. Taylor managed a few cordial words in his Berlitz

Russian but could not understand the thrust of the conversation. Within a few minutes a translator called and informed him that Rudenko was still sick but that Malyarov would see him if he could come over immediatley. Taylor found a translator and rushed over to the Procuracy, where Malyarov was waiting. After a few preliminaries Taylor turned to the business at hand and showed the Deputy Procurator General the powers of attorney signifying that he was the authorized legal representative of the prisoners' relatives.

"So an American lawyer comes to Moscow representing Soviet citizens," Malyarov said sardonically. "How did you obtain your information about these trials?" he went on. Taylor told him about our interviews in Israel. "What makes you think they are reliable?" Malyarov asked.

Taylor saw his opening: "We have cross-checked as carefully as we could, but I would welcome an opportunity to examine the trial records if they could be made available."

Malyarov shook his head. "You have your way of doing things, and we have ours." Taylor assured Malyarov that it was our intention to proceed in an entirely professional manner, eschewing publicity or open criticism *if* the Soviet authorities would receive our legal documents and promise to read and consider them. After some hesitation Malyarov gave Taylor permission to submit petitions on behalf of the prisoners and assured him they would be read and considered at the highest levels of the Procuracy. We were to be the first American lawyers ever allowed to participate formally in the Soviet legal process.

We were ecstatic about Taylor's success, but not at all sanguine about the eventual outcome of the case. Harking back to the old Russian joke, we had not only "talked to" the dead man but he had even "listened." Now the most difficult task at hand was to get him to rise up and do something!

"They Felt Like Brothers and Sisters"

After returning from our fascinating trips to Russia and Israel we felt it was time to get down to the hard work of preparing the legal documents that Malyarov had given us permission to file. Being responsible for overseeing this task, I arranged for office space, stenographers, typing facilities, and translators in a suite of offices at Harvard Law School. We scoured Cambridge and Boston for as many Cyrillic typewriters as we could find. We moved a substantial portion of the Harvard Law Library's Soviet collection into our suite. We secured the voluntary assistance of two Soviet-trained lawyers, several Russian typists and translators, and two recent law school graduates working at New York law firms. Our team—

more than a dozen strong—assembled in Cambridge on May 20, 1974.

For several hectic days and nights we ran an international law firm out of the cramped offices at Harvard Law School. Our task was prodigious. We had nineteen cases in all. Each required an individual petition and affidavits—in Russian and English. We also had to prepare extensive briefs covering the major legal issues. In all, we had to produce—literally from scratch—more than fifty separate documents.

As I got down to work I had a strange feeling: I had never met any of my imprisoned Soviet clients, yet they felt like brothers and sisters. It seemed as if I had known them for years. I found myself referring to them by their intimate nicknames—"Edik," "Yusi"—instead of by their formal names. Never had I so closely identified with my clients, despite the fact —perhaps, in part, because of the fact—that I had never met them. Deep in my heart I knew that someday I would meet them and like them.

In order to draft the petitions and memoranda we had to teach ourselves Soviet criminal law and procedure almost overnight. Fortunately for us, the Soviet legal system is based entirely on statutes and regulations, and not on the common-law development of cases. The statutes and regulations are relatively few in number and generally manageable, whereas the cases that have to be studied under a common-law system are legion. We were fortunate that the Harvard Law School Library has a full collection of them in English. And so, after a cram course in Soviet law, we were ready to write.*

We worked against a tight deadline, since Taylor was leaving for Moscow within a few days for a scheduled meeting with Procurator General Rudenko at which he would attempt to deliver our documents. We made it by minutes as we raced to Xerox our final petitions just before Taylor boarded the plane.

This time Rudenko was available and Taylor met with him for several hours. Rudenko accepted the legal documents.

Now we had to wait. We heard nothing for several weeks. On June 27 President Nixon was in Moscow for a Summit conference. We prevailed on his legal advisers to cable the President's party in Moscow and enlist them to advance our cases. Copies of our petitions were sent. We were later told that our cases had been brought up and discussed during the bilateral talks.

Silva Zalmanson's Release

We heard nothing until late August, when Silva Zalmanson was suddenly released from prison on health and humanitarian grounds—she was report-

*The resulting documents appear in *Courts of Terror* by Telford Taylor (New York: Knopf, 1976).

edly suffering from a peptic ulcer and tuberculosis. We were elated, although we had no specific reason to believe that it was our request that had done the trick, since there had been many public demands for her release. But it was impossible to be certain that her release was unrelated to our brief because in the petition we filed for her we had emphasized the "numerous detailed reports about her deteriorating health, both physical and psychological," and we had specifically requested the Procurator General "to exercise his power to inquire into her condition and do whatever is possible to improve it," including a recommendation for "either full or partial relief from unfulfilled portions of the sentence." As soon as she was free, Silva went to the summer home of Andrei Sakharov, where she issued a statement expressing "endless thanks" for the appeals from abroad on her behalf and asked for continuing outside support for "the liberation of my dear ones and all the prisoners of Zion."

Silva was permitted a brief visit with her husband Eduard before she was "deported" to Israel, where she underwent medical treatment. Shortly thereafter she came to the United States on a speaking tour in support of the remaining prisoners. Telford Taylor and I, along with several other lawyers who had worked on her case, arranged to meet her over lunch at Lou Siegel's, a kosher restaurant in Manhattan. It would be our first "reunion"—hopefully the first of many—with the clients we had never met. Our encounter was emotional and tearful. Knowing of Silva's love for things Jewish, we decided to order a real old-fashioned Jewish meal for our Friday lunch. The first dish was *cholent,* a delicious concoction of beans, potatoes, barley, and a small amount of beef, cooked for hours in a heavy sauce. When the *cholent* came, I turned to Silva and explained what it was—that it was a traditional dish served in Jewish homes on the Sabbath. She took one taste of it, and her face turned sad—and then she burst out laughing as she exclaimed, "Traditional *Jewish* food? This is Russian *prison* food! I've just been through eating food like this for four years!" Only then did we realize that the old-fashioned food, which was such a treat for us, *was* peasant food, designed to use the least amount of meat possible. The same economics that dictated the diets of our peasant forebears now determined the menus prepared by the prison authorities. We all had a good laugh, and I ordered a slice of rare roast beef for our guest.

She told us about her husband's condition and pleaded with us to persist in our efforts. She had no doubt that the prisoners wanted us to continue with our legal efforts. This was important, since it was our first direct confirmation that our clients themselves supported our legal intervention. She emphasized the importance of continuing our support for the two non-Jewish prisoners—Fedorov and Murzhenko—in our efforts. She also told us about several other prisoners who had been released or who were about to be released, and she urged us to make another trip to Israel to bring our information up to date.

The Pinkhasov Case

And so, over the Christmas vacation, we were off to Israel once again to conduct interviews and to learn of several new clients. Among the people we met was Yalta Pinkhasov, the wife of the one-legged carpenter from Derbent. She told us that her husband had been framed. As skeptical criminal lawyers, we took the familial assertion of innocence with a grain of salt. The charges in this case seemed inherently plausible, since overcharging of services is a widespread practice among tradespeople in the Soviet Union. But Mrs. Pinkhasov insisted: "Not Pinkhas, he never overcharged." We assured her that we would represent her husband even if he was guilty, since it seemed clear that the reason he was selected for prosecution from among so many who overcharge was his application to emigrate. And this made his case a political prosecution and made him a prisoner of conscience.

But this wasn't enough for his wife: "No, no, you must assert his total innocence." Finally, in desperation, she blurted out, "If you don't believe me, ask the judge." I smiled and said that it would be difficult to speak to the judge in Derbent. The Israeli translator who was with us seemed a bit upset at Mrs. Pinkhasov's reference to the judge and became even more so when she continued, "One of the judges that sat on my husband's case is here in Israel. She is a Jew, and several months after my husband's conviction she herself emigrated."

I decided that we had to meet this judge and inquired of her whereabouts. The Israelis were discouraging. "She will never talk to you. This whole thing has been a trauma for her. We promised her we would not raise the issue. She's here to start a new life, not to rehash her old one."

I persisted, as any lawyer must, especially a lawyer with a client in prison. "I must speak to her, even if I have to find her myself," I insisted.

The Israelis tried to dissuade me: "She's not really a judge, anyway. She was one of the two lay judges, really like your jurors." I was familiar with the Soviet system of one professional judge and two lay assessors who were part jurors and part amateur judges. An affidavit asserting his innocence from one of the lay assessors who sat on Pinkhasov's case would be invaluable, I assured the Israelis. Finally they agreed to help us find Riya Mishayeva.

All we knew about the woman judge's whereabouts was that she had been assigned to live in Shderot, one of the new Israeli development towns established for recent immigrants in out-of-the-way places. This one was located somewhere in the south of Israel, a long day's drive from Tel Aviv. I set out to find Riya Mishayeva, having no idea how we would do it, since she had no telephone and there was no way of reaching her in advance.

I arrived in Shderot and began looking. The town appeared to have sprung up from the desert sand. The buildings were made of a stucco substance similar to the sand on which they stood. There was a central market and a small playground. It was primitive, simple, and sparse—but lovely. I walked through the market asking about Riya Mishayeva, finally locating a man who said he knew where she lived. I hurried to the apartment, only to learn that she had just moved, but I was taken to the home of one of her friends and there found Mishayeva. The apartment was furnished with only a table, a few chairs, and some cots while the families awaited the shipment of their goods from the Soviet Union.

When I told Mishayeva why I was there, she became frightened and refused to talk. There was a hurried conference among her friends. Then one of them walked over to me and with a broad smile asked me to join them in some food and drink. I quickly accepted. Again I tried to bring up the purpose of our visit, but my hosts would have none of that while we were breaking bread together. I could sense that they were trying to feel me out, to see whether I could be trusted. They asked about my background, and I told them about my own Russian-Polish ancestry.

As we were talking the first course arrived. It was an enormous fish of an undetermined type, wrapped neatly in newspaper. I was startled to notice that the newspaper was Russian. I wondered whether the fish had traveled with our hosts from the Soviet Union. As nonchalantly as I could I asked when our hosts had arrived in Israel. "Several months ago" came the reply. The age of the fish thus having been established, I began to feel a bit nauseated. I decided that a good lawyer must sometimes eat bad food to avoid offending a source. I tasted the fish. It was delicious. I later learned that it had been dried in Derbent by a local process. In any event, after a few glasses of straight, warm vodka, it didn't much matter.

Finally Mishayeva said, "You have told us about your background. You seem like a decent person. Let me tell you about mine." She began to relate the story of her life, of her youth in the Komsomol, her membership in the Communist Party, and her appointment as a party official in the candy factory in Derbent. She was still a devout Communist and went out of her way to defend the party and the Soviet system at every opportunity. This led to some uncomfortable discussion among her friends, who obviously did not share her enthusiasm. She had emigrated to Israel, she assured us, for "personal reasons" and because there was still some anti-Semitism among the peasants and workers, though it was discouraged by the party.

Mishayeva told us about the system of lay assessors, how loyal party members took official turns serving as a "people's assessor." She had been serving in this capacity for "five years and judged many, many cases." Being a judge, she said, was her "second trade." She stopped at this point, almost to suggest that she had reached the end of her story.

"Can you tell us about the Pinkhasov case?" I asked. She sat silent, a tear forming in her eye. "What you tell us could save his life," I gently pressed. Still there was no reply. I pushed a bit harder. "Don't you think, perhaps, you owe him the truth at this point? There's nothing anyone can do to you here for telling the truth."

Immediately she responded, "You think it was I who got him in trouble. You're wrong. I saved him from worse." Then it began to come out in torrents.

She said she had been picked to serve on the Pinkhasov case because she was Jewish and might have a better chance of persuading him to change his mind about emigrating to Israel. She was assigned by the professional judge, a man named Rasmasanov, to speak to Pinkhasov and to offer him a deal: if he renounced his desire to emigrate and summoned his family back from Israel, all charges against him would be dropped and he would be given a new apartment. When Pinkhasov protested his innocence, Mishayeva told him, "That doesn't matter. The others will sentence you severely unless you do as I say." Pinkhasov refused, and the trial proceeded. Eleven witnesses were called by the prosecution, all local people for whom Pinkhasov had done carpentry work. Each asserted that the one-legged carpenter had done excellent work and had charged the official price. Several testified to having given Pinkhasov some food or drink or a tip for extra work. One said that he had given a small gift to Pinkhasov's son, who had helped him on a job.

Judge Rasmasanov and the other assessor wanted to sentence the carpenter to seven years of imprisonment. Mishayeva held out for a lower sentence. Eventually a prison term of five years was imposed, with the unanimous consent of the three judges. Mishayeva explained, a bit defensively, that if she had refused to sign, he would probably have received a seven-year sentence. Finally she told me, tearfully, that there was no question about Pinkhasov's innocence. She had studied the file and heard all the witnesses. "There was absolutely no evidence that he overcharged. The whole case was a fabrication. We were under instructions to find him guilty unless he renounced his application to emigrate."

I asked Mishayeva whether she would be prepared to repeat her story on a tape recorder and then sign an affidavit attesting to Pinkhasov's innocence. She wanted to know what we intended to do with the material. When I told her that we would submit it to the Soviet legal authorities, she again became hesitant. "What will they do to my friends who are still there?" she asked. I told her there could be no assurances, but that it was unlikely that any reprisals would be taken against nonrelatives. With a plaintive, almost resigned tone, she said, "You're right. I do owe it to him. I will do it. I have made my break with that country."

Assured of Mishayeva's cooperation, I drafted an affidavit based on our conversations, which she signed and had notarized. We then prepared a detailed petition on behalf of Pinkhasov. We cited various legal violations of the defendant's rights under Soviet law, but emphasized his factual innocence as confirmed by the affidavit of one of the judges herself.

We had greater hopes for the Pinkhasov appeal than for some of the others. We knew that the decision to prosecute the other defendants, particularly in the group trials, had been reached at the highest levels in Moscow. The probability of getting them to change their minds was slight. The decision to prosecute Pinkhasov had been reached—we surmised—at a local level. It was more likely, therefore, that the central authorities to whom we addressed our petition would be willing to reverse the locals, especially in a case containing such obviously embarrassing material as the Mishayeva affidavit presented.

This time the response was more immediate, and, it appeared, more direct. On September 24, 1975, several months after we filed the Pinkhasov petition, we received word that the Presidium of the Supreme Court of the Dagestan Autonomous Socialist Soviet Republic had decided "to reduce [Pinkhasov's] sentence to two years of deprivation of freedom." Since by this time the carpenter had already served almost exactly two years, he was released and allowed to join his wife and family in Israel.

After several months of silence concerning the remaining prisoners we decided to hold a press conference announcing the fact that we had undertaken to represent Soviet prisoners and that we had received permission to file, and had filed, numerous petitions and briefs on behalf of our clients.

"A Tale of International Intrigue"

Still there was no response from the Kremlin. This time we had to wait several years. And then on April 27, 1979, a Soviet airliner descended through the overcast skies at Kennedy Airport and pulled up at an outlying hangar protected from public view by a fence. Seven black limousines drew up to the back ramp of the Aeroflot plane. Five frightened people—unaware of their precise whereabouts—were taken out of the plane and led to the limousines. Two others were loaded onto the plane through its front ramp for the return trip to Moscow. The press had been alerted that "something big" was in the works, but no one was permitted near the plane. All that could be seen were some shadowy figures in the misty background. The limousines moved quickly off the tarmac and headed toward the United Nations Plaza, a plush East Side hotel. At 4:25 P.M. the limousines arrived at the hotel, and the passengers—thin, pale, tired, and with shaved heads—disembarked. One was Eduard Kuznetsov. Another was Mark Dymshitz. The three others were Aleksander I. Ginzburg, Georgi Vins, and Valentin Moroz. In a dramatic "tale of international intrigue out of the cold war days in Berlin"—as the *New York Times* characterized it—five political prisoners had been swapped for two Russians who had recently been convicted of espionage in a federal court and sentenced to fifty years imprisonment. It was the first time that Soviet citizens had been exchanged for Soviet citizens without any Americans being involved. (There were no Americans known to be in Soviet prisons at the time.)

Finally, after almost nine years of special-regime confinement, the two central figures in the plot to commandeer the Soviet aircraft were free. Soon they both settled in Israel. It had been a long journey from Priozersk Airport to Ben Gurion Airport.

Shortly after the swap I met Eduard Kuznetsov at the home of Andrei Sakharov's stepson, Alexei Semyonov, who now works at MIT (and whose wife's effort to emigrate from the Soviet Union has recently succeeded as the result of a hunger strike by Sakharov). Disappointment often follows great anticipation and I had certainly waited for this meeting a long time. As I drove up to Semyonov's home on a quiet street in Newton, Massachusetts, I wondered what Kuznetsov would be like. I knew the public figure, the brave man about whom we had written the briefs and petitions; the man who would not be silenced even while spending virtually all of his adult years in prison. (Between the ages of twenty-two and forty, he had spent sixteen of those eighteen years in prison.) Kuznetsov proved to be no disappointment. A smaller man than I had expected, "Edik" exuded intelligence, sensitivity, and judgment. He did not seem bitter that the Soviet authorities had, in effect, robbed him of his young adulthood. Although he looked older than his forty years, he retained an exuberance. Some released prisoners I have met spend much of their time railing against their former captors, but Kuznetsov did not want to harp on the past. To be sure, we discussed his imprisonment, primarily to gather information about his three co-conspirators who were still in prison. "Now that the big names are out," he insisted, "we cannot let the world forget about Fedorov, Murzhenko, and

Mendelevich." He was particularly concerned for the welfare of Fedorov and Mendelevich, who had serious health problems.

The discussion turned from prisoners to world events. I was surprised by his next comment: "Don't let the prisoners, and the human rights issue, stand in the way of détente and the SALT talks. That would play right into the hands of the Soviet hard-liners, who want more prisoners and no SALT. Press them hard about the prisoners, but do not use nuclear disaster as a bargaining chip." He then went on to say that "publicity is the air and water which keeps the prisoners alive. Unknown prisoners die every day in the camps. But they do not dare let a prisoner die if he is known in the West." He told us that our legal defense project was very important; that it had probably deterred the bringing of several prosecutions and may well have resulted in the earlier release of some prisoners.

Our meeting ended with a feeling of fulfillment—partial but real. Whether or not our legal defense project had made any difference, it had been one of the most enriching experiences of my life. I knew that I could never rest while there were still prisoners of conscience in Soviet, and other, prisons. My professional life would always include the representation of dissidents, refuseniks, and other political prisoners.

The Helsinki Monitors

During the years following the hijacking trials a new Jewish leadership began to emerge. It was more closely affiliated with the democratic movement headed by Andrei Sakharov, the noted Soviet physicist, but it retained its Jewish character and it continued to focus on emigration.

After the United States and the Soviet Union signed the Helsinki Accords in 1975, an informal group was established by Soviet dissidents, religious leaders, nationalists, and refuseniks to monitor Soviet compliance with its human-rights provisions. The Helsinki Watch, or Helsinki Monitors, as the group came to be called, first convened on May 12, 1976, in Moscow. Branches were soon opened in the Ukraine, in Lithuania, Georgia, and Armenia. During the next two years fifty-eight Soviet citizens risked their freedom by enlisting as public members of these groups. Periodically, the group would distribute reports on the condition of human rights in the Soviet Union. Almost 300 such reports, many of them with extensive documentation and painstaking detail, were issued between 1976 and 1978.

Not surprisingly, the Soviet authorities disapproved of this monitoring group and of its work. But there was nothing illegal about it. Indeed, the Soviet Constitution itself, adopted in October of 1977, protected such activities.

But neither the Soviet Constitution nor the Helsinki Accords deterred the Soviet authorities from initiating a massive legal war against members of the group. Between February 1977 and March 1978, the KGB arrested twenty of the group's fifty-eight members on trumped-up charges ranging from arson to espionage.

Among the Helsinki Monitors was a man named Anatoly Shcharansky, who had served as the representative of the Jewish refuseniks on the Moscow Helsinki group.

Shcharansky was a twenty-nine-year-old chess expert who had studied the application of computer technology to the Russian national game. Born into a poor family, young Anatoly was a devoted and vibrant student who received a gold medal for his achievements. A brilliant career in science or chess was predicted for him. When Anatoly was seventeen, one of his "best friends" found out that he was Jewish and beat him up, screaming "*Zhid, zhid.*" This event had a profound impact on Anatoly, stimulating in him an interest in Zionism and Israel. He adopted the name Natan and began hanging around in front of the Arkhipova Street synagogue. There he met a tall, strikingly beautiful woman named Natalia Steiglitz, who also wanted to emigrate to Israel. (She adopted the name Avital.) In 1973 Shcharansky applied for a visa but was refused.

Rather than join the growing list of vocal refuseniks, he decided to work within the Soviet system. He sought and obtained an interview with General Verein of OVIR, the visa office. Verein promised that if Anatoly remained quiet for two months he would receive a visa, on "a Communist general's word of honor." Anatoly remained silent, forgoing demonstrations and protests, but the general later informed him that the refusal was final. After that Anatoly decided to remain silent no more.

When I arrived in Moscow during the spring of 1974, Shcharansky's name was not among those known in the West. I had not been told of him. It is likely that he was in the groups I met during my visit, either in front of the synagogue or in the home of one of the refuseniks, but I have no memory of ever having talked with him individually.

In June of 1974 Avital received an exit visa for Israel, but Anatoly did not. Her visa was to expire on July 5 and she could not get an extension. Avital and Anatoly decided to get married before her departure, but the authorities refused to sanction the marriage of a refusenik and a woman who was soon to emigrate. On July 4 the couple participated in a Jewish marriage ceremony conducted by a rabbi in the presence of a minyan. The ritual glass was broken, and the couple looked into each other's eyes and whispered, "Next year in Jerusalem." Before the next dawn Avital was gone.

The solitary Anatoly soon became a central figure in the Soviet human-rights movement. He had several indispensable attributes: a perfect command of both written and spoken English; extensive contacts with American journalists; an inexhaustible supply of energy that he applied relentlessly to the cause of human rights; an ability to bring together the seemingly incompatible components of the broad human-rights movement; and a wonderfully warm sense of humor.

Andrei Sakharov insisted on using Shcharansky for simultaneous translations during press conferences. Visiting American dignitaries would ask for him by name when they wanted a guide to the human-rights movement. American journalists, such as Robert C. Toth of the *Los Angeles Times,* quoted him openly as a source of information on human-rights activities.

Not surprisingly, Shcharansky was frequently picked up for questioning and detention, especially when visiting dignitaries were expected or when press conferences were called. During one detention, two of his KGB captors challenged him to play chess. Anatoly agreed only on condition that the losers must crawl on the floor. Within a few minutes Anatoly was enjoying the rare sight of two KGB officers on their knees.

When the group called Helsinki Monitors was established in 1976, Yuri Orlov and Andrei Sakharov, its guiding spirits, proposed that Anatoly Shcharansky represent the Jewish emigration movement. Shcharansky participated avidly in the work of the Monitors, especially in publicizing the reports. He was aware, of course, that he was under the constant eye of the KGB. He knew that his phone was tapped, his walls bugged, and his movements followed. What he probably did not know was that his own occasional roommate, Sanya Lipavsky, was a KGB informant and *agent provocateur.*

In the beginning of 1977 the Soviet authorities began to escalate their attacks on human-rights activists. On January 22 an hour-long documentary was featured on Soviet national television. Entitled "Traders of Souls," it portrayed Jewish refuseniks, including Shcharansky, as "soldiers of Zionism inside the Soviet Union." It invoked traditional anti-Semitic stereotypes, such as the fat Jew doling out pound sterling to his Zionist followers. Then, in an action unprecedented in the Soviet Union, it gave the names and addresses of several of these "alien soldiers" with their faces featured prominently on the screen. Shcharansky was outraged. "It's a videotaped invitation to a pogrom," he told a friend. "They have applied the newest forms of technology to the oldest forms of discrimination." Then Shcharansky did something that Soviet citizens simply do not do: he filed a lawsuit against the television station seeking a formal "denial of the slanderous information defaming my honor and dignity," and demanded that "the denial be disseminated in the same way by which this information was distributed."

It was at this point that the KGB made a definite decision to construct a criminal case against Shcharansky. He was mocking the Soviet legal system by attempting to take it seriously.

Once the decision was made to go after Shcharansky it was only a question of time and a matter of selecting the appropriate crime. (As Lavrenti Beria, the head of Stalin's secret police, once put it: "Just let us have the man; we will find the crime.") Shcharansky's "friend," Sanya Lipavsky, was summoned to KGB headquarters and instructed to write an open letter suggesting that Shcharansky had attempted to recruit him into the CIA.

The Lipavsky letter was featured prominently in the Soviet press. On March 13, 1977—a week after the publication of the letter—Shcharansky drafted a public appeal in which he wrote: "The situation is such that [I] feel exactly like [a] hostage . . . in the hands of terrorists who acknowledge no laws, national or international, and who are ready to take extreme measures at any moment."

He also wrote a more personal letter to Avital in Israel:

> Natulya, my beloved, my joy,
>
> Thinking about it all, I regretted only one thing—so much so that I was ready to cry: I regretted that we didn't have any children. . . .
>
> I am living now at the Slepaks' apartment; my tails live by the door. . . .
>
> Papa is taking it very hard. He doesn't sleep, his heart aches, his blood pressure jumped way up and I fear that he won't live through all of this.
>
> After we talk on the phone I promise to sit down and write you a long letter and I'll send it so that it gets to you. . . .

But there was to be no phone call and no subsequent letter. Two days later, on March 15, 1977, Anatoly was bundled off in a KGB van and taken to the dreaded Lefortovo prison. His arrest became headline news throughout the West.

"Will You Become My Tolya's Lawyer?"

Within a few days of Shcharansky's arrest, I received a phone call in broken English from a woman who introduced herself as Avital Shcharansky, Anatoly's wife. She asked me to help her husband. We continued the conversation through a translator. "Will you become my Tolya's lawyer?" (Tolya was Shcharansky's diminutive name.) I told Avital that it was unlikely that the Soviet authorities would allow me to appear in a Soviet court on his behalf. She said that she understood, but that "Tolya needs an American lawyer, an advocate who could present his case *in* the United States—to the President, to Congress, to the media, and to the American people." Would I become that lawyer? she asked.

"It would be a great honor and privilege," I replied. I realized that she was right; that there was far more to being a lawyer—especially in a case like this—than simply appearing in court on the defendant's behalf. There were other forums to which briefs could be submitted and arguments directed. It would be a real challenge and I welcomed it. Soon afterward I also received a letter from Ida Milgram, Anatoly's mother, who was still in the Soviet Union, requesting me to act on her behalf as well, and enclosing her power of attorney.

Since the Soviet press was accusing Shcharansky of being a spy for the United States, I decided that the first step his American lawyer should take was to try to get the United States government to deny that charge. I knew this would be difficult, since it is the policy of both the State Department and the CIA not to issue denials in spy cases. The logic is that if denials are issued in some cases, the world will know that the charge is true whenever there is no denial. For the government to deny the charge in all cases—even those where it is true—would be to invite embarrassment and lose credibility. Nonetheless, I decided to try. I did some research and discovered that at least in one prior case, a President—John F. Kennedy—had issued a specific denial that Professor Frederick Barghoorn of Yale University was a CIA agent. Of course our situation would be even more difficult, since Barghoorn was an American citizen and Shcharansky was not.

Rather than attempt to wend my way through the bureaucracy of the State Department and the CIA, I decided to go directly to the White House. I made an appointment to see Stuart Eizenstat, a former student of mine, who was President Carter's chief domestic adviser, and Robert L. Lipshutz, who was the President's counsel.

I arrived at the White House on a balmy April day in 1977 and was shown into Eizenstat's office. We reminisced a bit about his days at Harvard Law School, about the Carter campaign, and about mutual friends. We talked about his new job—President Carter had then been in office only a few months. Lipshutz joined us. I briefed them about Shcharansky's situation, saying that Andrei Sakharov had characterized Shcharansky's arrest as a direct "challenge" to President Carter and "an attempt to blackmail the new administration . . . to give up its principled stand on human rights all over the world."

Lipshutz assured me that there would be no backing down or submission to blackmail. I told them I thought that President Carter's bold statements on human rights were a double-edged sword: "If he keeps it up it will be constructive, but if he lets up now it might be worse than if he had done nothing." I explained that dissidents and refuseniks such as Shcharansky had gone out on a limb partly in reliance on the President's firm commitments to support the human-rights activists. If Carter was now to remain silent, "the President would be cutting down that limb with Shcharansky on it."

They asked what specific action I thought the Administration should take on the Shcharansky matter. I said that I thought the President should issue a direct statement categorically denying that Shcharansky was an American spy or that he had ever provided any information to American intelligence. Lipshutz reminded me of the policy against denying that anyone was a spy. I told him about President Kennedy's statement on Barghoorn. They promised to take the matter to the highest authorities. As I was leaving, Stuart —who had been silent during most of the meeting—suggested that I prepare a memorandum outlining various alternative responses the Administration might consider.

I returned to Cambridge to draft the memorandum. It would serve, in reality, as the opening brief on behalf of my imprisoned client—not a brief to be presented to the Soviet authorities, but one addressed to American authorities who might have considerable impact on the case.

Assisting me in the preparation of the brief was Yuli Wexler, the young man I had met in the Moscow synagogue who was facing imprisonment for his refusal to be drafted. By the time Shcharansky was arrested, Yuli had managed to emigrate, as he explained in an article:

> Soviet officials tried to draft me into the army [but] I refused to go. The normal penalty is three years of camp imprisonment. Exactly at the time that I was expecting the trial, I met Harvard Law School Professor Alan M. Dershowitz. I described to him my case, and he later transmitted it to Senator Edward Kennedy, who mentioned my case during his first trip to Moscow. As a result of which, I am now finishing Brandeis University instead of finishing a prison term—a very fortunate tradeoff!

After he got out of the Soviet Union, Wexler moved into my house in Cambridge, where he lived for almost two years, helping with household chores in exchange for room and board. He also worked as a translator and helped gather documents and information for the Shcharansky briefs.

Our memorandum to the White House proposed that the State Department communicate to the Soviet governments the willingness of American diplomats, who were witnesses to Shcharansky's actions, to testify on his behalf, and of several prominent Americans to observe his trial. These requests, it was hoped, might pressure the Soviet authorities to drop the American espionage charges in order to avoid a direct confrontation with our State Department.

I received no direct response from the White House, but on June 13, 1977, President Carter issued the following statement:

> I have inquired deeply within the State Department, and within the CIA, as to whether or not Mr. Shcharansky has ever had any known relationship in a subversive way, or otherwise, with the CIA. The answer is "no." We have double-checked this, and I have been hesitant to make that public announcement, but now I am completely convinced, contrary to the allegations that have been recorded in the press, that Mr. Shcharansky has never had any sort of relation, to our knowledge, with the CIA.

I was elated. We later learned that the President had personally decided to issue the denial despite opposition from within the CIA and the State Department. The Soviets could not now charge Shcharansky with spying for the United States without, in effect, calling President Carter a liar.

We did not expect the Carter statement to result in Shcharansky's immediate release. We did expect, however, that this would make it more difficult for the Kremlin to charge him with the most serious crimes he had been accused of—crimes that carried the death penalty.

Throughout the next months there were repeated rumors about a possible prisoner exchange involving Shcharansky. "They're only waiting for the right moment," I kept hearing from informed sources. But nothing happened.

The TV Debate

I conferred with Avital and with other friends and supporters of Shcharansky. We decided that the pressure had to be maintained. In June 1977 a remarkable opportunity was offered to present Shcharansky's case to the American public. Several months earlier the Soviet Union—concerned about its deteriorating image among Euro-Communists—had proposed a debate on Italian television between three Soviet speakers and three Italian speakers on the issue of human rights. The debate proved to be a propaganda coup for the Soviets. Their speakers were articulate, well-prepared, and persuasive. The Soviets, pleased with their victory, then extended a similar challenge to the United States. Three Soviet debaters would confront three American debaters in a ninety-minute live television exchange on NBC. The United States accepted. I was asked to be one of the American debaters. The others were Father Theodore Hesburgh, president of Notre Dame University, and Robert Kaiser, the *Washington Post*'s former Moscow bureau chief. Since I was the only lawyer on our team, my role was to cross-examine the Soviet debaters. I had a long list of questions I was eager to ask about Shcharansky and other prisoners. But then, on the eve of the scheduled debate, the Soviet team received a cable from Moscow instructing them not to participate in a debate in which I cross-examined their team members. The program, which had been given considerable advance billing, could not be canceled. We felt double-crossed. After some negotiation, however, we worked out a compromise so that each team could ask a few questions of the other team—as long as they were not "cross-examination–type questions."

The debate was moderated by Edwin Newman, the NBC news commentator. The most effective debater on the Soviet side was a Soviet journalist and playwright named Genrikh Borovik. Borovik was brilliant, charming, and—as he told us all repeatedly—Jewish. ("Some of our best debaters are Jewish.") Our research had also disclosed that he was ruthless and, almost cetainly, a colonel in the KGB. Although the youngest man in the group, and nominally the lowest ranking, he was clearly in charge. I knew he would emphasize the role of the press, as he had done during the Italian debate, and I prepared to take him on.

When Borovik's turn came, he began by making repeated references to American newspaper accounts of unemployment, crime, and racial discrimination. I directed my first questions at him:

Q. Mr. Borovik, you mentioned "reading American newspapers." Can an average Soviet citizen walk over to a Soviet newsstand and freely ask for today's copy of the *New York Times,* which includes a criticism of the Soviet Union?

A. [There are stands] with many newspapers, except the *Washington Post* and *New York Times.* It's very expensive to buy those newspapers . . .

Borovik proceeded to argue that Communist newspapers were not available in the United States. I answered, however, by describing how I was able to purchase more than twenty-five different Communist newspapers in Harvard Square. He shook his head in disbelief as I took out copies of each of these papers from my briefcase and began to read off their names.

During my affirmative presentation I spoke of the arrests of the Helsinki Monitors:

> It is as if former President Nixon had ordered the arrest of the entire Board of Directors of the American Civil Liberties Union and the *Washington Post* in response to the Watergate allegations. [If Shcharansky's trial] will be fair, why not allow American observers to attend, especially since Americans have been implicated in his alleged crime?

As Borovik was answering, a sobbing voice could be heard from the studio audience: "It's a lie." The voice was that of Avital Shcharansky, whom I had invited to attend the debate, in the hope that she might be able to meet with the Soviet lawyers and request their assistance for her husband.

Borovik then mentioned instances of American deprivation of human rights to its own citizens—specifically the case of Johnny Harris, a black sentenced to death in Alabama for participating in a prison riot in which a guard had been killed. Instead of denying that the United States sometimes violates human rights, I was quick to agree that the Harris case did raise troubling questions. I told Borovik that I had, in fact, done some work on that case and proposed that Soviet and American lawyers and journalists join in working together to remedy human-rights violations in both countries.

Robert Kaiser summarized this point best when he said, "We've had a big advantage here. . . . Whenever we've been faced with a difficult question, we've been able to criticize our government. Unfortunately, [the Soviet debaters] don't have that privilege."

Our confrontation with the Soviet debaters was a success for us. We were able to bring Shcharansky's case to a large American television audience in a popular format. The *New York Times* said the following:

> [T]he "first meeting of its kind" . . . proved to be a fascinating confrontation. The Russians did not fare well against Father Hesburgh's projection of basic human decency, or Professor Dershowitz's aggressive defense of Soviet dissidents. . . . The broadcast constituted a splendid illustration of how the concept of freedom that is preached here is also practiced here.

William Buckley, my old adversary in the debate over obscenity, was even kinder:

> I propose Medals of Freedom for Robert Kaiser, Alan Dershowitz, and Father Theodore Hesburgh. Those poor Russians . . . Dershowitz who, though something of a fundamentalist in the matter of civil liberties, has the Soviet system right between the cross-hairs of his sights. . . . Thanks to the skill of the American team [the Soviet] performance proved pitiable. . . . It is exhilarating that the slave masters did so badly.

When the debate was over, we were taken to a reception at a Washington restaurant. I accompanied Avital Shcharansky. The next day's *New York Times* reported on the "dramatic confrontation":

> The exiled wife of a Soviet Jewish dissident, Anatoly Shcharansky, confronted two visiting Soviet lawyers at [the] reception.
>
> [W]ith Prof. Alan Dershowitz . . . leading the way through the crowded room, Mrs. Shcharansky came face to face with Prof. Samuil Zivs . . .
>
> Professor Zivs asked Mrs. Shcharansky for her maiden name, suggesting that she was the "girl friend" of Mr. Shcharansky, rather than his wife.
>
> At that point, the third Soviet debater, Genrikh Borovik, a journalist, noticed that a reporter from the *New York Times* was taking notes. The Professor then broke off the conversation and moved away after telling Mrs. Shcharansky that bringing in the newspapers "will not do well for your husband."

This was our constant concern. Would the escalating press coverage of Shcharansky's ordeal backfire and work to his disadvantage by making it impossible for the Kremlin to back down? We debated the issue among ourselves, but in the end Avital's view necessarily prevailed: "It is Tolya's way to be public, to confront, and not to hide. If he were here to give us advice, he would definitely want us to keep his case in the news as much as possible. That is his only hope." And so we continued to direct our efforts at the media and at public opinion.

By this time we had been able to surmise that the KGB's investigation was proceeding in high gear. The KGB had summoned dozens of witnesses, including many prominent refuseniks and human-rights activists, as well as an American journalist, Robert C. Toth, who was seized on a Moscow street and interrogated for several days. We had sent instructions to Moscow through the refusenik network that each of the witnesses should be debriefed as soon as he or she was released. I debriefed Toth myself upon his return to the United States. By learning the questions asked of the witnesses we were able to piece together the case the KGB was preparing against Shcharansky. Week after week, we received summaries of the questions. Two conclusions became clear: the KGB was preparing an espionage and treason case against Shcharansky, and the KGB was not allowing the witnesses an opportunity to give evidence favorable to Shcharansky.

"He Spoke the Truth, and He Spoke It in English"

We decided, therefore, to convene a commission consisting of distinguished Americans to assess the evidence the KGB was refusing to consider. The material would then be sent on to the Soviet Union for inclusion in the Shcharansky investigation. The commission consisted of the president of Columbia University, William J. McGill, Senator Frank Church of Idaho, and civil rights activist Bayard Rustin, among others. The hearing was held in the meeting room of the Senate Foreign Relations Committee.

As Shcharansky's American attorney I presented the case for the defense. Jack Greenberg, the director of the NAACP Legal Defense and Educational Fund, Inc., served as counsel to the commission. Chief Judge David Bazelon of the United States Court of Appeals for the District of Columbia formally swore in the witnesses, so that the testimony would be admissible in any proceedings in the Soviet Union against Anatoly Shcharansky. Soviet Ambassador Anatoly F. Dobrynin had been invited to send a representative, but did not respond.

I called as my first witness Avital Shcharansky and asked her whether her husband had been aware that he was under surveillance. She testified that Anatoly had written her "several times that he knows perfectly well those people who trace him, he knows their faces and he knows that the apartment is bugged."

My second witness was Congressman Robert Drinan of Massachusetts, who had spent time with Shcharansky in Moscow shortly before his arrest. Father Drinan testified that Shcharansky always "conducted himself openly."

The next witness was an expert on computer technology who testified that Shcharansky had no computer information of relevance to "the military might of the Soviet Union."

I then called Alfred Friendly, the deputy staff director of the Commission on Security and Cooperation in Europe, who described his contacts with Shcharansky:

> He walked in a way that was different from other Soviet citizens. He held his head up and his shoulders back. And he spoke. [H]e once

> suggested that I listen to the silence of the streets. His only crime was that he spoke the truth, and his worst crime was that he spoke it in English.

As my final witness I called a man who had spent the last several days before Shcharansky's arrest with him, an attorney who had just emigrated from the Soviet Union, Isaac Elkind. Elkind testified that Shcharansky was the initiator of seminars "composed of refuseniks who studied the Soviet law in order to familiarize all members of those groups to prevent any possibility of violating any Soviet law."

Several weeks after the close of the proceedings, the commissioners issued their findings:

> [T]he available evidence establishes that Anatoly Shcharansky has had absolutely no connection with the American CIA and did not engage in any act of espionage.

This conclusion was documented by evidence and testimony. The proceedings of the commission and its findings were published and sent on to the Soviet Procuracy.

The Soviets Appoint a Lawyer for Shcharansky

In June of 1978 the United States Commission on Security and Cooperation in Europe—the Congressional monitoring committee for the Helsinki Accords—decided to convene a hearing on the Shcharansky, Aleksander I. Ginzburg, and Yuri Orlov cases. I was invited to appear for Shcharansky, Edward Bennett Williams for Ginzburg, and Ramsey Clark for Orlov. The hearing represented an important opportunity to present my client's case, since the commission was formally responsible for assessing compliance with the Helsinki Accords.

I brought the commissioners up to date on the Shcharansky case by informing them that the Soviet authorities had appointed an attorney named Silvia Dubrovskaia to represent Shcharansky. I then read them a cable that Father Drinan had sent her:

> Professor Alan Dershowitz has been appointed by Shcharansky's mother, to represent his interest in the United States [and] has interviewed numerous witnesses . . . who have left the Soviet Union. [This] testimony is obviously not available to you, and yet it may prove crucial to the Shcharansky defense case. We do not seek to interfere with your representation or with any legitimate

> domestic affairs of the U.S.S.R. We seek merely to meet with you—lawyer to lawyer—and to share with you relevant information to which we have had unique access [and] we will make immediate plans to travel to Moscow in the spirit of cooperation and mutual understanding.

We never received a response from Dubrovskaia. We later learned that Shcharansky had rejected her as his lawyer.

While these and other public efforts were being made on Shcharansky's behalf, private efforts were being undertaken, as well. Meetings with Soviet officials were arranged. Diplomatic overtures were initiated. Prisoner exchanges were proposed. But nothing happened.

The Trial

And then, the Soviet authorities announced that Anatoly Shcharansky would be tried for high treason in July of 1978. The specific charge was that between 1974 and 1977 the defendant had supplied state secrets to "Western Diplomats, intelligence, as well as an agent of a foreign military-intelligence service who worked under the cover of a journalist in Moscow." The maximum punishment was death by firing squad. That was the news we had dreaded. Until the decision to try Shcharansky for treason was formally announced there was a glimmer of hope—however slight—that he might be released, or tried for a lesser crime. But once a treason trial was announced, the result was inevitable.

I requested permission to travel to the Soviet Union to represent my client, or at least observe the trial. Similar requests were made by Shcharansky's European lawyers, his Canadian lawyer, and others. All were either ignored or denied.

The days immediately preceding the trial were a frenzy of activity. I crisscrossed the country speaking on behalf of my doomed client at rallies, in legislative halls, and on television. During the trial Barbara Walters interviewed me for the ABC evening news, and asked whether Shcharansky was "being tried primarily because he is a Jew." I answered that he was being tried

> because he's a Jew; because he wanted to emigrate; because he spoke English beautifully and was one of the leaders of the Helsinki movement, and communicated effectively with the press; because he was the link between the various dissident movements; and because he was a very outspoken and courageous man.

Walters then asked me what the "importance of this trial [was] to other Soviet dissidents." I answered:

> It's a message to them that no matter how hard they try to remain within the spirit and the letter of the law they will be prosecuted and convicted if they speak out against the system or seek to emigrate.

As the trial drew to a close, my frustration mounted. Though supported by people throughout the world, Anatoly stood alone in the prisoner's dock, defending himself. He was not allowed to speak to his family, friends, or supporters. His mother was excluded from the courtroom, as were Andrei Sakharov and other human-rights and Jewish activists. The Soviets announced that the trial was "open," but that all the seats were "occupied by others." Only Anatoly's brother Leonid was allowed to take a back-row seat, and so he became Anatoly's sole link to the outside world. Several times the brothers passed in the hallway and were able to exchange greetings and smiles. Leonid was amazed: after nearly a year and a half of virtually incommunicado detention and interrogation, Anatoly had not lost his buoyancy, his enthusiasm, or even his sense of humor. The first thing he whispered to his brother as he passed him in the hall was "You're getting a bit fat out there," as he flashed him a crumpled photo of Avital, which he kept with him at all times. But his external calm masked an internal dread: Anatoly knew that his fate was sealed.

As I read the reports of the trial I decided to try one last desperate attempt to present a legal argument on my client's behalf. I worked all through the night drafting the closing argument I would have presented if I had been allowed in the Soviet court. I cabled it to the judges, and it was published in *Newsweek* and in the *Congressional Record.* This is part of my statement:

"Honorable Judges, I am here to speak on behalf of a man who has already been declared guilty by the Soviet press and by high-ranking officials of the Soviet Communist Party and government. I am acutely aware of the burden under which you labor. I know—as you know only too well—that no judge in the half century of Soviet history has ever voted to acquit a defendant charged with a political crime such as treason. But I ask you to throw off your yokes and to act as honorable members of the legal profession: by rendering a true and honest judgment.

"If the charges were not so serious, they would be comic indeed. Imagine how incompetent an American intelligence agency would have to be to have engaged someone like Shcharansky as a spy. His phone obviously tapped, his every movement openly under surveillance, his roommate a KGB plant, Shcharansky was the worst possible candidate for the espionage game. Imagine how incompetent the Soviet counterespionage apparatus would have to be to have let someone like Shcharansky—a man who had publicly declared his allegiance to Israel and who had demanded the right to emigrate there—*have access to* military secrets.

"When your country and mine brought the Nazi judges to trial at Nuremberg, one German judge—in defense of his decision to allow an innocent Jew to be executed—argued that by following the party's orders in one case he could slow down the process of genocide. The Nuremberg judges—from your country and mine—rejected his defense and jointly proclaimed that on the day that justice was perverted by the deliberate conviction of the first innocent victim, an irreversible step toward judicial genocide had been taken. I implore you to search your consciences before you take a similar tragic step here."

"I Have Nothing to Say to This Court"

While I was drafting my argument in the quiet comfort of my Cambridge home, Anatoly was at work in his tiny cell composing his argument—the one that would actually be presented to the Soviet court. At the close of the fourth and final day of trial Anatoly was given the opportunity to end his sixteen months of enforced silence. The statement he delivered is truly remarkable. Turning his back to the judges, he spoke directly to the one person in the entire courtroom who would listen to and transmit his courageous words—his brother Leonid. This is some of what he said:

> I understand that to defend oneself in a semi-closed trial such as this is a hopeless case from the very beginning.

At this point his speech was interrupted by a shout: "They ought to hang people like that!" Anatoly continued:

> Those who conducted the investigation warned me [that] I would receive either the death sentence or a minimum of fifteen years of prison [unless] I agreed to cooperate with the KGB organs in helping to destroy the Jewish emigration movement. They promised a speedy release and even a meeting with my wife.
>
> And now, when I am farther than ever from my people and from my Avital, when I face many difficult years of imprisonment, I say, addressing my people and my Avital:

> *"L'shana ha-baah b'Yerushalayim!"*
> "Next year in Jerusalem!"

Then Shcharansky turned abruptly to the three judges and looked them squarely in the eye and said contemptuously, "I have nothing to say to this court, which must confirm an already predetermined sentence." With that, he sat down and waited for the inevitable verdict and sentence.

Several hours later the judges returned to the courtroom and formally announced that Shcharansky was guilty of all charges and would be imprisoned for thirteen years. The only good news was that his life had been spared.

Several of the KGB cheerleaders who filled the courtroom yelled "Not enough!" Leonid yelled out to his brother, "Tolya, the whole world is with you," as the guards led Anatoly away. Leonid left the courtroom weeping and joined his friends on the street. They were anxious to hear how Anatoly had borne up. Leonid read them Anatoly's final remarks, as their mother sobbed hysterically. Andrei Sakharov moved over to comfort the grieving mother. KGB agents stepped between them. Finally the reserved scientist could not control his feelings. "You are not people!" he shouted at the KGB agents in an uncharacteristic burst of anger. "Hear me, a member of the Soviet Academy of Sciences, you are fascists." The crowd milled around the emptying courthouse, when suddenly one of Shcharansky's supporters started singing "Hatikva," the Jewish anthem of hope. All the supporters —Jew and non-Jew alike—joined in the melody, and the crowd slowly dispersed.

"Thus ended a Moscow show trial that had captured the attention of the U.S. and the world," reported *Newsweek.* And indeed it had, as the name of Anatoly Shcharansky became a household word for several weeks. His smiling, ebullient, yet intense, face appeared on the cover of almost every news magazine and newspaper in the Western world. But Anatoly would not see these magazines or newspapers unless he became a free man.

When the news reached Avital in Washington, D.C., her first reaction was, "In thirteen years I will no longer be able to bear children." Several days after the sentence Anatoly was given permission to write his first letter to Avital from prison. Characteristically, it minimized his own suffering:

> Natulenka, when a few days before my arrest I unsuccessfully tried to telephone you, sensing that this was the last opportunity to hear your voice, a "wise" man told me: "When it is very difficult for you, console yourself with the thought that it is even more difficult for

Natasha." He was right—of course it is much harder for you than for me. But he was a thousand times wrong—in no way can I console myself with that.

Avital, my beloved, my dear one, I believe that we shall yet enjoy genuinely happy days together—I repeat this hope every day in a prayer which I composed myself in my primitive Hebrew. . . .

[Y]ou are a great heroine and I am very happy and proud that I have such a wife.

Tolya

The Endless Wait

Since the trial, Avital has traveled all over the world seeking support for her imprisoned husband. Her lawyers have continued to work as well: an exhaustive brief was filed by Shcharansky's Canadian lawyer, Professor Irwin Cotler of McGill University; conferences and rallies have been arranged; prisoner exchanges have been proposed; and diplomatic efforts persist.

Anatoly languishes in prison. He has lost weight, suffered dizzy spells, and been injured in an accident. His father has died of heart failure. His mother has been denied numerous visits. In the spring of 1981 I met with Josif Mendelevich and Hillel Butman, who had recently been released from prison where they had seen Shcharansky. They told me that his spirits remained high despite his deteriorating health.

My involvement in the case continues unabated. I have traveled to Madrid to present Shcharansky's case—and those of Ida Nudel and the remaining Leningrad prisoners—at the International Helsinki compliance meetings.

In January of 1982, Shcharansky's mother and brother traveled for several days to spend two hours with him. Thin and pale, Anatoly reported that three years of his sentence had been changed from labor camp to prison—with much harsher conditions—because he had been found guilty of "continuing to consider himself not guilty." He had also been punished for lighting Hanukkah candles.

Whenever I begin to lose hope or motivation I recall a statement made by Genrikh Borovik, the Soviet journalist against whom I debated on NBC. At a reception at the Soviet embassy before the debate, I asked him why the Kremlin was prepared to endanger détente by incurring the wrath of the American government and the media over the Shcharansky case. He replied, "Within months after the Shcharansky trial the American press and the American people will forget him. The memory of your people is very short. Of course, we will be criticized during the trial and for several weeks before and after, but within a few months nobody will even remember his name. He will become just another faceless prisoner."

Anatoly Shcharansky cannot be allowed to become "just another faceless prisoner." The American memory must not be allowed to fade—not of Anatoly Shcharansky, whose name and face are known to millions, nor of the thousands of faceless political prisoners throughout the world.

8

Is the Threat to Bring a Lawsuit a Mental Illness Or a Crime?: The Cases of the Turnabout Judge and the Fenway Park Cop

I was sorting through my books and notes and getting ready to leave for an afternoon class on Psychiatry and Law when the telephone rang. I considered not answering it, since I was on my way to pick up my teaching colleague, Dr. Alan Stone, a psychiatrist who teaches at Harvard Law School. Stone and I had been teaching this course together for more than ten years. Our subject for that day's class was the politics of psychiatry. I was prepared to discuss the Soviet practice of committing dissidents to mental hospitals for asserting their legal rights. I was also going to say—as I have in the past—that commitment of the mentally ill in the United States, while it raises serious questions of law and policy, is not used in an overtly political manner.

But I did answer the phone, and the conversation that ensued caused me to change my lecture quite dramatically. "I've just been committed to a mental hospital by Judge Brewin," the caller said in an agitated voice. I receive many such calls over any given year and I asked the woman on the line to describe the situation. She told me that three weeks earlier she had come to Cambridge to visit a cousin. After a night of difficult and confused interaction the cousin had called the police and had her committed. She had been confined since that time until her court hearing, which had been held that morning in a makeshift courtroom on the hospital grounds.

Having been a prelaw student, and having taken a course in forensic psychiatry, the caller decided—quite foolishly—to represent herself at the hearing. She did quite well, up to a point. The government presented its case, which consisted largely of the testimony of a hospital psychiatrist who diagnosed the patient as paranoid schizophrenic. My caller, whom I will call Lauri, cross-examined the psychiatrist and exposed some soft spots in the testimony. After the close of the government's case the judge issued the following oral ruling: "On the basis of what I have heard, I order the patient released." This should, of course, have ended the matter, but some people don't know enough to shut up when they are ahead. Lauri then said:

> For the record, I want the psychologist to testify as to her findings regarding my diagnosis. I want to be vindicated . . . For the purpose of any future lawsuits which may be brought for me, I wish to go on with the hearing and to have this on record.

As soon as Judge Brewin heard the words "future lawsuits," he bristled. Turning to the patient, he said, "On the basis of these statements, I have decided to commit you." Observers in the courtroom thought at first that he was joking. But he repeated his conclusion, sternly: "The patient will be committed."

I have heard many strange stories from committed mental patients, and I have learned to listen to them with a shaker full of salt. I asked Lauri whether there was a transcript or a recording of the hearing that could establish the judge had done this. She told me there were no transcripts or recordings, but that a lawyer friend of hers had been in the hearing room and taken notes. I spoke to the lawyer, and she corroborated the substance of what Lauri had told me. I asked the lawyer to come to my office as soon as class was over.

When I arrived in class I described the phone call, saying that I might be interested in representing the patient, and asked if any of the students might want to help out. I said that if the facts were as Lauri and her friend had described them—a big "if" in my mind—then this might be an instance of political abuse of psychiatric commitment laws. It seemed clear that *if* the judge had been prepared to release Lauri at the close of the government's case and *if* he had changed his mind and ordered her commitment only after she had said that she might sue the hospital, then the basis for her commitment was the exercise of her rights to bring a lawsuit.

Dr. Stone and I then went on to conduct a dialogue about the ideological bases of mental illness and commitment. We talked about Dr. Benjamin Rush, the father of American psychiatry, who had been a surgeon in the Continental Army and a close associate of General George Washington. He had given diagnostic labels to all manner of political activities and beliefs: fervent supporters of revolution suffered from "revolutiona"; radicals were affected with "anarchia." I could not help thinking that if Rush were alive today he would perhaps diagnose a citizen who threatened lawsuits as being afflicted with "litigatia." The vivid image of Lauri being committed because she threatened a lawsuit hung over the entire class, as we continued our discussion of the potential abuses of psychiatry.

When I returned to my office after class, Lauri's friend was there. She had prepared an affidavit describing in detail the commitment hearing before Judge Brewin. I read it and decided that I would take the case and seek the patient's immediate release. The affidavit confirmed the arbitrary and abusive nature of Judge Brewin's change of mind. I was outraged, but not surprised. It is common for judges to protect other governmental institutions; there have been numerous instances of judges conditioning the dismissal of criminal charges on the agreement of the defendant not to sue the police. Judges often have a cozy relationship with "their" policemen. It is also common for judges to react personally and precipitously when they are angered by a litigant's assertiveness.

The call from Lauri provided a good opportunity to call this pattern of judicial arrogance and abuse to the attention of a higher court. It was also important to maintain the integrity of the psychiatric hospital system; to make certain that commitment of the mentally ill could not be used to *punish* patients for invoking their legal rights.

I had long been interested in the rights of the mentally ill. During my law school years, I had worked with several professors in that area, and upon graduation I clerked for Chief Judge David Bazelon who was the country's leading judicial authority on the relationship between law and psychiatry. In 1964 I developed and taught the first course offered at Harvard Law School on that subject. In 1968 I published my first law review article, entitled "Psychiatry in the Legal Process, A Knife that Cuts Both Ways." (The title was derived from *The Brothers Karamazov,* where Dostoevsky had said, "Profound as psychology is, it's a knife that cuts both ways . . . You can prove anything by it.") In that article, I criticized both psychiatrists and lawyers alike for neglecting the civil liberties of the mentally ill. I ended with a call for lawyers to become involved in defending patients at commitment hearings:

> [N]o legal rule should ever be phrased in medical terms; no legal decision should ever be turned over to the psychiatrist; there is no such thing as a legal problem which can not—and should not—be phrased in terms familiar to lawyers. And civil commitment of the mentally ill is a legal problem; whenever compulsion is used or freedom denied—whether by the state, the church, the union, the university, or the psychiatrist—the issue becomes a legal one: and lawyers must be quick to immerse themselves in it. The words of Brandeis ring true:

> "... Experience should teach us to be most on our guard to protect liberty when the Government's purposes are beneficent. Men born to freedom are naturally alert to repel invasion of their liberty by evil-minded rulers. The greatest dangers to liberty lurk in insidious encroachment by men of zeal, well-meaning but without understanding."

Since that time I had written and lectured extensively about the rights of the mentally ill, but I had never actually represented a defendant in a civil commitment case.

I decided to bring the matter directly to a justice of the state's highest court. Under Massachusetts law, a single justice of the Supreme Judicial Court has the power to issue a writ of habeas corpus—an order releasing a detained person from confinement—in extraordinary cases.

I was determined to act quickly, both to emphasize the importance of the case and to underscore the point that every minute of additional confinement following the judge's original order of release constituted a continuing abuse of the legal and mental-health systems. Setting ourselves a noon deadline for the following day, my students and I worked feverishly to produce the necessary legal research and documents. By the next morning we had completed a draft of the papers, and I informed the state Attorney General's office that we were suing Judge Brewin and the superintendent of the hospital.

At eleven-thirty we appeared in the Supreme Judicial Court and requested an emergency hearing. At first, the clerk's office was discouraging about our prospects of obtaining quick relief, but we pressed our claim. Finally, the presiding justice—Herbert P. Wilkins—indicated that he would hear us at one o'clock, following a hearing on a controversial challenge to a recently enacted statute mandating "voluntary" prayers in the public schools.

I went into the packed courtroom and listened to the prayer-case argument. When it was over everybody left the courtroom and I approached the lectern feeling a bit like a burlesque comedian performing to an empty house after the last stripper had completed her performance. I began my argument:

> Good afternoon, your Honor. This is an emergency application seeking the immediate release of a woman who was ordered committed to a mental hospital because she expressed the possible desire to exercise her rights to bring a lawsuit against the hospital. There are only three facts relevant to our application: 1) After hearing the entire government's case . . . the judge reached a decision [and] issued an

> oral order to release the patient; 2) At that point, the patient made various statements, [none of which] were in any way relevant to the issues of mental illness or . . . dangerousness. . . . All bore on her right to bring a lawsuit. The entire speech took approximately thirty seconds . . .; 3) The judge, on the basis of this thirty-second statement of a desire to bring a lawsuit, changed his mind, and changed his order of release to an order of commitment.
>
> Our country has been justly proud, as we compare our record of the use of mental hospitals to the records of other countries throughout the world. And many people have stated unequivocally that no people today are in mental hospitals in this country for the exercise of their political or legal rights. As I stand here now, your Honor, that statement can no longer be made. [Lauri] is in Westboro State Hospital solely as punishment for the exercise of her political and legal rights.

At this point Justice Wilkins interjected, inquiring about "how this proceeding for commitment got commenced."

I explained what I knew:

> Approximately twenty days ago this woman went to visit her cousin, a professor at Harvard College, and spent one night at the cousin's house and manifested behavior which to the cousin seemed disturbed. The cousin then called the police, took her physically to Cambridge City Hospital and sought her commitment. She represented herself at the hearing. She had a course in forensic psychiatry, a 700 on the Law School Aptitude test, and a prelaw education which made her feel that she was capable of representing herself. I'm not commenting on that, your Honor.

But the justice did comment on that. "There is a certain problem of a person subject to charges consisting of commitment being competent enough to represent oneself."

I agreed.

> Absolutely. And all those matters were taken into account, presumably by the judge. Nonetheless, in the face of the evidence against her and in face of her cross-examination, of her statements, the judge ordered her released. That is the order we are seeking to have enforced. It is as if, your Honor, the judge had said "released." And then the government had come in and said, "By the way, your Honor, do you know that this defendant is black rather than white?" and the judge said, "Oh, black rather than white, I'm ordering her commit-

> ted." At that point nobody would look at what went on thereafter. The reasons for reopening were invalid reasons, and the reasons for reopening in this case were entirely invalid reasons.

The justice then called on the assistant Attorney General to present the Commonwealth's position. The assistant admitted that my rendition of facts was accurate but argued that "there are simply no illegalities here, your Honor." Justice Wilkins disagreed:

> It sounds to me as if the judge took the position that he was going to go forward on the commitment because she was threatening litigation, and it seems to me that is an indefensible position.

The assistant Attorney General responded that Lauri's statement "may have indicated to him some additional evidence of mental illness."

Justice Wilkins then gave his tentative conclusion:

> Well, I certainly think she should be released . . . The question is what happens to the proceedings . . . from here.

He then asked me whether I could give him

> assurance that this matter was being dealt with by members of her family in the kind of way that would be helpful, that possibly that's the best solution?

I was not in a position to give that kind of assurance:

> Your Honor, I made efforts this morning to try to be able to answer that question, which I anticipated, and I have to report that I have not been able to receive those assurances. Part of the problem as I understand it is a substantial disagreement between this young woman and her family, who live in California, and I don't expect that there will be support from family directly. [It] is the current contention stated by the patient not to remain in the Commonwealth if she has that choice.

Justice Wilkins then ended the proceedings saying that he was "going to reflect on this matter."

Within an hour after returning to my office following the argument, I received a call from the court indicating that Judge Wilkins had issued an order directing the Superintendent of the Mental Hospital to release Lauri "forthwith" and with no conditions. His accompanying opinion contained the following crucial paragraph:

> The threat of litigation was not a valid basis for committing the petitioner, or for reopening the proceeding to take further evidence. Consequently, the petitioner should be released from the custody of the defendant superintendent. It is my hope that private efforts to assist the petitioner can be made.

Private efforts were, in fact, made to assist her in finding a place to live and in receiving emotional support and medical help. Within a week she boarded an overseas flight and moved to a kibbutz in Israel. She has since written several letters informing me that she is happy and doing well. The letters suggest that she may well be suffering from a mental illness, but she seems to be coping in the nurturing atmosphere of a rural kibbutz.

"Tell It to the Judge"

The threat to bring a lawsuit should never be considered by governmental authorities as a basis for committing or otherwise punishing a litigant. But the sad fact is that citizens are punished all the time for asserting their rights. It is common practice for courts and police officers to require arrested persons to waive their rights to sue the arresting officer as a precondition to their release. The arrested person is thus blackmailed into giving up his right to sue the policeman on the threat that if he refuses to do so he will be held in jail. Few such citizens are willing to endure further imprisonment, and so they "willingly" sign the waiver. I had been victimized myself by this practice just a few months before Lauri's case had arisen, and the memory of that outrage was still fresh in my mind when I decided to become her lawyer.

My case had arisen in the invigorating surroundings of Fenway Park during a Boston Red Sox–New York Yankees baseball game. A Yankees-Red Sox game always carries the risk of the unexpected, especially when Tommy John is on the mound against Dennis Eckersley. But what happened to me was far from my wildest dreams when a lawyer friend called me on a lovely Sunday afternoon and offered me tickets to the game. "I can't use my tickets. Can you be over in ten minutes?" It was half an hour to game time, but my son and I hustled into our best Fenway Park attire and made it to the game by the middle of the first inning. We had just about settled into our four-dollar grandstand seats behind first base when a burly fellow in a shiny bowling jacket rudely reached over me and asked my sixteen-year-old son for his ticket. Jamie showed it to him and the man said, "Give that to me."

Fearful that he would take the ticket and claim the seat was his, Jamie said, "No, it's mine."

The man said, "Oh, yeah, well I'm a cop and that's a stolen ticket. Come along with me."

Funny, he didn't look much like a cop, and so I said, "Wait a minute, let's see your identification."

"OK, mister, is this kid your son? You come along, too."

I asked if we were being arrested.

He said, "No, this is just an investigation."

In the meantime, Jerry Remy had just bunted his way onto first and Burleson was coming to bat with Lynn in the on-deck circle. I told the cop that the tickets were not stolen, but had been given to me by a reputable lawyer, and I would be delighted to cooperate with any investigation. I gave him my business card.

He took it and said, "OK, wiseguy, both you and your kid are guilty of receiving stolen goods."

I asked him what the goods were and from whom they were stolen, and he said, "The tickets for your seats have been pickpocketed from their rightful owners and you're in possession of them." I said that I didn't know anything about any pickpocketing. He grabbed us both and led us away.

As we were leaving, two people in the row behind handed me their business cards and offered to be witnesses to "this outrage," as one of them called it. On the way downstairs we passed some phone booths and I asked for permission to call my lawyer, but the policeman refused: "Your card says you're a lawyer, you don't need another one." Sure I'm a lawyer, I thought, but I didn't want a fool for a client.

When we got downstairs I asked the supervising officer whether I could explain the whole thing and get back in time for the rest of the game. He said no, I would have to explain it to the judge the next day. A wagon was on its way over and we would have to be handcuffed. I asked why they were taking my son. They said that he had refused to cooperate in the investigation. I assured them that he knew nothing other than that we were going to a ball game, and the policeman said, "That's enough." The supervising officer did allow me my one short phone call, which went to Harvey Silverglate, my attorney.

Off we went to the pokey. When we got there we were immediately separated. My son was taken away to a tiny juvenile holding cell, without even a chair, and locked up. I was asked whether I had a belt ("You can hang yourself with a belt," I was solemnly informed) and told I could keep my wallet and lawyer's diary. The arresting officer then informed me that I was being charged with "disturbing a public assembly," as well as receiving stolen goods. I asked whether he was claiming that I had raised my voice. He assured me I had not. (I hadn't even had a chance to cheer for our Fenway heroes.) "The fact that you had a conversation with me must have disturbed the fans." I reminded him that the fans were all on my side and that the whole incident took about a minute. "Tell it to the judge," he said with a smirk.

Like a good lawyer I took out my little notebook and started to write down what the policeman had said (especially his admission that I hadn't raised my voice). Upon seeing this the policeman said, "We've just rescinded our permission to let you keep your wallet and notebook. Now we're really gonna search you."

They took everything out of my pockets, out of my wallet, and out of the bagful of snacks I had quickly assembled to munch at the game. The search took about half an hour. Fifty-two sunflower seeds were carefully counted and sealed in an envelope. Two bananas and a chocolate chip cookie were added to the inventory. My glasses were confiscated. Finally, I was taken away. My jailer looked around for an appropriate cell and settled on one with an open and unflushable latrine into which the last prisoner had recently thrown up. My next-door neighbor was a homosexual charged with a stabbing. When he wasn't trying to reach his hands into my cell, he was banging on the wall and screaming "Let me out of here! Officer, I got to get out. I need a fix. I need some speed. Let me out!" My cell rattled from his constant assault on the walls. I sat on the hard bench for over an hour waiting (and wondering what had happened to Remy at first base; I later learned that he had been ingloriously picked off).

Finally, Harvey Silverglate's partner, Tom Shapiro, appeared and told me the whole thing was a terrible mistake and had been cleared up. It turned out that my lawyer-friend had found the tickets outside his law office on the night before the game—along with several other pairs of tickets to future games. He had tried to turn them over to the night watchman in the building, but then noticed that two of them were for the next afternoon and would obviously go to waste, so he decided to use them and then reimburse their owner when he was located on Monday. The owner, an insurance salesman, had apparently dropped them while making a phone call. Embarrassed by the loss of his company's tickets, he had concocted a story about being pickpocketed, which he proceeded to report to the police. The police, told of their exact location, were waiting to see who sat in the "hot" seats. I was unaware of all this until Shapiro told me about it.

I thanked my lawyer for clearing the matter up and getting me out. And then—like Lauri—I said, "Boy, am I gonna hit the cops with a whopping lawsuit." (I had spent the time in my cell fantasizing about the amount of the suit: $10,000? No. $100,000? Why not a million!) Shapiro responded soberly, "Alan, you know you can't do that."

"Why not?" I asked, incredulously.

"They won't let you or Jamie out unless you both sign waivers releasing the cops from all liability for false arrest," he told me.

"You must be kidding," I snapped. "I won't sign my release under any circumstances."

"Then they won't let you out until after you're arraigned tomorrow, and you'll both get arrest records for a felony," he said, shaking his head.

"That's goddamn blackmail," I answered, "and I won't have anything to do with it."

By this time my son had joined us. He was anxious to get out since he had an important exam the next morning. He urged me to sign the release. I proposed that he sign *his* release to get out, but that I would refuse to sign mine. Shapiro said that the cops wouldn't go for that: either I signed it or both of us would stay in jail. I thought about it for a few minutes and decided that the release probably wasn't binding, since it would be signed under the threat of imprisonment. I decided to sign it, get out, and then sue the bastards anyway.

As soon as I signed, the precinct captain appeared and apologized for the misunderstanding. He said he didn't realize that he "had a tiger by the tail," and he hoped the whole thing would be forgotten. "As far as we're concerned, you and your son were never arrested; it was all a mistake." I asked about any records. "There are no records," he assured me. "You weren't arrested or booked. If anybody ever asks you, you weren't arrested. Understand?" I said I understood, and left the police station still grumbling about a lawsuit.

Eventually, we decided not to sue, since my son had a job selling popcorn in Fenway Park that summer and he didn't want to alienate the arresting officer—who was on full-time season duty in Fenway. But I am still outraged at the policy of the police—and of many courts—in refusing to release innocent people unless and until they waive all rights to sue the people who detained them improperly.

My Fenway Park episode was, of course, the mirror image of what Judge Brewin had done to Lauri, and so our victory in her case gave me some vicarious vindication for what had happened to me and my son at Fenway Park and in the police lockup on that lovely Sunday in June.

— 9 —

Capital Punishment for the Sins of Their Father

It took me longer to get into the Arizona State Prison to visit Ricky and Raymond Tison than it had taken them to break their father Gary out of the same prison two years earlier. It was the eve of Halloween when I met Ricky and Raymond on death row. The ghost of their father hovered over the prison in which he had been an inmate for nearly twenty years. During the last eleven of those years he had been a "lifer," sentenced for the killing of a guard in an earlier escape. While there, Gary Tison had become the most important inmate at the Arizona State Prison—a prison organizer and leader. Then he became its most famous escapee.

The setting of the prison was appropriate for the season. Situated in Florence—the oldest town in rural Arizona—the high barbed-wire prison walls provided an eerie contrast to the flat, dusty cotton terrain of Pinal County. As I stood at the gate of the maximum security wing of the prison —"super-max," the inmates call it—I could barely see the top of the guard tower through the clouds of dust. It might have looked poetic in a movie. But in real life you breathed the heavy dust. It covered your lips, nostrils, and eyes. It remained with you for hours after you left. It was a relief finally to be allowed into the antiseptic corridors of super-max.

I had been driven to the prison by Dorothy Tison, the boys' mother, and Dan Deck, a journalism instructor at the prison, who had befriended the boys' father while he published the prison newspaper. Mrs. Tison, a slight, tight-lipped woman who reminded me of the wife in "American Gothic," was under indictment herself for helping to plan the escape. Dan Deck, a peripatetic character planning to write a book about the Tisons, was earning his living as an inventor. (His current project was a fluid vibrator that could replicate the sensation of the human tongue: "There's a hundred-million-dollar-a-year market out there for a tireless tongue," he assured me.) As we drove through the Arizona desert, Deck kept up a nonstop conversation about the life and exploits of Gary Tison. (I soon began to think of Deck as the "tireless tongue.") It seemed as if he was the authorized biographer of a great man. He knew everything about Gary Tison, and he spoke of him in reverential tones.

As the car drove into Florence—past its trailer parks, its $12-a-night motel, and its cotton fields—I could feel the drama coming alive. The participants I had read about in the trial transcripts and newspaper accounts were no longer abstract characters in a theoretical legal dispute. We approached the prison. Dorothy Tison began to cry. "They won't let me visit the boys today. Ever since my indictment I can only come with my lawyer. Can't a mother spend the remaining time with her sons before they take them away from me?" She wiped her eyes as her tears turned to anger: "You know I can never get this time back. If they kill Raymond and Ricky I'll have nothing left. That's why I'm fighting so hard. I won't let them take Raymond and Ricky from me."

In an obvious attempt to change the tone of the conversation, Dan Deck began to point out the important landmarks in the escape: the hospital parking lot where the escapees had switched cars; the dirt road they took out of town and into the desert; and then—as if to suggest the inevitable symmetry of justice—the Spanish-style courthouse in which Ricky and Raymond Tison were eventually tried and convicted of the jailbreak. In another courthouse, in a different part of the state, they had also been convicted of mass murder and sentenced to die in the gas chamber.

That was why I was in Arizona on that dusty autumn day. I had come to argue for the lives of the Tison brothers before the Arizona Supreme Court the next morning. The argument would take place on Raymond's twenty-first birthday; Ricky was eleven months older. They had both been teenagers at the time of the escape. I wanted to meet the two young men, to learn their story, and to try to understand what could have motivated them to participate in the most publicized jailbreak, mass murder, and manhunt in Arizona history.

Life Without Father

It had started without violence. The plans for a peaceful escape had been hatched during one of the visits the Tison brothers made to their convict father. These visits had become a weekly ritual during the many years Gary had spent in prison.

Raymond, Ricky, and Donald Tison had not known a real father—a "home father," rather than a "prison father," as they put it—for many years. Gary had spent nearly all of his adult life in the Arizona prison. Even before he met and married Dorothy, he had served two years for armed robbery. After just a few years of marriage, and three children in quick succession, Gary was again convicted of armed robbery. He had held up several stores with an army machine gun stolen from the local armory. This time he would serve five years. During that time, Dorothy took the boys to visit him every week. In the crowded visitors area, they would pray, play, and laugh together. Dorothy was determined to preserve the family in anticipation of her husband's return.

Gary's release brought a period of real happiness to the close-knit family. The waiting, the long, dusty trips to Florence, the stigma of Gary's imprisonment, had all been worth it. Over the next year, as the boys remember it, they had a real father. Gary took his boys—who were then eight, seven, and six—fishing, hunting, and camping. They played roughhouse, climbed trees, and did all the things sons and fathers are supposed to do together.

But whatever was inside of Gary had reared its ugly and uncontrollable head again. This time it was merely passing a bad check, but it meant more time in prison. Even though it would be only six months this time, Gary couldn't face it. Maybe it was the time he had spent at home with the boys and Dorothy. It had been a good time, better than he had ever imagined.

He was taken off to jail, but he knew he wouldn't stay. He waited for his opportunity. It came sooner than he expected. Usually when a prisoner is sent to court for a legal proceeding, two armed guards accompany him. But because Gary was trusted, he was sent with only one guard. On the way back from court Gary overpowered the guard, killed him, and took his gun Then he held up a family and demanded a dime to call some friends. When the frightened family offered up their wallets and jewels, Gary said that he didn't need those; the dime would be fine. His magnanimity earned him the title "Gentleman bandit."

Gary was recaptured and his six-month sentence became life without possibility of parole. Ricky, Raymond, and Donald were again without a home father—this time for good. At first, Dorothy could not face telling her nine-, eight-, and seven-year-old sons. But they learned: from classmates, from rumors, and finally from their mother. When Ricky found out that his father would not be coming home soon, he locked himself in the bathroom screaming, "I want my daddy . . ."

The boys readjusted to their fatherless home. They developed into likeable teenagers, with the usual interests in hunting, fishing, cars, and girls. Ricky spent a lot of time at his grandfather's gas station, establishing a reputation as an expert auto mechanic. Ray took on a series of odd jobs from loading bricks to installing can-openers. Eventually, he earned enough money to buy himself a car. Donny worked part-time at a pizza parlor and then joined the Marines. The boys were close. Dorothy told them that it was important for a family to love each other and that they needed each other. Ricky helped keep Donny, the most headstrong of the three, out of trouble. Many times the younger brothers waited to help Donny close up the Pizza Hut at night and left with him to meet friends for a beer or a swim. Through it all, Dorothy supported them by working as a secretary for an insurance agency.

Virtually every weekend over those years included a trip to see Gary. The family would stay with Dorothy's mother, who lived near the prison, and spend whatever time was permitted with Gary. As the boys grew older they sometimes saw Gary alone, or missed a weekend, but throughout all that time Dorothy made sure that Gary maintained as much of a father's role as possible. She lavished on him the intimate trivia of his sons' daily lives, from spelling-test scores to new shoes. As the years passed, she encouraged Gary to dispense discipline and praise, backing up his orders to terminate car privileges and deferring to his approval of Donny's desire to join the Marines. Gary came naturally to his role, for he was proud of his sons and frustrated by the tedium of prison life. His strong will and consummate skill at manipulating others found a ready outlet in his opportunity to influence his sons.

The boys had their share of trouble, of course, but it was relatively trivial. Ricky and Raymond once stole a few bottles of beer from a Mexican food store near their house. They were caught and made to clean up several miles of highway litter.

Donny, the eldest, wanted to become a lawyer. As a first step he thought he might become a policeman or an FBI agent. He took courses at Central Arizona College and had, as one of his instructors, a retired policeman who had twice arrested his father. Gary, the convict father, was proud that his eldest boy wanted to be on the other side of the law: "It doesn't matter what you do or which side you're on," he told his sons, "as long as you are the best at what you do." Ricky and Raymond were uncertain about their future. Their lives were consumed by the present reality of their father's imprisonment.

The visits continued. More and more the talk turned to the frustration of Gary's efforts to obtain parole. Friends offered him jobs. Politicians promised intervention. But nothing happened. Several times the boys had been led to believe that parole or commutation was imminent, only to have their adolescent hopes shattered by the political realities. It was becoming clear that nothing was going to happen—at least not lawfully. No one was prepared to take a chance on a four-time loser who had killed a prison guard.

Gary was a man of action. What he hated most was waiting. And that is what prisoners do. They wait, and they count, and they hope. They file briefs, and they write petitions—and they wait. Some of them plan escapes. For every attempted escape there must be a thousand plans. But Gary was not going to be one of the dreamers. He wanted out, and he set his plans in operation.

The first step was to get himself removed from the "escape risk" list and maximum security—to establish a sense of trust in him by the prison officials. When some young prisoners started a strike, Gary sided with the officials and helped to quell it. This, coupled with his exemplary record on the newspaper, television, and entertainment committee, earned him the right to have visits with his family in the outdoor recreation area. The weekly visits became picnics: fried chicken, rum cake, lemonade, and lots of laughter. It whetted the family's appetite for even greater intimacy that only release could satisfy. The talk turned to reunion. At first there were jokes about meeting in an exotic foreign land. Soon the jokes turned to serious talk. A decision was reached: the boys would help their father escape—a method of leaving prison that had worked for Gary Tison, at least temporarily, twice before. This time he would make it out of the country: the Arizona State Prison is only two hours from the Mexican border. They planned a summer breakout.

The Escape

Plans soon turned to action. And on a hot summer visiting day in July of 1978, the three Tison brothers arrived at Florence with their perennial picnic basket. But there were two differences: Dorothy was not with them; and in place of her fried chicken and rum cake, the basket was stuffed with pistols and shotguns.

The boys had planned carefully for the breakout. They had bought weapons; managed to have several shotguns sawed off; and arranged for a car to be parked in the lot of the local hospital. They knew there were risks. They might not make it. But they had no choice. If they did make it they would be together with their father and free. If they didn't make it they would be together with their father—in prison.

There were other dangers, of course. There could be shooting. They might be killed. Their father might be killed. But their father assured them—promised them—that nobody would get hurt. "The more firepower you have," he instructed them, "the less likely you'll have to use it."

"We told Dad," Raymond said, "we'll do this on one condition—that no one gets hurt."

Gary assured the boys, "We'll make it out without firing a shot or being fired at. And once outside, it will be clear sailing. I know how it works. I've been there before." He had been there before, and it had never worked, but the boys didn't doubt his word. They believed him and they believed *in* him. To them he was not a killer. A guard had been accidentally shot in a scuffle. It was not in cold blood. Their father was incapable of that.

When the boys had been growing up, Gary had gone so far as to tell them that his criminal conduct had been the product of secret training he had received in the "Service." It had all been top secret, he told them, but he wanted the boys to understand the background of his problems. They believed this fantasy like they believed everything else their father told them. "Nobody was going to get shot," their father assured them.

And their father was right—at least about the escape. It came off without a hitch or a shot. Raymond went to meet his father in the picnic area. Ricky and Donny went into the waiting room with their picnic basket. By prearrangement, a friend of Gary's, a killer named Randy Greenawalt, was in the adjoining control room. Despite his record he had been made a trustee. ("Killers make the best trustees," goes an old prison saw.) When the room was clear of all other visitors the boys pulled out their shotguns and held the guards at bay. Quickly the boys passed a shotgun to Randy. Raymond and Gary joined them in the lobby.

When two additional guards appeared they were ordered to lie on the floor. One who tried to turn on the walkie-talkie hanging from his belt was spotted by Gary, who had hurried into the room with Raymond. "If you touch the radio you're all dead," Gary warned as he ordered the guard to slide the radio across the floor.

The guards were quickly herded into a storage room, along with some frightened visitors who had chanced onto the scene. The door was locked and the power turned off. Then the five nonchalantly strolled out the front door.

A guard in the front control tower noticed that the intercom to the front office was not working. As he tried to tune it in he saw five men walking out the gate. One was twirling his keys. It seemed quite normal for a visiting day. They got into a green Ford and drove out the driveway. After a few more minutes of fiddling with the intercom, the guard in the control tower hailed another guard walking down below. He told him to check the front office. By this time the guards in the storage room had knocked a hole in the ceiling with a discarded metal pipe and had unlocked the door. The alarms were sounded. But the Tisons and Randy Greenawalt were gone.

The green Ford was found abandoned in the nearby hospital parking lot.

News of the daring escape blared from radio and television, and the manhunt was on. But the objects of the hunt were keeping to the back roads in the desert, heading west. They were in an old white Lincoln supplied by their Uncle Joe, a once-and-future felon whose business was importing marijuana from Mexico. But the car turned out to have bad tires. One went flat the next day and was replaced with a spare. Late that night, in the desert north of Yuma, another went flat. This time there was no spare.

Murder in the Desert

Earlier that evening John Lyons had arrived home after a trip to Los Angeles. He was a Marine stationed at the air base in Yuma and was taking his family home on leave to Omaha, Nebraska. His fifteen-year-old niece, Theresa Tyson (no relative of the Tison family), had been visiting them for a week, and was going to be dropped off in Las Vegas on the way. They had decided to leave that night to get an early start and to escape the desert heat.

While his wife Donnelda did some last-minute ironing, and two-year-old Christopher slept, John and his friend Nick packed the orange Mazda. Finally, the family, their suitcases, John's gun, and their chihuahua were loaded into the car. They left around ten-thirty, heading north.

About an hour later the silhouette of a man waving his arms appeared in John's headlight beams. At first John passed; then he stopped, backed up, and pulled next to the Lincoln. Four more men appeared out of the shadows with guns drawn. One of them ordered the Lyonses out of the car and motioned them into the back seat of the Lincoln. Two of the men got in the car with them, and the others got into the Mazda.

The Lincoln bumped along for several miles down the rocky dirt road, with the Mazda following behind. Gary stopped the Lincoln and told Greenawalt to turn the Mazda around so the cars would be trunk to trunk. The Lyonses were ordered out of the Lincoln and the men cleaned out the Mazda, put their guns in it, and loaded the Lyonses' suitcases into the Lincoln. Only the clatter of gun barrels and the soft thud of suitcases broke the silence.

Then Gary and Randy got into the Lincoln and drove it seventy yards farther into the desert. They shot some holes into the engine and told the boys to put the Lyonses into the Lincoln. After the Lyonses were transferred, Gary turned to Ricky and said, "You boys go back to the Mazda and get the water jug." Raymond and Ricky were relieved that the Lyonses would be left with enough water to survive until help arrived.

. . .

Donny, Ricky, and Ray walked silently back through the black desert night. They retrieved the water jug from the Mazda and were on their way back. Suddenly they heard the shotguns go off. They could see flashes of fire through the darkness. They stood transfixed. It seemed to last forever. Then there was silence.

The dim outlines of Gary and Randy, black against black, materialized on the road. As they came closer the boys could see the look on their faces, the sweat, and the shotguns slung under their arms. Gary looked Ricky straight in the eye and said, "It sure is hard to kill a Lincoln." Without a word they got in the car.

The boys were numb with disbelief. They had just seen their father murder an entire family—father, mother, baby, and niece—and for no apparent reason. They didn't know what to do, what to think, what to feel. They sat immobilized by horror as Randy Greenawalt drove them away in the orange Mazda.

The road was deserted as they drove north. Soon they began to think about what they had seen—and been a part of. "We have their car," Raymond thought. "Why did they have to be killed?" They were filled with disgust and fear.

They knew it was only a matter of time before someone started wondering where the Lyons family was. The next morning they stopped at a variety store in the little town of Wenden and bought six cans of silver spray paint for the car. It was only a holding action. They needed another car.

Greenawalt thought there was one person they could take a chance on, an old girl friend who lived near Flagstaff. They drove straight through, trying to balance speed with caution by sticking to back roads wherever they could.

The next morning they drove into Doney Park, just east of Flagstaff. Hunger got the better of caution, and they stocked up on hot dogs and beans at the market. When they came out they noticed an old dirt road across the main highway. They headed up into the hills, found a deserted campsite secluded by pine trees, and waited for dark.

That night Greenawalt knocked on Kathy Ehrementraut's door. He wanted her son's truck, but it was in bad shape. She agreed to buy him one the next morning, and went into Flagstaff with Donny, while Greenawalt stayed at Kathy's house with her grandchildren. Donny finally picked out a blue Chevy truck at Crazy Al's, and Kathy borrowed the money at the bank.

The truck could not be picked up until later in the day, so they drove back to get Greenawalt, gave him guns and ammunition, and dropped him off at the foot of the dirt road. Donny stayed with Kathy to get the Chevy. On the way she turned and asked him how he was. "I'm very, very tired and I wish I could sleep a long time," Donny answered. "When us boys got Dad out, Dad changed completely." He leaned back and lapsed into silence. She drove on and dropped him at the dealer's.

Now that they had the pickup, they could move on. But first they drove the Mazda behind a dead tree and covered it with pine brush. Then they headed in the direction of the Colorado border.

The Honeymoon Couple

At about the same time another car was heading for Colorado. Margene and James Judge had just gotten married in Texas. They had planned a honeymoon camping trip in the Colorado woods followed by a visit to Denver for an exhibition football game between the Broncos and the Cowboys. On the morning of the wedding, August 5, Margene's father gave her a hundred-dollar bill to spend in the city. After the reception the couple left in their new blue and silver van.

On August 8 Margene called her father and said they were going fishing near South Fork, Colorado, for a few days. Several days later they were seen buying supplies in a market near South Fork. That was the last time anyone ever saw the honeymoon couple. Their seats at the football game were empty.

On August 9 three very bedraggled men went into the same market near South Fork. They bought several cartons of cigarettes, and paid for them with a hundred-dollar bill. Later that day a heavy-set man dropped a blue pickup off for repairs at Gabriel Chevrolet in Cortez, Colorado. He left with several others in a blue and silver van. He never came back to get his truck.

It may never be known for sure whether the men who went into the market at South Fork were part of the "Tison gang," or whether the Tison gang ever encountered the honeymoon couple. What is known is that four months later, the decomposing bodies of the Judges were discovered partially covered with snow near Cabison Creek. A jar of fishing bait, a pair of glasses, and a wedding ring lay nearby. Each had died from a single shot in the back of the head. The police believe that Gary Tison killed the Judges and took their van.

The Chase

By the time the men were seen in the market near South Fork, Colorado, the Arizona police had found the Lyons family in Yuma. Mother and baby were in the Lincoln, shot to death. John Lyons was dead on the ground beside the car. Theresa was missing, giving rise to the fear that she was being held by the Tisons for sex or safety. Several days later she was found: she had been shot once in the hip and had managed to drag herself toward the main road before bleeding to death. The dog lay dead from dehydration a few feet away from her.

The disclosure of these gruesome crimes shocked the public, which had heretofore followed the news of the manhunt with a mixture of fear and admiration for the daring prison escape. Now revulsion and hatred replaced admiration. The crimes were characterized by the media as a "mad-dog murder spree," and a "death orgy," and a "ritualistic execution." The suspected killers were described as "crazed" and "desperate." Some people refused to drive at night until the Tisons and Greenawalt were caught.

The pressure on the police was intense, and they redoubled their efforts to track down the Tisons. The largest manhunt in Arizona history was under way: patrol cars, helicopters, police dogs, roadblocks, a massive communications network. Hundreds of state and federal law enforcement officials were working full time hunting the Tison gang.

Pressure was also mounting on the Tisons. They were in their fifth car since the escape, yet they spent every minute on the road expecting a police cruiser to round the turn and recognize them. They were numb with exhaustion, and low on money. Gary decided that they had to make a break for Mexico, even if that meant risking detection at the border.

On the night of August 11, three policemen were manning a roadblock south of Casa Grande. At 2:58 a van approached, and suddenly shots were fired, putting two holes in one of the police cars. Immediately the van sped up and crashed through the roadblock. The policemen jumped into their patrol cars and chased the van up a hill and through a pass. Traveling at close to a hundred miles an hour, one police car passed the other so that the third officer could use his shotgun. He fired several rounds at the speeding van.

Then the police let up on the shooting. They called in the helicopters that were on standby for just such an eventuality. They knew there was a second roadblock on the other side of the pass. The Tisons did not. For a brief instant, Gary, who was manning the gun out the rear window, thought he had made it. But Donny, who was driving, saw the second roadblock. He crashed through it, but not before four shots from the waiting police cars struck him in the head. The van swerved off the road and came to rest in the desert in a cloud of sand. Gary yelled, "Every man for himself," and ran into the desert. Ricky, Ray, and Randy Greenawalt followed. One of the policemen, dimly seeing Randy's outline, fired a shot. Ricky, Ray, and

Randy threw themselves to the ground. Gary kept going and vanished into the darkness.

The police advanced cautiously toward the van. They found Donny, slumped in the driver's seat, still breathing but unconscious from his head wounds. They handcuffed him, called an ambulance in Casa Grande, and left him there after removing the guns from the back of the van. It was 3:15 A.M. when the Aztec Ambulance Service received the emergency call. At 3:40, the ambulance arrived at the scene of the roadblock with lights flashing and sirens blaring. But the driver and medics were made to wait at the roadblock for over five hours. When they were finally allowed to go to Donny at 9:10, he was dead.

Shortly after the officers had made their initial search of the van, the helicopter arrived with its powerful floodlights. Two men were spotted lying beside each other with a third a little farther away. The nearest was ordered to stand up and walk toward the police with his hands up. It was Ricky, splattered with his brother's blood.

Next Raymond was ordered to get up. As he was being handcuffed he told the police he had a gun in his shoulder holster, under his shirt. After removing the gun and handcuffing him, two deputies went over to where Greenawalt was still lying in the desert. They bound him and brought him back to the roadblock. Where each man had been lying in the desert, they found another gun.

A shotgun was shoved against the back of Ricky's head. A pistol barrel was put in his mouth. His clothes—all of them—were cut off his body with a Buck knife. He was pulled by his hair into a police car surrounded by three officers and interrogated—naked and shivering—for five hours. When he expressed reluctance to talk, he was asked, "Do you want to see your dying brother?" The implication was clear: he would be shot and left to die if he did not confess. "I don't want to make a statement," he said. The police continued the interrogation. Donny, bleeding and unconscious, would receive no medical attention until his brothers confessed. Finally, Ricky confessed to his role in the events following the breakout. Raymond was treated the same.

As dawn approached, the police drove the boys to the Pinal County jail, pausing to give them blankets to cover up their still naked bodies as they approached a group of waiting reporters who had been alerted to the capture.*

Dorothy Tison learned about the shootout and her oldest son's death from a jubilant radio announcer.

*The foregoing account is that of Ricky and Raymond Tison.

For over a week no trace was found of Gary Tison. More than five-hundred armed vigilantes volunteered to comb every inch of desert near the scene of the shootout for this most wanted of fugitives. A helicopter-borne SWAT team was lowered into abandoned mines and caves. Police dogs were used. An eighty-year-old retired escape expert was called in. Psychics were consulted. A circus atmosphere surrounded the search. Rumors circulated about Gary's whereabouts. He was reported in dozens of locations ranging from the Grand Canyon to southern Mexico. Police set up a "dial-a-sighting" to handle the thousands of calls. He was "spotted" in Utah, and a search was conducted there. Another sighting was made in the Sawtooth Mountains, and a team of climbers and horsemen were dispatched to cover that area. After a week of intensive air and ground reconnaissance, the effort was scaled down. Ricky and Raymond hoped against hope that their father had survived the snake-infested terrain and made it to freedom.

But several days after most of the vigilantes had gone home, a Papago Indian smelled something foul in an underbrush. It was a badly decomposing body. The police were called, and the remains were identified as those of Gary Tison. He had been hiding out in the desert, just a mile north of the roadblock. The August heat proved too much for him. His end came in the Papago Indian Reservation, lying amongst the ironwood and the brush, with a sock full of cactus berries squeezed dry near his head. He was only a few yards from the fresh water he was trying to reach. Underneath him, half buried in the sand, was John Lyons' gun. Gary Tison had died within fifty miles of the prison from which he had escaped. The manhunt was over. It had not ended in a hail of bullets, but in a parched and lonely desert. Newspapers as far away as California ran two-inch banner headlines: "Tison Dead." Dorothy Tison believes he was found alive and murdered by the vigilantes.

A Deal Falls Through

From the time of the escape, and particularly after the discovery of the Lyons family, the hunt for the "Tison gang" had received unparalleled local press coverage. Newspapers compared them to the Manson gang, the Boston Strangler, and Murder Incorporated. Their escape led to a shakeup of the prison system: The warden was fired; lifers had their ground privileges revoked. It was disclosed that prison officials had been warned of a possible Tison breakout five months earlier, but had allowed Gary to retain his ground privileges after he had passed four lie detector tests.

Now that some of the culprits were dead, the full force of public outrage was focused on those who were still alive. Rational consideration of who had actually done what was subsumed by the recurrent vision of the murdered toddler and the view that "if they hadn't gotten Gary Tison and Greenawalt out, none of this would have happened." The press demanded the gas chamber. One editorial expressed chagrin that two of the Tisons had been captured alive. Perhaps sensing the public mood, or simply from desperation, Ricky escaped from the county jail. He remained at liberty for fifteen hours as bulletins announced his escape to angered—and frightened—Arizona residents. But Ricky was soon tracked down by police dogs in a corn field. He was bitten three times by the dogs and subdued. "Those are some bad dogs," he muttered as he was returned to prison.

Soon thereafter, Raymond, Ricky, and Greenawalt were tried in Pinal County and convicted of assault and escape charges stemming from the prison break. Each newspaper story recalled the fatal events of the past summer, further inflaming public opinion as the date for the Yuma County murder trials approached.

Against this backdrop, Ricky and Ray's court-appointed lawyers tried desperately to make a deal. Their ace in the hole stemmed from the fact that Randy Greenawalt was to be tried separately. As one of the two killers, and as one who had previously been convicted of murder (he was serving that sentence at the time of the escape), Greenawalt was the primary focus of the state's efforts. But since Greenawalt could not be forced to testify at his own trial, the only two available witnesses to the murder of the Lyons family were Raymond and Ricky. Perhaps, also, the prosecutor felt that what the boys had done did not merit the gas chamber.

In any event, an agreement was reached whereby Ricky and Raymond would testify at Greenawalt's trial in exchange for the state's promise not to ask for the death penalty. Following the formalizing of the agreement, the boys talked freely to the prosecutor and Greenawalt's attorney, and their lawyers turned their attention to other cases. There were rumblings of discontent, however, that the boys were "getting off." Editorial writers criticized the prosecutors who had made the deal.

Greenawalt's trial began in February 1979. The prosecutor's opening statement promised that the Tison brothers would testify, and attention was riveted on the courtroom. But the publicity reminded the public that the boys were not to be executed for the murders. It was apparently not enough that Ricky and Raymond were likely to spend the rest of their lives in prison. This was too good for them. What little public support there may have been for the plea bargain quickly evaporated as the lurid details of the crime were again recounted in the newspapers.

When Raymond finally rose to take the oath to tell "the truth, the whole truth, and nothing but the truth," he was fully prepared to testify about the night in the desert near Yuma—the only events for which Greenawalt was then standing trial. The plea agreement had stated that Raymond would testify "in any proceedings pertaining to criminal charges relating to an incident occurring on or about August 1, 1978, in which the John Lyons family . . . were killed." Having already undergone a separate trial and conviction for the prison escape, Raymond assumed that the Greenawalt trial would focus exclusively on the murders.

But the prosecutor started to ask him searching questions about the planning of the prison escape: who else was involved; what they had done. Raymond refused to answer. It is unclear why they were asked—maybe the prosecutor wanted to give "the whole picture" to the jury, maybe he was fishing for evidence of as yet unknown co-conspirators, or maybe he guessed that Raymond would not want to answer these questions. But it is fairly clear why Raymond, and later Ricky, refused to answer. They were not going to name the people who had helped them plan the escape. Perhaps they were trying to forestall their mother's indictment.

The judge declared a mistrial in the Greenawalt case. The plea bargain was rescinded. And the lawyers for Ricky and Raymond were given two weeks to prepare for the murder trial.

The Murder Trials

The lawyers stood before Judge Douglas W. Keddie on the morning of February 20. During the preceding days the publicity had been intense and had included two editorials in the *Yuma Daily Sun* that the judge himself said "shouldn't have been written." Ricky's trial lawyer argued that the trial should be moved to another part of the state. The motion was denied. He then argued that the trial should at least be delayed to lessen the effects of the publicity on the potential jurors. This motion was also denied. He did manage to persuade the judge that the gruesome photographs of the bodies should not be passed around to the jury, although pictures of the bloodstained seats of the Lincoln were admitted into evidence.

The Tison brothers were tried separately for the Yuma murders. Ricky's trial was first. He faced a jury of eight women and four men, all of whom regularly read the *Yuma Daily Sun.* One woman frankly admitted that she had decided that Ricky was guilty prior to the trial. "I think the one thing that sticks in my mind is the fact that the baby was killed. The baby could not identify a soul, and had not the baby been killed, perhaps I wouldn't feel as deeply as I do." But the judge took her at her word that she could "set aside her opinion" and decide the case on the evidence introduced at the trial. Other jurors who expressed similar views were seated as well. It was not an auspicious beginning.

The witnesses sounded like castoffs from a low-budget detective movie. One was "Uncle Joe" Tison, on leave from federal prison, where he was serving time for conspiring to import marijuana. He said that his "business" was transporting marijuana between Arizona and the East Coast, in the trunks of old cars that he bought for the occasion and discarded after three trips each. One of these delivery vehicles was the Lincoln that had experienced two flats within twenty-four hours. He testified that he provided the Lincoln for Gary's escape in exchange for a promise that the "Mexican Mafia" would convince a potential witness not to testify against him in the marijuana proceeding.

The trial soon turned into a recital of the grim facts. The doctor's technical testimony about the number and placement of the bullet wounds in the Lyons family filled in the gaps left by the photographs of the bloody car seats, etching deeply in each juror's mind the horror of the crime. The long line of police, sheriff's deputies, and detectives who had been involved in the case underscored its enormity. And even when there appeared to be some confusion about which policeman had picked up what gun where and done what with it, the impression left on the jury was not so much that the police had been inept, but rather that the Tisons' arsenal had been enormous. The steadily growing pile of weapons in evidence served as a visible reminder of that fact.

Ricky himself did not testify, but his confession was recounted to the jury. "It was all worthwhile," he reportedly said. "Just to have a father for ten to twelve days made it all worthwhile." Nobody was supposed to get hurt, Ricky had told the police. None of this was supposed to happen.

Ricky sat throughout the trial with a nervous smile on his face. Trying to counteract the unfavorable impression his smile was causing, Ricky's lawyer called to the stand a roofing contractor who had given Ricky jobs over the years. Mr. Howell explained that Ricky had worn braces on his teeth and that when he was under pressure "he looked like he was smiling when he was really not smiling at all." Mr. Howell also testified, along with Mrs. Tison's boss and some friends and neighbors, that Ricky was a "great kid," honest, hard working, and never violent. But it was too little too late. The sheer volume of testimony and the fact that under Arizona law Ricky need only have been involved in the escape to be guilty of the murders were enough to persuade the jury. On the same day they retired to deliberate, the jury returned with a unanimous verdict of guilty. Raymond's trial soon followed with the same result.

Throughout it all, Dorothy sat in the courtroom lending whatever support she could. Her devotion to her family had been sorely tried. Her sons had broken their father out of prison because they loved him, and whatever followed was out of their control. The questions remained. What if the boys had left their father in the hospital parking lot when the cars were switched? What if "Uncle Joe" had thrown in an extra tire? And what if Gary Tison were still alive to face the rage of the community instead of his sons?

The Punishment

Now the battle moved to a different arena, where the stakes were even higher and the outcome more uncertain. In Arizona, after the jury has returned a verdict of guilty, it is left to the judge to set the sentence. Each brother came before Judge Keddie convicted of four counts of murder, three of kidnapping, two of robbery, and one of auto theft. But murder is the only crime in Arizona for which the death penalty may be imposed, and to do so, the judge must make specific findings as to "aggravating" and "mitigating" circumstances and determine that the former outweigh the latter. Dorothy Tison hoped that because neither Ricky nor Ray had actually committed the murders, the judge might sentence them to life in prison. (No one had been executed for murder in the United States during the past twenty-five years who had not personally done the killing.)

But the prosecution, freed of its promise not to ask for the death penalty, made the most of the situation. The presentence hearing became a forum for a gory exposition of the murder of the young honeymooning couple in Colorado (a crime for which no one was ever tried). The woman's father took the stand. When asked if he had any children, he answered, "I have one left." A clerk at the Foothill Supermarket in South Fork, Colorado, remembered that Margene "was extremely beautiful, not just in looks. She had a glow to her that you could never forget." Then followed the grisly tale of the gangland-style bullet holes to the back of the neck, and the discovery of bones gnawed by animals strewn near a fishing stream. It was a horrible and tragic story, sure to disgust any listener. But the killers were not in the courtroom. Gary Tison was dead and Randy Greenawalt was undergoing his own private hell. Instead, two neatly dressed young men sat there, reaping what they had not sown. In a strange way, they were victims, too.

Eight character witnesses for Ricky and Ray followed, each stressing the boys' nonviolent natures and devotion to their father. An aunt recounted how she had once backed into Ray's new car, and had only provoked a polite offer to move her car for her. Friends and neighbors told how the boys had helped build fireplaces and repair cars, turning down offers of payment.

And finally, Dan Deck, the journalism teacher who had worked closely with Gary Tison at the prison, described how cleverly Gary had manipulated both inmates and officials, and how desperately he had wanted to get out of prison.

It was widely believed that the Tison brothers would be spared the death penalty and sentenced to life imprisonment. The probation department, while strongly recommending the gas chamber for Randy Greenawalt—who was characterized by them as "a dangerous threat to humanity"—was "torn between recommending the death penalty or a lighter sentence" for the younger men. It therefore made no recommendation at all. But editorial writers called for the gas chamber: no other punishment would "satisfy the vengeance the people of Arizona feel toward the two."

The anticipation was unbearable. Ricky was moved to say, "I don't like Donny being dead. But I'm glad he's not going through this."

On March 29, 1979, Ricky and Raymond stood together before Judge Keddie to be sentenced. The judge first began to read his special findings of fact. It was then that the boys discovered how truly they stood in their father's place. The judge found three aggravating circumstances. Each murder had created a "grave risk of death to others" (the other three victims); the murders were committed to get something of value (the car); and the crimes were committed in a "heinous and cruel" manner. The fact that Ricky and Ray had not committed the murders themselves was irrelevant to the judge. Their conviction under a theory of vicarious liability—of being held responsible for the crimes of other co-conspirators—had served in his eyes to erase the distinction between them and their father. Their clean records, youth, and the circumstances of their convictions were deemed insufficient to outweigh the enormity of their father's crime. The judge sentenced each of them to die in the gas chamber. They were to be executed for the sins and crimes of their father and his friend.

"Barbaric and Inhuman"

The abolition of capital punishment has long been a passion with me. From my earliest years on the high-school debating team I always argued the affirmative on the proposition: "resolved, that capital punishment should be abolished." (I still have a copy of the index card from my first debate on that subject. It says that most murderers are products of their "invirment" and that I am in favor of the "abolission" of "capitol" punishment.) In college I wrote a paper on the subject. And while in law school, I wrote a letter to the Prime Minister of Israel urging that even Adolf Eichmann should be spared execution.

During my first judicial clerkship with Chief Judge David Bazelon of the United States Court of Appeals for the District of Columbia Circuit, I worked on a capital punishment case involving a young black man who had accidently killed a policeman during a struggle over the policeman's gun. He had been sentenced to death under the "felony-murder rule," because the struggle had resulted from an attempted robbery of a liquor store. I worked with Judge Bazelon on an opinion to spare the defendant's life.

On the first day of my clerkship with Justice Arthur Goldberg of the United States Supreme Court during the summer of 1963, the Justice called me into his office and asked, "Have you given much thought to capital punishment?"

"I certainly have," came my enthusiastic reply.

"Well, I have an idea that I think will interest you," the Justice said. "I would like you to work up a memorandum for me on the constitutional issues surrounding the imposition of the death penalty."

"I'd love to," I said, unable to conceal my excitement.

Justice Goldberg said, "Let's talk it through a bit, before you turn to the books. I have some thoughts I'd like to test out on you."

I told the Justice that I, too, had been thinking about it, and had worked on a capital case the previous year for Judge Bazelon.

"Dave [Bazelon] has said some interesting things about capital punishment," the Justice remarked. "But neither he nor any other judge so far as I know has ever really addressed the question of whether capital punishment is constitutional." He continued, "The Eighth Amendment prohibits 'cruel and unusual punishment,' and what could be more cruel than the deliberate decision by a state to take a human life. If torture is cruel and unusual punishment, then certainly deliberate killing by the state should be no less."

The idea was bold and imaginative, but there was a lot of history against this view, as I reminded the Justice: "At the time the Eighth Amendment was enacted, the colonists were executing people all over the place. Certainly the framers of the Constitution did not regard the death penalty as unconstitutional."

Justice Goldberg was aware, of course, of my argument, and he had his response ready: "Therein lies the beauty of our Bill of Rights. It's an evolving document. It means something different today than it meant in 1792. The cruel and unusual punishment clause"—he said, pausing to take a book from the shelf—"must draw its meaning from the evolving standards of decency that mark the progress of a maturing society. That's what the Chief [referring to Chief Justice Earl Warren] said in *Trop* v. *Dulles.*"

I remembered that case in which the Supreme Court had held that depriving a person of citizenship was cruel and unusual punishment for a crime, but I also remembered that in his opinion the Chief Justice had given his personal opinion—lawyers call it *obiter dictum*—that "the death penalty has been employed throughout our history, and, in a day when it is still widely accepted, it cannot be said to violate the constitutional concept of cruelty." I reminded Justice Goldberg of the Chief Justice's statement, which had been made only five years earlier.

He shook his head sadly and responded, "I know what the Chief said. I wish he hadn't. It wasn't necessary to say anything about the death penalty in *Trop* v. *Dulles,* because that case did not involve the death penalty. The Chief's going to be a big problem. But I'm still convinced that we should start the ball rolling on this issue. Maybe we won't get a court [i.e., a majority] the first time around, but at least we will have gotten lawyers and judges to start thinking about raising constitutional challenges to capital punishment."

I left the Justice, wondering why lawyers and judges had not brought such challenges. I am reminded of my colleague Alan Stone's observation that there are no Nobel Prizes in law, because law is the only profession where you lose points for originality and gain points for demonstrating that somebody else thought of your idea first. Lawyers are prone to look to the "authorities"—to past lawyers and judges—for their ideas. Creativity in the law consists largely of analyzing past cases so as to get around a barrier or move the law incrementally. Rarely do lawyers indulge in bold leaps of faith, in grand conceptual breakthroughs. (I recall my high school Talmud teacher once putting me down with the following "Catch-22" response for claiming that an idea I had was original: "If what you're saying is such a good idea, then obviously the old rabbis, who were much smarter than you, must have thought of it first; and if the old rabbis, who were much smarter than you, didn't think of it first, then it can't be such a good idea.")

Justice Goldberg's idea about the unconstitutionality of the death penalty was a bold leap of faith. It was now my job to make it seem like a natural progression from existing law and authority. I turned to the books with a sense of mission. Our state and federal governments had executed several thousand people, most of them black, poor, uneducated, and unlucky. Here was a real opportunity for the Supreme Court to save countless lives.

After several weeks of research and writing, I prepared a long memorandum to Justice Goldberg discussing the constitutionality of the death penalty. The memorandum outlined the English and American history of prohibition against cruel and unusual punishments and surveyed every Supreme Court case in which the issue had been discussed. It concluded that a reasonable constitutional argument could be made against the death penalty. *I recommended that the Supreme Court should first "carefully* scrutinize the . . . capital cases which came before it, in an effort to define categories of cases where the death penalty is unconstitutional." I suggested that Justice Goldberg should make known his doubts about the constitutionality of the death penalty so that lawyers would begin to raise Eighth Amendment arguments in death cases. This would set in motion a process that could gradually chip away at the constitutional legitimacy of the death penalty and might culminate in a decision declaring capital punishment unconstitutional in all cases.

As soon as I gave Justice Goldberg my first draft he went to work revising and refining it. He decided that he would circulate his final version of the memorandum to the entire Supreme Court as a test balloon to see how many votes he could garner. I was ecstatic that my handiwork—even though the ideas and ultimate refinement were Justice Goldberg's—would find itself on the desk of each of the Justices.

After numerous revisions and redrafts Justice Goldberg circulated his memorandum. It expressed his own strong view that the "institutionalized taking of human life by the state" was "barbaric and inhuman." But it went on to recognize that the "Brethren may not agree . . . that capital punishment, as such, is unconstitutional." He offered for consideration, therefore, the proposition that "the infliction of death at least for certain types of crimes and on certain types of offenders violates the Eighth and Fourteenth Amendments."

The memorandum was a bombshell. It became the talk of the Court, both among the Justices and the law clerks. Not everyone, of course, was happy with it. The two Justices who were most perturbed were the grand old men of the so-called liberal wing: Chief Justice Earl Warren and Justice Hugo Black. Warren, the astute politician who was always concerned with public acceptance of the Court's opinions, was convinced that any suggestion that the death penalty was unconstitutional would undermine the credibility of the Court's decisions in desegregation and other controversial areas. Black, the constitutional literalist, was upset by Justice Goldberg's attempt to "rewrite" the Bill of Rights.

But Justices Brennan and Douglas agreed with Justice Goldberg, and Justice Stewart expressed some tentative, albeit skeptical, sympathy toward the approach.

Finally, at the behest of the Chief Justice, Justice Goldberg agreed not to publish his memorandum. I was heart-broken, fearing that all of our efforts would go for naught. But Justice Goldberg, along with Justices Douglas and Brennan, did decide to publish a short dissent in a case involving a black man who had been sentenced to death for raping a white woman. His idea was to alert the criminal defense bar to the fact that at least three Justices had some doubts about the constitutionality of capital punishment in some contexts.

The response, not only by the bar but by the press, was immediate and electric.

The *New York Times* described the Goldberg dissent as raising a "potentially far-reaching idea." The *Washington Post* praised it as "an appeal to the brooding spirit of the law, to the intelligence of a future day . . ." But not all the editorial writers were pleased. William Loeb, the ultraconservative publisher of the *Manchester Union Leader,* wrote a page-one editorial headlined: "U.S. Supreme Court Trio Encourages Rape."

> This incredible opinion, of course, can serve only to encourage would-be rapists. These fiends, freed from the fear of the death penalty and knowing the saccharin sentimentality of many parole boards, will figure the penalty for their foul deed will not be too serious and, therefore, they will be inclined to take a chance.
>
> No Communist activist could ever do a better job than these men in destroying and undermining the fundamental principles on which a sound society is based. It does not take many years of . . . fostering disrespect for our womanhood to completely reduce a great civilization to a shambles.

Loeb failed to tell his readers that his own state of New Hampshire has not had the death penalty for rape for at least a hundred years. Other newspapers, particularly in the South, ran similar—if less colorful—diatribes.

Nor did other courts welcome the Goldberg dissent. Few followed his lead, and some rejected it outright in quite flamboyant terms. For example, the Georgia Supreme Court:

> We reject this [attempt to reduce the protection of] mothers of mankind, the cornerstone of civilized society, and the zenith of God's creation, against a crime more horrible than death, which is the forcible sexual invasion of her body, the temple of her soul, thereby soiling for life her purity, the most precious attribute of all *man*kind [sic!].

But the purpose of the Goldberg dissent was to send a message to criminal defense lawyers to raise the issue of cruel and unusual punishment; to give the courts the legal, factual, and historical ammunition with which to fight the battle from within. That message was heard clearly and understood fully, particularly by two of the nation's leading advocacy organizations: the NAACP Legal Defense Fund, Inc., and the ACLU.

As Michael Meltzner, one of the lawyers who acted on the message, put it: "The [Goldberg] opinion awakened interest in the constitutionality of capital punishment . . ." It "jolted [us] into action."

The ACLU changed its formal policy, which had long been that capital punishment was "not a civil liberties issue," and began entering capital cases. The NAACP commissioned a study on the racial factors in capital sentences. By the mid-1960s a nationwide effort had begun, to stop all executions and to present the United States Supreme Court with a series of cases challenging the constitutionality of all capital punishment. The effort was led masterfully by Anthony G. Amsterdam, probably the most creative and energetic civil rights lawyer in the country. He flew from state to state, from prison to prison, from court to court, arguing tirelessly on behalf of the condemned. Building on the Goldberg dissent, he persuaded the courts to broaden the foundation constructed in that short opinion.

While this effort was being mounted, I joined Justice Goldberg—who had by this time left the Supreme Court—in writing an article for the *Harvard Law Review* entitled "Declaring the Death Penalty Unconstitutional." In the article we laid out a detailed constitutional argument calling for courts, legislators, and governors to refuse to permit executions on constitutional grounds.

Shortly after publication the article bore its first fruits: the Attorney General of Pennsylvania, citing our article in support of his actions, wrote a letter to the warden of the state prison directing him "to remove the electric chair from the Execution Room . . ."

There were other narrow victories as well: a court of appeals held the death penalty unconstitutional for rape; the Supreme Court held it unconstitutional to exclude all jurors who have conscientious scruples against the death penalty. But there were setbacks as well.

And then, on June 29, 1972, the monumental efforts of Arthur Goldberg, Anthony Amsterdam—and the cadre of colleagues including Michael Meltzner, Frank Heffron, Leroy Clark, and numerous others—were rewarded: the United States Supreme Court, in a 5 to 4 decision in the case of *Furman* v. *Georgia,* struck down as unconstitutional all existing death penalty statutes. Three of the Justices—Douglas, Brennan, and Marshall—adopted Justice Goldberg's argument that the death penalty is cruel and unusual punishment. Two others, Stewart and White, refused to go that far, concluding instead that the manner by which the death penalty was then imposed—at the discretion of judges and juries—results in death being imposed "so wantonly and so freakishly" as to operate in a cruel and unusual way. As Justice Stewart put it: "These death sentences are cruel and unusual in the same way that being struck by lightning is cruel and unusual."*

The opening battle had been won; the 600 people then on death row would be spared. Justice Goldberg called me within hours of the decision being announced. "We did it," he said. "It was all worth it." Never in the history of courts had a single decision resulted in saving so many lives. Never had so many laws—both state and federal—been struck down with one judicial pronouncement. And never before had so important a social change been accomplished by a court in so short a period of time.

But the war was far from over. In his dissenting opinion in the *Furman* case, Chief Justice Warren Burger (a supposed practitioner of judicial restraint) had advised the states to revise their statutes so as to satisfy the "swing justices," White and Stewart. As soon as the opinions had been delivered, many states began to do just that.

Within a few years, most states restored capital punishment and enacted death penalty statutes designed to satisfy Justices White and Stewart. In 1977 the United States executed its first prisoner in ten years—Gary Gilmore. But the war has continued.

In recent years the controversy has been like a game of ping-pong between state legislatures and courts. Legislatures have revised their death penalty statutes; courts have struck some of them down; legislatures have revised again. Several states responded to Chief Justice Burger's invitation by enacting "mandatory" death penalty statutes, requiring that *all* persons convicted of a particular crime must automatically be sentenced to death. But the Supreme Court soon held these unconstitutional as well, stating that such assembly-line treatment of human beings could not be squared with the "inherent dignity of man."

Other states tried to walk the tightrope between the need for consistency and the need for individualized treatment by devising elaborate "dual-tier" sentencing procedures. Following a conviction for a capital crime, a separate hearing would be held at which the judge or jury considered specific "aggravating" and "mitigating" factors about the defendant, such as whether he had previously been convicted of a serious crime or, conversely, was young, or had acted under duress. The presence or absence of each factor would be ascertained by the judge or jury and the sentence would state whether "aggravating circumstances" outweighed "mitigating circumstances." If they did, the death sentence could be imposed.

Several death penalty statutes of this variety came before the Supreme

*The analogy to lightning is wrong: lightning strikes people at random; the death penalty is imposed disproportionately on blacks, the poor, males, and those who refuse to plea bargain.

Court in another landmark case, *Gregg* v. *Georgia.* Deferring to the clearly expressed will of many state legislatures, the Court held that the death penalty could constitutionally be imposed, provided that the sentencer—whether judge or jury—exercised its discretion within such guidelines.

However, the opinion raised at least as many questions as it answered, including the all-important one of what crimes could constitutionally trigger the death sentence. In the cases decided under *Gregg,* it was clear that the convicted defendants had themselves deliberately murdered their victims.

Thus the issue presented by the Tison case was still unresolved: could someone who had not killed anyone himself, but who had been involved in a crime that resulted in murder, be sentenced to execution? The Court had not sustained a death sentence in such a case since it rendered the *Furman* decision in 1972. Although the issue had come before the Court several times, each death sentence had been overturned on the basis of some other error in the statute or proceedings.

I decided to work on the Tison appeal. I felt that if the case was to reach the U.S. Supreme Court, we would have a chance of getting the death sentences overturned. Justices Brennan and Marshall had consistently opposed capital punishment since *Furman* v. *Georgia.* Justice White had directly confronted the issue we were raising in another case, *Lockett* v. *Ohio,* and had stated his own view that the death penalty could not constitutionally be imposed upon one who did not fire the fatal shot or intend the death of the victim. But the Supreme Court had left this important issue open. The *Tison* case presented it sharply. I thought we had a chance of persuading the Supreme Court to forbid the imposition of the death penalty in a case where the defendants neither fired the fatal shots nor intended the deaths of the victims.

No matter how the Tison case was to be resolved, I could not turn down the request of these young men to help save them from the gas chamber. I had devoted so much of my life and energy to opposing the death penalty. This was an opportunity to persuade the courts not to permit the commission of judicial murder on two defendants who did not deserve to die.

In my brief to the Arizona Supreme Court, I reviewed the long history of Supreme Court decisions about the death penalty, emphasizing the central role the doctrine of proportionality between crime and punishment had assumed in recent cases. I particularly drew on Justice White's opinion that a defendant must be proved to have intended to kill before he could be sentenced to death, and underlined the fact that twenty-five years have passed since a state had actually executed a murderer who had not pulled the trigger himself. I hoped that the Arizona Supreme Court would be reluctant to have its state became the first to execute a defendant under these circumstances. I hoped that the judges would understand that to execute these two young men would truly be to impose the most extreme punishment on them for the sins of their father.

A Visit to Death Row

I had filed the brief and now it was time for me to travel to Arizona to argue the case before the Arizona Supreme Court. At the time I was preparing the case—the fall of 1980—I sported a beard and rather longish hair. A week before the argument, however, I happened to be talking to an Arizona lawyer. The conversation turned to the Supreme Court of Arizona and how conservative it was. "You know what the Chief Justice recently said," my lawyer-friend asked rhetorically. "When he was swearing in the most recent admittees to the bar, he expressed pleasure that this new group of Arizona lawyers didn't include any of those 'bearded, long-haired-hippies.' " Within an hour I was seated in my barber's chair. "Give me an Arizona haircut," I instructed the surprised Cambridge barber. "Make it short and neat and get rid of the beard." Ricky and Raymond had enough problems because of what their father had done. They were not going to have to suffer for their lawyer's appearance. I traveled to Arizona closely cropped, clean-shaven, and wearing a pinstriped lawyer's suit.

My first stop was death row. I had never met the Tisons. They had asked to see me before the argument.

When you meet criminals individually, they almost never look like criminals are supposed to look. Raymond and Ricky appeared to be typical small-town teenagers. Raymond is a good-looking and suave young man. His appearance, even in the denim prison uniform, made me think of an aspiring insurance salesman. Speaking softly, evenly, and sincerely, he immediately took charge. Taking out a bundle of newspaper clippings and legal documents, he proceeded to tell me the story of the case.

Ricky has a more interesting looking and expressive face. He smiled knowingly as he sized me up. Dimples formed on his cheeks, but they were not cute. Every so often he would interrupt his brother with a wisecrack or an insight. Ricky seemed far more episodic, far less predictable than Raymond. He was always smiling—or so it appeared. One local TV reporter characterized it as "the leering grin that thousands of Arizonans have come to detest." His brother Raymond reminded me that "Ricky's always had a dental problem with a bad overbite. It makes him look like he's smiling no matter what he's feeling."

After reviewing the factual and legal issues relevant to the next day's argument, the boys wanted to talk about personal things. "We know you very well," they told me. "Even though this is the first time we're meeting face to face, we've done a lot of checking up on you."

I knew they had been interested in my personal life because they had written several letters inquiring about me. But I had responded rather professionally and unrevealingly. "Dan Deck told us some things, Mom told us some things, some of the prisoners know about you. We saw you on a TV program arguing against the death penalty."

Ricky began to talk about his father: "He was the most efficient and determined person we ever knew. If he decided to do something, it got done. He didn't ever have to ask. He had a magnetic power. He could influence people without their knowing it. He would have been a great lawyer if he were on your side of the fence." I wondered how he could still believe that, after what they had been through, but filial devotion is often irrational.

"Ricky's right," Raymond added. "Dad never had to ask. You knew what he expected of you." The late Gary Tison had obviously been a powerful force. What truly amazed me is how powerful a force he remained —even in death and even after having committed such unspeakable crimes.

I asked the boys whether they ever thought of splitting from their dad and Randy Greenawalt. Raymond answered, "Near the very end. Just before the roadblock, we talked about it. It was clear that Dad was losing control. We discussed splitting up and going off separately, every man for himself. We had become a burden on Dad. He couldn't move as quickly with us as he might without us. He had to take care of us. After all, we didn't know what to do or where to go without him."

"Being on the lam was a totally new experience for us," Ricky explained. "We didn't know what to expect. Dad knew all about that. He was prison-wise. He had been on the lam before. He knew when to travel, what to avoid, how long to stay. All that kind of stuff." As he said this Ricky looked down again, and spoke in a disappointed tone. "But there were some things Dad didn't know about the outside world. He had been inside so long he had no idea how much food cost, how the police were equipped with electronics, how fast the word would spread. He was still living in the 1960s. He had become institutionalized. And that didn't help him once he got out."

I asked them how they assessed their own role in the crime. Raymond said that the killings were terrible, inexcusable—especially the baby. "The only possible way we could have prevented any of the murders was by killing our dad, and even that wouldn't have helped, 'cause it would have been too late." Ricky looked down at the ground as he spoke. "Some people think we should have killed our dad after the Yuma shootings. But I couldn't kill my own dad, no matter what he did. I couldn't put a gun to his head and pull the trigger. He was my father and I still loved him and respected him."

"They've sentenced us to die for *not* killing our father," Ricky added. "We're guilty of that, but we're not guilty of killing anybody. There's nothing we could have done to stop it. We wish it hadn't happened, but we couldn't stop it."

"You can't imagine what went through our heads when the shooting began," Raymond continued. "We had never experienced anything like it. It was god-awful." "I can still hear the shots," Ricky interrupted, the nervous smile still incongruously glued to his face. His dimples began to twitch as he took over the conversation. "We felt helpless and terrible. We couldn't believe something like this could happen."

"Especially the baby. Why the baby? He couldn't have identified anyone," Raymond remarked. "He probably would have died anyhow, but why did they have to shoot the baby?"

"You know, we still get death threats from other inmates because of the baby," Ricky added. "When we were first arrested, we would get death threats from lots of people—even a church group. Now it's mostly the inmates. Even inmates who did much worse things, they curse us, spit at us, and threaten us, on account of the baby."

Raymond offered his explanation: "No matter how terrible somebody may be, no matter what awful things they may have done, everybody has to set limits. Everybody has to be able to condemn people who they think are worse. For a lot of people, there's nothing worse than killing a baby. By condemning us, they say to themselves 'no matter what we did, at least we never killed a baby.' "

Raymond then asked me whether I was going to save them from the gas chamber: "Are we going to die in here, or will you save us?" The brothers looked intently at me, waiting for an answer. "There are no guarantees in the law," I said. I could promise only one thing: that I would not rest until they were no longer on death row.

As I got up to leave, Raymond turned on his bright optimistic face and gave me the thumbs-up sign: "You'll save us. I know it," he said. Ricky looked at me for the first time without a smile and said, "We're counting on you. You're our only hope of ever getting out of here alive."

The Argument

The scene the next morning could not have been more different from the setting of my meeting with the Tison brothers. The argument was heard at the University of Arizona Law School. The air of unreality was exaggerated by the fact that the argument was being held in the "moot court" room of the law school. Television cameras were set up so that the argument could be videotaped and transmitted throughout the law school. It was an educational event for the students; it was an entertainment event for the dozens of television reporters who were covering the argument for stations all around Arizona. For Raymond and Ricky Tison it was a matter of life and death.

The five judges entered. (All were clean-shaven and closely cropped.) The argument began. I decided that my strategy would be to emphasize the *Arizona* Constitution, the *Arizona* statutes, and the *Arizona* cases. I did not want to come off as an outsider trooping in waving a copy of the U.S. Constitution and telling the local folks how to conduct their business. I wanted to persuade the Arizona justices that their own law should be interpreted so as to forbid the imposition of the death penalty on the Tison brothers. In preparation for the argument I had read dozens of Arizona death penalty cases, and I had learned how the state justices thought about the issue of capital punishment.

I argued that the Arizona capital punishment statute did not contemplate the imposition of the death penalty in this kind of case: one involving young men with no prior serious criminal records who did not fire fatal shots, did not control the situation, and did not intend that anyone be killed. The Chief Justice immediately interrupted my argument and asked me what the boys' "intent" was in smuggling guns to known killers. I responded that the intent was to break their father out of prison—which was not a capital crime. The only capital crime in Arizona was aggravated murder, and the smuggling of guns did not necessarily mean that Ricky and Raymond intended to kill anyone. Indeed, all the evidence was to the contrary.

I pointed out that even the sentencing judge did not find that *these* defendants—Ricky and Raymond—had intended to commit an aggravated murder or had themselves committed such a murder. All the sentencing judge had found was that *the crime itself* was committed in "an especially heinous, and cruel and depraved manner." But these defendants—Ricky and Raymond—had done nothing to contribute to the heinousness, cruelty, or depravity of the murders. It was Gary Tison and Randy Greenawalt who had done the shooting, controlled the situation, and selected the victims—including the baby. The judge's finding of "heinous, cruel and depraved" could more appropriately have been made of Gary Tison and Randy Greenawalt than of Ricky and Raymond.

Indeed, I had discovered that morning—just hours before the oral argument—that the sentencing judge had lifted his wording about the heinousness, cruelty, and depravity of the crime verbatim from his own findings concerning Randy Greenawalt, whom he had also sentenced to death. I suspected that this might be the situation—judges can get awfully lazy even in important and highly publicized cases—and I called Greenawalt's lawyer at home to check. He confirmed that the words used by the sentencing judge to characterize Ricky and Raymond's participation in the murders of the Lyons family had been exactly the same—word for word—as those he had used to characterize Randy Greenawalt's participation in the same murders. Despite the fact that Greenawalt did the actual shooting and that neither Raymond nor Ricky had fired a single shot, the sentencing judge had used the same language to describe their entirely different roles. There could be no better proof that the sentencing judge had failed to consider each defendant as an individual in assessing the ultimate penalty.

The Arizona statute was clear. Before the judge could impose the death penalty on a particular individual, he had to find that "*the defendant* committed the offense in an especially heinous, cruel or depraved manner." It was not enough that "*the crime*" had been committed in such a manner by *other defendants.* And there had been no such individualized finding as to Ricky and Raymond. They were being sentenced to die because others —their dead father and his killer friend—had committed a heinous, cruel, and depraved crime.

When the argument was over I was inundated with TV microphones and cameras. The questions from the Arizona press were quite hostile: Why had I come all the way from Massachusetts to argue for these two boys? Did I realize what they had been responsible for? Did I make it a habit to defend baby-killers? Didn't I trust Arizona lawyers?

I had not realized the extent of the hostility toward the Tison boys. I became worried that it might influence the court's decision. Judges, after all, are affected by the passions and hostilities around them. They read the same newspapers, watch the same TV programs, and listen to the same local gossip as other citizens. Black robes do not make them different: they just make them look different.

I flew back to Cambridge to wait for the decision. I had no idea how long it would take the court to decide. It could be anywhere from a few days to a few months. My first night back I couldn't sleep. My dreams alternated between visions of the baby being shot and the Tison brothers being marched into the gas chamber. In the latter vision I saw Ricky Tison peering over his shoulder—his ever present smile contorted with fear—as if he was waiting for me to come running up to the door of the gas chamber carrying a writ that would stop his execution. But I was nowhere to be seen. The image of failure haunted me. I couldn't shake it.

I am still haunted by that image as I write these words. The Tison brothers are still on death row. The Arizona Supreme Court affirmed the death sentences during the summer of 1981. The court acknowledged that neither Ricky nor Raymond had fired the fatal shots or intended the deaths of the victims. But it ruled that under Arizona law, this made no difference:

> That they did not specifically intend that the Lyonses and Theresa Tyson die, that they did not plot in advance that these homicides would take place, or that they did not actually pull the triggers on the guns which inflicted the fatal wounds is of little significance. Ricky and Raymond Tison *associated themselves* with others who were willing to and had in the past committed homicidal acts.

Ricky and Raymond were to be executed for their guilt by association with their homicidal father.

The case is now on its way to the United States Supreme Court. Ricky and Raymond are waiting. I am waiting. But they are waiting in the valley of the shadow of death—just a few yards from the poised canisters of cyanide gas.

Three

OBSTRUCTING INJUSTICE

— 10 —

It Takes One to Catch One: The Case of Edmund Rosner v. the United States Attorney's Office for the Southern District of New York

The United States Attorney's office for the Southern District of New York is widely regarded as "the jewel of the federal system." The quality of the young lawyers in the office—most from Harvard, Yale, and Columbia—has always been uniformly high, and there has never been even a hint of financial corruption. A recent article described the office as having "a tradition of autonomy, incorruptibility, and righteousness that no other outpost of the Department of Justice can rival." The assistants in the Southern District, it reported, "practically whistle while they work."

This is the story of how the United States Attorney's office for the Southern District of New York relentlessly pursued an ambitious young criminal lawyer named Edmund Rosner. It is also about a policeman named Robert Leuci—the man sent to pursue him—whose experiences are recounted in a book and motion picture entitled *Prince of the City*. It tells a far different story of Robert Leuci than the one given in those authorized accounts.

Successful Young Lawyers

I first met Edmund Rosner in the spring of 1973, while I was trying the Jewish Defense League murder case. He was in Judge Bauman's courtroom awaiting sentencing, having been found guilty by a jury of attempting to bribe an agent in the United States Attorney's office for the Southern District of New York. Judge Bauman ultimately sentenced Rosner to five years imprisonment.

After the sentence was imposed and a new trial motion was denied, Rosner approached me in the hallway outside Judge Bauman's courtroom.

"I've been watching you for the last couple of weeks. I want a new lawyer to handle my appeal. Do you want the case?" I asked Rosner what the issues were, and he told me that he had been "entrapped" by a policeman into committing the crime. (Entrapment is a legal defense under which a criminal defendant can be acquitted if the idea for crime "originated" with the police—if the government "created" the crime.) He also told me he believed that the policeman who had entrapped him had lied to the jury about his own criminal activities.

Rosner was not denying that he had offered the money; the passing of the cash had been surreptitiously recorded on tape. Rosner—like Sheldon Seigel—wanted me to put the government on trial for its conduct. He wanted me to argue that the government had acted improperly by sending a police officer to entice him into committing a crime; and that the government had compounded its impropriety by allowing the officer to lie on the witness stand about his own previous criminal activities.

While I was deciding whether to take the case; I ran into an assistant U.S. Attorney whom I knew in New York. I told him that I was considering taking the Rosner appeal. He cautioned against it. "Rosner's a real bad character. When he was practicing here he was the most despised criminal defense lawyer in town. He's arrogant, obnoxious, and condescending. He's smart as hell, but he's dirty. He wins his cases by manufacturing evidence, especially alibis."

I asked him whether he thought there was a plausible entrapment argument. He told me that he didn't think that really mattered: "The Second Circuit's never going to reverse Rosner's conviction. Everybody around here has been waiting too long to get Eddie. He was a cancer in this courthouse. You don't put a cancer back once you've excised it."

My friend's observations—made entirely in good faith and in an effort to protect me from a hopeless situation—persuaded me to take the case. The challenge was irresistible. I told Rosner and his wife, Nancy, also an attorney, that I would argue the appeal.

Edmund and Nancy Rosner were clever and successful lawyers with opulent life-styles. They wore stylish clothes, drove flashy cars, and charged handsome fees. Just a few years earlier Edmund Rosner was doing volunteer work for the Civil Liberties Union and the Congress on Racial Equality. Among the cases he worked on was *Massiah* v. *the United States,* a famous Supreme Court case in which the Warren Court had freed a convicted drug smuggler because an undercover government agent had elicited incriminating statements from him without his lawyer present. (Ironically, the *Massiah* decision would figure in Rosner's own appeal.)

In 1966 Rosner opened his own law office, specializing in criminal defense work. He soon established a reputation as an aggressive lawyer, especially in difficult drug cases. On several occasions he won stunning victories by coming up with surprise alibi witnesses. As his reputation spread and his clientele increased, he hired a young honors graduate of the University of Chicago Law School named Nancy Packes to be his associate. Soon they were married and became partners.

Nancy Rosner, the daughter of a Bronx barber, became an extraordinary lawyer: clever, tough, articulate, prepared, and persuasive. She used her exceptional good looks to advantage. Her courtroom costumes were all of the same cut: tailored suits with tight skirts; a modest jacket worn partly opened over a low-cut and revealing blouse. She was the picture of controlled sexuality; the effect was as riveting as it was calculated.* Success had come quickly to the Rosners. Eddie was in his early thirties, Nancy not yet thirty when they reached the peak of their profession.

Pedro Hernandez and the CIA Alibi

Among Eddie's clients was an accused drug pusher named Pedro Hernandez, who faced federal prosecution in March of 1967. The government's case seemed airtight: agents had observed Hernandez making a heroin sale in New York on the day specified in the indictment. But Hernandez took the witness stand and testified that he had been in Miami that day, at an anti-Castro rally sponsored by the CIA. Travel receipts and hotel reservations were introduced to corroborate the alibi. But the jury found Hernandez guilty and the judge sentenced him to seven years imprisonment.

The government, which had Hernandez in a "squeeze" similar to the one in which it had placed Sheldon Seigel, proposed a bargain: "Give us" Eddie Rosner and we'll let you off the hook. Hernandez told the federal authorities exactly what they wanted to hear: that Rosner, along with his private investigator Nicholas DeStefano, had concocted the alibi and manufactured the documentary evidence. Rosner and DeStefano were indicted for subornation of perjury. Hernandez was freed.

Protesting his innocence, Rosner continued to practice law, but his clientele dwindled. His wife took over the practice while he devoted his energy to marshaling a defense in his own case. He hired Maurice Edelbaum, one of New York's most renowned senior criminal lawyers, to defend him.

*On August 22, 1976, *Parade* magazine carried a cover story about Nancy Rosner in which she describes how she got an acquittal in a difficult heroin-importing case because "she gained the sympathy of a strong-willed male juror 'who responded to me like gang-busters,' says Nancy, a dark-eyed brunette who wears her expensive silk blouses unbuttoned just to the point of discretion. She says she directed her case to him 'in the most subtle ways possible.' She won an acquittal in six hours."

Rosner was scared: he knew the government wanted him, but he did not know what the evidence against him was—other than the word of his former client who had been given an inducement to cooperate.

Enter "The Prince"

While Rosner worked on his defense, another drama—one that was to determine his fate—was secretly unfolding in another part of town.

In February of 1971 a thirty-one-year-old New York City narcotics detective named Robert Leuci was summoned to appear before a special commission established to investigate police corruption. Leuci belonged to an elite squad of narcotics detectives with broad jurisdiction to investigate cases involving major heroin deals—a group referred to as the "Princes of the City." Born in Brooklyn, he had been a star athlete at Brownsville High School. After a year of college football at Baker University in Kansas, he returned to New York to become a policeman. Within four years he had attained the rank of detective.

The Knapp Commission—as it came to be called, after its chairman, Whitman Knapp—was creating shock waves throughout the ranks of the police, and headlines throughout the metropolitan area, for its bold disclosure of police corruption. (Among the commissioners was an attorney named Arnold Bauman who, within a few months, would resign to become a federal judge.)

The investigation of Leuci was routine; the commission had nothing on him. He was summoned in the hope that he might provide information about other corrupt narcotics cops. The commission knew that the Narcotics Division of the New York City Police Department was a cesspool of corruption. As one experienced investigator put it, "It's hard to distinguish between the dope dealers and the policemen sometimes." The investigator who said that was the man assigned to question Leuci: Nicholas Scoppetta, a disarmingly shrewd lawyer who was eventually to become Commissioner of Investigations for the City of New York.

After several hours of routine questioning and banter, Scoppetta began to suspect that beneath Leuci's innocent exterior—he was known on the street as Babyface—there was a hidden layer of corruption. Denying any wrongdoing, Leuci deflected the conversation to corrupt defense lawyers and assistant District Attorneys. As Scoppetta probed, the denials became less assertive. Finally, Scoppetta offered the bait: if Leuci would cooperate, he could wipe his own slate clean. Leuci said he wanted to think.

Leuci came back the next day and began to talk—about other people. He admitted that there was corruption in the Narcotics Bureau. But, he added, there was corruption throughout the criminal justice system.

Scoppetta asked Leuci why he didn't do something about it. Leuci returned to his theme: he told Scoppetta that he could make cases against lawyers, judges, and people who paid off cops. Scoppetta began to lose patience as he reminded Leuci that the Knapp Commission was limited in its jurisdiction to exposing corruption among cops. Leuci exploded. "Fuck the Knapp Commission!" If Scoppetta really wanted to get at the root of the corruption he should leave the Knapp Commission and set up a separate office that had jurisdiction over defense lawyers, prosecutors, and judges.

Scoppetta saw the potential and tried to interest the United States Department of Justice in setting up a special office within the United States Attorney's office to make cases against corrupt lawyers and other participants in the judicial process. The Justice Department liked the idea and before long Scoppetta was sworn in as a Special Assistant U.S. Attorney in charge of "the Leuci investigation." Scoppetta, along with his prize canary, moved from the Knapp Commission to the United States Attorney's office.

Coordinating the Leuci operation within the United States Attorney's office was a suave Harvard-educated assistant United States Attorney named Edward M. Shaw, who stood six feet five inches and carried himself with patrician self-assurance.

Scoppetta and Shaw saw Leuci as the perfect candidate for making corruption cases. There was an aura of corruption surrounding him: his cousin, John Lusterino, was a "captain"—not in the police department, but in the Colombo organized crime family. Leuci eventually confessed to Scoppetta that he himself had been involved in some graft. A team of narcotics cops would conduct an investigation of a suspected drug dealer. If the police failed to produce enough admissible evidence to make a case, they would arrange for Leuci—because of his organized crime contacts—to approach the dealer and tell him that they had an airtight case against him, but would be willing to drop it for $10,000. The dealer almost always took the bait and paid the extortion. Leuci got a commission for his role as intermediary.

Scoppetta asked Leuci in how many such shakedowns had he been involved. Leuci admitted to three.* Scoppetta, a savvy investigator, suspected that there may have been more: the *modus operandi* seemed too inviting. But he did not want to press Leuci about his misdeeds for fear of alienating his prospective undercover operative. Nonetheless, he asked Leuci to talk

*Throughout the case there was some confusion about whether Leuci admitted to three or four separate shakedowns, since one of them involved two incidents. For purposes of consistency I refer to three rather than four, as does Robert Daley in *Prince of the City.*

into a tape recorder about his experiences with corruption, including his own involvement. Leuci agreed—but insisted on keeping the tapes after Scoppetta was finished with them. Leuci talked for days; the resulting tapes filled a large box. But it will never be known precisely what they contained, since they were eventually returned to Leuci, who says he unceremoniously incinerated them in his barbecue pit. The only remnant of Leuci's hundreds of hours of recordings is a two-page memorandum outlining the same three acts of corruption.

Manufacturing Crime

Scoppetta and Shaw now turned to their main task: making cases against suspected criminals. Shaw was not satisfied simply to *find* corruption; he wanted to *manufacture* it—so long as the targets were obvious hoodlums. According to an account written by Robert A. Daley, the former Deputy Police Commissioner of New York,* one of Shaw's first plans was

> to call in the leaders of each of the city's five Mafia families. We tell them, Shaw said, that they may be prosecuted for tax evasion. Then Bob [Leuci], here, reaches out to them through his organized crime connections. He lets it be known that he has access to the IRS files. Then he meets with them, and they bribe him to get the files. Then we arrest them for bribery of a police officer.

But the Shaw plan never went into effect because Leuci refused to participate in that kind of operation. "I can't do that," Leuci protested. "This income tax fabrication . . . that's a total frame." He explained that this kind of crime-creation would make criminals even out of the typical "accountant living in Scarsdale." "Tell a man he's being audited by the IRS, and he panics. Sure a Mafia guy would pay Leuci money. So would the accountant in Scarsdale."

That is precisely why the Supreme Court has recognized that crimes created by entrapment techniques cannot be prosecuted in federal court. In the leading case of *Sherman* v. *United States,* the Supreme Court, in an opinion written by Chief Justice Earl Warren, held that the "function of law enforcement is the prevention of crime and the apprehension of criminals, [not] the manufacturing of crime."†

*The book, entitled *Prince of the City,* was checked for accuracy prior to publication by Leuci and several government officials.

†In the *Sherman* case, a government agent named Kalchinian met the defendant, Sherman, at a doctor's office where both were seeking treatment for narcotics addiction. Kalchinian asked Sherman if he knew of a good source of narcotics. Sherman tried to avoid the issue at

There are two essential issues presented to the jury when the defendant raises a defense of entrapment. The first is whether a government agent *induced* the defendant into committing the crime. If he did, then a second issue arises: the defendant cannot be convicted unless—and this is a big unless—the government can prove that the defendant was *"ready and willing"* to commit the crime and was just waiting for an opportunity. If the government can prove that the defendant was thus "predisposed" to commit the crime, then it can convict him even if its agents "induced" him into committing it on that particular occasion.

Because of this "predisposition" exception, very few defendants prevail before a jury on an entrapment defense. It is known among criminal lawyers as a "defense of last resort," to be used only when there is no other chance of an acquittal. Because it is such a weak defense, many prosecutors are entirely willing to use inducements, especially against unsavory characters—such as organized crime leaders—since they are confident that any jury would find such gangsters predisposed to committing virtually any crime.

In this instance Leuci's somewhat more elevated street ethics prevailed over Shaw's questionable prosecutorial ethics. Shaw's Mafia scheme was dropped and a new flock of pigeons was sought.

The Baxter Street Gang

Shaw eventually settled on the "Baxter Street gang." This was neither a street gang nor an organized crime family. It was a group of criminal lawyers, bail bondsmen, and assorted judicial personnel whose offices were in and around the Baxter Street courthouse area in downtown New York and who were suspected of fixing criminal cases. One of the targets was a heavy-set bail bondsman named Nick DeStefano, who was already under indictment along with Edmund Rosner for subornation of perjury in the case involving Hernandez. But that case was not going well for the government. In July of 1971 Pedro Hernandez, the government's key witness, suddenly disappeared. The government did not know whether he was dead or alive. Without him the case against Rosner and DeStefano was in danger of falling apart.

---

first, but after repeated requests agreed to get some drugs for Kalchinian. A unanimous Supreme Court reversed the resulting conviction on the ground that Sherman had been unlawfully entrapped. The Court said:

> The case at bar illustrates an evil which the defense of entrapment is designed to overcome. The . . . Government plays on the weaknesses of an innocent party and beguiles him into committing crimes which he otherwise would not have attempted. Law enforcement does not require methods such as this.

Leuci was sent hunting into the Baxter Street jungle. It seems likely that his real prey was a few blocks uptown at 401 Broadway, where Rosner maintained his law office. If the prosecutors could not prevent the *Hernandez* case from falling apart, they could at least try to manufacture a new one, using as leverage Rosner's understandable anxiety about *Hernandez.*

On September 30, 1971, Leuci arranged to have lunch with Nick DeStefano and a New York City police detective named Nick Lamattina, at the New Lin Heong Chinese restaurant. Leuci, wired with a device capable of transmitting the conversation to a nearby tape recorder, told the bondsman and the detective that he had "a friend who works in the U.S. Attorney's office . . . [and] he's the kind of a guy like you can talk to. . . ." Then came the offer. "If anybody wants to do anything with this thing, let me know, I'll speak to this guy, and I'm sure something can be done. . . ."

Eventually, the discussion turned to the pending case against Rosner and DeStefano. Leuci offered to find out "whatever you want to know about it."

As soon as the meal ended, DeStefano raced over to Rosner's building and phoned him from the lobby. Rosner came downstairs and DeStefano told him about his conversation with Leuci and asked him whether he would be interested in meeting the source. Rosner said no. DeStefano then asked Rosner whether there was any information he wanted him to obtain. There was, of course, a great deal of information in the government's secret files that could have helped the worried Rosner prepare his case. But Rosner again declined the offer, saying that he didn't want to get involved in that kind of thing.

Leuci, DeStefano, and Lamattina met again the next day, DeStefano telling Leuci that Rosner wasn't interested because he felt that he had the *Hernandez* case beat.

The time had come for a new strategy—different bait had to be put on the hook if Rosner was to be snared. Leuci and his federal supervisors were not the only ones anxious to involve Rosner in the Leuci offer. DeStefano and Lamattina—unaware, of course, that they were dealing with a walking tape recorder—saw Rosner as capable of bankrolling the payment to Leuci's friend; they wanted the information that Leuci was offering, but they didn't have the money to pay the price Leuci was demanding. If they could get Rosner to believe that the information was crucial to *him,* then he might be willing to pay for it; and they—DeStefano and Lamattina—would get it for free or, at least, at a substantially reduced price. Lamattina urged Leuci "to put Rosner in deeper . . . to lean on this guy [because] he's the guy with the money."

With this in mind DeStefano again called Rosner after the second meeting with Leuci and told him that he—Rosner—had a big problem and was in deep trouble. Rosner rushed to Baxter Street where DeStefano dropped the bomb. The United States Attorney's office had information that the missing Pedro Hernandez—the key witness in its case against Rosner—had been killed and that it was Rosner who had arranged to have him "clipped." The government was gathering evidence, and within a week or so Rosner would be arrested for murder, his bail would be revoked, and he would be imprisoned.

Having dangled the bait, DeStefano again asked Rosner to meet with his friend who could fill him in on the details and get him any information he needed. Despite the enormous temptations Rosner again declined to meet with DeStefano's friend or to get involved.

But now Rosner was in an absolute frenzy. He drove home in a daze. He felt panicky. His head was swimming. He could not believe what was going on. He knew that he had not gotten Hernandez killed. What was the government up to? Were they trying to frame him? Where was Hernandez anyway? Wasn't his convenient disappearance suspicious? How would he explain it to a doubting judge? What evidence did the government have?

On Monday, October 4, DeStefano came to see him. He was on his way to a crucial meeting with Leuci and it was essential that Rosner come along because only he—as a lawyer—would know the right questions to ask. Finally, after again being told how important it was to find out exactly what the story was, Rosner agreed to accompany DeStefano to his meeting.

Setting the Trap

The stage was thus set for the initial encounter between Rosner and Leuci. Fortunately for Leuci and unfortunately for Rosner and for posterity, Leuci was not wired on the day of that meeting: Lamattina and DeStefano picked that occasion to search him for a transmitter. Finding him clean, they began to talk about the Hernandez case. Precisely what they said was to become a matter of critical dispute, since Leuci's testimony and Rosner's would differ sharply.

According to Rosner's version, Rosner asked Leuci about the missing Hernandez. Leuci replied that his friend in the U.S. Attorney's office had said that "they believe that you had this person killed." "This is ridiculous," Rosner screamed. "Well, they have information," Leuci said, "that this person has been murdered and they also are gathering evidence or interviewing witnesses and getting evidence that you had him murdered." Leuci then warned Rosner that the government was preparing to have his bail revoked. Leuci offered to do anything he could to help. Rosner replied, "If you hear anything, whatever you hear, let us know."

Rosner and DeStefano left the table, and DeStefano said, "I think we ought to give him something for what he has done."

Rosner refused. "I'm not going to give him anything. Forget it . . . Absolutely not." The meeting then ended.

Leuci's version was that Rosner asked him whether his friend could get copies of the statements made by the witnesses against him. DeStefano asked Leuci what his friend wanted in exchange for this information. Leuci responded that no figure had been mentioned but that his friend had extended himself already and something had to be done for him as soon as possible. Rosner and DeStefano left the table and Rosner removed money from his pocket and gave it to DeStefano. They returned to the table and DeStefano said, "I have four for you," and handed Leuci a roll of cash under the table. Leuci thought he was getting $4,000 and expressed disappointment in finding only $400. He approached Rosner and said, "My friend has gone through a lot for $400." Rosner replied, "Well, have your friend get what I asked you to get and there will be a lot more for him in the future."

It is evident that there are critical differences between the Rosner and Leuci versions of this first encounter. If Rosner is to be believed, Leuci convinced him that his bail was about to be revoked because he was suspected of killing Hernandez; and it was Leuci who offered to get the information as a favor. If Leuci is to be believed, it was Rosner who asked for specific material and paid for it. Eventually, the jury had to decide who was more believable—Rosner, the corruptible lawyer; or Leuci, the corrupting cop.

The next several meetings were also unrecorded. DeStefano agreed that Leuci would be paid $3,500, but that Rosner would be told that the figure was $5,000, of which he owed half. In that way the information would cost DeStefano and Lamattina only $500 each, while Rosner would be stuck with the remaining $2,500.

Taping the Trap Closed

Finally, the prosecutors decided to have Leuci wear a recorder for a meeting at Ruggiero's Restaurant. There were two reasons for this change. Since several encounters had already occurred and money had passed hands, it was assumed that the participants were comfortable with each other and that Leuci would not be searched. Even more important, from a legal standpoint, the prospective defendants had already been induced at the unrecorded meetings; there was no longer any need for Leuci to lie, threaten, beguile, or implore. It was now safe to turn on the tape, since all it would record would be evidence of the crime itself, and not evidence of the trap being laid, baited, and nibbled at.

This tactic of not recording the preliminary meetings where the alleged entrapment occurs, and then recording subsequent meetings where the already entrapped defendant provides evidence of the crime, is not uncommon. It is unfair to defendants, but those who use it justify it by a concern for the safety of the entrapper. One result of this tactic is that the jury is faced with the defendant's uncorroborated word against that of the policeman concerning the original entrapment, while the government has solid recordings of the commission of the crime itself. Given this kind of evidence, few juries will acquit.

The conversation at Ruggiero's began with Leuci saying that the "most important thing" was to keep his source happy "for the future." Leuci told Rosner that the government's perjury case against him was weak. "They think they ain't got a prayer; the only prayer that they thought they had was to show previous and subsequent criminal acts." Rosner was obviously relieved: "There's nothing there." Leuci told Rosner that the government was interviewing other potential witnesses, but had come up empty-handed.

Rosner then discussed the missing witness Hernandez.

ROSNER: Now they say Hernandez's being clipped. I don't know if he's been clipped. . . . *What I was told by you, they think I had this guy hit.* [My italics.]

LEUCI, aware that he is being recorded, immediately tried to deny he told ROSNER that the government believed he had Hernandez killed.

LEUCI: No, no, no. They didn't say, you know, our man was clipped.
ROSNER: . . . Because I didn't. I don't know. I was relying on what you . . .
LEUCI: . . . They're saying, they're saying according to him that they're sure that a guy's been clipped in this, because they just can't find the guy.

This conversation tends to support Rosner's contention that Leuci had told him the government suspected he was responsible for having Hernandez killed—a contention denied by Leuci.

Eventually, a price was agreed on for all the material with a "guarantee" that if anything important was missing—if there was "a sleeper"—the trio would "get the money back." Leuci reassured him that "You've got this thing beat. . . . All the U.S. Attorneys are saying that you got it beat."

Rosner then asked, "Why the fuck are they going ahead with it? Why don't they dismiss it?"

Leuci responded, "You're really at the mercy of a lot of people."

Rosner then said, "The whole case is bullshit, so help me, we're completely innocent."

The conversation then turned to the arrest of a couple of cops in Harlem, and Leuci asked Rosner whether he would defend them and how he could "beat that case." Rosner responded—with unsuspecting irony—that he would raise a defense similar to entrapment, explaining the legal significance of the entrapment defense and the "predisposition" exception. Leuci replied admiringly, "Well, God forbid if I ever get in a jackpot, Eddie, you're going to be my lawyer."

At the end of the meal Leuci and DeStefano adjourned to the men's room, where DeStefano counted out several hundred dollars and gave it to Leuci.

The dinner ended at about midnight and Leuci immediately went to Shaw's apartment to play the tape. The sound quality was poor, with Italian music and laughing in the background, people speaking over other people's voices and electronic static. Leuci and Shaw were listening hard for concrete evidence of a bribe offer by Rosner. After some confusing conversation, Leuci yelled, "There it is . . . hear it?" But Shaw hadn't heard anything clearly.

The tape was played again and again. After the sixth rerun, Shaw finally heard what he was waiting to hear. "I hear it," Shaw shouted. "That time I heard it. That's his voice. That's him. It's there, it's there." Shaw started to grin and clap his hands: "We got the son of a bitch."

But the tape was ambiguous at best and Shaw wanted better and clearer evidence that Rosner had actually offered a bribe. Two additional meetings were arranged at the Dayton, a Jewish dairy restaurant on the Lower East Side of Manhattan. Both its milieu and its food were familiar to me, since it is located down the street from where my father's haberdashery store used to be. Whenever I worked there my treat used to be a "chopped liver" sandwich on an onion roll with a Dr. Brown Soda at the Dayton. (The untutored may wonder how a kosher dairy restaurant could serve chopped liver. But the Jewish culinary imagination has never been constrained by facts: the "liver" was made exclusively of string beans, eggplant, mushrooms, onions, chopped walnuts, and hard-boiled eggs.)

Neither of the Dayton meetings, which were recorded, produced evidence of guilt. The government's bribery case against Rosner would have to rest on ambiguous and unclear tapes coupled with the testimony of Robert Leuci. On the critical issue of entrapment it would be Leuci's word, as corroborated by certain portions of the tapes, against Rosner's, as corroborated by other portions of the tapes.

Leuci's Slip

After Leuci completed his Rosner assignment he continued to meet with DeStefano and Lamattina in an effort to sell them information about other targets. One of Scoppetta's plans was to let word reach a reputed narcotics dealer that the government had incriminating tape recordings of him that he could obtain for $50,000. The dealer reached out for Leuci through DeStefano and Lamattina. It was agreed that Leuci would provide copies of the tapes to DeStefano and Lamattina, who would listen to them and have them tested for authenticity. If they were genuine the $50,000 would be paid. On December 19, 1971—two months after the last of the Rosner meetings—Leuci transferred the tapes from his car to Lamattina's. Lamattina asked Leuci for a box or envelope in which to place them. Leuci looked around and spotted what appeared to be an empty manila envelope in his car. He put the tapes in the envelope and gave it to Lamattina.

That envelope was to mark the beginning of the end for Bob Leuci as an undercover cop. Tucked into a corner of the envelope was a revealing scrap of paper: a memo from Nicholas Scoppetta to TPF-I, requesting information about three targets named Lamattina, DeStefano, and Bless. TPF-I was Leuci's code name during the investigation.

Lamattina took the tapes home to play, but he never got to listen. As he removed the first of the tapes, the telltale memo dropped out of the envelope. Lamattina read it and called DeStefano in a panic. They decided to arrange a final dinner with the unsuspecting Leuci.

When they arrived at the restaurant DeStefano glared at Leuci and threw the Scoppetta memo at him. Leuci instantly knew that he had been careless and that his life was on the line. He couldn't think of a convincing explanation. His first instinct was to shift the blame to one of his partners, a police detective named Stanley Glazer. "I knew that fucking Jew was a rat the moment I saw him." But neither DeStefano nor Lamattina was persuaded. They told Leuci to come along with them to the men's room, where they searched him for a wire. This time Leuci was wishing that he had worn a transmitter, so that his backup team of two IRS agents and one New York City policeman could be listening. But he was completely alone. The ever-present backup team was driving around the block not anticipating a danger signal from the restaurant where Leuci was meeting with his two familiar dining companions.

Leuci decided that his best chance was to frighten DeStefano and Lamattina. "You guys are in trouble," he said. DeStefano turned to Lamattina, the gun-toting detective, and ordered him to kill Leuci. Leuci did not flinch. Confidently he told his would-be assailants that he had dozens of FBI agents waiting outside with machine guns, adding that he could get them a deal. Leuci suggested that they leave the restaurant and talk about it outside. He desperately wanted to be in view of his backup team. As soon as they reached the street, Leuci began scratching his head furiously—the agreed upon rescue signal. But the team was out of sight. DeStefano became menacing again; there were no agents with machine guns; maybe Leuci was bluffing. Maybe they would be better off killing Leuci and taking their chances with a difficult-to-prove murder rap than with an open-and-shut series of bribery charges. Just then the backup team's unmarked car turned the corner. The cop saw Leuci scratching his head, but he wasn't sure. Not wanting to endanger Leuci's cover in the event that he was responding to an innocent itch, the cop put his hand in his gun pocket, walked up to Leuci, and inquired innocently, "Hey, don't I know you?" Leuci heaved a sigh of relief and ordered the cop to arrest DeStefano and Lamattina and take them to the U.S. Attorney's office.

Scoppetta and Shaw were waiting when Leuci arrived with the frightened and confused DeStefano and Lamattina in tow. Shaw told them that Leuci had recorded their various meetings and the cases against them were ironclad. Their only hope was to cooperate with the government by testifying against Rosner and by becoming "undercover agents." After several hours of negotiation DeStefano and Lamattina agreed to consider cooperating. They also swore that they would not tell Rosner about their discovery of Leuci's status or the fact that they had become government agents. Upon those conditions they were permitted to leave.

At this point DeStefano and Lamattina realized that their fates lay completely in the hands of the government; they had exposed their own corruption fully to their "friend" Leuci, who had duly recorded it all on tape for the federal prosecutors. DeStefano and Lamattina had no choice but to keep their promise: they never told Rosner they had discovered Leuci's status and agreed to work undercover for the government. Scoppetta made the terms of the bargain very clear. The more information they provided about Rosner and other cases, the more they could expect "to get in return."

In the meantime an unsuspecting Rosner was confidently "winning" his original subornation of perjury case involving Pedro Hernandez. On January 24, 1972—three months after the recorded meetings with Leuci—Rosner's trial lawyer persuaded Judge Charles Metzner to dismiss the subornation of perjury charges on the ground that the government had violated the defendant's Sixth Amendment right to a "speedy trial," because it was still not prepared to begin the trial more than a year after the indictment. The reason was that its key witness, Pedro Hernandez, was still missing.

Rosner left Judge Metzner's courtroom a happy man, confidently ready to resume his law practice. He had nearly forgotten about the dinner meetings with Leuci some three months earlier; the information he had obtained from the policeman's friend had done him no good and would not be needed, since the perjury case had been dismissed.

Rosner didn't notice that several of the prosecutors left the courtroom smiling that day, secure in the knowledge that their real case against the "cancer" of the U.S. Courthouse had not yet begun. The formal dismissal of the perjury charge was unimportant. That case was, at best, weak to begin with; and it had more than achieved its purpose by serving as potent bait for Leuci's trap.

Two months after Judge Metzner dismissed the subornation of perjury charges, and several days after the five-year statute of limitations on that crime had run out, the government finally located Pedro Hernandez. He had not been "clipped" after all; he was alive and well and living in Mexico City. The government had him returned to New York and attempted to bring Rosner to trial on the Hernandez case. But Judge Metzner refused to reverse his dismissal order.

The government was not yet ready to indict Rosner for the Leuci bribery attempt. Leuci was still working undercover on several other important cases; and there was no way of publicly charging Rosner with the bribery attempt without blowing Leuci's cover. But Leuci's cover was growing thinner by the day. Suspicion was increasing in the Baxter Street area. People were starting to avoid him. Rumors had begun to spread.

Finally, on June 15, 1972, the *New York Times* and the *Daily News* disclosed that Detective Robert Leuci had been posing as a corrupt policeman and had snared several important participants in the criminal justice system. When Rosner saw the headline he turned pale. It had been a trap, and he—one of the shrewdest lawyers in the city—had stumbled into it!

As soon as the story broke, Leuci was hustled into protective custody. Eventually, he was allowed to rejoin his family in a cabin he owned in the Catskills. (No one knew about Leuci's mountain retreat, probably because the ownership of two homes on a New York City detective's salary would have raised some eyebrows.) The cabin was guarded twenty-four hours a day and Leuci remained there until his testimony was needed in the city—at which time he was moved to a military barracks on Governors Island, near the Statue of Liberty.

The Second Trap

Leuci's first and most important case, the attempted bribery prosecution against Eddie Rosner, was presented to the grand jury by Edward Shaw at the end of June. Shortly thereafter, indictments were handed down against attorney Rosner, bail bondsman DeStefano, and detective Lamattina. Rosner was devastated. How could he and his pregnant wife endure another ordeal? For solace he turned, as criminal defendants often do, to his co-defendants. They were in this together, and each could understand what the other was feeling. They also had a common legal problem and a coordinated defense was essential. But the shrewd New York lawyer was again falling into a trap. Rosner was unaware that DeStefano and Lamattina were also government undercover agents desperately trying to earn favors from the prosecutors in exchange for information about him.

From the day of the first newspaper accounts of Leuci's undercover investigation, DeStefano and Lamattina—feigning ignorance and failing to disclose their arrangement with the government—met with Edmund and Nancy Rosner and with Albert Krieger, the trial lawyer the Rosners retained to handle the Leuci trial. Every aspect of the case was discussed: trial strategy, pretrial motions, possible defenses, investigation of Leuci's background and credibility, potential lines of cross-examination, and how to explain incriminating statements on the tapes. Little did Rosner suspect that these secret legal discussions were being attended by government agents.

As the trial approached, the government prosecutors began to debrief DeStefano and Lamattina about the Rosner case. The government's chief trial counsel, Robert Morvillo, conducted the interviews. Morvillo was aware that if DeStefano or Lamattina provided the government with specific information from the confidential meetings between Rosner and his lawyers, this might constitute an unlawful intrusion into Rosner's right to confer with his lawyer in confidence. In order not to jeopardize their case, while also assuring themselves the maximum advantage from DeStefano and Lamattina's information, Morvillo took two precautions. First, he advised DeStefano and Lamattina "not to volunteer" any information about discussions between Rosner and his lawyers. Second, he decided to keep no records of the extensive debriefing sessions. No tapes were made; no notes were taken; and no memorandum was written. The lack of records gave the government lawyers what is known as "deniability"—that is, the ability to deny a fact without fear of contradiction by hard evidence.

Morvillo and the other prosecutors obtained a great deal of valuable information from their double agents. Armed with this information, the tapes, and Leuci himself—and amidst a flurry of media coverage—the government brought Edmund Rosner to trial for attempted bribery. The district judge pulled out of the wheel to hear the case was Arnold Bauman, formerly of the Knapp Commission.

Leuci's Own Crimes: What the Government Really Knew

The government planned to present its case against Rosner through Leuci and his tapes. (DeStefano and Lamattina pleaded guilty just before the trial, but did not testify for either side.) Since there were no recordings of the early meetings involving Leuci and Rosner—the meetings at which the government alleged that the bribe offer was made and at which the defendant alleged that the entrapment occurred—the government had to rely on Leuci's credibility as a witness. The prosecutors realized that they had a problem, since Leuci's own character was sullied by three prior crimes. Would the jury believe the word of a cop who had admittedly engaged in corrupt acts, against the word of a lawyer who denied any prior wrongdoing?

But the prosecutors had no choice: the law unequivocably obliged them to disclose to the defense *all* of the acts of corruption admitted by Leuci, so that the defense lawyers could be prepared to cross-examine the government's star witness. The defense, aware of rumors concerning Leuci's past corruption, specifically demanded that the government disclose his entire sordid history. When Leuci learned of this, he panicked: he did not want to expose his history of corruption to public view.

On the eve of the trial Leuci stunned Elliot Sagor, the young assistant U.S. Attorney helping Morvillo try the case, by announcing he would deny all prior misconduct at the trial. Sagor, in a panic, reminded him of what he had told Scoppetta. Leuci responded that he had been "bullshitting." Scoppetta and Shaw were summoned. After some discussion they persuaded Leuci that he had to disclose the three crimes he had admitted to Scoppetta.

By the time Scoppetta and Shaw were convincing Leuci that he had to disclose the three crimes, these prosecutors had become aware that Leuci had in fact committed several more crimes. Despite this knowledge they remained silent while Leuci committed perjury at the Rosner trial by denying that he had committed any additional crimes. This prosecutorial complicity in Leuci's perjury was to become a central issue in our appeals.

The prosecutors had learned of Leuci's additional crimes in the spring of 1971, shortly after Leuci began to work for the federal prosecutors. Leuci told Shaw that several years earlier he had participated in a warrantless search of a reputed drug dealer's apartment. The police found no drugs, but they did find some cash. The police took the money and divided it between themselves. The illegal entry coupled with the theft of the money constituted the felonies of burglary and grand larceny (even though it was never reported by the victim). The relatively small amount of money taken—$200 by Leuci's account—did not diminish the seriousness of the crime. After all, they took everything they found.

During that same period Leuci was sent out to investigate a homicide. The prime suspect was a drug dealer named Richard Lawrence, also known as The Baron, who was one of Leuci's major narcotics informants. Scoppetta directed Leuci to make a surreptitious tape recording of his conversation with The Baron. The recording yielded no information about the homicide, but it suggested that Leuci and The Baron were up to their necks in narcotics corruption. Leuci asked The Baron whether "we ever made a case where you didn't get a piece of the package?" Leuci then suggested that "the easiest way" to "get your hands on something" was to make it understood to the narcotics agent you were working with "before you make the case" that you expected to get a piece of the action.

Finally, during the course of the Leuci operation, Scoppetta, Shaw, and the United States Attorney himself, Whitney North Seymour, Jr., learned of an extremely serious crime in which Leuci had played a central role. It had started two years earlier when Leuci and one of his partners had been investigating a suspected narcotics operation in the Bronx. They tapped the phone of a large discount store in which the police believed the drugs were stored. While the detectives were monitoring the tape, they overheard a call in which a man with an Italian accent informed the owner of the store that his premises would be used to warehouse several hundred hijacked television sets. A truck soon arrived and the sets were unloaded. Suddenly, a plainclothes policeman—unrelated to the narcotics investigation—wandered into the store. He saw what was happening and he immediately called in a report to the local police headquarters. Within ten minutes there were fifty cops in the store arresting the owner and the hijackers. Then, within minutes, a fleet of private cars—Volkswagens, station wagons—arrived. Virtually all the policeman in the local precinct came in private cars and started loading TVs into their trunks and onto the roofs. The police were waiting in line to steal the hijacked TV sets. But there were more TVs than the local police could carry; so several began calling their friends at other precincts to tell them the good news.

Unfortunately for the cops most of the calls were made from the telephone in the store—the phone that was tapped. Each of these felonious calls was being recorded on Leuci's tape.

When he realized what was happening, Leuci was horrified. If he turned in the tape, his fellow police officers would have to be prosecuted. He and the other detectives decided, therefore, to erase from the tape all of the voices of policemen engaging in the crime of stealing the TV sets. This cover-up constituted a conspiracy to obstruct justice; misprison (concealment) of a felony; and tampering with evidence.

But this did not end the matter. Two years later, when the case against the narcotics dealers in the Bronx was ready for trial and when Leuci was already working for the feds, he and the other three detectives agreed among themselves to *deny* that the tape had been erased. They concocted a story—reminiscent of a tale from the Oval Office—that the gaps and omissions on the tape were caused by a "defect in the machine." Indeed, Leuci went so far as to inform the District Attorney prosecuting the case that the gaps were caused by a mechanical malfunction. The D.A. asked the detectives whether they were prepared to swear in open court under oath that "the tape had not been tampered with." All of the detectives—including Leuci—said that they would swear to that in open court the following day. They were fully aware that they had agreed—conspired—to commit perjury.

On the day before the Bronx trial of the narcotics dealers, Leuci told Shaw and Scoppetta the story. Shaw informed Whitney North Seymour, Jr., of the dilemma. They traveled to the Bronx in order to persuade the District Attorney to keep Leuci and the other detectives off the witness stand. The D.A. agreed, and the next day, the defendants in the Bronx trial were informed that the felony cases against them would be dropped if they pleaded guilty to misdemeanors, which they appreciatively did. The U.S. Attorneys had prevented Leuci from committing the crime of perjury in court. But it was too late to prevent Leuci from having committed a series of equally serious crimes: when Leuci and the other detectives *agreed* among themselves to lie about the erased tapes and told the lie to the D.A., they had *already* committed the crimes of conspiracy to commit perjury; conspiracy to obstruct justice; and the crime of lying to a law enforcement official. Even if Leuci's disclosure of these crimes to Shaw undid these conspiracies, it was too late to undo the original crimes committed two years earlier, when Leuci and his partner had erased the tapes and permitted their fellow policemen to get away with stealing the television sets.

The Rosner Trial

Thus, as Leuci was preparing to testify about the three crimes he had originally confessed to Scoppetta, several prosecutors within the United States Attorney's office—including the U.S. Attorney himself—were aware that Leuci had committed other serious crimes, crimes that he had no intention of disclosing to the defense at the Rosner trial. The suppression of the tape erasure and the conspiracy to lie about it was particularly indefensible, since its disclosure would have shown the jury that the government's star witness had a *recent* history of tampering with tapes and a willingness to lie on the witness stand—a history directly relevant to the Rosner case.

Both the prosecutors and the defense attorneys fully understood that this case would turn on whether the jury believed Leuci or Rosner. The tapes were garbled and ambiguous. Without Leuci's explanations—especially of the unrecorded and crucial early meetings—these tapes would not be enough to ensure the conviction. Moreover, if the jurors were to become aware of Leuci's history of tampering with tapes they might discount them entirely, or at least wonder whether they were complete.

The trial itself proceeded along predictable lines. Morvillo had Leuci recount each of the meetings with Rosner; the tapes were played to the jury; and Leuci was cross-examined about his three admitted acts of corruption. Rosner's trial lawyer, Albert Krieger, tried desperately to get Leuci to confess that he had committed other acts of corruption besides the three he admitted. Leuci adamantly denied committing any other crimes; he repeatedly swore under oath that the three crimes—the last committed five years earlier—were the only ones he had ever committed in his life. Moreover, he justified these isolated acts as having been motivated by a desire to protect defenseless victims from overreaching by other corrupt police. Leuci testified that these victims felt that he "was sort of a breath of fresh air [whom] they could count on . . . to sit at a mediation or that sort of thing and give them a fair shake." The sum total of money that Leuci admitted receiving as intermediary in the three acts of corruption was $5,000 to $6,000. He denied under persistent cross-examination, both before and during the trial, that he had ever perjured himself; that he had ever taken any money from an informant; or that he had ever sold drugs to anyone.

The Government's Silence

It is interesting to speculate what must have been going through Edward Shaw's mind as he listened to Leuci swear under oath that he committed no crimes other than the three to which he admitted. Had he forgotten about the burglary that Leuci had admitted to him? Was he not aware of the incriminating statements he had made about drug deals on the recording with The Baron? Had he failed to recall the recent tape erasure and perjury conspiracy in the Bronx? Did he not realize that the erasure of the tape was a crime and that it was of potentially crucial relevance to the ongoing trial? Why had he—the lawyer responsible for disclosing evidence of Leuci's criminal past—failed to produce the information about these crimes?

Edward Shaw did not strike me as a man who forgets about crimes. The most plausible explanation for Shaw's conduct is that he must have decided that he was having enough trouble convincing Leuci to admit to the three original crimes, and to press him any further would be to risk a complete breakdown of communication. In order to preserve his star witness—and his prize case against Rosner—Shaw may have decided, in effect, to engage in an act of civil disobedience: conveniently to forget the other crimes that Leuci had admitted and to allow Leuci to commit perjury in the interests of a higher justice. It is possible, of course, that he actually did forget about these additional crimes or that he did not realize they were crimes. But this strikes me as unlikely.

The government's effort to portray Leuci as an enemy of corruption was not limited to the courtroom. The prosecutors orchestrated a public relations campaign in anticipation of the trial. In the days immediately preceding the trial, Morvillo devoted a considerable amount of his time to dealing with the press. In an extraordinary move, United States Attorney Whitney North Seymour, Jr., had approached *Life* magazine even before Leuci's cover was blown and offered them an exclusive story on the Leuci investigations. This kind of press manipulation by prosecutors is frowned upon because of the danger that it may prejudice potential jurors, but in this case Seymour encouraged it. Seymour was eventually criticized for his actions, but only because it was learned that the *Life* interview had led to Leuci's cover being blown before the completion of the investigation. The *Life* story characterized Leuci as an honest and compassionate cop who had acted as "go-between," but who had never been involved in extortion or the buying or selling of narcotics, who "has only contempt for the cop who is simply using his job as a cover for thievery." A *New York Times* profile of Leuci characterized him as a policeman who was pained by the problem of narcotics and who had demonstrated his toughness "by refusing to accept the corruption that he saw around him on the force."

At the trial the government assured the jury that since 1967 Robert Leuci had never strayed from the straight and narrow: even his candid and painful admissions of past misconduct cast an aura of truth over his testimony against Rosner. Prosecutor Morvillo repeatedly hammered home to the jury the absolute honesty of his star witness:

> Not once did Detective Leuci get caught in any lie, because he didn't lie.

Rosner testified on his own behalf. As expected, his version of the crucial unrecorded meetings was different from Leuci's. If Rosner was to be believed, he was clearly an unwilling dupe illegally entrapped by a lying government agent. If Leuci was to be believed, Rosner was the willing initiator and Leuci the reluctant supplier of the purchased documents.

Morvillo put the credibility contest to the jury: "Is Rosner telling the truth or is Detective Leuci, supported by those tape recordings, telling the truth?" Morvillo stressed the importance of the early unrecorded meeting between Leuci and Rosner at Ruggiero's. "The October 4th meeting is a very important meeting. [I]f you accept [Leuci's] version of what happened at the October 4th meeting, Rosner has committed a crime."

Judge Bauman agreed that the case turned on whether the jury believed Leuci or Rosner. He instructed the jury that the versions of Leuci and Rosner "are in such sharp divergence on key points, that it may be suggested that this irreconcilable conflict is not due to forgetfulness or lack of recollection. Both versions cannot be true."

After six hours of deliberation the jurors informed the judge that they wanted to "conduct [their] own review of [the] testimony" of Leuci and Rosner concerning the *unrecorded* meetings of September 30 and October 4. Four hours later, the jury sent a note to Judge Bauman reporting that while one of the jurors was in the subway he had overheard a conversation in which Leuci had been described as a cop who had been corrupt for "nine to eleven" years. The jury asked whether they could consider this. The request threw Morvillo into a rage. He jumped up and demanded that Judge Bauman direct the jury "in a very strong way" to ignore this conversation, since any information supporting the contention that Leuci's corruption extended beyond the three incidents early in 1967 would be completely "derogatory of the government's case and inconsistent with the detective's testimony." Judge Bauman properly instructed the jury to disregard the gossip about Leuci.

Shortly thereafter, the jury returned a verdict finding Rosner guilty on five counts of the indictment and not guilty on two counts.

Rosner was despondent but he was also determined. Within days after his conviction, he discovered several heroin addicts who claimed to have personal knowledge that Leuci was deeply involved in narcotics dealings.

His lawyer brought a motion for a new trial; the pitiful addicts were brought to the witness stand and testified. Judge Bauman ruled that their testimony was not worthy of belief and denied the motion.

Enter "The Baron"

During the time that this motion for a new trial was pending, another mysterious episode was unfolding within the confines of the United States Attorney's office. Robert Leuci's chief narcotics informant, Richard Lawrence—"The Baron," with whom Leuci had made the incriminating tape involving the sale of "packages"—mentioned to an assistant District Attorney in Manhattan that Leuci had repeatedly given him heroin to sell over the years and had shared in the profits. (Lawrence had apparently had a falling out with Leuci over money and was trying to ingratiate himself with the District Attorney's office.) Lawrence's information was exactly what Rosner had been trying to prove and what Leuci had repeatedly denied. The D.A. reported the conversation to the United States Attorney's office, and Robert Morvillo was given the assignment of investigating these allegations to determine whether they were true. If they turned out to be true, then it would be clear that Leuci had committed perjury at Rosner's trial, and Rosner's conviction would be in jeopardy.

Morvillo received the information and assignment in early January 1973 —at the very time that Rosner's trial lawyer was filing his new trial motion based on testimony by the heroin addicts who claimed knowledge that Leuci was involved in the sale of drugs.

The Baron's information was similar to the testimony of the addicts, but was far more important for several reasons: The Baron was neither a heroin addict nor even a user. He was a high-level registered government informant for whose credibility the government had vouched on numerous occasions. The Baron was so trusted and "outstanding" an informant that the Bureau of Narcotics had been paying him as much as $50,000 a year for his information. He was regarded by police officials as a "fantastic" informant whose reliable information was "at the root of all [Leuci's] major cases." Moreover, his information was not based on rumor or hearsay. It rested on years of direct dealings with Detective Leuci and it was corroborated with names, dates, amounts, and locations—in short, precisely the kind of evidence that is essential for a successful new trial motion.

The Baron's information put Morvillo on the spot. He had barely finished celebrating his victory against Rosner, and now it threatened to go down the drain. Morvillo could not have been surprised by the new information, since immediately after the Rosner trial—amidst the congratulations—he had warned Leuci that "It's not over for Rosner. Don't forget, you admitted to only three acts of misconduct." He advised Leuci to expect a motion for a new trial based on new evidence of other crimes.

Morvillo's first reaction to The Baron's allegations was—according to those close to him—a concern for his own reputation. How would it look in the newspapers? What would it do to his standing in the legal community? "If this is true," muttered Morvillo, "then all our cases will be bad."

Instead of disclosing this important witness to the defense so that the defense could conduct its own investigation—as the law obliged him to do —Morvillo decided to conduct his own secret inquiry in the hope that it would prove that The Baron was lying and that Leuci was telling the truth.

Morvillo's "investigation" was hardly worthy of the name. The Baron had provided information about two drug dealers with whom Leuci had engaged in illegal drug sales. He gave their street names, addresses, and, in one case, a phone number; in the other case, he gave the name of an assistant D.A. who could identify and locate him. Morvillo's investigation failed to identify or locate either dealer. Morvillo did not even call the phone number or the D.A., although each was easily reached in a matter of minutes when we subsequently tried.

The Baron also told the government that as partial payment for the narcotics Leuci had given him to sell, he had given Leuci three automobiles. The Baron produced documents to support the transfer of the cars. When Morvillo asked Leuci about this, Leuci produced one canceled check to The Baron in the amount of $400, dated September 1971. Leuci claimed that this check proved that he had paid for at least one of the cars—a 1966 Ford station wagon. A closer look at the documents proved exactly the opposite: the 1966 Ford was not transferred to Leuci until the spring of 1972—several months *after* the check was issued. Indeed, the Ford was not even owned by The Baron in September 1971 when the check was issued. The Baron first bought it—for $1,100—on October 28, 1971. But Morvillo was satisfied with Leuci's evidence and the investigation of the cars proceeded no further.

Finally, Morvillo decided that a lie detector test should be administered —not to Leuci, but to The Baron. Instead of using one of the dozens of reputable New York polygraph firms that the government usually retains, the government investigator decided to use an outfit that had just opened in Alexandria, Virginia (and that would go out of business within weeks). The test results were equivocal: several respected authorities who analyzed the charts later testified that "no expert could reasonably conclude on the basis of these charts" that The Baron was lying or being deceptive. But they were enough for Morvillo. He hastily concluded that The Baron was lying about each of his charges and that the investigation could now be closed.

Morvillo also decided that neither Rosner nor the court should ever be told about the investigation, about The Baron's allegations—or even about his very existance. Though Judge Bauman, in his denial of the motion for a new trial, concluded that the testimony of the addicts about Leuci's narcotics corruption was not worthy of belief, he also implied that if the evidence had been credible, a serious issue would have been presented. Morvillo sat back silent and satisfied.

Sentencing

The new trial motion having been denied, it was time for Rosner to be sentenced. In some states the judge imposes the sentence as soon as the jury has returned its verdict of guilty. In the federal courts, there is a hiatus of several weeks between the verdict and sentencing, to allow the Federal Probation Department—an independent arm of the court—to prepare a report about the defendant's past and his potential for rehabilitation. Many judges depend heavily on the recommendations of the Probation Department, since it is supposed to be staffed by experts in penology, who are independent of the prosecutorial establishment. On the day of the sentencing, Rosner was informed that Judge Bauman had been given two separate reports on his case. One was prepared by the Probation Department; the other by the prosecutor's office under the direction of Robert Morvillo. In a departure from accepted legal procedures, Morvillo had surreptitiously sent the memorandum to Judge Bauman more than two months before the sentencing date. Morvillo had failed to notify the defense of his extraordinary and irregular action. Nor had Judge Bauman informed the defense that he had received the memorandum.

Several minutes before the judge was to impose sentence, Rosner was handed a copy of Morvillo's lengthy memorandum. A quick glance revealed that it was nothing more than a collection of gossip and rumor about Rosner's reputation. For example, one assistant United States Attorney told about a case whose name he couldn't even remember, in which he believed that Rosner might have induced a witness to perjure himself, though he admitted that he "had no proof to substantiate this possibility."

Judge Bauman informed Rosner's lawyers that he might consider the Morvillo report in sentencing Rosner. Krieger requested an adjournment in order to investigate and answer the charges. Bauman denied the request and sentenced Rosner to five years imprisonment. Since the usual prison term for bribery in the federal courts is approximately a year and a half to two years—even when the bribery is committed by government lawyers or judges—it seems likely that Morvillo's memorandum had influenced Judge Bauman's judgment.

Investigating and Appealing

When Rosner retained me to argue his appeal, he knew that there would be more to the case than a simple brief and argument. "Leuci is the most corrupt cop in the City of New York," Rosner told me. "We can't prove it yet, but we're not going to rest until we can convince even his most skeptical friend that his testimony about those three little crimes was a load of shit."

We decided to wage a two-front war. I would prepare the appeal while Rosner would direct the investigation into the reports of Leuci's corruption. We would coordinate our efforts toward the common goal of reversing Rosner's conviction either on appeal or on the basis of newly discovered evidence of Leuci's perjury.

The appeal raised three major issues: 1) whether the evidence established that Leuci had unlawfully entrapped Rosner; (2) whether DeStefano's and Lamattina's presence at Rosner's meetings with his lawyers—after they had agreed to cooperate with the government—had denied Rosner his right to confidential communication with his lawyer; and 3) whether Judge Bauman's decision to consider the Morvillo sentencing memorandum had denied Rosner the due process of law. We could not yet raise the issue of Leuci's perjury, since we had no solid evidence that Leuci had committed crimes other than those he admitted.

I argued the appeal in July of 1973. In September a unanimous court of appeals rendered its decision. It found that the trial had been essentially a credibility contest between Leuci and Rosner and that Judge Bauman had properly "left to the jury the credibility of the witness." The jury had chosen to believe Leuci and, thus, "the defense of entrapment did not stand up."

Turning to the issue of intrusion into the privacy of Rosner's legal conferences, the court criticized the government for allowing DeStefano and Lamattina to continue attending such meetings after they had agreed to cooperate, but it found no specific prejudice to the defendant from the intrusions and debriefings.

As to the sentencing, however, the court concluded that Judge Bauman erred in relying on the Morvillo presentence report, without affording the defense an adequate opportunity to respond. It vacated the five-year sentence and ordered a resentencing before a different judge who had not already "made up his mind."

It was a partial victory. We were confident that the sentence would be reduced. But Rosner wanted vindication. As we prepared a petition requesting review by the United States Supreme Court, the search for the real Bob Leuci continued through the streets and back alleys of New York.

King Versus Prince

Eddie Rosner hired a private investigator—a former New York City police detective named Frank King, who was knowledgeable about the narcotics trade on the New York City streets. One day, as I was preparing Rosner's Supreme Court petition in my Cambridge office, Rosner called and told me to come quickly to New York: "I think we hit pay dirt." When I arrived at Nancy Rosner's office on Broadway, Edmund, Nancy, and Frank King were there—all smiles. King opened the meeting: "Hey Professor, you ever go to the movies?"

"Sure," I said, a bit bewildered.

"Ever see a picture called *The French Connection*—about a narcotics cop named Popeye Doyle and how he broke up a Marseilles-based heroin operation and seized millions of dollars worth of pure heroin?"

"Sure, I saw it. Gene Hackman played Popeye, didn't he?"

"What do you think ever happened to the heroin they seized in that case?" King continued.

"I don't know," I said, "I suppose it's been destroyed or it's in storage somewhere."

King turned to me challengingly: "What would you say if I told you it's been 'recycled'—that it's all back on the street?"

"They certainly didn't show that in the movie," I said.

"Well, it's true, Professor," King assured me. "The whole French Connection haul has been stolen from the Police Property Clerk's office near Little Italy—$70 million worth of 'Horse.' The largest single theft in the history of the world. And it's been resold on the street."

"Who could have gotten to it?" I asked naïvely.

"Cops, that's who," King replied. "And guess which cop was behind the whole thing?" King asked. Not waiting for me to answer, King screamed at the top of his lungs, "Bob Leuci, that's who!"

"Can you prove it?" I asked.

"Not yet," King whispered, "but we're almost there. We're getting close to an old informer of Leuci's who may have sold the drugs for him on the street. If we can get to him we may be home free." King mentioned the informer's name. It meant nothing to me or to the Rosners. The name was Richard Lawrence, The Baron.

I encouraged King to continue his search. If we could prove that Leuci had been involved in so recent and so serious a crime, we would have a good shot at getting a new trial. As we filed our petition for a writ of certiorari in the Supreme Court—an application for review by the High Court—King looked for The Baron, who had mysteriously disappeared from his usual haunts in the city. No one on the street had seen him for months. Finally, Eddie retained a new investigator—another former Police Detective named John McNally, who was reported to be a crackerjack at locating missing persons. Within weeks, McNally had interviewed forty people, and after following several blind leads, managed to find The Baron in the small town of Spencer, New York. We discovered Lawrence almost a year to the day after Morvillo had suppressed his existence and evidence at the new trial hearing before Judge Bauman.

Debriefing The Baron

The Baron was the Rosetta stone capable of unraveling the mysteries of Leuci's complex past. He knew everything about Leuci. He had been his alter ego—his street presence—for five years. Jeanne Baker, who was assisting me on the case, was dispatched to New York to debrief him. She met him in Nancy Rosner's office. The Baron was everything we had been led to believe: a tall, heavy black man with a scar running across his face; he sported an enormous white fedora, a full-length fur coat, and fluorescent-colored shoes, socks, shirt, and tie. His manner was ebullient; his presence was dominating; he exuded the kind of charm and self-confidence necessary for survival on the streets of uptown New York. He drove a bright green Eldorado convertible with a telephone in the back seat.

Baker spent dozens of hours with The Baron learning about his past and present activities, and especially about his relationship with Leuci. He regaled her with tales of duplicity, violence, and corruption. In the middle of the warring factions—cops, Mafiosi, pushers, informers, and addicts, each battling for their share of the valuable powder—stood The Baron, with his eyes and ears, not to mention his palms, wide open.

When Baker asked Lawrence whether Leuci would admit to knowing him, Lawrence pulled from his pocket several crumpled legal transcripts: "Read these and you'll see whether Babyface can forget about me." The transcripts showed that Leuci had recently testified under oath about his close relationship with Lawrence and his absolute trust in him. Leuci had described Lawrence as "tight," "close," and "quite a friend," whom he would "absolutely . . . trust with his life." He had told the jury that "in the period of . . . five years that I have known The Baron" he had taken forty pounds of heroin off the city streets "to save your children." It would be impossible for Leuci to deny that he had worked closely with The Baron. It would also be difficult for Leuci to label as a liar an informant whose word he had vouched for under oath. The pieces were beginning to fit into place.

Baker asked Lawrence to recount—with names, dates, and places—the occasions on which Leuci had sold him heroin for resale on the street. Lawrence said that over the years they worked together Leuci had supplied him with heroin "several times a month," and that he paid Leuci after he diluted it and sold it on the street. Lawrence also said that "on numerous other occasions" Leuci had sold him narcotics seized in police raids. Lawrence told Baker that he witnessed and participated in many transactions in which Leuci sold heroin to three other wholesalers known respectively as "Slim," "Cornbread," and "The Saint." The amounts of drugs sold by Leuci over the years, according to Lawrence, were staggering. If The Baron was telling the truth, then Leuci was among the biggest drug dealers in the city of New York.

While Baker was debriefing The Baron, Frank King—the former detective who had led us to The Baron—kept wandering in and out the office. He prodded Baker to keep her eye on the ball: "It's the French Connection theft that's gonna spring Eddie; make sure that you put that in your papers. Leuci did it, and we gotta be able to prove that." But The Baron was vague about Leuci's role in the French Connection theft. He believed Leuci was involved. That's what people on the street were saying. But he had no hard facts. King kept urging us to press on.

And then, on February 25, 1974, a front-page story in the *New York Times* disclosed that

> Investigators . . . are focusing on Frank King, a 39-year-old former narcotics detective, as the possible mastermind behind the theft of millions of dollars worth of heroin and cocaine [which] originally had been seized during the case upon which the film *The French Connection* was based.

I felt like a complete fool. Frank King had taken us in. We never saw him again. The government was never able to prove that King, or anyone else, had stolen the $70 million worth of drugs. But King was indicted for conspiracy, perjury, and contempt, based on his efforts to obstruct the grand jury investigation of the French Connection theft. After several years, the charges were dropped. King was convicted, however, of income tax evasion, on the basis of evidence that he had spent $110,000 the year after the French Connection theft, while reporting substantially lower earnings. To this day, the French Connection drug theft has not been solved. The Special Prosecutor's office still believes that King was the mastermind, but rumors persist that others were involved. Without definitive evidence from The Baron, however, we decided not to include this charge against Leuci in his affidavit.

Baron Versus Prince

On March 19, 1974, fifteen months after the jury had convicted Rosner, we filed our motion for a new trial. Appended to the motion was a fourteen-page affidavit by Richard Lawrence cataloging dozens of drug-related crimes by Leuci involving hundreds of thousands of dollars in illicit profits. We also submitted affidavits detailing our own investigations, which had corroborated many of the details of the transactions to which Lawrence had attested. We asked for a hearing in order to confront Leuci with his accuser.

On April 9, 1974, the government responded with its own set of affidavits, the thrust of which was to call Lawrence a liar. The government claimed that Lawrence's allegations had been thoroughly investigated by Morvillo and that "Lawrence was found to be a thoroughly discredited informant unworthy of credence." This was the first we heard about the Morvillo "investigation." The government strongly opposed a hearing; it did not want Leuci called to the witness stand and cross-examined under oath about The Baron's allegations.

By this time, Morvillo had left the prosecutor's office, and a new assistant United States Attorney had been assigned to the case: Joseph Jaffe, the surly junior prosecutor from the JDL case, had been appointed chief of the corruptions unit, and the Leuci investigation was turned over to him. Soon after we filed our new trial motion, Jaffe encountered Jeanne Baker in an elevator in the federal courthouse.

"Did you prepare The Baron's affidavit?" he asked her.

"I drafted it on the basis of what he told me," she replied. (Lawyers routinely draft affidavits of witnesses.)

"Have you ever heard of subornation of perjury?" he asked unpleasantly. "Lawrence is lying, and if you knew that, you may have a problem yourself," he said with a frown. "Before long *you* may find yourself in front of a grand jury," he said as he left the elevator.

After receiving affidavits from both sides, Judge Bauman agreed to convene a hearing on the afternoon of May 1, 1974. That morning, as I was preparing to leave my office for the trip to New York, I received a telephone call from Judge Bauman's law clerk. "The judge is indisposed," he said. "The hearing has been put off indefinitely." We wondered about this turn of events, but it seemed routine enough. Little did we realize the drama that was beginning to unfold within the closed corridors of the United States Attorney's office, a drama to which Judge Bauman had been made privy —once again without notice to the defense.

The Unmasking of Babyface

On April 17, two weeks before the hearing was scheduled to begin, Leuci began to drop hints that The Baron wasn't lying about everything. Leuci was terrified that the truth would come out, and that if it came out of someone else's mouth, the government would have little choice but to prosecute him. Leuci spoke to Joe Jaffe and another prosecutor named Rudolph Giuliani. He wanted to know what would happen to him if he was to admit—hypothetically, of course—that he had given drugs to informants. The prosecutors said that it was possible he could be indicted but that they would argue strongly against it. Leuci implied that Shaw and Scoppetta had led him to believe that if he cooperated they would never press him on his prior history. Giuliani shook his head and solemnly told Leuci that the moment he went undercover, it was inevitable that all his past dirt would eventually come out, since all the defendants he testified against would be motivated to dig it up. "Anybody who told you different was misleading you," Giuliani said with an apparent reference to Shaw and Scoppetta. Giuliani urged Leuci to tell the truth, even though it "would overturn the conviction of a miserable son of a bitch like Eddie Rosner."*

Finally, Leuci decided to confess. And what a confession it was! The Lawrence allegation, it turned out, was but the manhole cover of an enormous sewer. For several weeks Leuci recounted his life of crime. In the end, his catalog of corruption filled an eighty-four-page booklet. He had committed hundreds upon hundreds of crimes spanning his thirteen-year police career, and not just the three ending in 1967 about which he had testified at the Rosner trial. He was—by the sheer number of crimes he admitted to—one of the biggest crooks in the history of the New York City Police Department. Rosner's instincts had been on target from the beginning!

On April 23, 1974, a week before the scheduled hearing, the government sent another of its secret messages to Judge Bauman. They informed him that Leuci had admitted to numerous crimes that he had previously denied under oath. As a result of this letter, Judge Bauman postponed the scheduled hearing, claiming indisposition.

When, if ever, the government would have told us about Leuci's about-face is impossible to say, for on May 2, 1974, the *New York Times* broke the story that Leuci had confessed to the federal prosecutors that he had committed extensive crimes beyond those he had admitted to at the Rosner trial. The *Times* learned of Leuci's massive confessions as the result of a bizarre dispute between state and federal officials that eventually led to an

**Prince of the City*, pp. 298, 299.

unprecedented lawsuit brought by the state prosecutors against the federal prosecutors.

After Leuci began his marathon confessions on April 17, the federal prosecutors put him in protective custody and began to debrief him. Two days later the United States Attorney informed Maurice Nadjari, the Special State Prosecutor for corruption, of Leuci's about-face. Nadjari, wanting to be in on the action, demanded the right to interview Leuci, since Leuci had testified in several state cases, as well as in the Rosner case. The U.S. Attorney refused to permit Leuci to be interrogated by state officials until the feds had finished with him. This led Nadjari to charge that the U.S. Attorney's office was engaged in a "cover-up of information from Leuci to suppress his disclosures because of . . . the pending Rosner motion." The *Times* disclosed that "there are reports that [the U.S. Attorney] wishes to keep Detective Leuci from saying anything that could upset the [Rosner] conviction."

Nadjari filed a lawsuit to compel the United States Attorney's office to "share" Leuci with him. The filing of this lawsuit publicly disclosed the Leuci recantations for the first time. The U.S. Attorney was furious, arguing that Nadjari should have filed his lawsuit *in camera*—that is, secretly, so that the press (and presumably Rosner) would not have learned about it.

The Nadjari lawsuit—brought before Judge Bauman—became front-page news. It is not every day that the chief state corruptions prosecutor sues the chief federal prosecutor in open court about charges of extensive police corruption and perjury. After several hearings—at which I was a very interested spectator—the United States Attorney's office won and was allowed to continue its secret interrogation of Leuci without interference by the state prosecutors.

The federal debriefing lasted several weeks. Word began to leak out that Leuci was ratting on his closest friends and colleagues. On May 21, 1974, Detective William J. Cody—one of Leuci's partners on the narcotics squad—shot himself in the head with his service revolver. Just a few minutes earlier Leuci had called to tell him what he was reporting to the federal interrogators.

A week later I brought a lawsuit on Rosner's behalf against the United States Attorney's office demanding immediate access to Leuci and his new information.

Judge Bauman denied my request, but scheduled the hearing for July 1. "There will be no delays in that date, and I am going to tell you exactly why." He then announced that he had decided to retire from the bench on August 15 and enter private practice. And he wanted to decide this motion before then. The Rosner matter had been his first major case when he assumed the bench; it would also be his last case before he returned to private practice.

As we prepared for the hearing, we received word that the United States Supreme Court had denied our petition for certiorari but had expressly stated that its decision was not intended to preclude a hearing in the district court on the Leuci allegations.

A Cornucopia of Corruption

The time had come to put the government on trial for its misconduct in the Rosner case. Now, the defendants would be Shaw, Scoppetta, Morvillo, Sagor, and Leuci. As Rosner's lawyer, I would be the prosecutor. At stake was the continued freedom of Edmund Rosner, as well as the reputation of the United States Attorney's office for the Southern District of New York.

The courtroom was filled with newspaper and television reporters. Since no cameras were allowed in the courtroom, the first row was occupied by TV artists attempting to capture the drama in charcoal and crayon.

On the morning of July 1, 1974, a front-page story in the *New York Times* by Myron Farber foretold what the public would learn from the proceeding:

> [A] bizarre tale will unfold, with [c]harges of a 'coverup' by Government officials [and] a disputed lie-detector test given by a former official of the Central Intelligence Agency.
>
> Interest in the hearing goes well beyond Mr. Rosner's attempt to have his conviction overturned. . . .
>
> In effect, Mr. Rosner and his attorney, Prof. Alan Dershowitz of the Harvard Law School, are now trying to put the Government on trial for what they regard as gross misconduct in the Rosner case.

As always in a Bauman courtroom, the hearing convened at 10:00 A.M. sharp; at 10:02 we called our first witness, Detective Robert Leuci. He walked in from the witness room, surrounded by a small army of federal marshals. It was the first time the public had seen his face. Even the *Life* article had shaded his photograph to protect him from potential assassins. As Leuci took his seat in the witness box, the TV artists began to draw feverishly. The resulting picture was of a cherubic-looking young man in his middle thirties, with a kind and honest face that seemed lined from worry. Of average height and tending toward overweight, Leuci hardly looked the part of a tough street detective. He wore a tan sport jacket and a polyester shirt open at the neck; the prosecutors had evidently advised him to leave home his flashy clothes and glittering jewelry. He smiled nervously at me as I asked my first question.

"Mr. Leuci, will you tell us how long you have been a policeman?" The tone of his answer was sharp and aggressive, as if to signal that he did not intend to be pushed around: "I have been a policeman for approximately thirteen years." He remained belligerent as I took him—crime by crime—through his sordid history: the fifteen "seizures" of cash from suspected drug dealers; the nearly 1,000 instances of illegal distribution of seized heroin to addict-informers; the hundreds of times he had received heroin and cash payoffs from street pushers in return for allowing them to remain in business; the substantial amounts of heroin he gave to nonaddict dealers for resale to addicts; the selling of confidential information about ongoing police investigations—including wiretaps—to members of organized crime; the installations of illegal wiretaps for purposes of extorting money from the subjects of the taps; the acceptance of a bribe from a defense attorney to testify in a certain manner at a criminal trial (Leuci vigorously denied that he changed his testimony as a result of the bribe; he claimed that he was offered the money "so that I *wouldn't* perjure myself in order to put his [the attorney's] client away"); the payment of a bribe to an assistant District Attorney "not three feet from the bench" in order to receive lower bail for a defendant; the receipt of money from a restaurant owner for sending down some "strong-arm people" to protect him; the repeated fraudulent evasion of federal and state income taxes; and the countless examples of perjury and lying throughout his career, as recently as the previous week. (I could not question Leuci about the conspiracy to erase the tapes and commit perjury in the Bronx, since I did not know about it; the government continued to suppress this crime even during the hearing.)

As Leuci proceeded through this cornucopia of corruption, he became increasingly belligerent. Displaying no remorse, he repeatedly attempted to justify his crimes as helpful to people and as necessary to survive in the jungle he worked in.

Judge Bauman did not appear sympathetic, stating at one point: "Whatever Detective Leuci has undergone or is undergoing, he very richly deserves and has brought upon himself. So much for Detective Leuci."

Leuci had been brought to the dock and been found guilty. There could be no doubt that the detective had been among the most corrupt cops in the city's history; nor could there be any doubt that he had lied so often that his credibility was utterly demolished. The Prince of the City emerged from the hearing a toad.

But Leuci had not been the only culprit. Other law enforcement officials had been guilty of duplicity, lack of candor, and worse. The questionable conduct of these members of the respected United States Attorney's office for the Southern District of New York would also have to be exposed and condemned. In order to assure a new trial for Rosner, we would have to prove not only that Leuci had lied, but that the federal government was responsible for some of the detective's misconduct. This phase of our examination would be far more delicate. Now we were questioning the integrity of the very United States Attorney's office in which Judge Bauman himself had proudly served. One of the attorneys whose conduct we would question was Robert Morvillo, the man who, like Bauman, had once been chief of the Criminal Division. We knew we were in for a tough time.

Many defense attorneys shy away from cases in which they must attack the integrity of prosecuting attorneys. This is entirely understandable. The prosecuting attorney wields enormous power in the day-to-day life of a defense attorney and can exert considerable influence on the fate of his clients. Since plea bargaining is the dominant mode of resolving criminal cases, the defense lawyer must always look for a deal; and it is the prosecuting attorney who must agree to it. In some jurisdictions the prosecuting attorney also makes sentencing recommendations that often carry considerable weight with the judge.

On a more personal level the prosecutor can make the defense attorney's life pleasant or miserable in countless small, but important, ways: by agreeing to or by opposing continuances; by opening or closing files for discovery; by waiving or insisting on technical requirements; by recommending or denigrating the attorney to prospective clients; by being generally agreeable or disagreeable. And many prosecutors are not reluctant to exercise their power in order to exact favors from defense attorneys. I am not suggesting that there is anything improper in all this, although it is often unseemly and sometimes borders on the unethical. I am only suggesting how important it is to remain on the good side of the prosecutor's office.

Many prosecutors welcome a good fight—as long as it is over the guilt or innocence of the defendant. But when the fight concerns the integrity of the prosecutor himself, it is often difficult for the defense attorney and the "prosecutor-defendant" to remain on good personal or professional terms. It is not surprising that most defense attorneys will decline cases in which their clients want them to attack the prosecutor. At best they will simply deflect the attack from the prosecutor onto the "government" as an impersonal institution.

In this case it was essential to direct my attack against specific prosecutors, regardless of whether I made enemies. I had been told of Morvillo's notorious temper. I had once seen him outside a courtroom shouting at a defense attorney who had challenged his memory: "You son of a bitch. You're cut off. My office will never deal with you again." For a defense attorney who practiced in the Southern District of New York, these words could amount to a decree of bankruptcy: the criminal division of the U.S. Attorney's office—of which Morvillo was chief—would no longer negotiate pleas or make deals with this lawyer.*

Of course, no prosecutor would relish being subpoenaed to the witness stand and closely examined about what he knew about Leuci's other crimes, when he learned of them, and why he had not disclosed them. This was, after all, the final summer of Watergate. As our hearing was being conducted, a President of the United States was being pressured out of office for his role in a cover-up. In the process, the reputations of numerous lawyers—several of them present or former prosecutors—were being tarnished. Judge Bauman repeatedly drew analogies between the proceedings in Washington and those taking place in his courtroom.

I was prepared to take on the Southern District not because I am any more courageous than other lawyers. I simply had—or, at least, I thought I had—considerably less to lose. As a tenured professor and part-time lawyer from a different city, I did not depend as much as local practitioners do on the local prosecutors. I did not generally negotiate deals or enter into plea bargains. I litigated constitutional issues. I believed that my own relative insulation from possible reprisals gave me an added responsibility to take on the thankless task of calling prosecuting attorneys to bay for their misconduct. Moreover, as a teacher of legal ethics, I had been particularly appalled at the double standard practiced by many courts and ethics committees in evaluating the conduct of prosecuting attorneys and of defense attorneys. Rarely is a prosecutor disciplined, or even criticized, for overzealousness in prosecuting crime. But defense attorneys constantly place their licenses on the line—as I would soon learn—by defending their clients with too much zeal and vigor.

For these reasons, I have always been willing to challenge the conduct of prosecutors and judges. Indeed, that has since become an important part of my constitutional practice. But the Rosner case was the first in which I had directly confronted the integrity of the United States Attorney's office.

*During the Leuci hearing, even Judge Bauman virtually took "judicial notice" of Morvillo's temper.

MR. LEUCI: Bob Morvillo, far different than you, Mr. Dershowitz, didn't sit down and try to explain things to me in a quiet sort of way . . . he kind of jumped up and down, quite agitated.

THE COURT: . . . Anybody who is familiar with this building can almost take judicial notice of what Mr. Morvillo would have been like.

Prosecuting the Prosecutors: Robert Morvillo

Our first witness was Robert Morvillo. Short and pudgy, he has been described as resembling Buddy Hackett, but without a sense of humor. His voice was high-pitched and his tone was cynical. He had been the head of the criminal division and he wanted to be treated like a boss. He did not enjoy his role as witness.

Morvillo was being called on the carpet for his deliberate decision, in January of 1972, to suppress the fact that The Baron had accused Leuci of precisely the same kind of misconduct that the addict-witnesses had accused him of at the new trial motion hearing.

Morvillo was a cocky witness. He stated everything in categorical terms: the investigation of The Baron's allegations was "thorough"; "there was absolutely no support to the allegations of any kind"; they were "completely unfounded"; "they were just not reliable"; and in any event, The Baron "had failed, and miserably failed, the lie detector test."

Subsequent witnesses would demonstrate how unthorough the investigation had been. Virtually no leads were followed; eyewitnesses were not interviewed; arrest records were not checked; other investigative agencies with pertinent information were not contacted. Indeed, in one instance considered important by the government, the investigators looked for a store that The Baron told them was near Eastern *Parkway,* one of the major boulevards of Brooklyn. Instead, they went out looking for Eastern *Avenue* —a nonexistent thoroughfare. When they could not find the avenue they gave up.

The investigators tried to justify their sloppiness by pointing to The Baron's "failure" of the lie detector test. But here Morvillo's investigation reached its nadir. The nation's leading expert in polygraphy—an expert used by Arnold Bauman when he was in private practice—testified that the test administered by the Virginia agency was a sham, that the machine had not worked properly, that the questions were "very poorly formulated," that the results were "totally inconclusive," and that no expert could possibly conclude on the basis of the "very flat charts" that The Baron was lying. Finally, the president of the polygraph firm contradicted Morvillo's testimony that The Baron had "miserably failed" the lie detector test in all respects. He testified that the tests showed only that The Baron may have been "holding back" and not telling "the complete truth about everything." The examiner had never told Morvillo that The Baron "was lying about everything." Morvillo's testimony about the lie detector test seemed shattered.

Prosecuting the Prosecutors: Elliot Sagor

We were now coming to an even more difficult and delicate aspect of the hearing: the conduct of Assistant United States Attorney Elliot Sagor—the government's main lawyer in the current proceedings—during the most recent phase of the Rosner case. It was our contention that Sagor had continued the government's cover-up through to the most recent new trial hearing—and, indeed, even during the hearing itself. We believed that Sagor had even gone so far as to mislead the Solicitor General of the United States who, in turn, had unwittingly misled the Supreme Court of the United States on the crucial issue of what the government lawyers had known about Leuci's crimes and when they had learned of them.

Elliot Sagor was a likable fellow who tried hard to be tough. He modeled himself after Morvillo—ferocious temper and all—but it didn't quite ring true. He was a walking series of contradictions: though casual by nature, he affected the pompous and self-righteous manner so characteristic of young prosecutors, especially in the Southern District. Though essentially decent and honest, he conveyed to me an impression of conniving and turning sharp corners. He didn't lie, but you were never sure he was entirely on the level with you. As he approached the witness stand, he seemed to hiss with contempt for me.*

I began by asking him about the document that had come to be known as the "Goe memorandum." The Goe memorandum—which was to assume central significance in the next phase of the hearing—was a two-page account of Leuci's admission, made two years earlier, that he had participated in a warrantless drug search with three other officers in 1965 and had stolen $200 in cash from the premises. It was called the Goe memorandum because Leuci made his admission to a federal agent, Robert Goe. Edward Shaw, who was then in charge of the Leuci investigation, learned of the incident and Leuci's admission of it, soon afterwards. It had not been turned over to the defense at the time of the Rosner trial, however, and we had obtained it on the eve of this hearing.

The Goe memorandum was extremely important to our argument: it constituted indisputable documentary evidence that prior to the Rosner trial the government lawyer responsible for disclosing Leuci's crimes was aware that Leuci had, in fact, committed at least one crime in addition to

*My relationship with Sagor was perhaps best captured by some old movie dialogue that I recall:

FIRST LAWYER: "Don't you trust me?"
SECOND LAWYER: "Absolutely."
FIRST LAWYER: "Me neither."

the three he was prepared to admit. Moreover, the crime described in the Goe memorandum was of a different character from the other three. Leuci attempted to justify the three crimes he admitted to—the ones in which he had acted as an intermediary—as motivated by a desire to protect the defenseless targets of overreaching policemen. The crime reported in the Goe memorandum could not be similarly justified: it was an out and out burglary by a group of law enforcement officers entrusted with the power to investigate crime. Most jurors would identify more closely with the victim of a police burglary than with the "victims"—if there were any—of the intermediary crimes to which Leuci admitted. That only $200 was found did not alter the character of the crime. If more had been found, it too would have been taken. Moreover, a federal judge had just sentenced John D. Ehrlichman to a prison term for his complicity in the burglary of Daniel Ellsberg's psychiatrist's office—a burglary in which *nothing* had been taken.

But the significance of the Goe memorandum went beyond the specific crime it disclosed. It would have alerted Rosner's lawyers to an entirely different type of corruption by Leuci. They could then have investigated this *modus operandi*—the burglary of money from drug suspects. As it turned out, the crime admitted in the Goe memorandum was but the tip of a large iceberg. Leuci eventually admitted to more than a dozen similar burglaries with a combined take of up to a quarter of a million dollars. The suppressed Goe memorandum may have been an important key to uncovering the mysteries of Leuci's criminal career.

Nor could there be any doubt that the government had been obliged under the law to turn over the Goe memorandum to the defense prior to the commencement of the Rosner trial. Even Elliot Sagor grudgingly admitted on cross-examination that as soon as he discovered it he "realized right away that the Goe memorandum . . . should have been turned over to defense counsel at the time of trial." But Edward Shaw—the lawyer in charge of disclosing to the defense all information about Leuci's past crimes—had not turned it over.

Sagor admitted that he first came into possession of the Goe memorandum on or about April 8, 1974. This date was significant because on the following day, Sagor submitted an affidavit to Judge Bauman in which he swore that the allegations made by Rosner in his new trial motion were "totally devoid of merit."

I pressed Sagor on why he had failed to include any reference to the Goe memorandum in his affidavit. At first, he attempted to obfuscate the chronology by using faulty grammar: "The first time I saw the Goe memorandum was an hour or so *by the time* the five o'clock deadline that the government's papers were due in Judge Bauman's chambers on April 9." I pressed for a clarification and he finally admitted that he had read the Goe memorandum *before* he had signed the affidavit. His excuse for not mentioning it was that his investigation was "incomplete as to the validity of the Goe memorandum on that date."

Leuci's testimony undercut Sagor's account. According to Leuci, Sagor had an extensive conversation with him about the Goe memorandum "during the time he was preparing" his affidavit. Moreover, Leuci distinctly recalled that the conversation occurred late at night, and so it must have occurred at least one day before the five o'clock filing deadline on April 9. Leuci testified that Sagor asked him whether the allegation contained in the memorandum was true; Leuci admitted that it was. This was not just a casual conversation about an insignificant incident. Leuci testified that when Sagor discovered the Goe memorandum, he immediately summoned Leuci and yelled at him: " 'What fucking idiot knew about this and where has it been?' [H]e was up to the third story by that time."

We were thus able to prove that Sagor had made a calculated decision not to disclose the existence of the Goe memorandum either to the defense or to Judge Bauman at the time he filed his affidavit on April 9, 1974. But, in our view, he had done something far more serious than that: he had also made a decision to withhold this crucial document from the United States Supreme Court, which was then considering our petition for certiorari.

We established that Sagor had discussed his dilemma concerning the Goe memorandum with various legal experts within the United States Attorney's office—including John Gordon, the lawyer responsible for liaison with the Solicitor General's office, which handles all government business with the Supreme Court. Upon reading the Goe memorandum Gordon told Sagor that "it was very unfortunate that we had not turned this thing over."

On April 19, 1974—eleven days after Sagor received the Goe memorandum and the day after Leuci started to admit his perjury—the Solicitor General filed his response to Rosner's petition in the Supreme Court. The Solicitor General's office—which had not been told of the Goe memorandum—stated that "the United States Attorney denies . . . that there was knowledge on the part of . . . the prosecutors in connection with false testimony by Leuci." The Solicitor General also acknowledged that if there had been such "knowledge" or "wrongdoing" by any prosecutors, this would have been "critical." The Goe memorandum established, however, that there had been such knowledge on the part of prosecutor Shaw. Thus, the government of the United States submitted a false statement to the United States Supreme Court. It did so because its right hand in Washington had deliberately been kept ignorant of what its left hand in New York was doing.

At this point the story gets worse!

As Leuci continued to pour out the story of his crimes, John Gordon finally decided that the Solicitor General's office had to be told something in order to avoid a potential embarrassment. But what the Solicitor General's office was told was, in my view, at best a half-truth and at worst an out-and-out lie. Gordon told the Solicitor General's office that Leuci had begun to confess to more crimes than he had admitted at the former trial. But he then proceeded to claim that "the crimes that we discovered that Leuci had lied about *had not been known to us* at the time of Leuci's false testimony." This was simply not the whole truth. At least two of the crimes —the burglary admitted to in the Goe memorandum and the conspiracy to erase the tape and commit perjury in the Bronx—*were* known to Shaw. And Gordon was "quite convinced" that he had learned about the Goe memorandum *before* he called the Solicitor General's office. (We were not able to ask Gordon or Sagor whether they knew about the tape erasure, since we did not learn about that suppressed crime until after the hearing was over.) Yet Gordon did not tell the Solicitor General's office about the Goe memorandum or about Shaw's knowledge of the crime admitted in it. Indeed he communicated exactly the opposite message: that no one in the United States Attorney's office was aware of any crimes other than the ones that Leuci admitted to at the Rosner trial.

Now the story gets even worse—much worse!

The Solicitor General decided that in light of Leuci's newly admitted perjury, he was obliged to file an additional document in the Supreme Court, to ensure that the Supreme Court did not act on the basis of misinformation or incomplete information. Accordingly, he drafted a document alerting the Supreme Court that Leuci had lied about his past at the Rosner trial. The Solicitor General sent a telex of the draft to the United States Attorney's office in New York, so that Sagor and Gordon could review it for accuracy. In that draft the Solicitor General argued that a new trial should be granted to Rosner

> . . . only after hearing such new evidence as is available, including evidence bearing on [Rosner's] allegation which the U.S. Attorney denies and which is potentially critical to disposition of the new trial motion.

Sagor—in his own handwriting—*changed that statement* to read as follows (his additions are italicized):

> . . . only after hearing such new evidence as is available, including evidence bearing on [Rosner's] allegation *that the government "knew about Leuci's additional criminal conduct"* which the U.S. Attorney denies and which is potentially critical to the disposition of the new trial motion.

Sagor had thus "corrected" the Solicitor General's draft brief so that it told the United States Supreme Court that the United States Attorney *denies* that the *government knew about* Leuci's additional criminal conduct. At the time he made this handwritten "correction," Sagor had read the Goe memorandum, had discussed it with several legal experts, and had become fully aware of its significance. Yet he "corrected" the Solicitor General's brief so as to deny what the Goe memorandum proved.

The Solicitor General—totally in the dark about these crucial documents and facts—thus filed an entirely misleading brief in the United States Supreme Court.

When I learned about Sagor's machinations—two weeks *after* the Supreme Court had denied review—I was furious. He had not only misled the highest Court in the land about a critical fact, but he had denied us the ammunition with which to correct the misinformation. I was hell-bent to expose this cover-up—this corruption in high places—at the hearing before Judge Bauman.

"We Can Read in New York, Too . . ."

But when I tried to establish Sagor's misconduct, the government—represented by Joe Jaffe—threw up a barrage of objections designed to protect Sagor from having to testify about his actions. Judge Bauman, growing visibly irritated at my attack on government lawyers, sustained Jaffe's objections. With mounting frustration I requested permission to make "an offer of proof"—a preview of what I expected to prove if permitted to continue my examination. I stated my offer:

> We will argue that there . . . was a deliberate intentional attempt by the United States Attorney's office to keep information from the United States Supreme Court pending a petition for a writ of certiorari. . . . This Goe memorandum was not brought to the attention of the Supreme Court . . .

In light of the facts available to me, this offer of proof seemed reasonable enough. I did not anticipate Judge Bauman's reaction. He rose from his chair, glared down at me, shaking his finger in a threatening gesture: "I think that charge is of the utmost seriousness," he said, "and you had better be able to prove it." The threat was unmistakable. Again, as in the JDL case, Judge Bauman was resorting to a favorite gambit—threatening the defense attorney in order to deflect a serious attack on the government. He was attempting to put me on trial for my attempt to put the government on trial. He was turning the tables on me, as I had tried to turn the tables on the government.

The rest of the morning was hell for me. Each time I tried to develop a line of cross-examination Bauman would cut me off: "I am still waiting for testimony to the effect that the United States Attorney deliberately withheld information from the highest Court. I would like you to get to that immediately. . . . That may be tomorrow morning's headlines, but I want proof of it today." With that challenge he ended the morning session and "directed" me to prove "that particular accusation at two o'clock." He marched off his bench and slammed his robing-room door.

I later learned, through the courtroom grapevine, what happened in that robing room. Judge Bauman directed one of his law clerks, a recent law school graduate, to prepare formal charges against me for my "unwarranted accusations" against the United States Attorney's office. Bauman said that when he returned from lunch, he would review the charges and send them to the Bar Association Disciplinary Committee. With that, he left a bewildered clerk to write them up. When Bauman returned, the law clerk told the judge that he would not participate in the drafting of charges against me, since he did not believe I had done anything wrong. If Judge Bauman wanted to submit charges, he would have to draft them himself. Bauman, in a fury, said that he would.

As we entered the courtroom, Judge Bauman directed me to address myself "to the accusation you made." He ceremoniously raised a pencil, saying, "I want to be sure exactly of what you said. You said that the United States Attorney deliberately suppressed evidence in the Supreme Court of the United States." As he uttered these words, he wrote each of them down, in plain view of everyone in the courtroom. It was clear that he was setting me up for a fall. I proceeded with my examination of Sagor. But instead of answering my questions, Sagor followed Judge Bauman's lead in deflecting the proceedings against me. When I asked him whether he had checked a critical date he was supposed to look up during the luncheon recess, the judge permitted him to give the following answer: "Frankly, Mr. Dershowitz, I felt that your allegations were so outrageous, I preferred to eat lunch as to look into when the date was." At another point, he answered my question by saying that he could only base his statements "on what you have mentioned in open court, Mr. Dershowitz, and I wouldn't want to comment on what I think the accuracy of that is." When I began to read from the document that Sagor had changed, he cut me off with the statement, "We can read in New York, too."

The hearing was getting out of hand, and Judge Bauman made no attempt to maintain control. At one point, Sagor seemed to forget that he was the witness and not the judge, as he began barking orders at me: "Mr. Dershowitz, I'm familiar with the record. Get to a question. Don't sit here. . . ." Only when Sagor tried to reverse our roles completely by asking me questions did Judge Bauman finally turn to the witness and say, "Wait a minute, you are supposed to be answering the questions."

I asked Sagor whether he recalled my saying to him that the Goe memorandum "is the first hard evidence that we have of government knowledge." His answer was "Do you recall me laughing?" This led Judge Bauman into a tirade—not against Sagor, but against me:

THE COURT: There is nothing funny about that and I want that thoroughly understood. At the end of this, I want Professor Dershowitz to tell me how he has proved this dreadfully—

MR. DERSHOWITZ: I am prepared—

THE COURT: Please, don't interrupt me. Should he fail, I will then consider what disciplinary steps to take. . . . I, for one, will see to it that it does not go unchallenged in the appropriate place.

Ultimately I was able to prove, through Sagor's own testimony, that he was to blame for the decision not to bring the Goe memorandum to the attention of the Solicitor General or the Supreme Court; that it was he who had changed the Solicitor General's draft brief to include a denial that the government "knew about Leuci's additional criminal conduct," *after* he had learned that the government did know about the contents of the Goe memorandum. I had thus managed to prove exactly what I had offered to prove: that the suppression of the Goe memorandum "was a deliberate intentional attempt by the United States Attorney's office to keep information from the United States Supreme Court." Having proved this, I felt confident that Judge Bauman's threat of disciplinary action would be withdrawn.

I was wrong. No sooner had I demonstrated that Sagor had deliberately failed to bring the Goe memorandum to the attention of the Solicitor General and the Supreme Court than Judge Bauman began to feign ignorance that my claim of suppression referred to the Goe memorandum. "I decline to think that any person of intelligence would level a charge of deliberate suppression in the Supreme Court of the United States *based on the Goe matter. . . .* I surely assumed, and I take it you meant for me to assume, that it was infinitely more serious than some $50 payoff." But that was exactly what I had charged. My offer of proof had referred expressly and exclusively to the Goe matter: "This Goe memorandum was not brought to the attention of the Supreme Court." I could not have made myself clearer.

Judge Bauman was now changing the rules after I had succeeded in proving exactly what I had offered to prove. Now he wanted an "infinitely more serious" charge to be proved. He ruled that the crime admitted in the Goe memorandum was "trivial" and that "no more questions [would be permitted] about the Goe situation either directly or indirectly."

The television accounts that night were ominous. One local newsman ended his report on the day's proceeding by commenting that "If Dershowitz proves his charges, then his client may avoid jail; but if he fails to prove his charges, then he may join his client in jail."

I returned to Cambridge to plan my counterattack. I consulted with Harvey Silverglate and Jeanne Baker. Our first thought was that I should take the initiative and bring disciplinary charges against Judge Bauman for his repeated threats against me. We researched the disciplinary rules and found no basis for a judge threatening discipline against an attorney who tried to make a good faith offer to prove government misconduct, even if the attorney ultimately failed to prove the misconduct to the judge's satisfaction. Both Harvey and Jeanne assured me that I had proved exactly what I had offered to prove. We agreed that it was Judge Bauman's conduct, and not mine, that should be the basis for disciplinary charges; it was he who had made baseless accusations; it was he who had allowed Sagor to rant and rave against me on the witness stand; it was he who had stated that the burglary of $200 by police officials was "trivial" and not worthy of serious consideration by a court.

I telephoned Dean Monroe Freedman of the Hofstra Law School, the country's leading authority on legal ethics in criminal cases. When I told Dean Freedman what Judge Bauman had done, he expressed outrage: "These former prosecutors are always getting on defense lawyers who try to raise government misconduct. I don't see where you did anything even arguably wrong." I asked him what he thought of our idea of bringing charges against Bauman. He paused, then replied: "It would be a great idea to do that someday against some judge. But this is the wrong situation. Bauman has just announced his retirement. No disciplinary body will want to chastise a judge who has just left the bench. I think they would find some way to justify his actions." I asked him what he thought I should do, and he advised me that the best thing was just to try to get Bauman to change his mind and back down. I asked Freedman whether he would be willing to be my lawyer in the disciplinary matter and he said he would.

My Own "Trial"

When I next appeared in court, Dean Freedman was at my side. My own trial was about to begin. Dean Freedman asked Judge Bauman to specify which canon, Bar Association rule, or legal norm I had violated. Judge Bauman refused to answer. It was his intention to refer the matter to the Bar Association Grievance Committee and leave it to them "to determine whether the conduct of counsel has violated any of those canons." Freedman informed the court that he had researched all the applicable rules and said it was his professional opinion that not only was I *permitted* to allege deliberate government suppression on the basis of the information I possessed but indeed I was *required* to make the allegation if instructed to do so by my client. Freedman argued that neither United States Attorneys nor judges are above criticism. Referring to the recent jury acquittal of former Attorney General John Mitchell, Freedman made a telling point:

> In this very courthouse there was recently a charge of deliberate obstruction of justice against a former prosecutor, the Attorney General of the United States. The lawyers who levied that charge failed to prove it. I am not aware of any suggestion that they be disciplined for that.

Judge Bauman did not seem convinced by Dean Freedman. He invited him to submit a brief. The matter was continuing to escalate, but I thought I saw a chance to resolve it. Judge Bauman's pride was on the line and I felt that he might back down if he could save face. I asked for permission to tell the court what "my own state of mind was" when I had used the word "deliberate" in my offer of proof. The judge agreed to listen. I explained that when I had used the term deliberate, I was referring to the applicable legal standard:

> failure to disclose evidence with high value to the defense [that] could not have escaped the prosecutor's attention.

I did not intend to characterize Sagor's conduct as necessarily "evil," though it was "my own view . . . that the government had made not an accidental but a deliberate decision."

Although I had not really said anything different, I had put it in a more accommodating tone. That was enough for Judge Bauman, who said that "since the record is now clear as to what you meant to impute to the United States Attorney, and the sense in which you used the word 'deliberate,' I don't think I will pursue the matter any further." But before closing the matter, Judge Bauman could not resist paying deference to his former office:

> [I]t is not because I was a member of the United States Attorney's staff itself but because the United States Attorneys in this district over the years—and this one in particular I might say—continuously have set high standards of professional integrity. . . . The office has a very long tradition of integrity, and I really must tell you I have not seen one iota of evidence in this situation of any improper conduct.

The hearing soon came to a close. Judge Bauman went back to his chambers to write his final judicial decision. It would be a humdinger—his magnum opus.

To Prosecute or Not to Prosecute Leuci

While the Rosner hearing was being conducted in open court, another secret hearing was taking place behind the closed doors of the United States Attorney's office. Its purpose was to decide whether Robert Leuci should be indicted for his massive perjury—and for the numerous crimes he had recently admitted to. There were, reportedly, three views. The first was presented by agents from the Drug Enforcement Administration who despised Leuci and wanted him indicted as a lesson to drug-dealing cops. The second came from several junior attorneys within the United States Attorney's office who wanted him indicted as a lesson to perjurious policemen. They also thought an indictment against Leuci would strengthen their position in the Rosner case. The third was pressed by Leuci's allies, who were called the "I Love Leuci Fan Club." This group was headed by Shaw, Scoppetta, and Giuliani, who argued against indicting "their man" for fear that it would discourage informers from cooperating with the government.

The newly appointed United States Attorney, Paul Curran, decided not to prosecute Leuci. Shaw's emotional appeal was apparently decisive. He had told Curran that Robert Leuci—perhaps the biggest police crook in New York City's history—"is one of my heroes." As a result, the prince of police corruption was allowed to retain his position as a member of the New York City Police Department. Indeed, he was appointed to a newly formed division called the "integrity unit," which is supposed to be staffed by "integrity-minded officers." He was never prosecuted, disciplined, or even sued by any agency of government for his scores of crimes and his hundreds of thousands of dollars of illicit and untaxed gains.

Bauman's Final Opinion

Edmund Rosner was not as lucky. On August 15, 1974, Judge Bauman rendered a thirty-page opinion.

He found that the $200 described in the Goe memorandum had "no real significance." He also found that the tape of the Leuci-Lawrence drug conversation was "ambiguous," even though "there is no question . . . but that during the course of it Leuci demonstrated a familiarity with procedures whereby Lawrence would obtain 'packages' of heroin from arrests." He concluded, therefore, that the failure of Shaw and Scoppetta to turn this material over to the defense was inadvertent.

The critical finding on which the entire opinion rested, however, was that the jury's verdict against Edmund Rosner had not depended on Leuci's credibility as a witness, but rather on the tapes of those conversations that Leuci managed to record:

> I . . . find that no matter how much Leuci's credibility could have been undermined, whether by a single additional incident or the full range of his crimes, the jury's verdict could not possibly have been affected. . . . I do not believe that a diminution in Leuci's credibility would have been fatal to the government's case. [There] is not the slightest likelihood that the jury, having been appraised of the Goe incident and the transactions with Lawrence, would have reached a different verdict.

Judge Bauman denied our motion for a new trial in its entirety, going out of his way to characterize our argument about the Goe memorandum as "staggeringly disingenuous." His parting shot was loud and clear.

Judge Bauman's opinion seemed again to have changed the rules midstream. His denial of our new trial motion was not based on anything that had transpired at the hearing. Indeed, he had found that we succeeded in proving just about everything that we had alleged in our request for a hearing: Leuci's massive perjury; Shaw's pretrial knowledge of the Goe incident; and Scoppetta's pretrial knowledge of the taped Leuci-Lawrence drug conversation. The findings that he made against us—and that doomed our new trial motion—were all based on information that was available to Judge Bauman *before* the hearing. His decision rested on an assessment of the original trial and the insignificance of Leuci's credibility to the jury's verdict of guilty against Rosner. Since Judge Bauman could have reached the identical conclusion *without ever holding a hearing,* we wondered why he had wasted hundreds of thousands of dollars in legal resources to go through the motions of calling irrelevant witnesses and reading unnecessary documents. Ironically, prior to the hearing, the government had vigorously opposed holding one at all, precisely on the ground that Judge Bauman could decide the case on the basis of the original trial record without hearing new witnesses. Judge Bauman had ridiculed the government's argument.

Rosner, with his long experience as a jury lawyer, was furious at Judge Bauman's certainty that the jury would have convicted him even if they had known everything about Leuci's past. "That's not the way jurors think," he kept saying. "If they heard that this cop was getting a free ride after ten years of rip-offs, they would have been outraged at the government and they never would have voted to convict me for what I did."

What the Jurors Really Would Have Done

While I was planning the next step—our appeal to the circuit court of appeals—I kept thinking about how we might undercut Judge Bauman's conclusion about the jury.

Suddenly an obvious way occurred to me. Why not ask the jurors themselves? They certainly were in a better position to know what they would have done than was Judge Bauman.

The Rosner jury had, of course, disbanded and returned to the anonymity of their private lives. It would be difficult to locate them. There are also legal constraints on making contact with former jurors, since the law seeks to protect them from harassment and threats. The American Bar Association has recommended that before a defense lawyer begins to interview a former juror, he should notify the government of his intention so that the government might seek appropriate relief from the courts.

We notified the government, and it sought an injunction from Judge Bauman preventing us from contacting the former jurors. Judge Bauman declined to rule, however, on the government's request.

After considerable leg work, we located two former jurors and arranged to interview them. My first stop was an apartment building in the Bronx, where I was greeted by an effusive Sylvia Cohen, who immediately offered us cake and tea.

"That Rosner case was so interesting," she said. "That poor boy had everything; it was such a shame that he got into trouble the way he did."

Her husband interjected: "It was a long trial. That's all Sylvia talked about for weeks."

I asked Mrs. Cohen whether she remembered the evidence against Rosner.

"Sure," she responded. "It was that sweet-looking policeman name Leuci."

"What about the tapes," I asked.

"Oh, the tapes," she said, "I remember them. You could barely hear them. They were full of static and music. We tried to listen very carefully, but we couldn't hear much. You could barely hear Mr. Rosner on them at all. It was mostly Leuci and those two other Italian fellows."

I asked Mrs. Cohen to tell me what went on during the jury deliberations.

"We argued a lot about whether Mr. Rosner had been trapped into committing his crimes by the officer. Rosner said one thing, and Leuci said another. One of them had to be lying. In the end I believed the officer's version. He seemed more honest. He even admitted that he had done some bad things when he was a young policeman."

I took out Judge Bauman's opinion and asked her to read the pages on which the judge summarized Leuci's newly admitted crimes. She read them slowly, her lips moving with each word. I could see her becoming visibly embarrassed as she read on.

Finally, she turned to me and asked, "Is this true? Did Officer Leuci do all of those things?"

I told her that he admitted to each of those crimes, including the perjury at the Rosner trial.

"That's terrible. He sure fooled us," she whispered with obvious embarrassment. "He seemed so nice, it's hard to believe."

I asked her whether her vote would have been the same or different if she had known the truth about Leuci.

"Oh, I never would have voted for conviction if I knew about the officer's crimes, especially if I knew he had lied to us about them. We believed he was telling the truth. I think that if I knew all that about Officer Leuci, I wouldn't believe him. I would believe Mr. Rosner instead."

The other juror was Seymour Mizner. I showed him the pages from Judge Bauman's opinion cataloging Leuci's newly admitted crimes. As he read them, he kept saying "Wow!" "My God!" "I can't believe it!" "This guy's a bigger crook than Rosner." Mizner then turned to me quietly and asked, "Have they put him in jail?"

I began to tell him that Rosner was still on bail, but he interrupted, "No, no, not Rosner. What about Leuci?"

I explained that Leuci was still a cop and that he had not been indicted.

"Well, I don't need a map to see the roadway," Mizner snapped. "When a crook gets a free ride for testifying, I wouldn't believe a word he said."

I reminded Mizner that Leuci had admitted at the trial that he had committed three crimes and that he did not expect to be prosecuted for them.

"Yeah, but those were old crimes that he couldn't be prosecuted for. We didn't think he was testifying in exchange for a free ride. Now it's clear he was."

I told Mizner that the government claimed it was not aware of the newly admitted crimes at the time of the Rosner trial, so there could not have been a deal for testimony in exchange for immunity from prosecution for crimes the government was not aware of.

"But Leuci knew he had committed all those crimes. He's a smart cop. He knew he might get caught some day, and then he'd be able to point to all the cases he made for the government. And I guess it worked. He's getting a free ride."

I showed Mizner the portions of Judge Bauman's opinion that concluded that the jury would certainly still have voted for conviction even if they had known about Leuci's crimes.

"How does he know?" Mizner asked. "Was he in the jury room with us? How does he know how we would have voted?"

I pressed Mizner: "Do you know for sure how *you* would have voted if you had known about all of Leuci's crimes?"

He thought for a moment and then he answered: "If I had known the truth about Leuci's criminal past and known that he had committed numerous crimes and had lied, I would not have believed in Leuci's testimony and I would not have voted for conviction." He paused another moment: "The nerve of that judge. Telling me how I would have voted."

I favored telling the court of appeals the results of our interviews with the two former jurors. I knew that our biggest legal hurdle in the appeal would be Bauman's "finding of fact" that "the jury's verdict could not possibly have been affected" by knowledge of Leuci's perjury and criminality. Courts of appeals rarely disturb "findings of fact" by lower courts. Although it is hard to characterize an unfounded speculation about what the jurors would have done as a "finding of fact," Judge Bauman had gone out of his way to make it appear as though he had based the conclusion on his observation of the trial. He had prefaced it with the statement that "as the judge who presided over the trial and carefully observed its course and conduct, I do not believe. . . ." This kind of statement is designed to make it more difficult for the judges in the court of appeals—who have not "presided over the trial"—to second-guess the trial judge. I believed that the affidavits of the jurors might provide something of an antidote to Judge Bauman's finding.

Nancy Rosner disagreed with me. She thought that the juror interviews sounded "hokey" and unprofessional, and that they would undercut the strength of our legal position. She also stressed the fact—of which I was painfully aware—that the government's tactic throughout this litigation had been to deflect the attack away from itself and onto Rosner and his lawyers; the jurors' affidavits—Nancy argued—would simply provide more ammunition to the government for this tactic in the court of appeals. I understood these risks, but I was not convinced. We argued, and Nancy's view prevailed—at least for the moment.

Rosner's Resentencing

As we began preparing the appeal, we were summoned before another judge: the Honorable Inzer Wyatt, who had been assigned to resentence Rosner after the court of appeals—on the first appeal—had vacated Judge Bauman's five-year sentence because of the Morvillo memorandum.

We submitted an extensive presentence memorandum of our own, citing federal sentencing statistics that demonstrated that when federal officials—such as judges and prosecutors—had been convicted of bribery, their sentences rarely exceeded two years.

I urged Judge Wyatt not to sentence Rosner to a prison term in excess of those given to corrupt judges and prosecutors. He nodded his head in apparent agreement when I made this argument, but when the time came for him to pronounce sentence he said that he had

> taken into account, as a factor, Judge Bauman's sentence [but that] taking all the other factors to which Mr. Dershowitz has directed to my attention in the memorandum and this afternoon, I do disagree with Judge Bauman as to the length of imprisonment which should be required.

He then sentenced Rosner to three years imprisonment. It was my impression that Judge Wyatt added an extra year in deference to his retiring colleague, Judge Bauman. We did not think that Judge Wyatt should have "taken into account" the concededly illegal sentence of Judge Bauman. Rosner was pleased, however, that the original sentence had been reduced, since three-year sentences could be served at Allenwood Penitentiary, a white-collar minimum-security facility, whereas five-year sentences are generally served at Lewisburg, a tougher facility for more dangerous criminals.

Judge Wyatt granted a stay of Rosner's sentence pending the outcome of our appeals.

The Second Appeal

The panel this time consisted of Judges Henry Friendly, a well-regarded jurist, William H. Timbers, a conservative judge from Connecticut, and Murray Gurfein, the district judge who had written the opinion in the first Rosner appeal and who had recently been promoted to the court of appeals. We were pleased that Judge Gurfein was on the panel, since we planned to rely heavily on portions of his opinion in the first appeal.

I argued for Rosner. Sagor argued for the government. I reminded the court—especially Judge Gurfein—that in its opinion on the original appeal the court had described the case as a "credibility" contest between Leuci and Rosner and had recognized that the early unrecorded meetings were "crucial to the jury's determination" of the entrapment issue. For the court now to accept Judge Bauman's "finding" that the jury's verdict rested exclusively on the tapes and not at all on its assessment of Leuci's credibility, would require a complete about-face from its earlier opinion.

Several weeks after the argument we received word that the judges wanted to hear all the tapes of the Leuci-Rosner conversations. Sagor and I went to the court of appeals conference room, which was equipped with five sets of headphones. The three judges and the two lawyers began to listen to Leuci conversing with DeStefano and Lamattina. Then we heard Rosner. His conversation was vague and elliptical, but he seemed to be agreeing to pay for information about his case. The rest was uncertain. The judges were straining to hear. On several occasions one of them would ask to have a conversation replayed. They kept shaking their heads in confusion as if to say, "What are they saying? Who is that speaking?" We left the conference room convinced that no reasonable person could decide, on the basis of the tapes alone, whether or not Rosner had been entrapped.

More weeks went by without further word. And then on April 29, 1975, five months after the argument, the court of appeals rendered its unanimous decision. Rosner lost again. This opinion, like the first, was written by Judge Gurfein; but it was difficult to tell that the two opinions had been written, or even read, by the same judge. Whereas the first opinion repeatedly emphasized the jury's reliance on Leuci's in-court testimony and credibility, the second opinion agreed with Judge Bauman's conclusion that "Leuci was not the linchpin of the government's case; the tapes were." The court thus concluded that if the Goe memorandum and the Leuci-Lawrence tape had been turned over to the defense—as they should have been—they would not have so altered a juror's perception of Leuci's credibility as "to induce reasonable doubt of Rosner's guilt on the basis that he had been entrapped." In addition to being speculative, Gurfein's focus on the Goe memorandum and the Lawrence tape avoided the crucial question: what would the jurors have done if they had known about *all* of Leuci's crimes, including his repeated perjury. Inexplicably, Judge Gurfein never addressed this central question.

Instead, he shifted his focus to the post-trial suppressions by Morvillo and Sagor. Here he agreed with our analysis. He concluded that Morvillo had "erred seriously"—strong words for a court—"in failing to notify the defense about the Lawrence situation." The court found that we were "right that the prosecutors should not have made a unilateral determination of the credibility of Lawrence when what Lawrence was alleging fitted into the very pattern of conduct suggested by Appellant's [new trial] motion." The court also assumed that Sagor may have improperly withheld the Goe memorandum from the Supreme Court. But it found—with little discussion or analysis—that Rosner had not been prejudiced by these errors:

> Thus, while Appellant's counsel has argued forcefully and well, he has been unable to demonstrate any ultimate prejudice to Appellant by the government's alleged misconduct.

We interpreted this statement as meaning that nothing was going to stop Rosner from going to prison and being disbarred. (Judge Gurfein later expressed that view in a private conversation with a mutual friend.)

That belief was confirmed by another decision rendered by a panel of the same court just six days before Judge Gurfein rendered the Rosner decision. In that case the government's key witness had admitted at trial that "he had used opium; that he had been addicted to and had sold heroin; that at the time of the trial he was taking methadone." After the trial it was discovered that in addition to these serious hard-drug problems, the witness had also once been convicted of "possession of marijuana." The information about this possession conviction had been "misfiled" by the government and was not known to the United States Attorney's office at the time of the trial. In that case the court of appeals held that although "the import of past possession of marijuana pales in comparison with [the witness'] extensive involvement with hard drugs"; nevertheless the conviction must be reversed since the jury's knowledge of the negligently suppressed marijuana conviction might have tipped the balance in the defendant's favor.

The facts of the Rosner case cried out far more convincingly for reversal than did the facts of that case. But Gurfein argued—in a footnote—that the cases were distinguishable on the ground, among others, that in the other case "the government was at fault in not discovering the past criminal record, a situation which *concededly* did not exist in the Rosner case." This last sentence was simply untrue. Rosner never conceded that the government was not at fault in failing to discover Leuci's past criminal record: to the contrary, his lawyers had spent hundreds of hours, tens of thousands of dollars, and dozens of pages of briefs in attempting to prove that the government was directly at fault in not discovering Leuci's criminality. If a lawyer had made such a statement in a brief, he would risk discipline for his mendacity; but three judges of the court of appeals were prepared to make that false statement in a published opinion. This episode persuaded me that the court of appeals was prepared to twist the law and the facts beyond all recognition to avoid reversing Rosner's conviction.

We immediately filed a petition for rehearing addressed to all nine judges of the court of appeals. In the petition we challenged Gurfein's statement about Rosner having conceded that the government had not been at fault and argued that the decisions reached in the two cases "are in irreconcilable conflict." The court denied our motion, and we turned to the Supreme Court of the United States as our last resort. In our petition we argued that this case was "uniquely suited for Supreme Court review," since our claim was that the "United States Attorney's office deliberately withheld relevant information from *this very court* during the pendency of a previous certiorari petition." We noted that this was "the first case" ever to raise this issue. The Supreme Court denied our petition without opinion on June 30, 1976.

By this time—with no recourse remaining—I was able to convince the Rosners that we should disclose the results of our interviews with the two jurors. We submitted their affidavits to the Supreme Court, arguing that they undercut the opinions of Judge Bauman and the court of appeals and raised a significant possibility that the jury verdict would have been different had the jurors known the truth about Leuci's crimes. The Supreme Court issued an order requesting the government to respond. This was unusual—and encouraging—since the vast majority of petitions for reconsideration are decided out of hand. In its reply, the government again went on the offensive, charging me with violating accepted legal standards by "approaching the trial jurors without the consent of the district court." We filed a reply pointing out that the government had tried, and failed, to get the district court to issue an injunction against our interviewing the jurors. But the government succeeded in convincing the Supreme Court that to consider juror affidavits would only open up a can of worms, and our petition for reconsideration was denied.

Finally, in 1977, after five years of litigation and more than a dozen separate court proceedings, Edmund Rosner was ordered to surrender and begin serving his three-year sentence at Allenwood.

EPILOGUE

Robert Leuci: The Prince of the City has become a hero again. He no longer makes cases, conducts investigations, or entraps defendants. But he is the central figure in a book—appropriately entitled *Prince of the City*—which became a best seller and a major motion picture. The money from these ventures coupled with the thousands of dollars he apparently amassed while he was a cop have certainly made him one of the wealthiest policemen in history. Robert Leuci recently retired from the police department with a twenty-year pension.

Seven years after my cross-examination of him, I met Leuci at the Boston premiere of the film *Prince of the City.* We had both been invited to participate in a panel discussion following the screening.

"Hiya, Alan, you look younger than ya did seven years ago," he said, putting his arm around me as if he was searching for a hidden recorder.

Leuci looked about the same, except that his clothing was more stylish and less garish. We gossiped about Rosner, Bauman, and the prosecutors. I told him that it was hard for me to believe that Shaw didn't know about the other crimes prior to the Rosner trial. "I'm convinced that in his heart he knew that I had committed more crimes," Leuci said. "He had to. Mike [Shaw] is no fool."

"Then how could he sit there and watch you lie on the witness stand?" I asked.

"He didn't consciously know for sure I was lying," Leuci continued. "He certainly suspected it and he probably believed it, but I had told him not to press me and he didn't. I said 'three crimes' "—Leuci raised three fingers and smiled broadly—"and he had to accept that."

"Prosecutors suborn perjury every day, Alan. You know that," Leuci continued. "They ask the cops to change their testimony to make a better case. How do you think the cops learn to do it—from the prosecutors. And in ninety-nine percent of the cases they do it with good intentions. That's a hell of a lot better than what defense lawyers do. They suborn perjury just for the money, and they put guilty guys back on the street. Our job—cops and prosecutors—is to see that doesn't happen."

The film itself strongly suggested that Shaw knew that Leuci had given drugs to addict-informers and had sat by silently when Leuci denied it under oath. If that was true, it would probably constitute subornation of perjury—ironically, the same crime Rosner had originally been charged with. When I asked Leuci about that after the screening, he said, "As far as I'm concerned, Shaw can do no wrong. He's God. He's like Thomas Jefferson to me." The point was clear: whatever Shaw did was, by definition, correct; his actions defined rightness for Leuci.

But Leuci has been critical of other prosecutors. In a recent interview he observed that "the cops would never have done what they did unless they knew they could get away with it . . . ." The Princes of the City could not have functioned without prosecuting attorneys "knowing that they were using illegal wiretaps or using perjured warrants . . . ." Leuci then talked about the pervasiveness of perjury in the criminal justice system:

> Cops are almost taught how to commit perjury when they are in the Police Academy. Perjury to a policeman—and to a lawyer, by the way —is not a big deal. Whether they are giving out speeding tickets or parking tickets, they're almost always lying. But very few cops lie about the actual facts of a case. They may stretch an incident or whatever to fit it into the framework of the law based on what they consider a silly law of the Supreme Court.*

As this book was going to press, I obtained some revealing new information about Leuci's perjury. I met with another law-enforcement official who was present at the first taped meeting between Leuci and the prosecutors who debriefed him prior to the Rosner trial. According to the official version of this meeting—sworn to by several government witnesses—Leuci told the prosecutors that he had committed only three crimes during his career as a policeman and that in each of those crimes he had served as an intermediary between other police and organized-crime figures. Also according to the official version, the tapes of these debriefing sessions were returned to Leuci, who burned them in his barbeque.

The law-enforcement person to whom I recently spoke told a very different story. In the presence of a witness he stated catagorically that he heard Leuci tell the prosecutors about many more crimes than the three to which he admitted at the Rosner trial. "He told them all about Pleasant Avenue, about how they sold big cases, about how they sold drugs. It was quite a story." The law-enforcement person also told me that it was widely believed within the police department that Leuci never burned the tapes: "He'd be crazy to do that. The tapes are his ace in the hole. The feds could never indict him for perjury as long as he held on to those tapes. Leuci's tapes would prove that he told the prosecutors more than the three crimes and that if *he* was committing perjury, so were *they.*" Finally, the law-enforcement official told me that after the publication of *Prince of the City,* he had taken this information to an assistant United States Attorney who told him to "forget it" because it "was stale" and it wouldn't "do anybody any good to wash the dirty laundry in public." The law-enforcement official to whom I spoke, concerned for his own future, has authorized me to publish his disclosures, but has asked me not to identify him by name.

Robert Morvillo: Several years after the Leuci-Lawrence incident, I discovered another—far more serious—instance of prosecutorial misconduct

*See rules IV and XI in Introduction at p. xvi.

and cover-up by Robert Morvillo. I was representing a defendant who had been convicted of stock fraud on the basis of testimony by a man named Michael Hellerman. Just as the prison doors were about to clang shut on my client, I learned that Hellerman was publishing his memoirs—after clearing the content with Morvillo.

The book disclosed that while Hellerman was working for the government, he and a colleague were swindling a bankrupt Long Island corporation of $80,000. The colleague took the stolen money to the Bahamas for laundering. Hellerman desperately needed the money to pay off loan sharks. Hellerman asked Morvillo to help him get the $80,000 in stolen funds to pay the sharks. Morvillo arranged for the FBI to seize the funds. At this point the money should either have been held by the federal government as evidence or returned to its rightful owner—the bankrupt company and its creditors. But instead, Morvillo and Hellerman worked out a complicated series of transactions that resulted in Hellerman obtaining the stolen $80,000 for his own personal use.

I realized that this story, if true, would make Robert Morvillo guilty of aiding a thief to obtain funds belonging to someone else. I requested a hearing on the issue and again confronted an angry Morvillo on the witness stand. The federal district judge concluded that the "bizarre story" had indeed occurred. He found "that it should have been readily apparent to the government, when it did release these funds, that the money inevitably would end up in Hellerman's pocket. In effect, the government chose to look the other way [and by] conscious avoidance the government thus intentionally eased the way for Hellerman to benefit from the decision to release the $80,000 in stolen funds . . ."

The judge was so incensed by Morvillo's actions that he went out of his way never to mention him by name in the course of his fifty-page opinion. He referred to him only by his title "the Chief." But in order to avoid any public criticism of Morvillo, the judge refrained from publishing his opinion.

The *Village Voice* subsequently published an account of this caper as its lead front-page story. Its bold headline was: "A Prosecutor Beyond the Law? Robert Morvillo: His Informant Raided a Bankrupt Firm." The story characterized the incident as a "scandal" and a perversion of the law. Morvillo's answer was that "Alan Dershowitz runs around the United States accusing every prosecutor he litigates against of impropriety. I can give you a list of fifty cases where he's made those allegations." When the reporter checked with me, I told him—and, after confirming its accuracy, he reported—that I had made allegations of impropriety in a total of five cases and had been "proven correct each time." The story concluded that

Morvillo's "accident"—his failure to censor the $80,000 incident from the draft of Hellerman's book—had probably cost him a federal judgeship or "the immediate prospect of becoming United States Attorney for the Eastern District." It was not surprising, therefore, that shortly after I exposed his shenanigans with Hellerman, Morvillo told a lawyer friend of mine that if he ever saw me outside the courthouse, he would "deck" me.

After leaving the United States Attorney's office, Morvillo entered private practice and was appointed chairman of a "select group of prosecutors and defense attorneys" to "investigate charges of unethical conduct by lawyers." The person who made the appointment was his former boss, Whitney North Seymour, Jr.

Arnold Bauman: While we were in the process of unsuccessfully appealing Judge Bauman's decision, Judge Arnold Bauman was resigning from the federal bench amidst a flurry of media hoopla about unlivably low judicial salaries (then $40,000 a year, now in excess of $70,000). He is currently senior partner in one of the largest law firms in the world, Shearman and Sterling, where he insists on being called "the Judge"—certainly an improvement over "the Court"—and where his annual earnings are thought to be in the area of a quarter of a million dollars.

Edmund and Nancy Rosner: After eight months at Allenwood, Rosner was released to a halfway house in Manhattan where he spent several nights a week while working for a legal publishing company during the day. In May of 1979 Rosner was featured in a *National Law Journal* article on disbarred lawyers. He said that being disbarred had been worse than going to jail. He spoke about his crimes and subsequent conviction, "wringing a table napkin in his hands until it was shredded." He told the paper, "The law was really a jealous mistress for me."

Edmund Rosner's conviction and disbarment cost him not only his "mistress," but also his wife. Nancy left him while he was in prison. For several years Nancy's career skyrocketed, as she defended big-time criminal defendants, including organized crime figures. At the height of her career, she appeared on the cover of *Parade* magazine. She put in twelve-hour days preparing briefs and arguments, but these long hours had their rewards, she said, pointing to the loyalty of her clients, who "would lay down their lives for me." Indeed, she made such an impression on one of her clients that they ran off together after she got his conviction reversed by the federal district court on a writ of habeas corpus. Unfortunately, the court of appeals reversed the district court and ordered Nancy's companion to prison. Nancy is now back in New York selling real estate.

Edmund Rosner is determined to return to the practice of law. He recently brought another motion for a new trial based on the disclosures contained in *Prince of the City.* That book revealed—for the first time—the remarkable story of Leuci's conspiracy to erase the tapes of the Bronx policemen systematically looting hundreds of TV sets, and his agreement to commit perjury at the trial. The government's suppression of that crime —a suppression that began before the *Rosner* trial and continued throughout the hearings and appeals—was the most serious suppression of all, because the undisclosed crimes bore directly on the way Leuci handled tapes, and the tapes of Rosner were—according to the government, Judge Bauman, and the court of appeals—the "linchpin" of the case against Rosner.

But as soon as Rosner filed his new motion based on the conspiracy to erase the tapes, the government changed its tack again. The United States Attorney's office—in a sworn affidavit—asserted that "as far as [Rosner's] defense at trial was concerned, tape recordings played *no part* at all." The trial court also concluded—this time—that the "tapes played *no part* whatever in the entrapment because the meetings with Leuci at which Rosner claims he was entrapped were not tape recorded." In the earlier opinions, the courts had concluded that the tapes were the "linchpin" of the government's case; now these same tapes played "no part" in that same case. The only constant among the opinions was the conclusion that "Rosner loses." As my friend had warned me before I took the case: "You don't put a cancer back once you've excised it"—even if you have to perform radical surgery on the facts of the case to avoid that result.

Rosner appealed—for the fifth time—to the court of appeals. In December 1980 a unanimous court of appeals affirmed the district court in an order relying "on the opinion below"—the opinion that had said the tapes had played "no part whatever" in the entrapment defense. Attached to the court of appeals' order was a stamped form warning that its statement "shall not be reported, cited or otherwise used in unrelated cases before this or any other court." The decision would mean that "Rosner loses," but the reasoning could not be used as precedent in any other case. It was almost as if the court of appeals was ashamed of its performance in the Rosner case. That would be entirely understandable.

The United States Attorney's office for the Southern District of New York: Despite repeated instances of misconduct of the sort uncovered in the Rosner and Hellerman cases, the United States Attorney's office for the Southern District of New York is still widely regarded as "the jewel of the federal system." But it is a tarnished gem. An aura of respectable corruption —corruption in the name of a higher justice—permeates many of its antiseptic corridors at Saint Andrew's Plaza in downtown Manhattan. The prosecutors who practice this brand of corruption would never dream of taking a bribe or manufacturing evidence. Nor would they tell a direct lie under oath. But some are prepared to close their eyes to perjury; to distort the truth; and to engage in cover-ups—all in the name of defending society from the obviously guilty. They practice this elite corruption with the knowledge and blessing of certain judges—some with the highest reputation for integrity and honesty.

The young assistant United States Attorneys are not only taught how to "cheat elite," but—much worse—they are taught that such cheating is acceptable, indeed desirable. They are taught by the examples of "heroes" like Robert Morvillo, Edward M. Shaw, and Whitney North Seymour, Jr. They are taught by the examples of former prosecutors who have become district judges and who continue to play the game from the bench. They are taught that the game of "cheat elite" pays off, by the court of appeals that continues to affirm convictions—to give the U.S. Attorneys victories —in the face of incontrovertible evidence of improprieties, and by the kudos and successes of those assistants who have developed the art of "cheat elite" to its highest form. Some assistants teach these lessons to their successors, and they take them into private practice and onto the bench. No one dares tell these elite members of the bar that what they have been doing is cheating.

In a recent case, for example, two former U.S. Attorneys—one of whom was Henry Putzel, who had prosecuted the Seigel case—learned from their clients that the government's key witness in an ongoing trial was a crook and a liar. In order to score negotiating points for their clients, these erstwhile prosecutors told the chief of the criminal division that they had proof that a government witness was a crook. But they did not want to make the government's job any more difficult by disclosing the *name* of the crooked witness while the trial was still going on. The former prosecutors realized that if they did so, the government would be obliged to call the trial to a halt and inform the judge and the defense attorneys of the new evidence. Accordingly, the former prosecutors—well versed in the ways of the Southern District—played a little charade: they told the current prosecutor that they "preferred to wait a few days before disclosing the name of this individual." It would take little imagination for an intelligent prosecutor to conclude that the mystery witness had testified in an ongoing trial that would be over within "a few days." But the prosecutor kept his blinders on and waited. Lo and behold, immediately after the jury returned its verdict of guilty, the former prosecutors told the current prosecutor the name of the government's crooked witness. It was too late to bring the new evidence to the attention of the jury—and that was exactly the point of the charade.

One would hope that a court concerned with encouraging compliance rather than defiance of the Constitution would be outraged at this little game between former and present U.S. Attorneys. But when I argued this case before a three-judge panel—a panel comprised of three former United States Attorneys—they expressed not a word of concern about the end run around the Constitution. They reserved all their criticism for me, for asking for a hearing merely on the basis of "smoke" without positive proof of fire.

The message this kind of attitude sends to prosecutors is clear: continue to cheat elite, and don't worry if you have to create some smoke. But make sure you do not create the kind of fire that even judges cannot ignore.

Nor can the type of cheating sometimes engaged in by these prosecutors be excused as the slips of a "bungling constable." The assistants I am referring to are not bunglers. They are shrewd, highly educated, and calculating lawyers. Their decisions to tolerate entrapment, to close their eyes to perjury, and to cover up the corruptions of their cooperating witnesses cannot all be accidental. Some of their decisions, at least, seem carefully worked through, either at a conscious or an unconscious level of calculation. They may believe they are doing the right thing. They are, after all, bringing guilty criminals to justice. They are defending the public against unscrupulous defense attorneys who invoke legal technicalities to free guilty defendants. They justify their deviations from legal and ethical norms as a sophisticated form of civil disobedience in the name of a "higher justice."

In my own experience, this type of elite corruption is most prevalent when the prosecutor is out to get a particularly "bad" defendant: where the office has "targeted" an organized crime leader, a corrupt public official, or —as in the case of Edmund Rosner—a despised lawyer suspected of dishonesty. A "war mentality" sometimes takes over in this kind of case, and all is deemed fair on the battlefield of justice. The desired end—conviction of the targeted bad guy—is seen as justifying the questionable means sometimes required to counteract the clever maneuvers of the defendant and his "hired gun." Prosecutors begin to behave, quite understandably, like defense attorneys, forgetting that their roles in the adversary system of justice are supposed to be quite different.

When a criminal defense lawyer exposes the corruption, the assistants dismiss it as the ranting of a hired gun. The judges, for the most part, go out of their way to protect the assistants. When, on occasion, an assistant is criticized by a judge, the criticism is regarded as the price one sometimes has to pay for overzealousness.

This is not to say that all, or even most, assistants are involved in this brand of elite corruption. I have encountered several who refuse to go along. But enough of them are involved at sufficiently high levels so that it permeates the office. Nor is it to say that matters are not worse elsewhere. That is precisely the point. Everybody knows that it is worse in many other prosecutor's offices, both state and federal. The United States Attorney's office for the Southern District of New York may well deserve its reputation as among the best and the least corrupt prosecutor's offices in the country. That is why so little criticism is directed at it. That is why elite young lawyers are sent there to learn. That is why it serves as a model of integrity. And that is why it is essential to disclose the sad reality behind its façade of incorruptibility.

—11—

Defending the Defenders

When F. Lee Bailey was indicted in 1973 for conspiracy to commit mail fraud, he quoted an aphorism popular among attorneys to the effect that England and the United States treat their criminal lawyers quite differently: in England they are apt to be *knighted;* in the United States they are apt to be *indicted.* There is some truth to the second part: a considerable number of American criminal lawyers have been charged with criminal conduct. Sometimes the public has to be reminded that the word *criminal* in criminal lawyer—like the word *baby* in baby doctor—is a description not of the professional, but rather of the clientele.

The image of lawyer as criminal has been etched indelibly into the American consciousness by such highly publicized prosecutions as those growing out of Watergate and Abscam, where many of the defendants were lawyers themselves. Indeed, in recent years I have begun my opening criminal-law lecture by reminding the first-year students that "statistically, more of you may end up as criminal *defendants* than as criminal *lawyers.*"

About half my clients have been lawyers, many of them criminal lawyers. The crimes they have been accused of have ranged from bribery and embezzlement to murder. For the most part, the criminal charges have grown out of their practice, such as those for which Edmund Rosner was convicted. Several have been cited, as I nearly was in the Rosner and JDL cases, with contempt of court or unprofessional conduct for overzealous representation of clients. Some have been charged with crimes unrelated to their legal work. In one case, a lawyer had invested in a furniture company. The business began to fail. The lawyer helped take out a million-dollar insurance policy on the life of the furniture company's president in order to satisfy the demands of certain creditors. The president was subsequently gunned down, gangland style. There was no proof that the lawyer had anything to do with the killing, but he was convicted of insurance fraud. I wrote the appeal brief, arguing that the jurors never should have learned that the insured had been murdered because once they learned this prejudicial fact, they inevitably would assume that the person who took out the insurance policy was responsible for the murder. That's the way it is on TV, and that's the way jurors understandably think. It is precisely the role of the trial judge to filter the evidence so that jurors cannot employ TV logic. Since there was absolutely no *evidence* that my client had anything to do with the killing, the jurors should not have found out about the murder. The appeals court agreed and reversed the conviction. The cases of most lawyers do not involve gangland murders, but they do range over the entire breadth of the criminal code.

In this chapter I will describe several types of criminal lawyers I have represented or encountered in my practice. Some "types" tend to get into more trouble than others. But some who never get into trouble may be the worst possible criminal lawyers from their clients' point of view.

The Criminal Lawyer Who Gets in Bed with the Client

Many of the problems encountered by lawyers are the result of a temptation to which lawyers—some good and some not so good—all too often fall prey: they fail to draw a line between representing a client and becoming his associate. Many lawyers, even the most distinguished partners in Wall Street firms, become associated in business with their clients. The association may assume a variety of forms: taking fees in the form of stocks, partnerships, or other financial interests in the company; giving business advice in addition to legal advice; and serving on the board of directors of a client-corporation.

F. Lee Bailey's problem with the law grew out of his business relationship with a flamboyant young Southern businessman named Glen Turner.

I first met Bailey in 1965, when his younger brother Bill was a student in my first-year criminal law class. I had been teaching the Sam Sheppard case, the case that had first thrust Bailey into the public eye. Sheppard, a wealthy osteopathic doctor from a Cleveland suburb, had been convicted, after a highly publicized trial, of murdering his wife. Bailey, then a fledgling lawyer, persuaded the Supreme Court to grant Sheppard a new trial on the ground that the publicity—much of it orchestrated by the prosecution—had denied the defendant a fair trial. On the retrial Bailey secured an acquittal. It was a spectacular win for the young lawyer, and it assured his national reputation as a premier defense attorney.

On the day I was discussing the Sheppard case, Bill Bailey brought a friend and they both sat in the back of the classroom. Playing the devil's advocate, I called on Bill and asked him to assume that Sheppard had, in fact, been guilty: "Would the Supreme Court decision reversing the conviction be justified if the Justices had been convinced of his guilt? Or does it make sense only if he had been falsely convicted?"

After the class Bill came up to the lectern and introduced his friend: he was Sam Sheppard's son. The young man told me how disturbed he was at my question. "How could you even assume that my father was guilty?" he asked plaintively. I apologized for my insensitivity, and explained that I had no idea that anyone personally involved in the case was in class. (This kind of embarrassment is an occupational hazard at Harvard, where the children of many prominent people are students.)

Bill invited me to come to court with him to observe his brother try a case. My first opportunity came in January of 1967 when Bailey was defending Albert DeSalvo, the alleged Boston Strangler. I took the students in my Law and Psychiatry seminar to watch Bailey cross-examine a hostile psychiatric witness. The cross-examination was masterful. Bailey had obviously done his homework before coming to court. Many of the questions were based on facts uncovered by his investigators and unknown to the psychiatrist. Bailey had mastered the art of combining extensive pretrial investigation—an occupation he had engaged in before becoming a lawyer—with slashing cross-examination. This combination distinguished him from most other criminal lawyers, who come into court relatively unprepared and must rely on their forensic skills and experience in examining a hostile witness. These skills are important, but without the investigative background material even the best lawyer can be tripped up by a clever witness.

Shortly after the Boston Strangler trial, Bailey asked whether I wanted to come down from my ivory tower and help him draft a certiorari petition to the Supreme Court in another murder case reminiscent of the Sheppard prosecution. This time it was an adulterous wife, who was accused of murdering her dentist husband by putting him in the family Volkswagen and pushing it over a cliff in an effort to make the death appear accidental. To complicate matters, the woman was pregnant during the trial, but the prosecutor still demanded the death penalty. The case was the stuff of which novels and movies are made. (Joan Didion's account of it is included in her best-selling collection, *Slouching Towards Bethlehem.*) The jury, which had been "cleansed" of all persons with conscientious objections against capital punishment, convicted the wife of murder, and she was sentenced to life imprisonment. I drafted the petition for certiorari and it was granted.

Eventually, the woman served a prison term, and then returned home to take care of her child.

After that case I worked on several other small matters for Bailey's office. And then on May 18, 1973, a federal grand jury indicted Bailey himself. The charge was conspiracy to commit mail fraud. At the center of the alleged conspiracy was Glen Turner. Turner had operated several large "pyramid" schemes, ostentatiously named "Dare to be Great" and "Koscott Interplanetary."

A pyramid scheme is a high-priced variation of the common chain letter. For a fee of $4,500 Turner and his companies would sell an investor the right to become a distributor of whatever product was being sold—cosmetics in one instance, and a Dale Carnegie-type motivational course in another. More important than the right to sell the product, however, was the right to sell new distributorships to other investors for $4,500. Part of the fee obtained from the second customer was given to the first customer, and the rest was sent to Turner and his company. The second customer could then recoup some of his costs by selling a new distributorship to a third customer, who could then sell a new distributorship to yet a fourth, *ad infinitum.* The only problem was that there was indeed a "finitum." Moreover, the government claimed that Turner and his companies did not have any genuine product to sell—that there were no salable cosmetics or motivational courses. The government claimed that Turner was really selling worthless distributorships, empty shells that could be sold and resold to naïve purchasers looking to make a quick buck. Most of these quick bucks were made, however, by Turner, who profited from every sale of a distributorship regardless of whether the distributor ever sold any cosmetics or motivational courses.

By the late 1960s Glen Turner had become a legend in the Southeast. The uneducated son of a sharecropper, Turner had amassed a fortune. He was like a cult leader, with thousands of believers in his gospel of success. Word of Turner's fame and wealth began to spread across the country and the world, as he sold more and more distributorships and built monuments, in the form of castles, to his own success. But the saturation point was being reached in several states. Dissatisfied customers were beginning to complain that not only were they unable to recoup their investments by selling new distributorships but they were also not receiving cosmetics or motivational courses to sell.

State and federal law enforcement officials undertook investigations and began obtaining injunctions against Turner's operations. "Koscott Interplanetary" and "Dare to be Great" were threatened with bankruptcy as the cash flow from the sale of distributorships began to dwindle. Now it was time for Glen Turner to seek out the best lawyer in America. He sought advice from his public relations director who recommended F. Lee Bailey. Turner's first reaction was, "Who's he?" But he agreed to interview Bailey.

Turner told Bailey that in his legal battle "It's me against the United States."

Bailey replied, "Good, I always like a fair fight."

After considerable discussion Bailey agreed to become Turner's lawyer, and they worked out an unusual fee arrangement—one which reveals something about each of their personalities. Turner would pay all the legal expenses of the case plus the cost of running Bailey's rented Lear jet. Moreover, if Bailey could solve Turner's legal problems, Turner would pay a substantial contingency fee. (A contingency fee is paid to the lawyer only if the lawsuit is won; it is perfectly proper in most civil cases.) The contingency fee was to be a spanking new Lear jet for Bailey. Bailey could not resist, and the deal was struck.

But here is where Bailey made the error that even good lawyers often fall prey to: he failed to draw a sharp line between representing a businessman and becoming his associate.

Turner wanted Bailey not only for his considerable legal talents but also for the prestige and legitimacy he could lend to the operation. He asked him to attend recruitment meetings as an assurance to his potential customers that everything would be fine. There is a dispute about precisely what role Bailey did play over the next several months, but it is clear that he did more than appear before courts and other governmental agencies on behalf of his client. There is nothing legally or ethically wrong, of course, with a lawyer performing functions outside the courtroom. Wall Street lawyers do it all the time. The point is, however, that the closer a lawyer gets to the boardrooms and salesrooms of a business, the more vulnerable he becomes to indictment if the business turns out to be fraudulent or illegal.

In May 1973 a federal grand jury in Florida indicted Glen Turner, three of his companies, eight of his business associates, and his lawyer, F. Lee Bailey, on charges of using the mail to engage in a conspiracy. The object of the alleged conspiracy was to defraud persons "too numerous to mention."

The inclusion of attorney Baily and his client Turner in a single indictment—and the government's decision to place them on trial together in a single proceeding—presented a perplexing and novel issue of both law and legal ethics. Bailey retained me to brief and argue this issue.

The problem can only be understood against the background of the attorney-client privilege. That privilege assures a client that whatever information or advice has been exchanged between the client and his lawyer will be kept in confidence by the lawyer and not revealed to anyone else. There are, of course, certain limitations: the information must have been exchanged in the process of obtaining legal advice; it must have been exchanged with the lawyer (and his staff) alone and not within the hearing of outsiders; and it must not be information about a future crime or fraud. Subject to these limitations (and a few more technical ones), all information exchanged between a lawyer and his client must be kept confidential by the *lawyer.* (The client, however, is absolutely free to disclose it.)

In the Turner-Bailey situation, Bailey had served as Turner's lawyer for more than a year. During that time, Turner had many confidential communications with Bailey. I don't know the content of those communications. Though I was *Bailey's* lawyer, he did not feel free to disclose them to me, since I had never been *Turner's* lawyer. But it did not take much imagination to surmise what the general nature of those communications may have been. I could easily imagine a typical conversation:

Lawyer: "All that puffing and exaggeration that goes on at the sales meetings—it has to stop. You can't tell potential distributors that they're going to make $50,000 a year. The record just doesn't bear that out. And you can't lead them to believe there is an unlimited pool of potential purchasers for distributorships out there. There just isn't. You know darn well there's a saturation point."

Client: "I don't write the scripts for the sales meetings. Some of my salesmen out there may get carried away on occasion, but what can I do about it?"

Lawyer: "You damn well better do something about it. What your boys are doing out there is fraud. And if it doesn't stop, you're going to be in big trouble."

I don't know what advice Bailey actually gave to Turner. But if there had been a conversation something like the one I imagined, it would clearly be to Turner's *disadvantage* to have it disclosed, since it would establish that his lawyer had told him that his employees were engaged in fraud. Turner's failure to stop such conduct *after* being told it was fraud would hurt Turner in the eyes of the jurors.

But disclosure of the very same conversation would be to Bailey's *advantage.* It would show that Bailey had advised Turner to put an end to the fraudulent activities. Giving advice, after all, is all a lawyer can realistically do. If the client fails to follow the advice, the lawyer cannot be held responsible—especially if he was not aware that the advice had been disregarded.

The dilemma of the lawyer being tried jointly with his former client is that if he discloses the conversation, he helps himself but hurts his client; if he withholds the conversation, he helps his client but hurts himself. What should he do? Bailey called me soon after the indictment was handed up and asked me to think about that perplexing question.

My answer was that he should do neither. He should seek to be tried *separately* from his former client so that he could disclose the conversation to the jury trying *him,* but withhold the conversation from the jury trying *his client.* Bailey had, of course, thought of that, but he wanted me to write a brief in support of a severance. Severance means that the trials of two defendants—in this case Turner and Bailey—would be conducted separately.

I wrote a lengthy brief arguing that to try Bailey and Turner together would set a precedent that would create an irreconcilable conflict between attorneys and their clients, and would

> encourage prosecutors to indict attorneys along with clients. [This] would have a severe chilling effect upon the willingness of the attorneys to represent unpopular clients and of clients to trust their attorneys with secrets.

The judge convened a hearing for June 13, 1973—the day after I argued the appeal for Sheldon Seigel in the JDL murder case. The Bailey hearing was scheduled to begin at seven-thirty in the morning, to minimize the effects of the stifling heat of the Orlando summer.

As I walked into the Orlando courtroom, the assistant U.S. Attorney was pointed out to me. He was wearing a fluorescent-blue polyester suit and white shoes. But any hope that this garb—which seemed so unlawyerlike to a Northeasterner—would prejudice him in the eyes of the court was quickly dashed when the judge entered the courtroom: underneath his robe, I could plainly see that he, too, was wearing a light-colored suit and white shoes. In addition to sharing similar tastes in clothing, the prosecutor and the judge also shared a common accent and relaxed manner. Beneath these casual exteriors were a tenacious prosecutor and a shrewd judge.

As soon as I began to speak, the judge pressed me for specifics. He challenged me to give him "several" examples of conversations the disclosure of which would be helpful to Bailey and harmful to Turner. I was not in a position, of course, to be specific, since Bailey had deliberately refused to brief me on the content of these privileged conversations. I did suggest, however, the general tenor of such conversations and offered to have Bailey disclose some of them to the judge privately in his chambers, outside the presence of the prosecutor.

The prosecutor took the position that none of the conversations between Turner and Bailey came within the lawyer-client privilege, since they were all part of an ongoing fraud—a continuing crime.

He argued that "Mr. Bailey should not be [allowed to hide] behind the privilege of . . . the client." I saw my opening and responded:

> Mr. Bailey is [not] trying to hide behind the privilege. [But he is obliged] to claim his client's privilege whenever he is asked a question which might breach that sanctity.
>
> Now, the reason why this motion for severance is being brought is precisely because Mr. Bailey . . . wants to bring everything out into the open and wants to testify as to every conversation he had.

The judge decided to hold our motion for severance "in abeyance" until later in the trial when it might become clearer whether there was an actual —rather than a theoretical—conflict between Bailey and Turner. In reserving this crucial decision, he planted the seeds that would eventually blossom into a practical victory for Bailey—albeit a costly one. Addressing the government's decision to try Bailey and Turner together, the judge cautioned:

> Now, the Government proceeds . . . at its own peril . . . because of the duration of the trial, if the case goes eight to fourteen weeks. . . . It might be that [if a severance has to be granted after that period of time, this] might preclude a retrial.

The judge's statement was prescient in one respect, but dramatically wrong in another. The government's case did not take eight to fourteen weeks to present to the jury; it took nearly thirty weeks. And after all the grueling weeks of trial (during which Bailey represented himself), the judge finally did what he should have done thirty weeks earlier: he granted Bailey a severance from the other defendants and declared a mistrial as to him.

The case went to the jury without Bailey, and after seven days of deliberation, the jury remained deadlocked. The entire thirty-week trial had been for naught. The defendants were told to prepare for a new trial.

But what about Bailey? The court had warned the government that a long trial culminating in a severance "might preclude a retrial" of Bailey. But the court refused to intervene, and the prosecutors kept Bailey up in the air for several months, "twisting slowly, slowly in the wind," as he put it in an affidavit. They refused to drop the charges or set the case down for a speedy trial. Bailey's practice began to disintegrate: his law firm fell apart; his wife fell ill; he suffered continuing anxiety.

Finally, in July of 1975 all charges against Bailey were dismissed by the district court. Several of the remaining defendants, including Turner, agreed to plead guilty to misdemeanor charges and received probationary sentences.

The dismissal of the charges against Bailey permitted him to resume the full-time practice of law, but the stigma of indictment still hung over him. Glamorous clients were no longer knocking at his office door. Bailey told journalist Shana Alexander that he had to borrow $400,000 just to stay afloat: "It was the worst thing that ever happened to me. I couldn't try any cases. I couldn't get any income. People stayed away in droves."

But all this was to change, unexpectedly, and dramatically. On September 18, 1975—just weeks after Bailey was cleared of all charges in the Turner case—the news came over the wires that the most famous, enigmatic, and controversial kidnapping victim in recent history had been captured by the police. Nineteen months after her abduction from a Berkeley apartment, Patricia Hearst was under arrest in San Francisco. An emergency phone call reached Bailey at the state penitentiary in Jackson, Mississippi, where he was interviewing a woman on death row. The caller was Randolph Hearst. After some negotiation the Hearst family retained F. Lee Bailey to become their daughter's chief counsel in her upcoming federal trial for participating, ten weeks after her abduction, in the Symbionese Liberation Army's robbery of the Hibernia Bank. Bailey's handling of the Hearst case generated more controversy than any other in his controversial career, and highlighted another important problem that certain kinds of defense attorneys encounter—or generate—in highly publicized cases.

The Media-Oriented Defense Lawyer

Bailey retained me to help prepare the legal briefs in the Hearst case. As he told Shana Alexander, "In a heavy case, I'm apt to send it over to Alan." And this was certainly a heavy case—both for Patricia Hearst and for F. Lee Bailey. It was Bailey's opportunity to put the Turner debacle behind him and to reassert himself as America's top criminal-trial lawyer. The trial was among the most widely covered legal events in history. As one journalist put it, the Hearst case promised to become "another Trial of the Century—the fourth or fifth in [Bailey's] sixteen-year legal career."

The basic issue at the trial was whether Hearst had voluntarily participated in the Hibernia robbery, or whether she was still under the control and domination of her abductors at the time she entered the bank carrying a gun. The press referred to this as the "brainwashing" defense.

Bailey asked me to coordinate the legal research on that defense. I hired half a dozen law students to dig up every case in Anglo-American legal history in which a defendant had been abducted and had then joined the abductors in the commission of criminal acts. We drafted several detailed legal memoranda on various aspects of the psychological defenses, and sent them off to San Francisco, where Bailey and his staff were in the last stages of pretrial preparation.

I submitted another memorandum analyzing whether the government could cross-examine Patricia Hearst about what she had done during the year and a half *between* the bank robbery and her capture. The government would argue that if she had willingly participated in "revolutionary" acts during the months after the Hibernia robbery, then that willingness would constitute some proof that she also voluntarily participated in the previous Hibernia holdup. The defense would argue that subsequent events would not prove anything about her state of mind on the day of the robbery, since there had been an important intervening development between the Hibernia robbery and the others: the Attorney General of the United States, William Saxbe, had told the press that as a result of the bank robbery, Patricia Hearst was considered "nothing but a common criminal." Her SLA captors kept telling her, "You have been defined as a criminal by your country, and now you have no choice but to join us!"

Bailey was worried about the jury hearing Patricia Hearst admit that she had willingly engaged in revolutionary crimes after the Hibernia job. He realized that even with the explanation of the Saxbe statement, they would try her not for what she *did* in the bank on that day in March, but for what she later *became*. Bailey referred to these incidents as "skunks" that should be kept out of the courtroom at all cost: "Once you let a skunk into the courtroom," according to an old country lawyer's saying, "you can't ever completely remove its stink."

My memorandum recommended that the judge be requested to make a ruling *before* Hearst was put on the stand as to whether the government would be permitted to cross-examine her about events after the Hibernia robbery. In this way, Bailey could make the judgment about putting her on the stand with full knowledge of whether she would be exposed to dangerous cross-examination. (This was a variant on the procedure we had used in the Sheldon Seigel case in seeking an advance ruling from Judge Bauman as to whether Seigel would be held in contempt if he refused to become a government witness.)

The best-laid plans of lawyers often go awry in the unpredictable frenzy of a trial. Bailey did seek an advance ruling. The judge refused to give a formal ruling, but he did state his opinion that the defendant could not be questioned about possible crimes committed after the Hibernia robbery unless she testified about that period of time during her direct testimony. In reliance on the judge's opinion, Bailey put Hearst on the witness stand and carefully avoided any reference to the events following Hibernia. But after Hearst completed her direct testimony, the judge apparently changed his mind and allowed the government to cross-examine her about everything. Bailey tried to prevent any questioning about crimes committed after Hibernia by having Hearst invoke her privilege against self-incrimination outside the hearing of the jury. The judge ruled, however, that by testifying as she had done, Hearst had waived her privilege and had to answer the questions or invoke the privilege in front of the jury. Patricia Hearst thus got the worst of all possible worlds: she was asked dozens of incriminating questions and was required to invoke the privilege against self-incrimination repeatedly in front of the jury; and the jury was told that since she had waived the privilege, it could draw adverse inferences from her improper invocation of it.

In the end the cross-examination of Hearst was a disaster for the defense. Many observers believe that it sealed her fate. Dozens of criminal lawyers, adept at the fine art of Monday-morning-quarterbacking, publicly castigated Bailey for his decision to put his client on the witness stand and then have her plead the privilege in the presence of the jury. I am confident that if Bailey had *not* put her on the stand, and if the jury had still returned a guilty verdict, many of the same lawyers would still have criticized Bailey for not having her testify. "He tried half a case." "He got lazy." "You can't expect to win a case involving a psychological defense without putting the defendant on the stand."

"Would *you* have put Patricia Hearst on the witness stand, knowing everything you know now?" That is a question I have been asked dozens of times. I'll try to answer, at the risk of being labeled a Wednesday-morning quarterback. I offer my answer recognizing that no lawyer can make the crucial decision that Bailey had to make without being there—without experiencing and appreciating the subtleties and complexities that pervaded the trial at the crucial moment.

When Bailey had to decide whether to put Patricia Hearst on the witness stand, the trial judge had already allowed the government to introduce evidence—through means other than Hearst herself—of Hearst's participation in additional crimes during the year and a half following Hibernia. This evidence included tape recordings and diaries of Hearst declaring her commitment to revolutionary doctrine, and strongly suggesting that her conversion had preceded the Hibernia robbery. The judge had also forbidden the defense psychiatrists from playing for the jury the more recent tapes of their interviews with Hearst during which she expressed remorse about her life as an urban guerrilla. Thus, when the time came for Bailey to make the difficult decision, he was confronted with an unenviable dilemma: If he did not put her on the stand, the jury would decide her guilt after having heard extremely damaging evidence from her own mouth about her state of mind after the Hibernia robbery, but without any explanation from the defendant. If he did put her on the stand, she could be cross-examined, but the judge seemed to have ruled that she could—outside the presence of the jury—lawfully claim her privilege against self-incrimination regarding the events following the Hibernia holdup.

Viewed from this perspective, the decision Bailey faced about Hearst taking the stand assumed the dimensions of a Hobson's choice. There was no risk-free resolution. Knowing everything I know now, including what several jurors told interviewers after their verdict, I would probably not have put her on the stand. (Several jurors apparently voted to convict because they simply did not believe the defendant's testimony.) But knowing what Bailey knew *at the time* he had to make his decision, I might well have done the same thing he did.

That is not to say that I would have tried the Hearst case the way Bailey did. I would not have! I would not have held press conferences before trial announcing the defenses I expected to use. Indeed, the government pointed to one such press conference in arguing that Bailey had opened the door to the introduction of evidence about the events subsequent to Hibernia. Thus, the dilemma that Bailey faced may have been partly of his own making.

No two lawyers would ever try a complicated case the same way. Bailey tried it in the Bailey manner. The basic decision faced by the Hearsts was not *how* the case should be tried *by Bailey.* Once they hired Bailey, the die was cast. That is how F. Lee Bailey tries cases. Had the Hearst family retained Edward Bennett Williams—the lawyer they approached *before* they retained Bailey, but who turned them down—the case would have been tried differently. It would have been tried in the Williams style: low-keyed, methodically researched, and mapped out play-by-play like a National Football League game plan, with contingency responses for every possibility. I don't know whether Williams would have put Patricia Hearst on the witness stand. I do know the decision would have been a careful and studied one based on the best information available—plus a good bit of instinct. Had Williams lost the case, however, he would not have been as soundly criticized by his fellow lawyers as Bailey was. Bailey's flamboyance and the attention he receives from the media invite jealousy and criticism from his brothers and sisters at the bar.

His showmanship also invites the suspicion—voiced by some, including Hearst's subsequent lawyers—that Bailey's trial tactics may have been influenced by his desire for personal publicity. It is perfectly proper for a lawyer to use the press—if done to further his *client's* interests (and if not in violation of any legal or ethical rules). But it is always wrong for a lawyer to subordinate a client's interests to his own desire for attention. The line is not always clear-cut, and the publicity-oriented defense lawyer will often believe—or rationalize—that press coverage will help *both* the client *and* the lawyer. Sometimes it will. Sometimes it won't. Even a good lawyer, with an eye to the media, will not always be able to tell the difference.

Patricia Hearst is now a free woman. Her sentence was commuted by President Carter after she had served twenty-three months of a seven-year term. Shortly after her release she married one of her bodyguards, and has had a child with him. She also wrote a book about her nineteen months with the Symbionese Liberation Army. In it she castigates Bailey for putting her on the witness stand, claiming that he had "promised" to keep her off and had misled her. She also criticizes Bailey for "overextending himself" during the trial by flying off to Las Vegas to give seminars to other lawyers at the end of the court day.

Indeed, Hearst eventually hired a new lawyer who filed a motion for a new trial on the ground that Bailey's defense had been inadequate and ineffective. But on January 6, 1982, Hearst dropped the lawsuit, citing her "desire to put this litigation behind me."

F. Lee Bailey is back in the business of defending criminals. His involvement in the Hearst case certainly had one effect: it made everyone forget about the Turner trial. Glen who?

The Criminal Lawyer Who Serves as "House Counsel" for Professional Criminals

In the Glen Turner case, F. Lee Bailey never had to resolve the difficult dilemma of whether to testify against his client to help himself. But James Lawson, a young lawyer just a few years out of law school, did have to confront that criminal lawyer's recurrent nightmare when a federal judge ordered him to provide certain testimony and information against his client or face imprisonment himself. Lawson refused to incriminate his client, and the judge sentenced him to prison "until such time as he is willing to provide [the] testimony and information." He came to me for advice and representation.

The case arose in a familiar context. Several people had been indicted by a federal grand jury in Washington state for a federal conspiracy to sell "Thai sticks"—a type of high quality marijuana. Two of the defendants retained the services of Oteri and Weinberg, a small Boston law firm with an excellent reputation for defending persons accused of marijuana offenses. Lawson, who was then an associate of the firm, was assigned the case. He flew to Washington and arranged a plea bargain: his two clients pleaded guilty and were sentenced to prison for a year.

The prosecutors suspected, however, that neither of Lawson's defendants was the kingpin of the operation: they believed that a man named George Bradley, who had not been indicted, was the real boss. In order to gather information in support of their suspicions, the prosecutors subpoenaed Lawson's defendants to appear before a grand jury, granted them immunity from further prosecution, and asked them a series of questions about their relationship with Bradley and with the law firm of Oteri and Weinberg. One of the questions was whether they had paid their own legal fees to the Oteri and Weinberg law firm. They testified that they had not. They also testified that they did not know who had paid the fees.

A few days later Lawson was subpoenaed before the same grand jury and asked "who paid your or the firm's fees" for the two defendants. Lawson realized, of course, that by identifying the source of the fees, he would be telling the prosecutors exactly what they wanted to know: who the real boss of the marijuana ring was.

But Lawson could not tell the government what it wanted to know, because the person who had paid the fee was *also* Lawson's client. He had paid the fee—and thus disclosed his role in the marijuana conspiracy—under an assurance of confidentiality. Now Lawson was being told to break that confidentiality and turn in his client. Lawson refused to answer the question, invoking the attorney-client privilege. Although the name of a client and the fee arrangement are generally not included within the lawyer-client privilege, Lawson argued that such information should be included when its disclosure would incriminate his client. The judge directed him to answer, but he persisted in his refusal, was held in contempt, and sentenced to jail. He told the court that he would appeal the contempt finding, and requested a stay of his sentence. The government opposed a stay, and urged the judge to jail him immediately. The judge granted a stay pending appeal.

In our brief before the United States Court of Appeals for the Ninth Circuit, we put the dilemma squarely in the laps of the judges:

> A young lawyer of the highest integrity and standing has been held in contempt of court and confined to custody because he has refused to disclose information about his client(s) that he sincerely believes—and has been advised by experts and his attorneys—he is not permitted to disclose because of his ethical and legal obligations as an attorney.
>
> The attorney now faces an impossible dilemma: he cannot in good conscience disclose the information . . . and he faces imprisonment

> unless he makes the disclosures. He respectfully petitions this Court to aid him in complying with his ethical and legal obligations as an attorney.*

The court of appeals reversed the contempt order, holding that Lawson "had a just reason to assert the attorney-client privilege," since the names of Lawson's "undisclosed clients, and fee arrangements involving other conspirators, would implicate those persons in the past conspiracy." Lawson was free. He did not have to go to jail to protect his client.†

This was neither the first nor the last time I represented the law firm of Oteri and Weinberg. Being subpoenaed to testify against one's clients is an occupational hazard for criminal lawyers, but especially for lawyers who specialize in drug cases. One reason is that drug rings generally operate in a hierarchical structure with the boss at the top and the drug carriers—or "mules" as they are called—at the bottom. Naturally, it is the mules who take the greatest risk and who, in fact, are most often arrested. They generally do not have the funds to retain able lawyers. It is often part of the deal that if they are caught, the boss will provide lawyers for them. Providing these lawyers—who are often quite expensive—is hardly a demonstration of altruism on the part of the bosses. The bosses have an interest in assuring that their own lawyers—lawyers they are paying—are representing the mules. The last thing the boss wants is for an independent lawyer—or worse, a lawyer friendly to the prosecutors—to encourage the mules to buy their freedom in exchange for turning in the boss. Part of the mule's job is to be "a stand-up guy"—to "take the heat and do his time" without informing on the boss.

The boss, in turn, has a stake in assuring his mules the best possible representation consistent with that understanding. A good lawyer will raise the odds that the mules will be acquitted, or if convicted, will get a light sentence. If the mules were to get long sentences, their incentive to sell out the boss would increase. Thus, a smart boss will generally try to retain the best possible lawyers for his mules. But he will try to get lawyers who will

*The dilemma faced by lawyers was highlighted in the notorious Leo Frank case in which an innocent Jew, falsely accused of murdering a young girl, was lynched by a mob in Atlanta, Georgia. A distinguished member of the Atlanta bar, Arthur G. Powell, related in his autobiography that prior to the lynching, he learned who had really killed the girl, but that he could not reveal the information—even though it might have saved Frank's life—because he had learned it as part of a confidential communication. See Powell, Arthur G., *I Can Go Home Again.* University of North Carolina Press, 1943, pp. 287–292.

†As my "bonus" for winning his case, Lawson gave me two tickets to a Red Sox–Yankees game. I have already told the story of what happened to me and my son when we used those tickets.

urge the mules to "fight rather than switch" allegiances. The government, for obvious reasons, disapproves of lawyers who represent both the boss and the mules. It often asks the court to disqualify such lawyers on the ground that there is a "conflict of interest" between the clients, since it may be in the best interest of a mule to cooperate and testify against his boss. The government, of course, is not really concerned about the best interest of the mule. It has its own interest in mind: to get the boss.

A variation on the confidentiality issue arose in another case involving Oteri and Weinberg. In that case the senior partners—Martin Weinberg and Joseph Oteri—were subpoenaed to disclose the *amount* of the fee they had received from a client who was charged with being a large importer of marijuana. They refused to disclose the amount of their fee on the ground that it was privileged information that could incriminate their client. It is not difficult to imagine why a criminal defendant charged with marijuana importation would not want the legal fee disclosed. Many marijuana importers are young people—in their twenties—with no visible source of legitimate income. If it became known that a suspect had paid a legal fee of, say, $100,000, then it would become clear that the government's suspicions were correct. The fact that he paid $100,000—a fact learned from his own trusted lawyer—would be overpowering evidence of his guilt. (It could also expose the client to a tax evasion charge, since it is unlikely that the money would have been reported as income.*)

Oteri and Weinberg persisted in their refusal to provide the requested information about the fees. I represented them throughout the litigation. (Martin Weinberg had been a student at Harvard Law School, and I tell my students that my criminal-law class comes with a five-year warranty on parts and labor.) In the end the government gave up, and the lawyers did not have to go to jail for refusing to incriminate their clients. But this occupational hazard remains a nightmare for many criminal lawyers.

Certain kinds of "drug lawyers" invite this nightmare more than others. They represent the same drug dealers on a continuing basis. They become the dealer's lawyer in much the same way that a Wall Street lawyer may become "house counsel" to a corporation (or the way a "consigliere" may become a legal advisor to an organized crime family). They give advice

*Another intriguing problem faced by the "drug lawyer" is how to deal with a client who has made a lot of money selling drugs, does not want to be caught, but does want to pay income taxes on the money he has earned. This comes up more frequently than one would expect, and various approaches have been tried. For example, a tax return may be filed that truthfully discloses everything but the *name* of the taxpayer, and that includes a cashier's check for the tax due. There is, however, no foolproof way of paying the taxes without exposing the client to some risk of prosecution on drug charges.

about ongoing transactions; their business cards and home phone numbers are given to the mules in the event of an arrest; they are "on call" any time a problem arises; they socialize and become friendly with the dealers; some even obtain drugs from their clients for personal use. These drug lawyers are regarded by the government as being in business with their drug-dealer clients, and several have been subpoenaed and even indicted. Though certain practices are unquestionably illegal, the line between proper representation of a drug dealer and improper participation in his business is not always a clear one. That is why many criminal lawyers shy away from drug clients altogether, while others specialize in them. Many of the specialists clearly remain on the proper side of the line; some play close to the edges; a few cross over and become part of the business. The temptations are great because the profits are enormous. But so are the risks.

It is understandable that the government goes after drug lawyers who are suspected of being in business with their clients. A law degree is not a license to join criminal enterprises. But prosecutors sometimes *pretend* to suspect wrongdoing as an excuse for going after entirely legitimate, but vigorous, drug lawyers. The Oteri and Weinberg firm has, for example, been repeatedly subpoenaed, investigated, and audited. No wrongdoing has ever been found. But because they continue to represent marijuana and cocaine importers with great success, some prosecutors persist in treating them as if *they* were the defendants and their clients potential witnesses against them.

The Prosecutor in Defense Attorney's Clothing

They may look like defense attorneys. They may talk like defense attorneys. They may even have defendants as clients. But they are really prosecutors at heart.

In my practice I have encountered many such lawyers. They practice in every major city. Many are former prosecutors who are biding their time —and earning their living—between stints in government by serving temporarily as defense attorneys. Most of those I have encountered are former assistant United States Attorneys. After several years in that position, they leave to enter private practice. Since their experience and expertise has been in criminal law, some choose to remain in that area. But a lawyer cannot prosecute criminals privately. So they become defense attorneys—at least in name. But their hearts are not in defending guilty criminals. Nor is it their ambition to spend their lives on what they regard as the "wrong side" of the law. They hope, someday, to return to the prosecutorial establishment in senior positions, perhaps as United States Attorney or chief of an important division.

Many of these once and future prosecutors develop a specialized type of "defense" practice. For the most part, they represent government informers, cooperating witnesses, and defendants looking for a deal. They rarely litigate cases; they would never publicly criticize prosecutors. On the contrary, their primary legal tool is their friendship with the current prosecutors.

Potential defendants who are thinking about cooperating with the government are often referred to these lawyers by current prosecutors in the United States Attorney's office. Referrals are made because prosecutors are generally not supposed to deal with potential defendants who have no lawyer, yet they are wary of allowing a potentially cooperative witness to retain an independent defense lawyer, who may advise against cooperation. By recommending a "trustworthy" attorney, the prosecutor is satisfying the letter of his ethical obligations, while assuring that he will not lose the cooperation of the witness. This charade enables the prosecutor to present a formal appearance of independence between the government and the witness, while maintaining a realistic degree of control over the situation.

The United States Attorney's office for the Southern District of New York used to keep a list of "approved" lawyers to whom it would refer cooperating or potentially cooperating defendants and witnesses. These lawyers, most of whom are former assistant United States Attorneys, can be trusted to encourage their "clients" to cooperate. If any of these lawyers begin to develop a reputation for independence or antagonism to the government, he or she is stricken from the list.

Inclusion on the list—membership in the club—is a lucrative source of business, since cooperating defendants in white collar cases are often wealthy and capable of paying handsome fees.

Membership in the club is seen as entitling the lawyer to a sentencing discount for his client: former prosecutors who remain in good standing with the current prosecutors often get, or at least appear to get, sweetheart deals for their clients.

It is important, both for the government and for the "prosecutors in defense attorney's clothing" that it be widely believed that these former prosecutors generally get good deals for their clients (especially since they rarely win litigated cases in open court). In that way, clients will be encouraged to turn to these lawyers and accept their advice to cooperate with the government (and the lawyer will be able to add another victory to his win-loss record).

Some prosecutors and law enforcement officials also keep a list of hostile lawyers who generally recommend against cooperation with the government. Some officials have been known to urge defendants to fire such lawyers or risk bringing down upon themselves the wrath of the government.

I recently learned of a variation of this game currently being played by the United States Attorney's office in New York. Each day the clerk's office posts the name of the defense lawyer who will be appointed to represent indigent witnesses subpoenaed to appear before the grand jury; the assistant U.S. Attorneys wait for a day when one of "their" lawyers—one of the "prosecutors in defense attorney's clothing"—is to be the appointed lawyer; they subpoena potential cooperating witnesses on *that* day to increase the chances that they will be "advised" to cooperate by the appointed "defense" attorney. The witness is unaware, of course, that "his" lawyer has been selected for him by the government precisely to assure that he will not receive objective advice.

It may sometimes be in the interest of a defendant to retain and follow the advice of one of these "defense" attorneys. Exchanging cooperation for a lenient sentence (or no sentence at all) may be in the best interest of a particular defendant. But the decision to go that route should *never* be made without the advice of a truly independent lawyer who can assess objectively the advantages and disadvantages of each alternative. An independent lawyer may conclude that the best course *is* to cooperate and seek a deal through the "old prosecutor's network." But in some cases he or she will surely conclude that a more adversary stance is to the advantage of the client.

No defendant should ever rely on the advice of a lawyer with a hidden agenda. The agenda of a "prosecutor in defense attorney's clothing" generally includes getting the best possible deal for the client, but it may also include a desire to remain in the good graces of the current prosecutor, even at the expense of a particular client.

The "Perry Mason" Lawyers

The Perry Mason image of the defense lawyer is that of a clever strategist subtly weaving a psychological net around the lying prosecution witness. In real life, however, such stratagems generally backfire. Cross-examination rarely succeeds in getting the witness to admit that he lied. One of the hardest lessons for a lawyer—or law student—to learn is when *not* to cross-examine; when to leave well-enough, or even bad-enough, alone.

The typical criminal trial is not the taut, tense confrontation portrayed on TV; it tends to be a slow-moving and tedious series of obvious questions and predictable answers.

Lawyers' stories about the backfiring gambit are legion. A defense attorney friend told me about the time he put his client, who had a criminal record, on the witness stand. Eager to show the jury that he was not trying to hide anything, the lawyer asked his own client whether he had ever been convicted of a crime. "Yes," the client answered. The lawyer asked whether he had ever been convicted of a felony. The client again answered "Yes." The lawyer then asked the client to tell the jury the exact number of felonies he had been convicted of. The client paused and started to count on his fingers. Finally, he looked his lawyer in the eye and said, "This one will make four."

Another defense lawyer's "war story" is about the case of a man on trial for murdering his wife. No corpse had been found, but the circumstantial evidence was convincing. During his closing argument the defense lawyer told the jurors that they were in for a great surprise: when he counted to ten, the allegedly murdered wife would walk through the courtroom door. "One, two," the lawyer began. By "seven" every juror had his eyes riveted upon the door. "Eight, nine, ten," the lawyer counted. The jurors waited expectantly, but the door remained closed. The defense attorney smiled, and explained to the jurors, "See, each of you turned your eyes to the door. You each must have had a reasonable doubt about whether the wife was really dead. My little experiment," the lawyer declared victoriously, "proved that you had a reasonable doubt and that you must acquit the defendant." Despite this logic the jury convicted the defendant. Afterwards, the disappointed defense lawyer asked one of the jurors how she could have voted for conviction after the jurors had all looked at the door. "Yes, *we* all looked to the door," the juror explained, "but we noticed that the *defendant* did not look to the door. *He* knew nobody was going to walk through it."

Occasionally a legal stratagem really works. The cross-examination of Parola during the JDL case, when he was misled into believing we had tapes of certain conversations, is an example. Often, as in that case, the immediate consequence is a rebuke from the trial judge. My friend and colleague Harvey Silverglate—a uniquely resourceful and gutsy defense lawyer—has been rebuked on several occasions, and has asked me to represent him. Once, a client of his was charged with a drug sale. The arresting officer swore that he could positively identify the defendant as the one who had made the sale. What the officer did not know was that the defendant had a twin brother who lived with the defendant in the apartment where the arrest had been made. On the day of the trial Harvey arranged for the other twin to appear in place of the defendant and sit in the front row of the court traditionally reserved for the accused. The object of this twin-switch was to see if the officer would be able to tell that the person he would be asked to identify was not the person who had made the sale. When this ploy was used by Perry Mason on television, the policeman failed to identify the innocent defendant. But when Harvey tried it, the assistant United States Attorney demanded that he be disciplined. Eventually, the matter was dropped, but not without considerable concern that Harvey might be held in contempt of court or subjected to disciplinary proceedings.

The stratagems made famous by Perry Mason are fraught with danger for the real criminal defense lawyers who attempt them: generally they backfire, and when they work, the lawyer is often criticized for using them. Rarely, if ever, do they produce the Perry Mason result: acquittal of the innocent client; confession by the guilty witness; and praise from a grateful judge.

The Integrity Lawyer

There are a handful of defense attorneys in most major cities who are regarded as "models of integrity." These are distinguished lawyers who see themselves as above the fray. Their hallmark is absolute candor with the court and with the government. They generally understate their cases and argue in unemotional tones. They would never dream of using a stratagem or trick, no matter how essential to their clients' case. Nor would they attack the government or the court. They win through respect rather than through intimidation or artifice. They are judicial statespersons whose names are often included on lists of potential judges.

These integrity lawyers generally place their own reputations—their standing at the bar—above the immediate needs of a particular client. They rationalize this by believing that in the long run their clients, as a group, will benefit from their reputation for integrity and candor. This "future clients" perspective has been presented most articulately by my former Harvard Law School colleague, Judge Robert Keeton, a renowned expert on trial tactics:

> From a long-range point of view, as distinguished from concern with the immediate case only, you have an interest in avoiding customary use of methods designed to win cases on grounds that may be regarded as unfair, though legal. A reputation for this type of practice becomes a handicap to you in representing your clients *in future cases.* [The] aim of the trial system to achieve justice, *the interests of future clients,* and your legitimate interest in *your own reputation* and future effectiveness at the bar compel moderation of [the] extreme view [that the lawyer is] obliged to raise every legal claim or defense [My italics].

This attitude is probably correct: an attorney's clients *as a group* may well benefit from a reputation for "moderation" and "fairness." But in *any particular case* a *given* client may suffer grievously by the lawyer's refusal to play tough when toughness is demanded.

The integrity lawyer's general reputation may be built on the imprisoned lives of those defendants whose short-term interest in freedom may have been sacrificed to the lawyer's own long-term interest in developing a reputation for integrity.

Before an integrity lawyer is retained, it is crucial to be certain that the lawyer will be using his reputation for integrity to help *this* defendant, rather than using this defendant to help build the lawyer's reputation for integrity.

The temptation to trade off one client against another or against one's reputation for integrity is often difficult to resist. It is said that Earl Warren, when he was a District Attorney in California, would call in each new public defender and offer him a deal: if the public defender really believed that a particular defendant was innocent, he should tell that to Warren, who would then show the lawyer the entire file on the case. If the public defender still persisted in his belief after reading the file, then Warren would dismiss the case. Consider the dilemma into which this humane-sounding deal placed the public defender: every time the defender did *not* say he believed one of his clients was innocent, he acknowledged, in effect, that he believed him guilty. But in order to preserve his integrity with Earl Warren, and thus help some future innocent client, a well-intentioned defender could not assert his belief in the innocence of every client.

Once a criminal defense lawyer begins to worry excessively about his or her reputation for moderation and integrity (as those words are defined by judges and prosecutors), the temptation to sacrifice individual clients—particularly poor or despised ones—can become overwhelming. In this respect, the integrity lawyer who subordinates the interest of a client to that of his own reputation may not be so different from the media-oriented lawyer who subordinates his client's interest to that of his own desire for publicity. Yet the organized bar condemns the latter, while praising the former.

The Defense Attorney Who Places Causes Before Clients

Some defense attorneys practice criminal law primarily to further certain causes. They oppose capital punishment; they abhor police violence; they believe in equal justice for the poor or racial minorities or women; they seek to expand the protections of the Bill of Rights; they advocate prison reform;

or they favor even more fundamental and radical reforms in our system of government. These causes may be noble, but each can—at least on occasion—conflict with the interests of a particular client in a specific case.

William M. Kunstler is an example of a lawyer who boasts of his primary commitment to causes and to those individuals who embody them.

"I only defend those whose goals I share. I'm not a lawyer for hire. I only defend those I love," he has declared. "I feel alive when I have a cause."

He describes himself as "a people's lawyer," who regards "the law as an enemy" and "a living lie." He identifies so closely with his clients and their causes that he feels uncomfortable if one of his clients faces imprisonment and he himself does not undergo the same risk. (He claims that he once shot up heroin with Lenny Bruce in a men's room so that he could better identify with his client's feelings.)

I have known Kunstler for many years, and I was part of the team of lawyers that wrote the brief in the appeal from his contempt conviction growing out of the "Chicago 7" trial. Kunstler was the lead trial lawyer in that case and also participated in some of the obstreperous behavior that characterized the trial.

The original defendants were eight "leaders" of the various demonstrations that accompanied the 1968 Democratic Convention: Tom Hayden, Rennie Davis, David Dellinger, Abbie Hoffman, Jerry Rubin, John Froines, Lee Weiner, and Bobby Seale. (Seale's case was ultimately severed, thus leaving seven defendants.) Since there was no federal law prohibiting rioting or incitement to riot—those activities are generally left up to the state to prohibit—the defendants were tried under the antiriot provisions of the 1968 Civil Rights Act, charged with conspiring to cross state lines to incite a riot. The prosecution admitted that the "conspirators" had never met together as a group before the convention, and Bobby Seale had never even met any of the others. The eight defendants, whose political views ranged across the political spectrum from political radical (Hayden), to cynical Yippie (Rubin and Hoffman), to black power activist (Seale), were at first amused to be charged with conspiring together. As Abbie Hoffman remarked, "Conspire, hell, we couldn't agree on lunch." Rennie Davis struck a more serious note: "In choosing the eight of us, the government has lumped together all the strands of dissent in the sixties. We responded by saying the government of the past decade is on trial here."

The pyrotechnics of the trial were in part a result of the defendants' decision to mount a "political" defense, orchestrated in part by Kunstler, in which they tried to attack the political and judicial hypocrisy they believed existed in the United States. Much of the disorder was also attributable to other personalities in the case. Chief among these was Julius J. Hoffman, the feisty seventy-four-year-old judge who regarded himself, according to a Chicago lawyer, "as the embodiment of everything federal." Even before it began, defendant Abbie Hoffman predicted that the trial was going to be "a combination Scopes trial, revolution in the streets, Woodstock festival and People's Party." It turned out to be a latter-day Roman circus, with Judge Hoffman in the role of tyrannical emperor, denying virtually all of the defendants' motions and requests, and openly chastising the defendants and their lawyers. The prosecutors were no better, feeding the judge his lines and taking every opportunity to abuse the defense. For their part, the defendants baited the judge mercilessly. And Kuntsler contributed to the chaotic atmosphere.

Abbie Hoffman, who was not related to the judge, called him his "illegitimate father" and made repeated reference to their common ethnic background, shouting in broken Yiddish: "*You schtunk! Vo den! Shanda fun de goyem.*"

Other defendants behaved similarly, rolling jelly beans on the floor, bringing birthday cakes into the courtroom, and dressing in outrageous costumes.

Kunstler did not directly participate in any of these antics, but he did repeatedly employ the rhetoric of his radical clients. He characterized Judge Hoffman's rulings as "an unholy disgrace," as "inhumane," as "childish," and as "the most outrageous statement I have ever heard from a bench." He described the court as "a medieval torture chamber." He "invited" the judge to hold him in contempt, "because what your Honor is doing is a disgrace in this court."

For his part, Judge Hoffman repeatedly insulted Kunstler and accused him of "fanning the flames of disorder." The interchanges developed into a burlesque of pettiness, as when some defendants "groaned" at one of the court's rulings:

(Groans)

JUDGE HOFFMAN: Mr. Marshal, I wish you'd take care of that.

MR. KUNTSLER: Your Honor, those groans are highly appropriate. I get no help from you, so a groan of a client once in a while at least keeps my spirit up.

JUDGE HOFFMAN: I note that you approve of the groans of the client in open court.

MR. KUNTSLER: I approve of those groans, your Honor, when your Honor does not admonish [the prosecutor].

JUDGE HOFFMAN: I note them, I note them, sir.

It may have been the first time in American history that a highly publicized criminal trial had been turned into such a farce. The legal establishment was outraged; mainly by the antics of the defendants and their lawyers, but also by Judge Hoffman's willingness to take the bait.

During the course of the trial, a forum was conducted at the Harvard Law School on defending political cases. The two main speakers were William Kunstler and Leonard Boudin, a great civil liberties lawyer, who had represented Dr. Benjamin Spock in an earlier antiwar prosecution. I was the moderator. As was his custom, Kunstler was late, and the forum began without him. Boudin began by predicting that when Kunstler arrived, he would immediately approach the platform and plant kisses on both Boudin and me. Sure enough, that was exactly what happened—to the amusement of the audience.

Boudin took the position that a lawyer should limit his role to the legal defense of his clients, eschewing a politicization of the trial. Kunstler took the political approach, advocating the direct involvement of the lawyer in the political means and ends of his clients, and the use of the trial itself to further political goals. He closed his remarks by predicting that he would probably be held in contempt by Judge Hoffman. He then turned to me and asked whether I would come to his assistance if he was held in contempt. I smiled and answered, "Bill, I have to confess that I don't love you, but I would be prepared to help you." He said that he would not demand love from me, only good advocacy.

Several weeks later, Kunstler, his co-counsel Leonard I. Weinglass, and all of the defendants were held in contempt of court for committing one-hundred and seventy-five "contemptuous" acts, ranging from addressing the judge as "Mr. Hoffman" instead of "your Honor" (six months in jail for Dellinger), to baring a ribcage in the courtroom (four days for Hoffman), to clapping in the courtroom (fourteen days), to laughing (fifteen days). The charges against Kunstler were far more serious, including encouraging disorder, violating the court's direct orders, shouting inflammatory statements in the presence of the jury, and encouraging "groans from the defense table." Judge Hoffman sentenced him to four years and thirteen days imprisonment for his numerous contempt citations. (The jury acquitted all the defendants of the conspiracy charges, and acquitted Froines and Weiner of all charges against them, but convicted Hayden, Davis, Dellinger, Hoffman, and Rubin of crossing state lines with intent to incite a riot at the convention. All of the convictions were ultimately reversed, with the court of appeals going out of if its way to comment that "The demeanor of the Judge and prosecutors would require reversal if other errors did not.")

I was asked to become one of the lawyers for Kunstler and Weinglass on the appeal of their contempt citations. Morton Stavis, a brilliant and dedicated lawyer from Newark, New Jersey, argued the appeal. In May of 1972—almost four years after the Democratic Convention and more than two years after the end of the trial—the court of appeals rendered its decision: it reversed all of the contempt convictions against the defendants and the lawyers. The court found that some did not constitute contempt as a matter of law, and that others required a new trial before an unbiased judge.

Several years later the contempt cases were tried before Judge Edward Gignoux. He found that most of the alleged contempts by Kunstler and Weinglass were within the bounds of zealous advocacy, while a few engaged in by Kunstler exceeded those bounds. The judge concluded, however, that much of the fault for the circus atmosphere of the trial was attributable to Judge Hoffman and the prosecutor. Accordingly, he decided that "no purpose other than . . . vindictiveness" would be served by sentencing any of the defendants to imprisonment. Kunstler was free to continue his radical ways.

In recent years Kunstler has taken to attacking many of his former colleagues as sellouts. He described Mark Lane—the peripatetic lawyer who has made a career out of finding conspiracies in every assassination—as a "diseased human being, so concerned with a desire for public notoriety that he will take any case where there's guaranteed publicity." He has condemned Michael Tigar—one of the original Chicago 7 lawyers—for defending a congressman convicted under Abscam: "I think it's a horror, just a horror . . . I would not work with him again." He has attacked Joan Baez for criticizing human rights violations by North Vietnam and Cambodia. And he has chastised me for "pointing [a] finger at the Soviet Union for the Shcharansky trial." It is Kunstler's position that no "progressive" person—whatever that means— should ever publicly criticize a "socialist" government regardless of how oppressive it has been.

Kunstler's own most recent "causes" have been somewhat out of character for a "people's lawyer." He has represented a bullying, corrupt former policeman named William Phillips, who used to shake down drug dealers, pimps, and prostitutes, and who was convicted of murdering a pimp and a prostitute. Kunstler took the Phillips case without meeting his client, explaining that he doesn't "know a soul who doesn't like him. He's supposed to be a delightful rogue."

Kunstler's other recent "cause" involves rogues whom few would regard as delightful. It is the cause of organized crime. Not content to represent persons suspected of organized crime activities on the ground that every defendant is entitled to a lawyer, Kunstler has tried to make a cause out of organized crime. "Representing the mob is a Civil Rights issue," Kunstler has proclaimed. "Raymond Patriarca [the reputed head of organized crime in New England] is just like Martin Luther King in one sense. He's an unwanted person by those who are in authority. . . ." Kunstler acknowledges that he may be "over-romanticiz[ing]" Patriarca: "Maybe I see him as the Godfather, as Marlon Brando, [but] I find it hard to put him in the real big category of villains in my world." The mob, he says, is "more honest than the major American corporations, which do just as much killing—even more." He will not represent just anyone suspected of organized-crime connections: "They have to be of a certain caliber." His organized-crime clients may not satisfy his "love" test, but he says he finds them very "likable, personally." I suspect that most of his new clients are not interested in using their cases to further any cause. They just want to get off.

Indeed, Kunstler's orientation toward causes rather than clients recently generated an embarrassing conflict. During his representation of some reputed organized crime figures in Rhode Island, Kunstler learned that the offices of a local lawyer had been bugged by the FBI. Without consulting the lawyer, Kunstler announced to the national news media that he was bringing a $100 million lawsuit against the federal government, and proceeded to challenge the bugging in federal court. The local lawyer was furious: "I opposed both of those things and disagree with his role in the suit," the lawyer has said, "because it compromises the position of some of my clients who have cases pending and investigations ongoing." Kunstler's actions, allegedly on behalf of the lawyer, got the lawyer in trouble, as well: the court hearing disclosed that the lawyer himself—and not only his clients—was among the targets of the bugging.

When Kunstler was asked to explain how he could take legal action that could hurt the client on whose behalf the action was taken—without the permission of the client—he said, "I just think it was a different philosophical approach to the whole thing . . ." But the real question is whether any lawyer has a right to impose his "cause" approach on an unwilling client. To that question there can only be one answer: an unequivocal NO!

The Overzealous and Underzealous Defense Lawyer

I have been accused several times of overzealousness. I confess my guilt. In a world full of underzealous, lazy, and incompetent defense lawyers, I am proud to be regarded as overzealous on behalf of my clients. I do resolve doubts in favor of my clients and in favor of zealous representation. This approach almost got me into trouble with Judge Bauman in the JDL and Rosner cases, but I have no regrets and would do it again.

About a year after the Rosner case, a criminal lawyer in Boston was charged with misconduct by Judge Andrew Caffrey, chief judge of the Massachusetts Federal District Court, for alleging that government attorneys "may have" planted a spy in the defense camp of a criminal defendant who was awaiting trial. In support of his allegation, the defense lawyer submitted an affidavit of a Boston police officer and requested additional time to investigate the matter. But the judge—like Judge Bauman—said that the lawyer would have to prove his serious allegation right there and then. After a hearing, Judge Caffrey rejected the allegation and formally charged the defense attorney with "unprofessional conduct" and "a dereliction of his duties as an officer of this court." The Bar Counsel—the agency that initiates disciplinary proceedings in Massachusetts—prosecuted the lawyer and sought sanctions against him. These could have included suspension or even disbarment.

I urged the Civil Liberties Union to become involved, and volunteered to write the brief on behalf of the lawyer.

The disciplinary committee eventually ruled that "no professional misconduct has occurred." Out of obvious deference to the chief judge, however, the committee said that "the question is close," and that the lawyer's conduct "went to the very edge." My own view is that the only close question was whether Judge Caffrey's submission of a wholly unwarranted charge against a zealous defense lawyer went over the "edge" of proper *judicial* behavior. The question of how far a defense attorney can go in challenging the government without going over the undefined edge is still very much unresolved.

I hope that dedicated defense lawyers will not be deterred by threats of discipline from raising the kinds of well-grounded allegations that so angered Judges Bauman and Caffrey.

The real problem with many criminal lawyers is not overzealousness; it is underzealousness. Too many criminal lawyers are simply lazy. Their primary concern is their legal fee. They demand their fee in advance, and they know that the "up front" payment is all they are going to get, regardless of how long or complex the case becomes. Once they get their fee their prime concern is in disposing of the case as quickly as possible so that they can take new cases and earn new fees. These criminal lawyers regard clients the way a department store regards merchandise: the more quickly turned over at a profit, the better.

I have experienced many such underzealous lawyers. Occasionally, I have written appellate briefs in cases where the trial lawyers were regarded as underzealous by their clients. One case involved Arnold Bauman when he returned to private practice after his stint on the bench. His first major criminal case involved several defendants—one a graduate of the Harvard

Law School—who were accused of conspiracy to pay a one-million-dollar bribe to the mayor of Fort Lee, New Jersey, in order to obtain a zoning variance for construction of a quarter of a billion dollar office complex. There was no question that the bribe had been offered by a man named Arthur Sutton: the mayor had been wearing a recording device provided by the FBI and Sutton was caught in the act. After being arrested and conferring with his lawyer, Sutton decided to seek a deal. He told the government that three executives of a major real estate investment company—the company financing the project—had put him up to the bribe. The three executives were indicted, and one of them hired Arnold Bauman to represent him.

The trial was essentially a credibility contest between the defendants and Sutton; there was no hard evidence that the executives had put Sutton up to the bribe. It was his word against theirs.

During the cross-examination of Sutton, a young man named James Silver approached Bauman's client and told him that he had evidence proving that Sutton was a liar and a crook who had been in the habit of bribing officials. Silver had worked for Sutton for several years and was intimately familiar with his practices and history. Even more important, Silver told Bauman that he—Silver—had disclosed the story to the United States Attorney before the trial. This was important because the defendants had made pretrial motions demanding all information in the government's possession that might discredit Sutton. In violation of the law, the government had suppressed the information given to it by Silver.

Bauman decided to ignore this bombshell. It may have been too late in the trial to take the chance of calling a witness like Silver to the stand. But Bauman could, at least, have called the prosecutor's misconduct to the attention of the trial judge. For reasons best known to Bauman, he did nothing, and neither the judge nor the jury learned of Silver's information.

The jury, deprived of significant evidence discrediting the prosecution's key witness, convicted the defendants on three counts. The judge sentenced them to five years imprisonment—an extremely long sentence for this kind of bribery by private citizens. (Most of the public officials convicted in Abscam received sentences of approximately three years.) When Bauman's client asked him to complain about the sentence, Bauman refused, telling his client that when he was a judge, he had sentenced a lawyer to five years for attempted bribery as well. This was obviously a reference to the Rosner case. What Bauman neglected to tell his client was that the court of appeals had reversed that sentence and another judge had reduced it to three years.

Following the sentencing, I was retained to represent one of the defendants—the Harvard Law School graduate. After long and heated litigation, in which I did accuse the government of unlawfully failing to disclose the

Silver information before trial, we obtained reversals of two of the counts and a hearing on the remaining one. Eventually, we settled the case: our clients agreed to drop their charges of prosecutorial misconduct in exchange for a reduction of their five year sentences to six months.

The most egregious case of underzealousness I have ever been involved in concerned a criminal lawyer in a capital case against an illiterate black man from Lanier County, Georgia. The lawyer's name is Edward "Piggy" Parrish. He represented Son Fleming, who was accused of participating in the murder of a white police chief named James Giddens. The murder occurred shortly after an armed robbery of a 7-11 grocery store near the rural town of Adel, Georgia. Son Fleming was not involved in the robbery; it was committed by his nineteen-year-old nephew Larry Fleming and his nephew's twenty-one-year-old friend Henry Willis. After the robbery the two young men apparently picked up Son in their car and were soon spotted by Chief Giddens. After radioing that he was going to stop the car, Giddens pulled it over, was overpowered, and eventually shot to death. All three of the car's occupants were tried for murder. The case against Son Fleming was the weakest, since he had not been involved in the robbery and there was no credible evidence that he participated in the shooting of the police chief. The trial—and pretrial preparation—was a textbook study of incompetence, sloppiness, and underzealousness.

Parrish actually fell asleep in court during an important pretrial proceeding. He conducted no investigation of the circumstances surrounding the murder. He filed no pretrial motions seeking to inspect the government's evidence. He did not know until the trial itself that his client had made several statements to law enforcement officials about his role in the crime. He was aware that his client had made one statement before trial, but he did not obtain a copy of that important document or inquire whether it had been accompanied by a waiver of rights. As a result of his failure to find out about the statements, the defense presented contradictory "defenses" to the jury. Parrish also failed to make a dozen or so other motions that would be obvious to any dedicated defense lawyer and necessary to preserve the issues for appeal.

Perhaps the most striking example of Parrish's defense technique was in his closing argument to the jury. The defendant had testified that he had been beaten by several white policemen. The prosecutors disputed this and argued that the defendant was lying. This is what Parrish—Son Fleming's *defense* lawyer—argued to the jury on his client's *behalf*: "Now [the prosecution] have said much about Son's not telling the truth. I don't know but that I agree with them . . . I don't think Son was beat by those policemen. I don't believe it, not one bit in this world."

Finally, after the defendant was convicted of murder, Parrish was given an opportunity to offer evidence in mitigation of punishment—evidence designed to show that Son Fleming should not be executed. Although there was evidence available—his mental and emotional problems, his minor participation in the events, his general background, and other favorable material—Parrish introduced no mitigating evidence. The sentencing judge himself concluded that the facts of the case do not "foreclose all doubts respecting the defendant's guilt." But in the absence of mitigating evidence, he sentenced Son Fleming to death. Fleming is now on death row awaiting the outcome of federal challenges to his conviction and sentence. I am his lawyer, along with a law firm in Atlanta, Georgia. We are desperately trying to undo the damage done by his trial lawyer.

Parrish's underzealous—indeed incompetent—representation of Son Fleming may well have made the difference between life and death. Yet nobody has cited Parrish for unprofessional conduct or underzealousness.

The message to criminal defense lawyers is clear. Given the choice between overzealous and underzealous representation, a lawyer concerned for his own safety and security should opt for underzealousness. Few defense lawyers have ever gotten into trouble for *failing* to accuse the government of misconduct even where warranted or for *failing* to defend a client with zeal. But defense lawyers have gotten into trouble for accusing the government of misconduct even where warranted and for defending a client with too much zeal.

Despite this double standard there will always be some defense attorneys who will understand that in defending criminals, the best defense may often be a vigorous and zealous offense.

The Best and Worst Defense Attorneys

The best defense attorneys will always be those who are able to adapt their styles and techniques to the needs of a particular client at a given time. In the preceding pages I have described various "types" of criminal lawyers. I am often asked "which type is the best?" There is no general answer to that question, but there are some guidelines.

The first and most important rule in selecting the best defense attorney is to be certain that he or she is interested *only* in achieving the best legal result for the client and not in serving some other personal or professional interest (such as exposure to the media, or enhancing a reputation for integrity, or maintaining a cozy relationship with the prosecutor).

The second rule is that the lawyer must have a diverse array of weapons in his professional arsenal. He or she must be a lawyer for all seasons. The lawyer who is known solely as a plea bargainer has few chips to bargain with. The most feared trial lawyer will generally be the best plea bargainer. The lawyer with a reputation for integrity will often be in the best position to surprise an opponent with a clever ploy when necessary to serve the client's interest.

Although there is no all-purpose best type of defense lawyer, there are certain types that must be avoided at all cost: the lazy or busy lawyer who simply fails to devote sufficient time or energy to the case; the lawyer who makes the same "canned" arguments without regard to the facts or law of the case; the lawyer who neglects to preserve pretrial and trial errors for appellate review.

Most important, of course, is to avoid the crooked lawyer—or the lawyer who falsely claims he is crooked. There are a few defense lawyers who really do bribe judges and/or prosecutors; every so often one is convicted of bribery. The problem used to be widespread, but it is now diminishing. There are, however, still some defense attorneys who claim or imply to their clients that they can "get to" the judge or prosecutor. They demand excessive fees which, they say, will be "spread around." More often than not, the lawyer is bluffing and will keep the money. (This is reminiscent of the story about the court clerk who used to separately approach both litigants in a civil lawsuit and tell each that he could "probably" fix the case with the judge for $1,000. The clerk obtained each $1,000 in advance, promising that he would refund it if he failed to fix the case. In this way, the clerk would get $1,000 from each of the litigants; he would not say anything to the judge; after the judge had ruled, he would return the $1,000 to the losing litigant, telling him that he had not been able to get to the judge. But he would keep the $1,000 from the winning litigant, who was happy to pay to have had the case "fixed.") Beware, therefore, of the criminal lawyer who promises too much.

The Last Bastion

The zealous defense attorney is the last bastion of liberty—the final barrier between an overreaching government and its citizens. The job of the defense attorney is to challenge the government; to make those in power justify their conduct in relation to the powerless; to articulate and defend the right of those who lack the ability or resources to defend themselves. (Even the rich are relatively powerless—less so, of course, than the poor—when confronting the resources of a government prosecutor.)

One of the truest tests of a free country is how it treats those whose job it is to defend the guilty and the despised. In most repressive countries there is no independent defense bar. Indeed, a sure sign that repression is on the way is when the government goes after the defense attorneys. Shakespeare said, "The first thing we do, let's kill all the lawyers." Hitler, Stalin, the Greek Colonels, and the Chinese Cultural Revolutionaries may not have killed all the lawyers first, but they surely placed defense attorneys—especially vigorous and independent ones—high on their hit lists.

One of the surest ways of undercutting the independence of defense attorneys is to question the propriety of their representing the guilty. Those who argue that defense attorneys should limit their representation to the innocent, or indeed to any specific group or category, open the door to a system where the government decides who is, and who is not, entitled to a defense. Granting that power to the government, to the bar, or to any establishment, marks the beginning of the end of an independent defense bar—and the beginning of the end of liberty.

The role of the defense attorney who defends guilty clients is the hardest role in the criminal justice system to explain to the public. In 1980 I traveled to China to advise the People's Republic on its criminal justice system. Most Chinese lawyers seemed to understand the need for free and independent judges and prosecutors. But hardly anyone—even those lawyers who had suffered most under the Cultural Revolution—seemed willing to justify the actions of a defense attorney representing a client whom he knew to be guilty and "counterrevolutionary." (Every society has its own favorite epithets for those it most despises.) "Why should our government *pay* someone to stand in the way of socialist justice?" was the question I was most often asked. I tried to explain that justice—whether socialist, capitalist, or anything else—is a *process,* not only an end; and that for the process to operate fairly, all persons charged with crime must have the right to a defense. Since not all defendants are created equal in their ability to speak effectively, think logically, and argue forcefully, the role of a defense attorney—trained in these and other skills—is to perform those functions for the defendant. The process of determining *whether* a defendant should be deemed guilty and punished requires that the government be put to its proof and that the accused have a fair opportunity to defend.

I also tried to explain to the Chinese lawyers that laws that are today directed against counterrevolutionaries may tomorrow be directed at them. As H. L. Mencken once put it: "The trouble about fighting for human freedom is that you have to spend much of your life defending sons of bitches; for oppressive laws are always aimed at them originally, and oppression must be stopped in the beginning if it is to be stopped at all."

To me the most persuasive argument for defending the guilty and the despised is to consider the alternative. Those governments that forbid or discourage such representation have little to teach us about justice. Their systems are far more corrupt, less fair, and generally even less efficient than ours. What Winston Churchill once said about democracy can probably also be said about the adversary system of criminal justice: It may well be the worst system of justice, "except [for] all the other [systems] that have been tried from time to time."

Attorneys who defend the guilty and the despised will never have a secure or comfortable place in any society. Their motives will be misunderstood; they will be suspected of placing loyalty to clients above loyalty to society; and they will be associated in the public mind with the misdeeds of their clients. They will be seen as troublemakers and gadflies. The best of them will always be on the firing line, with their licenses exposed to attack.

There will never be a Nobel Prize for defense attorneys who succeed in freeing the guilty. Indeed there are few prizes or honors ever bestowed on defense lawyers for their zealousness.

The ranks of defense attorneys are filled with a mixed assortment of human beings from the most noble and dedicated to the most sleazy and corrupt. It is a profession that seems to attract extremes. The public sometimes has difficulty distinguishing between the noble and the sleazy; the very fact that a defense lawyer represents a guilty client leads some to conclude that the lawyer must be sleazy. Being so regarded is an occupational hazard of all zealous defense attorneys.

The late Supreme Court Justice Felix Frankfurter once commented that he knew of no title "more honorable than that of Professor of the Harvard Law School." I know of none more honorable than defense attorney.

Index

ABOUT THE AUTHOR

ALAN M. DERSHOWITZ was born in Brooklyn and was graduated from Yeshiva University High School, Brooklyn College, and the Yale Law School. He clerked for Judge David Bazelon of the United States Court of Appeals and for Justice Arthur Goldberg of the United States Supreme Court, and was made a full professor at the Harvard Law School at the age of twenty-eight, the youngest in the history of the school. Professor Dershowitz has served on the National Board of Directors of the American Civil Liberties Union and as consultant for various foundations and presidential commissions. He received a Guggenheim Foundation Award in 1979 to study human rights. In 1981 Professor Dershowitz was honored by the New York Criminal Bar Association for his "outstanding contribution as a scholar and dedicated defender of individual liberty and human rights." In 1979 *Time* magazine included him among its "50 Faces for the Future" in recognition of his defense of civil liberties. His columns and articles appear regularly in newspapers and magazines, and he comments frequently on national television. He lives in Cambridge, Massachusetts.

VINTAGE POLITICAL SCIENCE AND SOCIAL CRITICISM

V-568 **ALINSKY, SAUL D.** / Reveille for Radicals
V-736 **ALINSKY, SAUL D.** / Rules for Radicals
V-726 **ALLENDE, PRESIDENT SALVADOR AND REGIS DEBRAY** / The Chilean Revolution
V-286 **ARIES, PHILIPPE** / Centuries of Childhood
V-604 **BAILYN, BERNARD** / Origins of American Politics
V-334 **BALTZELL, E. DIGBY** / The Protestant Establishment
V-571 **BARTH, ALAN** / Prophets With Honor: Great Dissents & Great Dissenters in the Supreme Court
V-791 **BAXANDALL, LEE (ed.) AND WILHELM REICH** / Sex-Pol.: Essays 1929-1934
V-60 **BECKER, CARL L.** / The Declaration of Independence
V-563 **BEER, SAMUEL H.** / British Politics in the Collectivist Age
V-994 **BERGER, PETER & BRIGITTE AND HANSFRIED KELLNER** / The Homeless Mind: Modernization and Consciousness
V-77 **BINZEN, PETER** / Whitetown, USA
V-513 **BOORSTIN, DANIEL J.** / The Americans: The Colonial Experience
V-11 **BOORSTIN, DANIEL J.** / The Americans: The Democratic Experience
V-358 **BOORSTIN, DANIEL J.** / The Americans: The National Experience
V-501 **BOORSTIN, DANIEL J.** / Democracy and Its Discontents: Reflections on Everyday America
V-414 **BOTTOMORE, T. B.** / Classes in Modern Society
V-742 **BOTTOMORE, T. B.** / Sociology: A Guide to Problems & Literature
V-305 **BREINES, SIMON AND WILLIAM J. DEAN** / The Pedestrian Revolution: Streets Without Cars
V-44 **BRINTON, CRANE** / The Anatomy of Revolution
V-30 **CAMUS, ALBERT** / The Rebel
V-966 **CAMUS, ALBERT** / Resistance, Rebellion & Death
V-33 **CARMICHAEL, STOKELY AND CHARLES HAMILTON** / Black Power
V-2024 **CARO, ROBERT A.** / The Power Broker: Robert Moses and The Fall of New York
V-862 **CASE, JOHN AND GERRY HUNNIUS AND DAVID G. CARSON** / Workers Control: A Reader on Labor and Social Change
V-98 **CASH, W. J.** / The Mind of the South
V-555 **CHOMSKY, NOAM** / American Power and the New Mandarins
V-248 **CHOMSKY, NOAM** / Peace in the Middle East? Reflections on Justice and Nationhood
V-815 **CHOMSKY, NOAM** / Problems of Knowledge and Freedom
V-788 **CIRINO, ROBERT** / Don't Blame the People
V-17 **CLARKE, TED AND DENNIS JAFFE (eds.)** / Worlds Apart: Young People and The Drug Problems
V-383 **CLOWARD, RICHARD AND FRANCES FOX PIVEN** / The Politics of Turmoil: Essays on Poverty, Race and The Urban Crisis
V-743 **CLOWARD, RICHARD AND FRANCES FOX PIVEN** / Regulating the Poor: The Functions of Public Welfare
V-940 **COBB, JONATHAN AND RICHARD SENNETT** / Hidden Injuries of Class
V-311 **CREMIN, LAWRENCE A.** / The Genius of American Education
V-519 **CREMIN, LAWRENCE A.** / The Transformation of the School
V-808 **CUMMING, ROBERT D. (ed.)** / The Philosophy of Jean-Paul Sartre
V-2019 **CUOMO, MARIO** / Forest Hills Diary: The Crisis of Low-Income Housing
V-305 **DEAN, WILLIAM J. AND SIMON BREINES** / The Pedestrian Revolution: Streets Without Cars
V-726 **DEBRAY, REGIS AND PRESIDENT SALVADOR ALLENDE** / The Chilean Revolution
V-638 **DENNISON, GEORGE** / The Lives of Children
V-746 **DEUTSCHER, ISAAC** / The Prophet Armed
V-748 **DEUTSCHER, ISAAC** / The Prophet Outcast
V-617 **DEVLIN, BERNADETTE** / The Price of My Soul

V-671 **DOMHOFF, G. WILLIAM** / The Higher Circles
V-812 **ELLUL, JACQUES** / The Political Illusion
V-874 **ELLUL, JACQUES** / Propaganda: The Formation of Men's Attitudes
V-390 **ELLUL, JACQUES** / The Technological Society
V-143 **EMERSON, THOMAS I.** / The System of Freedom of Expression
V-396 **EPSTEIN, EDWARD JAY** / Between Fact and Fiction: The Problem of Journalism
V-998 **EPSTEIN, EDWARD JAY** / News from Nowhere: Television and The News
V-405 **ESHERICK, JOSEPH W. (ed.) AND JOHN S. SERVICE** / Lost Chance in China: The World War II Despatches of John S. Service
V-803 **EVANS, ROWLAND JR. AND ROBERT D. NOVAK** / Nixon in the White House: The Frustration of Power
V-802 **FALK, RICHARD A.** / This Endangered Planet: Prospects and Proposals for Human Survival
V-2002 **FERNBACH, DAVID AND KARL MARX** / Political Writings Vol. I: The Revolutions of 1848
V-2003 **FERNBACH, DAVID AND KARL MARX** / Political Writings Vol. II: Surveys from Exile
V-2004 **FERNBACH, DAVID AND KARL MARX** / Political Writings Vol. III: The First International and After
V-225 **FISCHER, LOUIS (ed.)** / The Essential Gandhi
V-927 **FITZGERALD, FRANCES** / Fire in the Lake: The Vietnamese and the Americans in Vietnam
V-316 **FREEMAN, S. DAVID** / Energy: The New Era
V-368 **FRIEDENBERG, EDGAR Z.** / Coming of Age in America
V-409 **FRIENDLY, FRED W.** / Due to Circumstances Beyond Our Control
V-378 **FULBRIGHT, J. WILLIAM** / The Arrogance of Power
V-846 **FULBRIGHT, J. WILLIAM** / The Crippled Giant
V-491 **GANS, HERBERT J.** / The Levittowners
V-167 **GANS, HERBERT J.** / More Equality
V-862 **GARSON, DAVID G. AND GERRY HUNNIUS AND JOHN CASE** / Workers Control: A Reader in Labor and Social Change
V-2018 **GAYLIN, WILLARD** / Partial Justice: A Study of Bias in Sentencing
V-183 **GOLDMAN, ERIC F.** / The Crucial Decade—and After: America 1945-1960
V-31 **GOLDMAN, ERIC F.** / Rendezvous With Destiny
V-174 **GOODMAN, PAUL AND PERCIVAL** / Communitas
V-325 **GOODMAN, PAUL** / Compulsory Mis-education and The Community of Scholars
V-32 **GOODMAN, PAUL** / Growing Up Absurd
V-932 **GRAUBARD, ALLEN** / Free the Children: Radical Reform and The Free School Movement
V-457 **GREENE, FELIX** / The Enemy: Some Notes on the Nature of Contemporary Imperialism
V-430 **GUEVERA, CHE** / Guerilla Warfare
V-33 **HAMILTON, CHARLES AND STOKELY CARMICHAEL** / Black Power
V-453 **HEALTH/PAC** / The American Health Empire
V-635 **HEILBRONER, ROBERT L.** / Between Capitalism and Socialism
V-283 **HENRY, JULES** / Culture Against Man
V-482 **HETTER, PATRICIA AND LOUIS O. KELSO** / Two-Factor Theory: The Economics of Reality
V-465 **HINTON, WILLIAM** / Fanshen: A Documentary of Revolution in a Chinese Village
V-328 **HINTON, WILLIAM** / Iron Oxen
V-2005 **HOARE, QUINTIN (ed.) AND KARL MARX** / Early Writings
V-95 **HOFSTADTER, RICHARD** / The Age of Reform: From Bryan to FDR
V-795 **HOFSTADTER, RICHARD** / America at 1750: A Social Portrait
V-9 **HOFSTADTER, RICHARD** / The American Political Tradition
V-686 **HOFSTADTER, RICHARD AND MICHAEL WALLACE (eds.)** / American Violence: A Documentary History
V-317 **HOFSTADTER, RICHARD** / Anti-Intellectualism in American Life

V-540 **HOFSTADTER, RICHARD AND CLARENCE L. VER STEEG (eds.)** / Great Issues in American History: From Settlement to Revolution, 1584-1776
V-541 **HOFSTADTER, RICHARD (ed.)** / Great Issues in American History: From the Revolution to the Civil War, 1765-1865
V-542 **HOFSTADTER, RICHARD (ed.)** / Great Issues in American History: From Reconstruction to the Present Day, 1864-1969
V-385 **HOFSTADTER, RICHARD (ed.)** / The Paranoid Style in American Politics and Other Essays
V-591 **HOFSTADTER, RICHARD (ed.)** / The Progressive Historians
V-201 **HUGHES, H. STUART** / Consciousness and Society
V-862 **HUNNIUS, GERRY, DAVID G. GARSON AND JOHN CASE** / Workers Control: A Reader on Labor and Social Change
V-514 **HUNTINGTON, SAMUEL F.** / The Soldier and the State
V-566 **HURLEY, ROGER** / Poverty & Mental Retardation: A Causal Relationship
V-17 **JAFFE, DENNIS AND TED CLARKE (eds.)** / Worlds Apart: Young People and The Drug Programs
V-241 **JACOBS, JANE** / Death and Life of Great American Cities
V-584 **JACOBS, JANE** / The Economy of Cities
V-433 **JACOBS, PAUL** / Prelude to Riot
V-459 **JACOBS, PAUL AND SAUL LANDAU WITH EVE PELL** / To Serve the Devil: Natives and Slaves Vol. I
V-460 **JACOBS, PAUL AND SAUL LANDAU WITH EVE PELL** / To Serve the Devil: Colonials and Sojourners Vol. II
V-2017 **JUDSON, HORACE FREELAND** / Heroin Addiction: What Americans Can Learn from the English Experience
V-790 **KAPLAN, CAROL AND LAWRENCE (eds.)** / Revolutions, A Comparative Study
V-337 **KAUFMANN, WALTER (trans.) AND FRIEDRICH NIETZSCHE** / Beyond Good and Evil
V-369 **KAUFMANN, WALTER (trans.) AND FRIEDRICH NIETZSCHE** / The Birth of Tragedy and The Case of Wagner
V-985 **KAUFMANN, WALTER (trans.) AND FRIEDRICH NIETZSCHE** / The Gay Science
V-401 **KAUFMANN, WALTER (trans.) AND FRIEDRICH NIETZSCHE** / On the Genealogy of Morals and Ecce Homo
V-437 **KAUFMANN, WALTER (trans.) AND FRIEDRICH NIETZSCHE** / The Will to Power
V-994 **KELLNER, HANSFRIED AND PETER AND BRIGITTE BERGER** / The Homeless Mind: Modernization and Consciousness
V-482 **KELSO, LOUIS O. AND PATRICIA HETTER** / Two-Factor Theory: The Economics of Reality
V-708 **KESSLE, GUN AND JAN MYRDAL** / China: The Revolution Continued
V-510 **KEY, V. O.** / Southern Politics
V-764 **KLARE, MICHAEL T.** / War Without End: American Planning for the Next Vietnams
V-981 **KLINE, MORRIS** / Why Johnny Can't Add: The Failure of the New Math
V-361 **KOMAROVSKY, MIRRA** / Blue Collar Marriage
V-675 **KOVEL, JOEL** / White Racism
V-459 **LANDAU, SAUL, PAUL JACOBS WITH EVE PELL** / To Serve the Devil: Natives and Slaves Vol. I
V-460 **LANDAU, SAUL, PAUL JACOBS WITH EVE PELL** / To Serve the Devil: Colonials and Sojourners Vol. II
V-560 **LASCH, CHRISTOPHER** / The Agony of the American Left
V-367 **LASCH, CHRISTOPHER** / The New Radicalism in America
V-46 **LASCH, CHRISTOPHER** / The World of Nations
V-987 **LEKACHMANN, ROBERT** / Inflation: The Permanent Problem of Boom and Bust
V-880 **LERNER, GERDA (ed.)** / Black Women in White America: A Documentary History
V-280 **LEWIS, OSCAR** / The Children of Sanchez

V-634 **LEWIS, OSCAR** / A Death in the Sanchez Family
V-421 **LEWIS, OSCAR** / La Vida
V-370 **LEWIS, OSCAR** / Pedro Martinez
V-533 **LOCKWOOD, LEE** / Castro's Cuba, Cuba's Fidel
V-787 **MALDONADO-DENIS, DR. MANUEL** / Puerto-Rico: A Socio-Historic Interpretation
V-406 **MARCUS, STEVEN** / Engels, Manchester and The Working Class
V-480 **MARCUSE, HERBERT** / Soviet Marxism
V-2002 **MARX, KARL AND DAVID FERNBACH (ed.)** / Political Writings, Vol. I: The Revolutions of 1848
V-2003 **MARX, KARL AND DAVID FERNBACH (ed.)** / Political Writings, Vol. II: Surveys from Exile
V-2004 **MARX, KARL AND DAVID FERNBACH (ed.)** / Political Writings, Vol. III: The First International and After
V-2005 **MARX, KARL AND QUINTIN HOARE (trans.)** / Early Writings
V-2001 **MARX, KARL AND MARTIN NICOLOUS (trans.)** / The Grundrisse: Foundations of the Critique of Political Economy
V-619 **McCONNELL, GRANT** / Private Power and American Democracy
V-386 **McPHERSON, JAMES** / The Negro's Civil War
V-928 **MEDVEDEV, ROY A.** / Let History Judge: The Origins & Consequences of Stalinism
V-112 **MEDVEDEV, ZHORES A.** / Ten Years After Ivan Denisovitch
V-427 **MENDELSON, MARY ADELAIDE** / Tender Loving Greed
V-614 **MERMELSTEIN, DAVID (ed.)** / The Economic Crisis Reader
V-307 **MIDDLETON, NEIL (ed.) AND I. F. STONE** / The I. F. Stone's Weekly Reader
V-971 **MILTON, DAVID & NANCY AND FRANZ SCHURMANN (eds.)** / The China Reader IV: People's China
V-905 **MITCHELL, JULIET** / Woman's Estate
V-93 **MITFORD, JESSICA** / Kind and Usual Punishment
V-539 **MORGAN, ROBIN (ed.)** / Sisterhood is Powerful
V-389 **MOYNIHAN, DANIEL P.** / Coping: On the Practice of Government
V-107 **MYRDAL, GUNNAR** / Against the Stream: Critical Essays on Economics
V-730 **MYRDAL, GUNNAR** / Asian Drama: An Inquiry into the Poverty of Nations
V-170 **MYRDAL, GUNNAR** / The Challenge of World Poverty
V-793 **MYRDAL, JAN** / Report from a Chinese Village
V-708 **MYRDAL, JAN AND GUN KESSLE** / China: The Revolution Continued
V-834 **NEWTON, HUEY P.** / To Die for the People
V-2001 **NICOLOUS, MARTIN (trans.) AND KARL MARX** / The Grundrisse: Foundations of the Critique of Political Economy
V-377 **NIETZSCHE, FRIEDRICH AND WALTER KAUFMANN (trans.)** / Beyond Good and Evil
V-369 **NIETZSCHE, FRIEDRICH AND WALTER KAUFMANN (trans.)** / The Birth of Tragedy and The Case of Wagner
V-985 **NIETZSCHE, FRIEDRICH AND WALTER KAUFMANN (trans.)** / The Gay Science
V-401 **NIETZSCHE, FRIEDRICH AND WALTER KAUFMANN (trans.)** / On the Genealogy of Morals and Ecce Homo
V-437 **NIETZSCHE, FRIEDRICH AND WALTER KAUFMANN (trans.)** / The Will to Power
V-803 **NOVAK, ROBERT D. AND ROWLAND EVANS, JR.** / Nixon in the White House: The Frustration of Power
V-689 **AN OBSERVER** / Message from Moscow
V-383 **PIVEN, FRANCES FOX AND RICHARD CLOWARD** / The Politics of Turmoil: Essays on Poverty, Race & The Urban Crisis
V-743 **PIVEN, FRANCES FOX AND RICHARD CLOWARD** / Regulating the Poor: The Functions of Public Welfare
V-128 **PLATO** / The Republic
V-719 **REED, JOHN** / Ten Days That Shook the World

V-791 **REICH, WILHELM AND LEE BAXANDALL (ed.)** / Sex-Pol.: Essays 1929-1934
V-159 **REISCHAUER, EDWIN O.** / Toward the 21st Century: Education for a Changing World
V-622 **ROAZEN, PAUL** / Freud: Political and Social Thought
V-204 **ROTHSCHILD, EMMA** / Paradise Lost: The Decline of the Auto-Industrial Age
V-954 **ROWBOTHAM, SHEILA** / Women, Resistance and Revolution
V-288 **RUDOLPH, FREDERICK** / The American College and University
V-226 **RYAN, WILLIAM** / Blaming the Victim, (Revised edition)
V-130 **SALE, KIRKPATRICK** / Power Shift
V-965 **SALE, KIRKPATRICK** / SDS
V-902 **SALOMA, JOHN S. III AND FREDERICK H. SONTAG** / Parties: The Real Opportunity for Effective Citizen Politics
V-375 **SCHELL, ORVILLE AND FRANZ SCHURMANN (eds.)** / The China Reader, Vol. I: Imperial China
V-376 **SCHELL, ORVILLE AND FRANZ SCHURMANN (eds.)** / The China Reader, Vol. II: Republican China
V-377 **SCHELL, ORVILLE AND FRANZ SCHURMANN (eds.)** / The China Reader, Vol. III: Communist China
V-738 **SCHNEIR, MIRIAM (ed.)** / Feminism
V-375 **SCHURMANN, FRANZ AND ORVILLE SCHELL (eds.)** / The China Reader, Vol. I: Imperial China
V-376 **SCHURMANN, FRANZ AND ORVILLE SCHELL (eds.)** / The China Reader, Vol. II: Republican China
V-377 **SCHURMANN, FRANZ AND ORVILLE SCHELL (eds.)** / The China Reader, Vol. III: Communist China
V-971 **SCHURMANN, FRANZ AND NANCY AND DAVID MILTON (eds.)** / The China Reader, Vol. IV: People's China
V-89 **SENNETT, RICHARD** / Families Against the City: Middle Class Homes of Industrial Chicago 1872-1890
V-940 **SENNETT, RICHARD AND JONATHAN COBB** / The Hidden Injuries of Class
V-308 **SENNETT, RICHARD** / The Uses of Disorder
V-974 **SERRIN, WILLIAM** / The Company and the Union
V-405 **SERVICE, JOHN S. AND JOSEPH W. ESHERICK (ed.)** / Lost Chance in China: The World War II Despatches of John S. Service
V-798 **SEXTON, BRENDAN AND PATRICIA** / Blue Collars and Hard Hats
V-279 **SILBERMAN, CHARLES E.** / Crisis in Black and White
V-353 **SILBERMAN, CHARLES E.** / Crisis in the Classroom
V-850 **SILBERMAN, CHARLES E.** / The Open Classroom Reader
V-681 **SNOW, EDGAR** / Red China Today: The Other Side of the River
V-930 **SNOW, EDGAR** / The Long Revolution
V-902 **SONTAG, FREDERICK H. AND JOHN S. SALOMA III** / Parties: The Real Opportunity for Effective Citizen Politics
V-388 **STAMPP, KENNETH** / The Era of Reconstruction 1865-1877
V-253 **STAMPP, KENNETH** / The Peculiar Institution
V-959 **STERN, PHILIP M.** / The Rape of the Taxpayer
V-547 **STONE, I. F.** / The Haunted Fifties
V-307 **STONE, I. F. AND NEIL MIDDLETON (ed.)** / The I. F. Stone's Weekly Reader
V-231 **TANNENBAUM, FRANK** / Slave and Citizen: The Negro in the Americas
V-312 **TANNENBAUM, FRANK** / Ten Keys to Latin America
V-984 **THOMAS, PIRI** / Down These Mean Streets
V-322 **THOMPSON, E. P.** / The Making of the English Working Class
V-810 **TITMUSS, RICHARD** / The Gift Relationship: From Human Blood to Social Policy
V-848 **TOFFLER, ALVIN** / The Culture Consumers
V-980 **TOFFLER, ALVIN (ed.)** / Learning for Tomorrow: The Role of the Future in Education

V-686 **WALLACE, MICHAEL AND RICHARD HOFSTADTER (eds.)** / American Violence: A Documentary History
V-957 **WHALEN, CHARLES** / Your Right to Know
V-313 **WILSON, EDMUND** / Apologies to the Iroquois
V-483 **ZINN, HOWARD** / Disobedience and Democracy